SYSTEM
DEVELOPMENT

Prentice-Hall International
Series in Computer Science

C. A. R. Hoare, Series Editor

Published

BACKHOUSE, R. C., *Syntax of Programming Languages: Theory and Practice*
de BAKKER, J. W., *Mathematical Theory of Program Correctness*
BJØRNER, D. and JONES, C., *Formal Specification and Software Development*
DROMEY, R. G., *How to Solve it by Computer*
DUNCAN, F., *Microprocessor Programming and Software Development*
GOLDSCHLAGER, L. and LISTER, A., *Computer Science: A Modern Introduction*
HENDERSON, P., *Functional Programming: Application and Implementation*
JACKSON, M. A., *System Development*
JONES, C. B., *Software Development: A Rigorous Approach*
REYNOLDS, J. C., *The Craft of Programming*
TENNENT, R. D., *Principles of Programming Languages*
WELSH, J. and ELDER, J., *Introduction to Pascal*, 2nd Edition
WELSH, J. and McKEAG, M., *Structured System Programming*

SYSTEM DEVELOPMENT

M. A. JACKSON
Michael Jackson Systems Limited

based on the work of
M. A. JACKSON *and* J. R. CAMERON

Prentice/Hall International

ENGLEWOOD CLIFFS, NEW JERSEY   LONDON   NEW DELHI
SINGAPORE   SYDNEY   TOKYO   TORONTO   WELLINGTON

To Judy, Daniel, Tim, David and Adam

Library of Congress Cataloging in Publication Data
Jackson, Michael, 1936–
    System development.

    Bibliography: p.
    Includes index.
    1. System design.   I. Title.
QA76.9.S88J33   003   82-619
ISBN 0-13-880328-5   AACR2

British Library Cataloguing in Publication Data
Jackson, Michael
    System development.
    1. Systems engineering   2. Business
    I. Title
    658.4'032   TA168

    ISBN 0-13-880328-5

© 1983 by PRENTICE-HALL INTERNATIONAL, INC.

ISBN 0-13-880328-5

PRENTICE-HALL INTERNATIONAL INC., London
PRENTICE-HALL OF AUSTRALIA PTY., LTD., Sydney
PRENTICE-HALL CANADA, INC., Toronto
PRENTICE-HALL OF INDIA PRIVATE LIMITED, New Delhi
PRENTICE-HALL OF JAPAN, INC., Tokyo
PRENTICE-HALL OF SOUTHEAST ASIA PTE., LTD., Singapore
PRENTICE-HALL INC., Englewood Cliffs, New Jersey
WHITEHALL BOOKS LIMITED, Wellington, New Zealand

Printed in the United States of America

10 9 8 7 6 5 4 3 2 1

Contents

v

4   JSD Development Procedure   38

PART II   JSD DEVELOPMENT STEPS   59

5   Three Applications   61

6   The Entity Action Step   64

7   The Entity Structure Step   84

8   Initial Model Step   121

9 The Function Step 171

10 The System Timing Step 246

11 The Implementation Step 256

Preface

1   SCOPE OF JSD

This book is about a system development method. The method, known by the acronym JSD, is a method for specifying and implementing computer systems. We use the general term 'development' to cover a range of activities usually carried out by people whose job titles are 'systems analyst', 'system designer', 'program designer' or 'programmer'. These activities include requirements specification, functional specification, logical system design, application system design, physical system design, program specification and design, program implementation, and system and program maintenance. The book is addressed to people, whatever their job titles, who engage in any of these activities, or want to understand how they may be approached.

There is very little agreement on the definitions of these activities, and even less on the meanings of the job titles 'analyst', 'designer' and 'programmer'. JSD cuts across even the very small area of agreement that does exist, redrawing the boundaries between activities and between jobs, so that the existing names and titles become almost entirely inappropriate. So we shall refer to the activities by the general term 'development', and we shall use the title 'developer' to mean whoever is doing the activity currently under discussion.

Within JSD the primary distinction is between specification and implementation. The JSD development procedure has six steps, of which the first four are concerned with creating a specification of the required system, and the last two with implementing that specification. What is often called 'design' has largely been absorbed into the implementation part of JSD. This division of development into two major parts—specification and implementation—seems to be beneficial in many ways. One of the most important of these is that it encourages recognition of what has arguably always been the major division between people working in system development: the division between those whose primary interest lies with the system user and those whose primary interest lies with the computer.

JSD does not encompass every activity associated with system development. It excludes activities such as project selection, project planning and management, and cost/benefit analysis; it excludes procedures for system acceptance, installation and cutover; it excludes the whole area of human engineering in such matters as dialog design. JSD also excludes specialized application skills. In a system concerned with controlling inventory, JSD has nothing to say about the question of whether it would be better to provide an improved service to customers or to reduce the size of the total inventory. For example, in a system concerned with controlling elevators in a building, JSD provides no guidance towards a decision whether the pattern of elevator movements should follow one algorithm or another, or whether the system should provide gentle music to soothe the impatience of waiting customers.

2　THE SYSTEM AND THE REAL WORLD

The word 'system' can be used extensively, to include computer procedures, manual procedures, all or part of the user organization, everything and everyone that directly affects or is affected by the result of the development work. So, in an application concerned with control of aircraft engines the system includes the engines themselves and the devices which increase or reduce flow of air or fuel; in a purchasing application, the system includes the suppliers, the delivery trucks, the suppliers' documents, the receiving bays, the warehouse locations, the clerks in the purchasing department.

In JSD we restrict the use of the word 'system', referring essentially to what is created by the development activity; we distinguish the system from the real world outside. The real world provides the subject matter for the system: it contains the engines to be controlled, the employees to be paid, the customers and suppliers whose transactions are to be accounted for. The system itself consists of computer and manual procedures and hardware; we think of it as having a definite boundary—the system boundary—across which inputs and outputs flow between the real world and the system. This view is pictured in Fig. 1. In an old-fashioned batch data processing system, the system boundary was almost a physical boundary, enclosing the data preparation and the computer departments, and the mail room, together with some clerical departments that interfaced with data preparation on one side and the organization's customers, employees and suppliers on the other. In on-line and embedded systems, the boundary is less tangible, but still there.

In JSD the real world is regarded as given, a fixed starting point. This view reflects the exclusion from JSD of specific application knowledge; it is no part of JSD to choose the most economic policy for stock replenishment, or to negotiate with labor unions to determine rules for overtime payments, or to decide the algorithm for computing the movement of an airplane's control surfaces to correct a deviation from course. Our concern in JSD is to ensure that the system correctly reflects the real world as it is, and to provide the functions requested by the user, to a specification in which the user has the determining voice.

Although we regard the real world as given, we do not, of course, exclude the possibility that some or all of the real world must be invented or changed. For the most part, the invention or change is not itself an integral part of the JSD development. An extreme illustration is the general functional requirement: develop a good video game. The appropriate expert—if one exists—might determine that a certain psychological pattern would be good, a certain progression of success and reward, expectation and fulfilment, tension and satisfaction; and that the game should be about an intricate and difficult search for some treasure. Here, then, is the real world for this system. The JSD developer helps to specify this real world, working in cooperation with the expert and

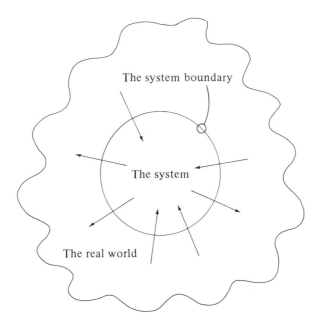

Fig. 1

providing concepts and notations in which the specification can be clearly expressed. The expert does the invention, and the JSD developer does the description. At a later stage of development, especially in the implementation stage, some technical invention is necessary within the system; that is a part of the developer's task.

3   APPLICABILITY OF JSD

JSD is used to develop systems whose subject matter has a strong time dimension. For example, the subject matter of the elevator control system is the real elevators, the real customers, the buttons they press to summon the elevator, and so on. To describe this subject matter properly we must place a major emphasis on its time dimension: the customer presses the call button before the elevator arrives; the doors open after the elevator arrives; the elevator leaves the floor after the doors close. In a data processing system for a bank, the subject matter is the real customers, their checks, their bank loans, their repayments, the interest charges, and so on. Here again, the time dimension is of central importance. A loan must be granted before repayments begin; repayments are credited before interest charges are applied; the checking account is opened before any checks are written.

Because of its emphasis on the time dimension, JSD is very widely applicable. Certainly it may be used for developing embedded systems, switching systems, control systems, and all kinds of data processing systems, both on-line and batch. All of these are concerned with real worlds in which the time dimension is of central importance.

4   JSD AND JSP PRINCIPLES

The system development method JSD has grown out of JSP, a program design method which has been widely taught and used over the past ten years. JSD may be seen as an enlargement of JSP, applying the same principles to a larger class of problems and to a larger part of the development task.

The starting point for JSP is a full specification of the program to be designed. A JSP program is a sequential process, to be eventually implemented in a sequential programming language such as PL/I, COBOL, Fortran, Pascal, or assembler language. Its inputs and outputs are viewed as sequential streams of records: a magnetic tape file or a line printer report is obviously a sequential stream of records; but so also is a set of segments retrieved from a database, or a set of terminal input messages in a conversation. A simplified form of the JSP program design procedure is:

(a)   describe the structure of each input and output data stream;
(b)   combine these structures to form a program structure;
(c)   list the operations which the program must execute to produce the outputs from the inputs, and allocate each operation to its proper place in the program structure;
(d)   write the program text, adding the necessary conditions to control execution of iteration components (loops or repetitions) and selection components (if–else or case constructs).

An essential principle of JSP is that the subject matter of the computation is described first, in steps (a) and (b), while the detailed function of the program is dealt with later, in step (c). This principle is central also in JSD. The subject matter in JSD is the real world, strongly ordered in time, outside the system; the detailed function is the production of system outputs. In JSD the early development steps are concerned with describing the real world, and explicit consideration of system function is deferred until later.

A program to satisfy a realistic specification usually needs to be decomposed into two or more sequential processes: at step (b) of the JSP design procedure, the developer recognizes that there are structural conflicts, or clashes, among the descriptions of the data streams. JSP provides a classification of these structure clashes into boundary, ordering, and interleaving clashes. For each type of clash there is a prescribed decomposition into a pattern of sequential processes connected by data streams internal to the program.

JSD does not start from a given specification, nor does it decompose the system into sequential processes. Instead, JSD development begins by creating a specification for the system, building it up from parts which are themselves sequential processes: the activity is therefore one of synthesis rather than decomposition.

Where a program is decomposed into connected sequential processes, JSP provides an implementation technique for recombining these processes into a single executable program. This technique, known as program inversion, is a transformation of a sequential process text into the text of an equivalent subroutine; the processes can then be combined into a hierarchical structure of subroutines. Combining processes in this way is regarded as an implementation activity, to be carried out at the end of program development: the hierarchical structure is devised purely for purposes of efficient execution, and is not considered in the earlier design steps.

In the same way, JSD provides an implementation technique, based on program inversion and other transformations, for combining the sequential processes of the system specification into an efficiently executable system.

5   SYSTEM DEVELOPMENT AND PROGRAM DESIGN

Conventionally, program design and programming are thought of as the final stages in system development. The earlier activities of system analysis, specification, and design produce a higher-level structure of the system whose lower levels remain to be completed by programmers. From this point of view, organizations that have adopted JSP as their program design method might hope to find that JSD is a 'front-end' to JSP: JSD would create the specifications for programs which would then be designed using JSP.

But it is not so. Aspects of JSP are diffused through the JSD development procedure. The early steps of JSP are concerned with the structure of sequential processes. They are directly relevant to the development of a JSD specification, which is composed of sequential processes. The implementation techniques of JSP are embodied in those of JSD. The JSP identification of structure clashes has a part to play in the JSD description of its real world subject matter. Certainly, there are some parts of a JSD specification—especially batch reporting programs and batch or on-line treatment of the system inputs—which can be handed over to a JSP program designer in the traditional way; and there are tasks in the JSD implementation stage which are very close to conventional program design tasks. But much of the traditional work of program design has already been incorporated in the development of a JSD specification. This is one example of the way in which JSD redefines the boundaries between development activities.

It is not necessary to know JSP to read this book. Those parts of JSP which are incorporated into JSD are explained as they arise, and JSP notations are included, with JSD notations, in an appendix. A full account of JSP from a program design point of view is given in M. A. Jackson, *Principles of Program Design*, Academic Press; another account is given in Leif Ingevaldsson, *JSP: A Practical Method of Program Design*, Studentlitteratur.

6   ARRANGEMENT OF THIS BOOK

The book is arranged in three major parts. In Part I, the JSD development method is introduced. The underlying principles of JSD are explained and justified by general arguments in an informal way; the development procedure, divided into six steps, is described, and is illustrated by a tiny example. Readers who want only a broad understanding of JSD may find that this part of the book is sufficient for their needs.

Part II is a series of chapters following the sequence of the JSD development steps. Three applications, introduced at the beginning of Part II, are used to provide illustration of the points arising in each development step. This interleaved treatment of the three applications allows technical material to be placed where it arises most naturally. To help the reader to follow the development of each application, the main results for each are gathered together in appendices and should be referred to as necessary to reestablish the context of the application as it progresses.

Part III contains material on some general aspects of development, such as errors and system maintenance, and a retrospective view of JSD in the light of the material in this part and in Part II.

In addition to the appendices, there is a glossary of JSD terms and a summary of notations used in JSD and in JSP at the end of the book.

It is hoped that the repeated discussion of main points of principle and practice will help those readers to whom the ideas are unfamiliar and hard to grasp, without irritating those for whom they are more quickly and easily digestible.

7   EXAMPLES

The examples used are very small; certainly they are smaller than any system that is likely to be put into productive use. Even in these small examples, some detail, especially of documentation, has been omitted from the discussion.

Of course, this is inevitable. In a book of this size, there is too little room for even one complete realistic example. Some authors solve this difficulty by presenting examples of a realistic size but limiting their discussion to fragments rather than complete examples; this is often done where the method presented is top-down. But JSD is not a top-down method, and in a section at the end of the book we discuss why we believe that top-down approaches are essentially inadequate. We prefer instead to limit ourselves to small examples which can be treated fully, omitting nothing that the reader might find difficult to supply or that might invalidate the treatment given.

We hope that the reader will not conclude that JSD is a method for developing very small, toy, systems. E. W. Dijkstra once observed that it is hard to give a talk: if you use no examples, most of the listeners will fail to understand the subject; if you do use examples, many of the listeners will conclude that the examples are themselves the subject. The subject of JSD is the development of a wide class of systems, including very large systems. The examples given are small, because they are intended to illustrate the exposition of the method, not to delimit its applicability.

Acknowledgements

The ideas in this book take their form from work done by John Cameron and myself over the past four years. We have worked together both in developing the ideas and in presenting them on courses, so in that sense the book is as much his as mine. He has also commented extensively and carefully on an earlier draft of the book, saving me from many mistakes: but the words are mine, so any defects of detail and expression are mine too.

I have never found it easy to recognize, and so to acknowledge, the sources of ideas I have worked on and promulgated. The influence of Tony Hoare's work on communicating sequential processes will be obvious, and also the influence of Rod Burstall and John Darlington's work on program transformation. But I have also been influenced, without doubt, by many other people. A paper presented at a conference, a book partly read, an informal discussion at a meeting, can all impart the germ of an idea without a conscious awareness of the debt. I hope that anyone who recognizes the influence of his own work in this book will accept these words as an explanation and an apology.

Cliff Jones and Mike McKeag have given me generous encouragement and valuable comments on an earlier draft of the book. So too have Barry Dwyer and Hans Nägeli. Tony Hoare, the editor of this series, first invited me to write the book, and then sustained me with encouragement and support when I needed it most. Among the few people who have made fundamental advances in software engineering, he is distinguished by his readiness to listen seriously, with care and interest, to ideas that are so much less exact and elegant than his own. Without his help this book would not have been written.

PART I

INTRODUCTION TO JSD

This part of the book is arranged in four chapters. The first three chapters explain and discuss the fundamental principles of JSD, and the fourth chapter describes the JSD development procedure.

Chapter 1 is about the distinction between model and function and the priority given to modelling over functional considerations in JSD. In JSD, development does not begin by specifying the function of the system to be developed: instead, it begins by describing and modelling the real world which provides the subject matter of the system. The functions of the system are specified on the basis of this model. A JSD system may be regarded as a simulation of the relevant parts of the real world outside the system; system functions are regarded as providing outputs derived from the behavior of this simulation.

Chapter 2 is about process models. The JSD method is concerned with applications in which the real world is dynamic, with events occurring in time-ordered sequence. Most data processing applications are of this kind, as also are applications in process control, embedded systems, and switching systems. To model such a dynamic reality adequately, it is necessary to use a modelling medium which is itself dynamic. JSD models are therefore built from sequential processes, rather than from the components of a database. The term 'sequential process' has a strong flavor of programming and technology: but in essence a sequential process is no more than a statement of the time-ordering of events.

Chapter 3 is about implementation. Because a JSD specification, both of model and of function, is expressed in terms of sequential processes, it is in principle capable of direct execution on the computer (or computers) on which the system is to run. But there is often—in typical data processing systems, always—a mismatch between the number and characteristics of the processes in the JSD specification and the number and characteristics of those which can be conveniently executed on readily available computers and operating systems. The implementation step in JSD is therefore centrally concerned with transforming the specification to make it convenient to execute. By regarding the implementation task as one of transformation, we narrow the gap between the specification and the executable system which implements it.

Chapter 4 describes the JSD development procedure, step by step. A brief example is used to illustrate the content and method of each step. The purpose of this chapter is to give a framework of the development procedure rather than to explore detailed considerations and questions arising at each step: that is the purpose of the second part of the book.

1

Model and function

1.1 FUNCTIONAL SPECIFICATIONS

Traditionally, the starting point in system development is the functional requirement. The developer begins by establishing the system's function, determining what the system is to do and what outputs it is to produce. The essential content of the system specification is the statement of system function.

This tradition has deep roots. In the earliest days of electronic computing, the computer was regarded as a machine which could be commanded, instructed, or ordered, to perform certain elementary functions. Thus we spoke of an 'add command', or a 'move instruction', or a 'multiply order'. A program or a system consisted of a set of these commands, commanding the computer to perform elementary functions in a pattern which amounted to the performance of larger, composite, functions. A suitable pattern of add, subtract, multiply, divide and move commands amounted to the calculation of gross pay for an employee in a payroll system. The invention of the subroutine in 1949 allowed larger functions to be conveniently specified in terms of smaller functions. It was then a relatively short step to view a program or system as having a single function which could be successively decomposed into smaller functions until the level of the already available machine functions was reached.

There is an obvious and attractive common sense about this. The purpose of the system is to do something, to perform some function, and that provides an apparently natural starting point for development; not merely natural, but convenient too, since the activity of decomposition, detailing, or refinement, can then lead to the final product of development, the finished system.

This is essentially the view on which 'functional decomposition' is founded. The system function is organized as a hierarchy of functional procedures, and development consists of elaborating this hierarchy from the top downwards. It is also the view underlying 'structured systems analysis and specification' (see, for example, Tom de Marco, *Structured Analysis and System Specification*, Yourdon, and Chris Gane and Trish Sarson, *Structured Systems Analysis: Tools and Techniques*, Prentice-Hall). In that approach, the system function is organized as a hierarchy of processes connected by data flows: each process performs a part of the system function, and is itself decomposed into a set of processes connected by data flows, each one performing a sub-part of the function. But whether the medium is procedures or processes, subroutine calls or data flows, the message is function.

1.2   MODELLING REALITY

JSD relegates consideration of system function to a later step in development, and promotes in its place the activity of modelling the real world. The developer begins by creating a model of the reality with which the system is concerned, the reality which furnishes its subject matter, about which it computes.

Every computer system is concerned with a real world, a reality, outside itself. A telephone switching system is concerned with telephone subscribers, telephone handsets, dialling, conversations, conference calls. A payroll system is concerned with employees, the work they do, the pay they earn, the tax they must pay, the holidays they are entitled to. A process control system for a chemical plant is concerned with the vessels, pipes and valves of the plant, the flow of liquids and gases, the temperatures and pressures at the various points in the plant. A sales order processing system is concerned with customers, the orders they place, the products they order, the deliveries they receive, the payments they make.

It is a fundamental principle of JSD that the developer must begin by modelling this reality, and only then go on to consider in full detail the functions which the system is to perform. The system itself is regarded as a kind of simulation of the real world; as the real world goes about its business, the system goes about simulating that business, replicating within itself what is happening in the real world outside. The functions of the system are built upon this simulation; in JSD they are explicitly added in a later development step.

In JSD, we use the word 'model' to mean a model of a reality outside the computer system which is being developed. There is some scope for confusion here, because the same word is used by other writers with other meanings. Some writers use the word 'model' to denote a somewhat abstract description of the system itself or of its function. When they speak of 'modelling' they mean describing the system function in 'logical' rather than 'physical' terms, describing what the system does without giving detail of how it does it. Other writers speak of 'modelling the system' in terms of its performance characteristics: the model describes system behavior in a way which permits them to apply mathematical tools such as queuing theory in order to determine how fast the system will execute and how much space it will use in main and backing storage. Other writers again use the term 'system model' to mean a prescription for the development procedure, showing the structure of the activities to be carried out by the developer.

Our usage in JSD is different. By 'model' we always mean a model of the real world outside the computer system; we never mean a model of the system itself, nor of any of its attributes or characteristics, nor of the development procedure used to create it. Making a JSD model of the real world involves two distinct tasks:

— first, making an abstract description of the real world, and
— second, making a realization, in the computer, of that abstract description.

The realization in the computer is then a model of the real world in the same sense that an architectural model is a model of the real building, or a naval model is a model of the real ship, or an econometric model is a model of the real economy, or a map is a model of the real terrain. The abstract description of the real world is simply a description in which relevant aspects are described and irrelevant aspects omitted: thus the abstract description of a real building might describe the shapes of the main masses, their relative sizes, and their relative positions and orientations; but it may omit to describe the material from which the walls are built, the water, electrical and other services, the parts of the building that are underground, and the internal structures of the building. The realization must satisfy the abstract description closely enough for the purpose the model is to serve: thus, the architectural model must contain the same number of main masses, with the same relative sizes, positions and orientations, as the real building.

1.3   FUNCTION BASED ON MODEL

The JSD idea of a model, and its relation to function, can be illustrated by a simple example.

A system is required to control traffic on a certain part of a railroad network. A suitable abstract description of the relevant part of the railroad is made:

> The railroad consists of three tracks, each divided into segments. Trains travel on these tracks, and can move from a segment to an adjacent segment of the same track. Trains moving east can move from the second segment of track A to the second segment of track B, and from the third segment of track C to the third segment of track B; trains moving west can move from the second and third segments of track B to the second and third segments of tracks A and C respectively.

This description can be realized in an electronic model. The apparatus might consist of a number of circuits, connected to each other and to the real tracks. Pulses sent from the real tracks to the apparatus indicate the movements of trains from

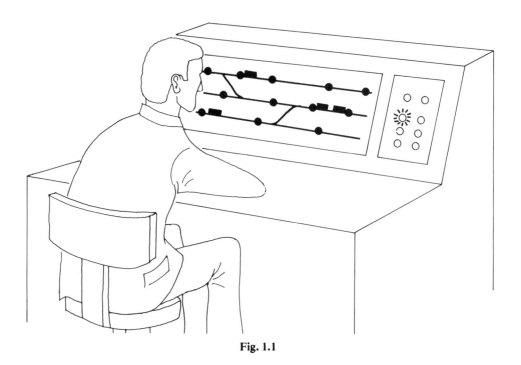

Fig. 1.1

segment to segment. The circuits are designed so that a movement of a real train from one segment of real track to another is modelled by some suitable change in the states of the circuits.

This electronic model has, in itself, no function. It does nothing except fulfil its role as a model, faithfully simulating the described behavior of the real world. But although the model has no function, it provides the basis on which various functions can be built. Figure 1.1 illustrates two functions added to the system. The first function is to make available to a human traffic controller a continuous display of the state of the real world tracks. The left, and larger, part of the console is an animated schematic picture of the tracks; when a train moves into a track segment, a small rectangle is lit up in the corresponding segment of the schematic picture. The controller can thus observe the movements of real trains by observing the movements of these rectangles in the display. The second function is provided by the outputs on the smaller panel on the right of the display. When two trains are in the same segment of track, a warning light is illuminated in this panel. This function is, as it were, a 'management exception report'. It could be modified into a control function by arranging that in addition to illuminating the light the system cuts off the electric power from the segment of track containing the two trains. Other functions can be readily imagined. Perhaps the controller needs a continuously refreshed summary display showing how many trains are currently under his control. Perhaps another warning light should indicate when a train has spent more than two minutes in one segment and may be presumed to have broken down. All of these functions can be provided on the basis of the model that has been built. In JSD we will base system functions on a model in exactly the same kind of way. Given a computer model which simulates the real world, we will be able to add functions for displaying the state of the real world, either continuously or on request, for producing exceptional outputs to indicate the occurrence of particular conditions, and for producing outputs that can be fed back to the real world to affect its subsequent behavior.

1.4   MODEL AS THE CONTEXT FOR FUNCTION

One reason for starting development with modelling rather than functional considerations is that the model provides the conceptual, as well as the computational, basis for the system functions.

There are two stages in modelling. First, we make an abstract description of the reality we are concerned with; then we determine how that abstract description can be realized in a working computer model. In JSD, the abstract description is carried out in two steps, and its realization in a third step of the development procedure. It is not until the fourth step that we come to consider explicitly the functions of the system.

An abstract description of the real world is, as we have seen, a partial description: we choose to describe certain parts of reality and to omit others. In the railroad model, the developer apparently chose to describe the arrangement of the tracks in segments, the connections between segments, and the movements of trains over the segments; the curvature of the main segments, their physical construction, the varying gradient of the track, the size of each train, the distinction between passenger and freight trains, the weight of each train, and an infinity of other aspects of reality have all been omitted. This kind of selectivity is inevitable in any description: the only complete description of reality is the reality itself, as the Ruritanian map-makers learnt when they set out to construct a perfect one-to-one scale map of their country.

To make a realized working model corresponding to the abstract description requires that we establish some connection between the real world and the model. In the railroad model, the tracks and trains must be connected to the parts of the electronic apparatus which simulate their behavior, ensuring that when a real train enters a real segment of track the states of the circuits corresponding to the train and track segment are correspondingly changed.

The abstract description and its realization together provide the context for functional specifications. They define a set of words—train, track, segment—to be used in specifying system functions; the meaning of each word in the real world is given by the connections between the real world and the model. Once the model has been created, we can be in no doubt about the meaning, for example, of 'train'. In the model itself, a train is that part of the circuitry which realizes the description of a train; in the real world, a train is whatever is connected to that part of the model. Functions concerned with trains can then be specified unambiguously: any ambiguity must perforce have been resolved when the abstract description and its realization were made and agreed with the user of the system.

By contrast, a development procedure starting with functional specifications is inevitably dealing in undefined terms. In a banking system, a function specified as 'report when a customer's account is overdrawn' relies in an obvious way on the meanings of the words 'customer', 'account', and 'overdrawn'. If these meanings have not been defined in an earlier stage of development, the functional specification is necessarily ambiguous. Of course, as this illustration shows, we may well suppose that the meanings of the terms are so clear and so well known that no explicit definition is necessary. The consequence of this supposition is often that hidden ambiguities in functional specifications remain to plague the later stages of development. In JSD we ensure that functions can be unambiguously specified in terms of a previously created model.

1.5   FUNCTION IMPLIED BY MODEL

A related, but different, reason for starting JSD development with modelling reality is that the model implicitly defines a coherent set of possible system functions. In the railroad control system, we are able to specify functions which can be expressed in terms of trains, tracks, and segments; but we are not able to specify functions in terms of passengers, track gradients, or freight trains. By creating the model we have, as it were, constructed a dictionary of words to be used in functional specifications: we can then specify any function which can be specified in words appearing in that dictionary.

Defining a coherent set of related functions is always hard if development starts by considering function directly. One of the difficulties in functional specification is that the specification is always liable to change. Even if changes are prohibited during system development, or strongly discouraged by tightly worded contracts, we must always allow for changes to be made after development is completed: the large, and increasing, proportion of system engineering effort devoted to system maintenance is well known. Often an apparently small change to the functional specification proves to be surprisingly expensive and difficult. Part, at least, of the high cost of maintenance is due to this vulnerability of the specification.

One possible response is to try to specify and build systems which provide more function than the user has yet requested. The hope is that most of the early requests for functional change will already have been provided in the initial system, waiting only to be activated for the benefit of an amazed user and the good repute of a gratified developer. But it is not easy to anticipate requests for change; often the user exercises what seems to be a perverse ingenuity, asking for changes that are actually made more difficult by the provision for anticipated but unwanted functions.

The source of the problem is the exclusive attention paid to function in the initial stages of development. A system development method concentrating on function is always liable to produce a system that is difficult to maintain. Here is a small illustration—almost a program rather than a system—of why this is so.

1.6   AN ILLUSTRATION

A company operates boats for hire on a pleasure lake. The customers come to the boathouse to ask the boatman whether he has a boat available for a session of sailing. If so, he makes the boat ready, helps the customer aboard, and keys a message into an on-line terminal. The message contains an identifier of the session and a code (S) to indicate that the session is starting; the terminal automatically adds the current clock time to the message. When the session is finished, the customer returns the boat, the boatman calculates the session time and receives payment from the customer, and keys another message into the terminal. This message again contains the session identifier and the clock time, and the code E to indicate that the session has ended.

(We may note that the management of the company has already chosen and purchased the terminal hardware, although the system specification is not yet written. This conforms to a practice widely established among some organizations.)

The manager of the operation wants some management information. He wants a report on each day's activity, in the form:

NUMBER OF SESSIONS = nnn

AVRGE SESSION TIME = mmm

where the average session time is, of course, the total of all session times divided by the number of sessions.

The system developer sees immediately that the required function has two parts: compute the information from the available input stream, and print it. Computing the information consists of counting the sessions, totalling the time, and calculating the average. Counting the sessions is easy: the number of sessions is the same as the number of S messages. Totalling the time is not much harder:

$$totaltime = (endtime\ of\ session\ 1 - starttime\ of\ session\ 1)$$
$$+ (endtime\ of\ session\ 2 - starttime\ of\ session\ 2)$$
$$+ (\ldots)$$

or, more conveniently,

$$totaltime = (endtime\ of\ session\ 1 + endtime\ of\ session\ 2$$
$$+ endtime\ of\ session\ 3 + \ldots$$
$$- starttime\ of\ session\ 1 - starttime\ of\ session\ 2$$
$$- starttime\ of\ session\ 3 - \ldots)$$

The resulting solution, functionally designed and implemented in structured code, looks like this:

```
begin open message stream;
      get message;
      number := 0; totaltime := 0;
      do while not end-of-stream
         if code = 'S'
           then number := number + 1;
                totaltime := totaltime – starttime;
           else  totaltime := totaltime + endtime;
         endif
         get message;
      enddo
      print 'NUMBER OF SESSIONS =  ', number;
      if number ≠ 0
        then print 'AVRGE SESSION TIME =  ',
                   totaltime / number;
      endif
      close message stream;
end
```

The system goes into production, and everyone is happy. The solution provides exactly the function that is required. But soon the manager comes to the developer with a request for a 'functional enhancement'. He wants the report to contain a third line:

LONGEST SESSION TIME = ppp

Careful examination of the existing system convinces the developer that the requested enhancement cannot be made except by throwing away what has already been done and building a completely new system. The reader should also examine the system as shown above, and convince himself that this is indeed so.

Fortunately, the developer persuades the manager that there are technical reasons, to do with the machine's operating system, why the requested change cannot be made: the manager is dazzled by the technical brilliance of the developer's explanations, and agrees that the change was not crucially important anyway. (Notice that no costs are debited to the system maintenance account: calculations of maintenance costs often omit the cost of not doing maintenance.)

Less fortunately, the manager is back soon with another request. This time he is sure the change will be easy, because all he wants is two reports, each one exactly like the report he is already receiving. One report should deal with the sessions starting before noon, and the other with the remaining sessions of the day. Once again the developer (and, I hope, the reader!) sees that the change cannot be made to the existing system. This time he devises an excuse based on the recent introduction of the fixed-block disks; the manager is somewhat less dazzled by the developer's technical brilliance than he had been before, and is definitely dissatisfied with the service he is getting. Soon, he returns with yet another request. This time the change is vitally important: the telecommunication line is defective, and has been dropping some of the messages. As a result, there are some sessions for which only one message, either the S or the E message, is received. The system must be changed to exclude these sessions from the calculation of the report.

Unfortunately, this change is no easier than the first two: it simply cannot be made without abandoning the system and creating a new one. Neither the time nor the budget is available, and there is no way out. The developer's explanations (something to do with the new compiler) fall on deaf ears, and he is soon updating his résumé and seeking another job.

1.7   MAINTAINABILITY AND MODELS

This system is difficult—or even impossible—to maintain because its development was based on purely functional considerations. A system developed in this way is always vulnerable: each new functional requirement will be arbitrarily difficult or easy, arbitrarily expensive or cheap.

The developer of the boating lake system would claim that he was very unlucky. His manager might have asked for a report showing the maximum number of sessions concurrently in progress at any time during the day (observation of this point by W. Turski is gratefully acknowledged). It would then have been easy to introduce a variable which is initialized to zero, incremented by 1 for each S record and decremented by 1 for each E record; the maximum value attained by this variable would then have been the required maximum number of concurrent sessions. He was also unlucky with the second request, asking for two reports, one dealing with sessions starting before noon and the other with the remaining sessions. If the session identifiers were allocated in ascending sequence from the beginning of the day, it would be possible simply to remember the identifier of the first session starting at or after noon: the two reports then deal with sessions having identifiers less than this remembered value and greater than or equal to this remembered value respectively. Either the identifiers are not allocated in ascending sequence, or the unfortunate developer failed to think of this solution.

However, he was not unlucky: he simply produced a bad solution. The defect of the functionally developed solution is that it fails to model the real world with which it is concerned. The real world for this system was certainly about sessions of boating: the customer buys a session of boating; the first line of the management information report is a count of sessions; the second line is an average time for the sessions. So the specification should have been, at least in part, a model of sessions, and the system structure should have been based on that model. But there is nothing in the solution which models a session: there is no part of the program text we can point to and say 'that part corresponds to a session'; there is no variable we can point to and say 'there is one of these for each session'.

Clearly, the idea of a session is an important ingredient in the manager's view of reality: that is why he asked for functional changes which were all concerned with sessions. The JSD insistence on starting development by explicitly modelling the real world ensures that the system user's view of reality is properly embodied in the specification and, eventually, in the structure of the system itself. The developed system can then be expected to allow easy enhancement for functions consistent with this view of reality.

Many experienced system developers would claim, with justice, that they would not have developed the bad solution we are castigating. They would have recognized that the rearrangement of the computation of *totaltime* was a dangerous optimization, and would have developed the system differently. Quite so. A good 'functional designer' is, in fact, applying criteria to system development which lie outside the realm of functional decomposition itself. JSD analyzes those criteria, places them in the appropriate early stage of the development procedure, and makes them fully explicit: they amount to a requirement that the system must embody a suitable model of reality.

1.8   MODEL MORE STABLE THAN FUNCTION

It might be objected that the model, embodying the user's view of his real world, is no less vulnerable to change than the system functions. This is not so. Model is more stable than function.

The greater stability of the model is a consequence of the fact that the system functions must be expressed in words whose meaning depends upon the user's view of reality. If the view of reality changes, the functions must change, but not vice versa: function can change while the underlying view of reality remains constant.

Consider an analogy. The view of the world is like a road map; the functions are possible journeys on the roads. If a relevant part of the map is changed, that is, if some of the roads are closed and some new roads are built, then any journey over the changed part of the map is necessarily affected: the journey cannot remain unaffected if the map is altered. But the converse is not true: there is a whole universe of possible journeys for a given map, and the traveller may devise new journeys and alter the routes of old journeys without affecting the map at all. In the same way, the system user can devise new functions and alter the definition of old functions without changing the underlying model.

In building a JSD model of reality, we are concerned to establish the base on which a set of functions can be subsequently specified and built. Explicitly, we reach agreement with the system user on a view of the real world; implicitly, we are agreeing on the definition of a set of possible functions. The developer of the boating lake system should have started by modelling the real world. He might have asked the manager: 'what is a session?'; 'do you want to include boats in the model?'; 'do you want to model the customers?'. He could then have explored with the manager the implications of the agreed model. If the model includes sessions, then the system will be able to support functions about sessions. If the model excludes customers, then the system will not be able to support functions about customers. The developer would say to the manager: 'you have told me to leave the customers out of the model; you must realize that this means that you cannot ask for reports about customers unless you are prepared to pay a high price for changing the system model of reality; on the other hand, we are including boats, so you will be able to get information about boats at a low price.' The developer does not have to say exactly what information functions will be provided; only to point out the general implications of the chosen and agreed model.

1.9   MODEL AND FUNCTION INTERDEPENDENT

Model and function are intimately connected. It is, of course, impossible to construct a model of reality without some idea of the purpose to which the model is to be put; we cannot carry out the first three steps of the JSD development procedure, in which we build the model, without some anticipation of the fourth step, in which we add the functions to the model.

If the user of the boating lake system were a biologist instead of a commercial manager, he would no doubt want the developer to build a model of the plant and animal life in and around the lake. If he were a sociologist he would want a model of the social interactions among customers and between the customers and the boatman. With different functions in mind the developer would build entirely different models.

This does not imply that the initial concentration on modelling in JSD is spurious, that it is simply a cloak for a secret addiction to functional specification. Model and function are inseparable: we cannot say anything about system function without implying a model of the real world; we cannot say anything about the real world without implying some purpose in our view. The question is: where should we begin? In the functional approach, the model of reality is implicit in the functional specification, and is never fully articulated. In JSD, the functional capability of the system is implicit in the model; but in the steps which follow the modelling, system functions are fully specified to whatever extent they can be known during development.

1.10   USER COMMUNICATION

There is another important reason why development should start by describing and modelling the real world rather than by specifying the system function. It concerns the communication between the system developer and the user.

Where users have been dissatisfied with the system development process and its product—and dissatisfaction is not rare in some organizations—two complaints have been loudly and commonly voiced. The first is that the system developer 'doesn't understand the business'. This complaint was heard so loudly and so often at one time, that a major topic of discussion was the question whether a systems analyst should be a computer technician trained in the user application or a user staff member trained in computing. The burden of the complaint is simply that the developer has failed to understand how the user sees the real world: that is, he has failed to articulate and agree an explicit model of reality. The result of this failure is that the system, even when its functional specification appears to satisfy the user's needs, is somehow not quite right: it embodies distortions of the reality seen by the user, and these distortions give rise to operational and maintenance difficulties. In the trivial illustration of the boating lake system, the user sees the world as one in which there are a number of sessions, each with a beginning and ending; but the developer sees it as one in which there are a number of events, each of which is either an *S* event or an *E* event. The difference is in some ways subtle; but it is enough to make the system absurdly inflexible.

The second complaint is that the system developer produces specifications which are excessively technical. This complaint was manifestly justified when system specifications typically included file and record layouts, system flow diagrams, and even logic flowcharts. Discussion between the developer and the user was conducted entirely on the developer's chosen ground of computer technicalities, leaving the user to make what he could of the documents (if any) which emerged. The same complaint remains valid, although to a lesser extent, when system specifications and communication between developer and user are based entirely on function. Detailed system function is necessarily intricate; unless the system is simply mechanizing what the user currently does by other means, these intricacies will be largely an artefact of the evolving computer system design, and will therefore be difficult for the user to understand.

In JSD, the initial communication between the developer and the user is all about the user's real world. The developer is approaching the user with a request to be informed about what the user already knows well, to learn to see the world the way the user sees it. Although the abstract description being developed may be more formal and exact than the user is accustomed to, it need not be expressed in technical language or formal notations. This initial communication has two good effects. The developer is seen to be coming right away from the computer and the computer department, moving into the area of the user and making an explicit effort to learn about the reality of the application. He cannot be accused of hiding behind technicalities or trying to dazzle the user with the power of the computer. The user, for his part, can gain confidence in the developer and in the effectiveness of their communication: initially, the user's role is virtually the role of a teacher, teaching what he knows best; only after the description of the real world has been agreed does discussion turn to the necessarily more technical subject of the system function.

1.11   DESCRIPTION BEFORE INVENTION

Finally, we may observe that to model the real world is to describe what already exists, while to define and specify system functions is to create something new. Of course, sometimes the system function will be no more than a reproduction of the function of an existing system, whether manual or automated; and sometimes a part, at least, of the real world for a system will need to be invented rather than merely described. But the point remains true for most systems.

In JSD, recognizing that the developer must practise both description and invention in producing the specification, we adopt a procedure in which the description comes first and the invention afterwards: the developer first models the real world, then defines the system function.

SUMMARY OF CHAPTER 1

Traditionally, system development starts by considering the functional requirements. This is merely common sense because the function of the system is the embodiment of its purpose (1.1).

JSD development starts differently, by building a model of the real world which provides the subject matter of the system and in which it is embedded. The model is a realization, in the computer, of an abstract description of the real world: in a sense, it is a simulation (1.2).

The functions of the system are then added to the model. The system can produce a visible display of the state of the model (and hence of the state of the real world); it can produce outputs when particular circumstances occur, and these outputs can be used for information or for control purposes (1.3).

The abstract description of the real world and its realization in the model provide a context in which functions can be unambiguously specified. The model is, in effect, an implicit definition of the set of functions which can be provided by the system (1.4, 1.5).

It is therefore easier to build maintainable systems. Because the system embodies the model and the model defines a set of possible functions, the developer and the user can agree on a set of functions which are to be supported in original development or in later maintenance. By contrast, a system which is not based on an explicit model of reality will be less maintainable: required functions may be arbitrarily cheap or expensive to add to the original system (1.6, 1.7).

The model of the real world is a stable basis for development: it is less subject to change than the functions built upon it (1.8).

Function and model are interdependent: a model implies a set of possible functions, and the words used in specifying a function imply some model. To make the model explicit, it should be considered first (1.9).

Communication between the developer and the user is improved because the developer is seen to be seeking knowledge from the user and consciously starting development from the user's point of view. He is explicitly 'understanding the business'. A description of what the user already knows precedes invention of functional or technical novelties (1.10, 1.11).

2

Process models

2.1 THE TIME DIMENSION

The real worlds we wish to model in JSD are always worlds in which the time dimension is of central importance: the importance of the time dimension is, in fact, the defining characteristic of the class of applications for which JSD is intended to be used.

In a payroll system, the employee must join the company before he can start work; he works for a week, or a month, before he receives pay for his work; he must reach the age of retirement before he receives his pension. In a system to control pumps at a filling station, the customer presses the reset button on the pump before he withdraws the nozzle from its housing; he inserts the nozzle into the car's filling pipe before he pulls the trigger; he pays the bill after he has completed the filling. In an on-line bank terminal, the customer inserts his card before keying-in his identifying number; after that he can enter a transaction code; then, if the code is for cash withdrawal, he keys-in a cash amount; after receiving the cash he can withdraw his card. In a financial system, goods or services are delivered before they are billed; the customers receive the bills before they pay; if a bill has been sent and no payment received within thirty days, then a reminder may be sent.

In systems like these, we are centrally concerned with realities in which events occur in a certain order. The order may, of course, vary: perhaps some goods or services are billed before they are delivered; perhaps a filling station customer wrongly pulls the trigger before pressing the reset button on the pump. But whether the ordering of events is fixed or variable, it is always of central interest and importance.

2.2 STATIC AND DYNAMIC REALITIES

A real world in which the time dimension is of such importance may be called dynamic. By contrast, we may use the word 'static' to describe a real world in which there is no time dimension, or in which the time dimension is unimportant to our purposes.

Static realities, as subjects for computer systems, come to mind less readily than dynamic realities; but they do exist. One example is provided by a national census, of the kind carried out in the UK in 1981. Each household was required to answer questions about the state and circumstances of the household and its members on a particular date, and to enter the answers on a census form. The quetions covered topics such as the number of members of the household, the sex and age of each member, their educational qualifications, and whether they were in full-time or part-time jobs. Suppose that a system is to be developed to hold the census results in an accessible form and to respond to queries that may be put by sociologists, planners, demographers, civil service departments, and other interested parties. A sociologist might enquire how many households consisted only of members of one family; the social security department might enquire how many households had only one member in a full-time job, and so on.

For this system, the real world is entirely static. It is a particular state of the UK at a particular moment in time. Within this world, nothing changes, nothing happens, and there is no time dimension: there is no before and no after.

Another example of a static reality is provided by the artificial intelligence problem of scene analysis. A scene, perhaps composed of some everyday objects on a table, is recorded by an electronic camera as a two-dimensional pattern of bits or pixels. The requirement is for a system, or a program, to analyze this pattern and to recognize the objects appearing in the scene and their relative positions. The output of the system might be, for instance: 'here is a cup; here is a bottle partly hidden by the cup; here is a book; here is another cup, standing on the book.'

Again, this real world is entirely static. It has no time dimension, and no events occur in it.

2.3 STATIC AND DYNAMIC MODELS

Static and dynamic real worlds need different techniques of description and modelling. For a static reality, assuming it to be discrete rather than continuous, it is appropriate to describe the world in terms of entities having fixed properties and fixed relationships to one another. For a dynamic reality, again assuming it to be discrete, it is appropriate to describe the world in terms of entities which perform or suffer certain actions in a certain order, and have varying properties and relationships.

The appropriate medium for modelling a static reality is a database. A database is essentially a snapshot; it captures a single state of the reality it models, just as a photograph captures a single state of its subject at a single moment in time. Because a static reality has, by definition, only one state, it can be appropriately and completely modelled by a database.

A fundamental principle of JSD is that a dynamic real world cannot be adequately modelled by a database: a dynamic reality requires a dynamic model. The difference between a static and a dynamic model can be illustrated by two familiar devices, both models of a dynamic reality which is the passage of time itself (Figs. 2.1 and 2.2).

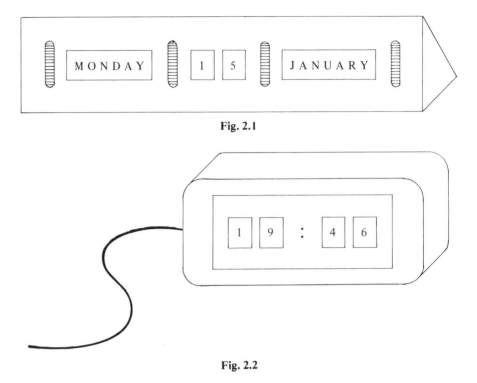

Fig. 2.1

Fig. 2.2

The first device is a desk calendar, consisting of a small metal box containing four cylinders arranged on a horizontal spindle. The first cylinder carries the names of the days of the week: Sunday, Monday, Tuesday etc. The second carries the digits 1, 2, and 3, and also has a blank area. The third carries the digits 0–9. The fourth carries the names of the months: January, February, March etc. This calendar is, like a database, a static model. To model the passage of time, it is necessary for the user of the calendar to update it. When the date changes from Monday, 15 January, the user must rotate the first cylinder so that it shows Tuesday instead of Monday, and the third cylinder so that it shows 6 instead of 5. When the date changes from Wednesday, 31 January, the user must update the calendar by rotating the first, second and fourth cylinders. Because the calendar itself is a static model, it requires an extraneous updating by the user, just as a database requires the provision of updating programs.

The difficulty created by this need for extraneous updating is, of course, that the updating may be done incorrectly. The user may wrongly change the date from Monday 15 January, to Tuesday 14 January, which is not a date in the current year; or from Monday 15 January, to Tuesday 35 January, which is not a date in any year; or he may even rotate one of the cylinders to a position midway between two days, causing the calendar to take a value which is not a date at all. In database parlance, this is an aspect of the database integrity problem: how to ensure that the contents of the database are meaningful, self-consistent, and consistent with the reality that is modelled.

The second device is a digital slave clock. It is of similar physical construction to the calendar, having four cylinders; the first cylinder carries the digits 0, 1 and 2; the second and fourth cylinders carry the digits 0–9; and the third cylinder carries the digits 0–5. The first two cylinders show the hour, and the last two show the minutes, in a 24-hour representation of the time. The cylinders are connected by an internal mechanism which ensures correct relative movement: after the clock shows 19.46, the next pulse must cause it to show 19.47; after it shows 23.59, the next pulse must cause it to show 00.00. There is no possibility, unless the clock is broken, that after 23.59 it will show 24.59 or 23.69, or any other wrong reading. The clock is a dynamic model, containing within itself the mechanisms that in the calendar were provided by extraneous updating rules.

Because the clock is a dynamic model, a large part of the database integrity problem is avoided. We need not worry, once the model has been built and we are satisfied of its correctness, that it may reach an invalid state, or a state that is not self-consistent, or that it may go through an incorrect sequence of states. Of course, we still need to ensure that the pulses from the master clock arrive at the appropriate intervals: connecting the model to the reality which it models is a problem that cannot be solved within the model itself. But, because we have built a dynamic model, we have been able to capture the dynamics of the reality, the sequences of events that can occur in the real world.

2.4   SEQUENTIAL PROCESSES

Some database development methods compensate for the static nature of the database model by specifying updating constraints as a part of the database definition. Thus, for the calendar illustration, we might specify that when the value shown by the third cylinder (the units digit of the day number) is 9, the next value must be 0 unless the second cylinder shows 2 and the fourth cylinder shows February, in which case the next value of the third cylinder must be 1.

This approach can be regarded as follows: first we make a static model, then we elaborate the model to cater for the dynamic aspects of the modelled reality. This is not the approach taken in JSD. In JSD we begin by making a dynamic model directly, based on a dynamic description of the real world.

The dynamic model in JSD is composed of a number of sequential processes. The form of a sequential process is that of a simple structured program: it is called sequential because there is no notion, within a single sequential process, of concurrency, parallelism, or multitasking; only one thing can happen at one time within one process. Within the whole model, there can be many things happening at one time, because there are many processes in the model.

Here is a sequential process which models time in the way it was modelled by the slave clock (for simplicity and brevity the first two cylinders (tens and units of hours) have been modelled together, and the last two cylinders similarly):

```
do forever
   begin hours := 00;
         do while hours ⩽ 23
            begin minutes := 00;
                  do while minutes ⩽ 59
                     receive 1 pulse;
                     minutes := minutes + 1;
                  enddo
                  hours := hours + 1;
            end
         enddo
   end
enddo
```

Evidently, this sequential process is a correct model of the passage of time in the 24-hour representation. The sequence of value-pairs of the variables hours and minutes is, as required: 00.00, 00.01, ..., 00.59, 01.00, ..., 23.59, 00.00, 00.01, and so on. The events occurring in the real world are the pulses emitted by the master clock and received by the process. The process keeps in step with the real world because the operation 'receive 1 pulse' cannot be completed until the pulse is emitted by the master clock: the model must wait for the next real world event to occur.

We may think of this sequential process as a program capable of being executed on a suitable computer system. It differs from most conventional programs in two ways. First, it will spend most of its life waiting for the next pulse to occur: the operations executed between one pulse and the next need at most a few microseconds of computer time; the remainder of the minute is spent waiting for the next pulse. Second, the elapsed time for execution of this process is very large: in fact, the process as specified will run indefinitely.

As we shall see, a very long execution time, composed chiefly of waiting for the next relevant event to occur in the real world, is typical of the sequential processes which make up a dynamic model of reality.

2.5   A DATA PROCESSING EXAMPLE

Here is another, somewhat more practical, example of a model composed of sequential processes.

A bank operates a deposit scheme. Customers enter the scheme by making an initial investment; subsequently they may withdraw or pay in money, until eventually they terminate their membership of the scheme. Overdrafts are permitted, and, unrealistically, no interest is charged on overdrafts and none paid on credit balances.

Events in this real world are ordered for any one customer; the initial deposit must be the first, and termination the last, event for each customer. But the customers act independently and, in principle, concurrently. We shall therefore require one sequential process for each customer. Each customer process is considered to have its own input stream of messages, analogous to the pulses received by the slave clock, carrying information to the process of the actions performed by the customer in the real world. The text of the process for one customer is:

```
begin open message stream;
      read message;
      simulate invest;
      read message;
      do while withdraw or pay-in
         begin if withdraw
                  then simulate withdraw;
                  else  simulate pay-in;
               endif
               read message;
         end
      enddo
      simulate termination;
      close message stream;
end
```

The *simulate* operations in the text are place-holders to indicate the points where the model process execution corresponds to the real world actions of the customer. In the standard form of process text, used in the later parts of this book, these place-holders are not necessary.

Like the clock process, the customer process has a long elapsed time of execution. If a typical customer of the bank is a member of the scheme for fifty years, then a typical instance of the customer process will take fifty years to complete its execution. Like the clock process, the customer process spends most of its elapsed execution time waiting: it is held up at each *read message* operation until the next input message becomes available; that is, until the customer performs his next action.

It is important to remember that the texts of these processes form a part of the system specification: they specify what a customer does, and in what order, and, in execution, they model the behavior of the customers of the bank. There are many reasons why they cannot be directly executed on the computer: these reasons include the very large number of the processes, their very long elapsed execution times, and the very high proportion of waiting time. The work of the developer in the implementation stage of JSD includes the transformation of these processes into a form that allows them to be conveniently and efficiently executed.

2.6   ADDING FUNCTION TO A PROCESS

The model process for the bank customer is so far little more than a skeleton. Its structure shows the actions which the customer may perform, and the ordering of those actions; but it does not show the effects of those actions, either on the state of the customer model or on possible system outputs. However, by constructing the framework of the process first, we make it easy to add those things later.

System outputs are invariably associated with system functions; in JSD any discussion of system output is deferred to the fourth step in the development procedure, the function step. The same is mostly, but not invariably, true of elaboration of the model by adding attributes to actions or processes.

Suppose, for example, that we wish to add a function to the model: we wish to produce a report whenever a customer overdraft occurs. This function is definable, as it must be, in terms of the model we have built. Each of the actions, *invest*, *withdraw*, and *pay-in* has an *amount* attribute; the customer process has a *balance* attribute, which is the cumulative sum of the action *amount* attributes, taking these to be negative for *withdraw* and positive for *invest* and *pay-in* actions. The report is to be produced when a *withdraw* action results in a negative *balance* value.

Adding this function to the model gives the process text:

> **begin** *open message stream*; *balance* := 0;
>   *read message*;
>   *balance* := *balance* + *amount of invest*;
>   *read message*;
>   **do while** *withdraw or pay-in*
>   **begin if** *withdraw*
>   **then begin** *balance* := *balance* − *amount of withdraw*;
>   **if** *balance* < 0
>   **then** *print report*
>   **endif**
>   **end**
>   **else** *balance* := *balance* + *amount of pay-in*;
>   **endif**
>   *read message*;
>   **end**
>   **enddo**
>   *simulate termination*;
>   *close message stream*;
> **end**

The process text now contains both a specification of the model and a specification of the function which has been added to the model. The model itself has been elaborated to include the *balance* attribute needed for the function.

2.7   PROCESS CONNECTIONS

Adding the overdraft report function to the customer model was particularly simple: the function, in the form of operations to produce the report, was embedded directly in the model process. In a realistic system we will have to work a little harder to add functions to the specification.

Sometimes the function will require a new process which is not one of the model processes. For example, if the system must produce a report giving the total of the balances for all customers, then clearly this function cannot be added to any one of the customer processes, or even to all of them: we must add a function process to the system which is separate from the customer model processes but connected to all of them.

Connections between processes can be made in two ways in JSD specifications. Both of these ways can also be used to connect model processes to the real world. We have already seen how the customer model processes are connected to the real world by sequential message streams; this form of connection is called data-stream connection. The other form of connection is called state-vector connection. The state-vector of a process is the set of all the local or internal variables of the process, such as the variable *balance* in the customer process. When state-vector connection is used between two processes, one of them directly inspects the state-vector of the other. So, for example, a function process connected to the customer process by state-vector connection could directly inspect the value of the *balance* attribute of the customer.

The two different forms of process connection used in JSD have different characteristics, which are discussed and illustrated in Part II. Both forms may be used in realizing the model of reality, and also in adding function processes to the model.

2.8   ENTITIES IN JSD

In the first two steps of the JSD procedure, an abstract description of the real world is made in terms which can lead to the specification of a realized model in the third step. The real world is described in terms of entities, actions they perform or suffer, and the orderings of those actions. For the simple bank example, the entities are the customers; the actions are *invest*, *withdraw*, *pay-in*, and *terminate*; the ordering of the actions is *invest* first, then any number of *withdraw* and *pay-in* actions, then, finally, *terminate*. In the third step, the customer entity is modelled by the customer process.

The meaning of the word 'entity' in JSD is closely associated with the idea of the process model, and with the idea of an ordered set of actions. It is therefore different from the meaning used in database methods, where an entity may have no real world actions, either suffered or performed. For example, we might wish to describe the fact that each customer is located in a certain town, each town in a certain county, and each county in a certain state; the towns themselves may have attributes, such as distance from our organization's nearest branch. In a relational database analysis we would be led to identify town, county, and state as entities, to be represented by relational tuples in the database. In JSD, town, county, and state are not entities unless they perform or suffer actions in the real world, and those actions are significantly ordered. A JSD model has, in general, fewer entity types than a database model.

Database definition in JSD is a part of the implementation activity, not of the specification. The content of the database is determined essentially by the state-vectors of the model and function processes; broadly, each state-vector constitutes a 'master record' that must be stored, in some form, in the database. The fields of the state-vector are derived chiefly from attributes introduced for functional purposes, as the balance attribute of the customer process was introduced. In the implementation stage, the developer may choose to hold the state-vector of one process in one, two, or many database segments or records; sometimes it will be efficient to combine the state-vectors of two or more processes into one database record. The access paths needed in the database are determined by the connections among processes and the order in which those connections are to be used; for example, a function process which inspects the state-vectors of many model processes will inspect them in some particular order, and this order will determine one of the access paths needed in the database.

SUMMARY OF CHAPTER 2

JSD is concerned with systems for which the real world has an essential time dimension. The description of such a real world is in terms of events occurring in a time-ordered sequence (2.1).

We may contrast such a dynamic reality with a static reality, in which there is no time dimension, and no event can be said to occur (2.2).

A dynamic reality requires a dynamic model. It is inappropriate to try to model a dynamic reality by a database, because a database is inherently a static model. Much of the 'database integrity' problem can be ascribed to the attempt to model a dynamic reality in a static medium (2.3).

The appropriate dynamic modelling medium for computer systems is the sequential process. A sequential process captures the time-ordering of the real world quite directly. It keeps in step with the events of the real world by receiving sequential input, each message indicating the occurrence of an event (2.4).

In a simple data processing example (which is used as the illustration of the JSD development steps in Chapter 4), we see how the lifetime of a bank customer can be modelled by a sequential process. The elapsed execution time of the process is necessarily the same, approximately, as the lifetime of the real world customer (2.5).

A simple function can be added to the model process by embedding the operations necessary to produce the function output directly into the process text. A variable required by the function becomes an attribute of the model, summarizing the previous actions of the customer (2.6).

A slightly more difficult function requires the addition of a new process to the system. It can be connected to the model processes by direct inspection of the state of the model process. There are thus two kinds of process connection used in JSD: data stream connection, and state-vector connection (2.7).

A JSD description of the real world is in terms of entities and their actions. A JSD entity is modelled by a sequential process, and is very different from a database entity. Database definition in JSD is regarded as a part of the implementation stage, at the end of development; the content and access paths of the database are determined by the model and function processes and their connections (2.8).

3

Implementing the specification

The gross division of system development into the two stages of specification and implementation is widely accepted. We first determine the 'what', and then determine the 'how'. In JSD, as we have seen, the 'what' is further divided into specifying a model of the real world and specifying system functions based on that model. In this chapter we will turn our attention away from this division of the specification into model and function, and concentrate on the relationship between the specification and its implementation.

3.1 THE 'WHAT' AND THE 'HOW'

A prime issue in system development methodology—that is, in the invention and study of system development methods—is how to divide the decisions which the developer must make between the two stages of specification and implementation. At some point, the developer must decide on the arrangement of records in files or in a database, on the decomposition of the system into on-line transaction modules and batch programs, on the use of intermediate files between programs, on decomposition of programs into modules, subprograms and tasks. Are these decisions to be treated as part of the specification or part of the implementation activity?

Sometimes such decisions are considered to be a part of an activity called design, which is neither specification nor implementation but an intermediate stage. In JSD they are firmly placed in the implementation stage: effectively, much of what is sometimes called design is, in JSD, treated as an integral part of implementation.

To some extent, this is merely a matter of terminology; but there is a substantive point here as well. Much of the progress that has been made in programming and in systems development has consisted in deferring certain decisions from the earlier to the later stages of development, of purging the specification stages of constituents that belonged more properly to the implementation. A programming example illustrates the point. On the earliest drum machines, the available main storage was so small that instructions had to be fetched singly or in small groups from the drum into the main store where they could be executed. Programmers were therefore concerned, in the early stages of planning a program, to ensure that when an instruction was to be executed it was likely to be already in main store or, failing that, to be just about to come under the drum's read head. It became recognized that this concern militated against other, more fundamental, concerns of program structure; techniques were devised of rearranging program texts for efficient use of the drum, thus freeing the program designer from this implementation concern. Later, as larger main stores became commonly available, programs grew correspondingly larger, and the same drama was re-enacted with overlay segments playing the part that had previously been played by individual instructions.

The point is easily misunderstood, because the decisions have often been deferred, not to a later stage of consideration by the developer, but to compile time or run time, where they are taken automatically by the compiler or operating system. In a virtual storage system, the decomposition of a program into pieces that can be efficiently loaded for execution is no longer a concern of the developer, but is performed automatically while the program is being executed. The allocation of machine registers for addressing and data manipulation is performed automatically by the compiler, as is the choice of machine representation for different data types. To concentrate on the automation of the decisions is to miss the point: what matters more is that the decisions are deferred, that the concerns are removed from the specification to the implementation stage. A system developer who chooses file designs and decomposes the system into runnable programs at an early stage is behaving like the programmer on the drum machine, prematurely making decisions that properly belong to a later stage and that can only distort the early stages of the work: he is rearranging the system before it is clearly determined what system is to be rearranged. It is true that these decisions are not, and perhaps can never be, automated: they must be taken, sooner or later, by the developer—but it is far better that they be taken later.

3.2   THE HIDDEN PATH AND PROGRAM PROVING

Given a satisfactory division between specification and implementation, between the what and the how, we are then faced with two important questions of methodology. By what path does the development proceed from the specification to the implementation, and how can we convince ourselves that what is implemented is what was specified?

Traditionally, the path from specification to implementation has been obscure, hidden in the minds of the developers. A system designer is given a narrative specification of an application problem, and eventually produces a system flow diagram in terms of programs and files, some file definitions, and some program specifications. What path did he follow in doing this work? The program specifications, perhaps again in narrative form, are handed to a programmer who produces a program in COBOL, PL/I, Pascal or Fortran. The path followed by the programmer is no clearer. It is not known how the work was done, and it is not known whether it has been done correctly.

One approach to this difficulty relies heavily, or even entirely, on testing. For a chosen set of input data, the specification defines what output should be produced; if the implemented system or program does produce that output when executed with the chosen input, we have some confirmation that the implementation corresponds correctly to the specification. But it is a very weak and incomplete confirmation. The test has not demonstrated that the implementation is correct; it has merely not demonstrated that it is incorrect. The inadequacy of testing is far greater for systems than for programs: there are many more possible combinations and sequences of input data, and the cost of each test is much higher. A batch system may contain errors which will be revealed only after the year-end program has been run twice: the necessary test would require two executions of this program and one hundred and four executions of the weekly batch updating program.

Another approach relies on proving correctness of the implementation by logical deductions based on the texts of the programs. The proof of correctness may be developed along with the program itself, and can thus help to guide the work of implementation. This approach has had some considerable success with small programs, but it is far from clear that it can be extended to large programs or to systems. It is most effective when the specification is very short compared with the length of the program text, specifying succinctly the relations that should hold between the inputs and the outputs.

Suppose, for example, that we wish to construct a subroutine which, given a positive integer X, finds the square root of X rounded down to the nearest integer. If we call this result Y, the specification of the subroutine is to find Y such that:

$$Y^2 \leqslant X \quad \text{and} \quad (Y + 1)^2 > X.$$

This specification is much shorter than the implementation; we do not need to refer to it while we read the text of the subroutine, along with the proof of its correctness. Instead, parts of the specification are incorporated into the proof, reappearing in successive steps, until the whole specification appears once more in the triumphant last line of the proof. A proof of the square root subroutine might run:

... so now we have $Y^2 = 0$ and $X \geqslant 1$

... so $Y^2 \leqslant X$

... now we still have $Y^2 \leqslant X$

... but $(Y + 1)^2 \leqslant X$

... and now we still have $Y^2 \leqslant X$ and also $(Y + 1)^2 > X$, so the subroutine is correct.

It is essentially this ability to carry the specification along with the proof that makes a convincing proof possible.

System specifications, whether for data processing systems, control systems, switching systems, or other kinds of system, are not short and simple in this way. They are full of detail, and approximately the same size as their implementations. Checking such a specification against the proof of its implementation would not really be easier than checking it directly against its implementation. The benefit of the proof would lie mainly in redundancy: the problem has been addressed three times instead of twice. Probably the additional effort could be better directed elsewhere.

3.3   ABOLISHING IMPLEMENTATION

An ideal approach to the difficulties of carrying out the implementation work and convincing ourselves of its correctness would be to abolish implementation altogether. This can be done if the specification can be directly executed on the computer. (We are, of course, thinking of the computer as the combination of hardware and software rather than as the hardware alone.)

Suppose, in the example of the square root subroutine, that we have a programming language with a built-in function INT, whose definition is that

INT(Z)

means 'Z rounded down to the nearest integer'. Suppose also that fractional exponents are allowed, so that

$X^{1/2}$

means 'the square root of X'. Then we could write our specification in the form:

Y := INT $(X^{1/2})$

and this specification would be directly executable on the computer. There would then be no implementation work to do, and hence no need to convince ourselves of its correctness. The specification is the program.

Notice the crucial difference between saying 'the specification is the program' and saying 'the program is the specification'. It would not be helpful to present the text of the square root subroutine, an elaborate structure of additions, subtractions and multiplications, to the user, saying 'here is your specification'. But this is what some developers have done in the past. Having studied the application, they produced a document containing system flow diagrams of programs and files, file and record layouts, and program flowcharts; this document was then offered to the unhappy user as a 'specification', which he was expected to 'sign-off' as confirmation of his acceptance of the specification. To be useful, a specification must be written in the user's terms, structured as his world is structured and not in accordance with the needs of the computer implementation.

3.4   DIRECT EXECUTION OF A SPECIFICATION

JSD specifications are written strictly in the user's terms, specifying a model of his real world and functions defined by reference to that model. At the same time, they are in principle directly executable.

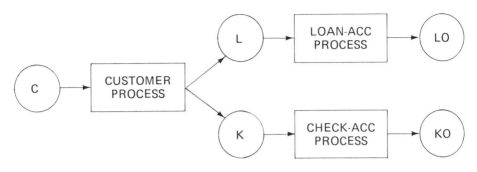

Fig. 3.1

Imagine a modest elaboration of the bank example, in which a customer has both a loan account and a checking account. As we will see later, this means that there are three entities for each customer, connected by sequential data streams (Fig. 3.1). The data stream C contains messages corresponding to the actions of the customer. The data streams L and K contain copies of those messages which refer respectively to the loan account and to the checking account. The outputs LO and KO are produced by functions embedded in the loan account and checking account processes: for example, LO might contain acknowledgements of loan repayments and KO might contain account statements produced whenever enough transactions have occurred to fill a page.

For the moment we will imagine, quite unrealistically, that the bank has only one customer. We could then execute the specification directly on a hardware system composed of the following devices:

— three microprocessors, one for each process of the specification;
— one input device, either a card reader or a keyboard terminal, for input of the data stream C;
— two communication buffers, one for each of L and K;
— two printers, one for LO and one for KO.

All of these devices would require to be highly reliable, capable of running without breakdown for the fifty years or so that the customer is active.

Each microprocessor would execute the text of its associated process, communicating with the others and with the world outside by sequential 'read' and 'write' operations. When a microprocessor is executing a read operation, and no message is available in the input stream, it waits in the conventional way; since the customer performs, on average, only one action every two days, most of the time is spent waiting for input. A write operation does not cause waiting: the buffers for L and K absorb any mismatching between the speed of the customer process and the speeds of the account processes, and the output printers for LO and KO are assumed to be similarly buffered.

The internal storage of each microprocessor contains two things. The first is the text of the process being executed on that processor: that is, the control structure specifying the ordering of the actions performed or suffered in the real world by the entity modelled by the process, together with the executable operations simulating those actions. The second is the state-vector of the process: that is, the internal variables representing the attributes of the entity, whose values give the current state of the entity at any moment. So, for example, the loan account processor storage contains the state-vector of the loan account process, including perhaps a variable *outstanding-balance*, a variable *years-to-run*, and so on. One variable which is of particular importance, and is in every state-vector, is the *text-pointer*. This is a variable which shows the point in the text that is currently being executed; when a processor is waiting at a read operation because no input message is available, the text-pointer will have a value pointing at that read operation. In the usual hardware terminology, the text-pointer is the instruction address; we will think of it, however, not as a hardware storage address but as a place in the process text.

Notice that each process is executed once only, during the fifty years of the system's lifetime. This point is no doubt already obvious; but it is of such fundamental importance that we would rather risk laboring the obvious than allowing it to pass unnoticed. The customer lives his life only once; so the process which models him is executed only once. The customer's life, so far as the bank is concerned, stretches over fifty years; so the customer process takes fifty years to run. When the customer process is waiting for an input message, it is waiting at a particular place in the text; when the awaited message arrives, execution of the customer process continues from that place, as indicated by the value of the text-pointer.

In a JSD system, processes always have these characteristics: each one is executed only once, and its execution takes as long as the lifetime of the entity it models. In some approaches, described by some writers, the word 'process' is used to mean 'what a clerk can do in five minutes'; it corresponds to what might perhaps be implemented by a sub-routine or procedure. This is not the meaning used in JSD.

3.5   PROCESS SCHEDULING

Suppose now that we require to execute the same specification on a single processor rather than on three. It is then necessary to find some way of sharing the power of a single processor among the three processes, of scheduling the processes so that they can take turns, according to suitable rules, at using the single processor. This process scheduling problem is central in JSD implementation; different choices of rules for process scheduling can give radically different implementations to the same specification.

One very simple and attractive solution is to use a generalized operating system, providing some kind of multi-processing or multi-tasking facility. Each of the three processes of the specification could be a separate task; the communication buffers, L and K, would be internal queues managed by the operating system; we would retain the two output printers for LO and KO. We would still require extreme reliability over the fifty years of system execution, but no doubt we could make fruitful use of the check-point and restore facilities of the operating system.

We are still executing the specification directly, without any explicit implementation step. Essentially, the operating system on the single processor is emulating the three microprocessors and the two communications buffers: it is providing us with three virtual processors and two virtual buffers.

The process scheduling rules built into the operating system are largely hidden from us. We may be able to affect the scheduling, perhaps by stating relative task priorities, but only in a very indirect and obscure way. However, for a system as small as this, on a dedicated computer, we might assume that any reasonable scheduling rules will be satisfactory. Since the customer performs so few actions over the fifty year lifetime of the system, there is a huge surplus of processing power. What we require of the scheduler is therefore something like this: that if a process can run—that is, it is not held up waiting for an input message that is not yet available—then it will be allowed to run within a short time (say, within one second).

Each process, of course, is still executed only once: when the scheduler allows a process to run, it allows it to continue execution from the place in its text it had previously reached. Execution does not restart from the beginning of the process any more than a human being, on waking in the morning, restarts his life from the moment of birth.

3.6   MACHINES NOT MATCHED TO SPECIFICATIONS

The bank system will be more realistic if we allow the bank to have a large number of customers, perhaps as many as 100 000. It would be very attractive if we could share the power of the single processor among the resulting very large number of processes, in the same way as we shared it among the three processes of one customer.

For our present purposes, we will set aside the potential difficulties posed by the presence of 100 000 input streams C, assuming that all C input records will arrive, in chronological order, on a single input device. Similarly, we will assume that only two line printers will be needed: on one, the 100 000 LO output streams will be printed, and the 100 000 KO output streams on the other. If we can arrange that each repayment acknowledgement and each page of checking account statement can be output by a single uninterrupted burst of printing, this assumption is reasonable. The real difficulty arising from the 100 000 customers lies in the very large number of processes to be executed. We are now demanding much more from the generalized operating system than it is designed to provide. We are asking it to run 300 000 concurrent tasks, and to manage 200 000 internal queues. This raises a number of difficulties, some of which are likely to prove insuperable.

One difficulty is that there may be stringent limits set to the number of concurrent tasks, perhaps by sizes of internal tables within the operating system. It might be that for each task a control block of something like 128 bytes is needed, and the table of these control blocks must be entirely within real main storage. The necessary 38.4 Mbytes is unlikely to be available, certainly not at a cost that would be reasonable for the use that would be made of it.

Another difficulty is the huge amount of process text: 100 000 copies of the text of each process type (customer, loan account, and checking account), each with an associated state-vector. This difficulty can be overcome if the state-vectors can be separated from the process texts: it would then be possible to keep only one copy of each of the three process texts, and to keep the 300 000 state-vectors in backing storage.

A more serious difficulty is posed by the computational overhead cost of scheduling so many processes, together with the cost of activating and suspending each process (that is, each task) when necessary. Because the table of control blocks is so large, assuming that it can be accommodated at all, it is expensive to search even a very small part of the table in determining which process is to be activated next. Each process activation and suspension requires the retrieval of the appropriate state-vector from backing store, loading hardware registers from the state-vector, storing the registers in the state-vector, and storing the new value of the state-vector in backing store.

Yet another difficulty is lack of control over the scheduling. Suppose that during some period of the day many messages are input in the data stream C. A message arrives pertaining to customer X; the customer process X is activated, and writes a message to its output stream L; meanwhile another C input message has arrived for customer Y. Should the loan account process for customer X now be activated, or the customer process for customer Y? A generalized operating system is ill-equipped with mechanisms for controlling such decisions. But if they are left to the uncontrolled vagaries of the scheduling rules implemented in the operating system, they are likely to result in unpredictable and undesirable consequences. Sometimes large numbers of L and K messages will be unnecessarily buffered, degrading system performance and delaying the production of outputs. Sometimes the system will be very slow to accept input messages in the C data stream. It may be that some customers seem to be treated much better than others, perhaps because their identifiers have lower values and hence their task control blocks are closer to the start of the table.

The heart of the problem is this. The JSD specification is written as a set of communicating, concurrent, processes; and the operating system is designed to run a set of communicating, concurrent, processes. But there is a severe mismatch between the dimensions of the two sets. The specification, for a typical data processing problem, has a very large number of processes, each of which requires small amounts of processor time spread over many years; the operating system is designed to handle a set containing a very small number of processes, each requiring a relatively large amount of processor time concentrated into a small elapsed time that is measured in seconds, minutes, or hours, not in years.

The implementation step of JSD development is concerned to overcome this mismatch between the specification and the machine on which it is to be executed.

3.7   PROCESS SCHEDULING AT BUILD TIME

The techniques used in JSD implementation have a common theme. They allow the developer to make decisions when the system is built that might otherwise not be made until the system is run. Having particular knowledge of the specification and of its desired execution characteristics, the developer can use that knowledge to make better decisions than could be made by a generalized operating system.

Many of these decisions are about process scheduling. As we have seen, process scheduling accounts for a substantial part of the mismatch between the specification and the machine on which it must be executed. Differences in process scheduling also account for a large part of the difference between a batch and an on-line implementation, and between one batch implementation and another.

Possible scheduling decisions in the bank example include the following.

(a) Run the customer processes as soon as input is available, but run the loan and checking account processes only after the end of the day's business. Messages written to the L and K streams by the customer processes are to be held in serial files in disk backing storage. At the end of the day, run the loan account processes before the checking account processes, so that one printer can be used for both LO and KO outputs, with only one change of printer set-up.

(b) Run every process as soon as input is available. When a running customer process produces an L or K message, suspend the customer process while the loan or checking account process is run for which the L or K message has been produced. Use two printers, so that LO and KO outputs can be produced continually.

(c) Save the C inputs during the day. At the end of the day, run every process for which input is available, as in (b) above.

Decision (a) gives a system which is partly on-line and partly batch. Updating for customers is on-line, but updating for accounts is performed in batch. Decision (b) gives a completely on-line system. Decision (c) gives a completely batch system.

These different scheduling decisions give different implementations, but they do not change the specification. Whatever scheduling choice is made, the customers in the real world still perform the same actions in the same order, and the customer processes still model those actions and their orderings. The process texts are unchanged: the scheduling decisions affect only the provision of processor time for the execution of those texts.

3.8   IMPLEMENTING BY TRANSFORMING

Process scheduling is usually thought of as being the province of those who design and build operating systems. It is carried out at the level of machine language, or very close to it; it deals in machine registers, instruction addresses, program status words, and other such things. It is largely hidden from those who design and implement application systems.

In JSD implementation, we need to be able to grasp the process scheduling quite directly, so that we can implement the scheduling decisions we make. To do so, we need not resort to machine language; we can do everything we require at the level of languages such as COBOL, PL/I, Pascal or Fortran. The techniques of JSD implementation include:

— writing process texts in a form which allows them to be easily suspended and reactivated, so that their execution may be scheduled explicitly;

— designing and writing special-purpose scheduler programs to control the scheduling of the system processes;

— separating process state-vectors from process texts, so that one copy only need be kept of the text of each type of process, while as many copies of the state-vector are kept as there are real world entities modelled by the process;

— breaking process texts into pieces which can be more conveniently loaded and executed in a conventional environment.

The results of applying these techniques are the familiar components of data processing systems. A process text that can be suspended and reactivated is, more or less, a module or procedure to handle a single transaction. A special-purpose scheduler program may turn out to be a transaction-handling monitor, or the skeleton of a batch program. Separating the state-vectors from the process texts gives the separation of master records from the procedures which update them. Breaking texts into convenient pieces converts programs which run for fifty years into programs which can be run for a few seconds, minutes, or hours at a time.

The route by which we reach these familiar components in JSD is largely one of transformation. We transform the specification processes to run on one machine rather than another: to run on the hardware and software which is actually available to us, rather than on the conceptual machine which provides a microprocessor for each process and a communication buffer for each data stream. If each transformation is systematic, and follows rules which guarantee its correctness, we will be confident that the final implementation is correct. It will implement the specification just as the machine code produced by a correct compiler implements the program written in the input source code.

3.9 A BASIC TRANSFORMATION

The various JSD transformations are discussed in detail in later chapters of this book. Perhaps the most significant is the transformation which allows processes to be easily suspended and reactivated, and hence to be easily scheduled: we give a short outline description of it here.

Suppose that we are considering the customer process in the bank example. It has one input data stream, C, and two output data streams, L and K (Fig. 3.2). We will assume here either that only one customer exists or that the state-vector has already been separated from the text of the process; we need therefore consider only one customer process to be scheduled.

The process is, as it were, a program which consumes the whole of the stream C and produces the whole of the streams K and L. To obtain a grasp of the scheduling, we would like to transform it into a subroutine of the scheduler, which the scheduler can call by the normal subroutine calling mechanism; when called, the subroutine will continue execution of the process text and, at some point, return to the scheduler. The call

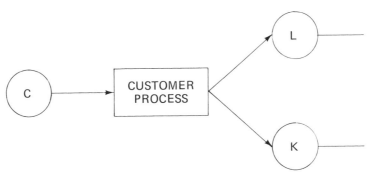

Fig. 3.2

of the subroutine by the scheduler is equivalent to activation of the process; return to the scheduler from the subroutine is equivalent to suspension of the process.

At what points should the process be suspended and reactivated? For several reasons, the most convenient points are those at which there is some input or output activity in the process; the points at which there is a 'read C message' operation, or a 'write K message' or 'write L message' operation. So these operations will be implemented by the 'return' statement which causes control to return to the scheduler from the subroutine.

Merely coding read and write operations as 'return' statements is not enough. We must also arrange that when the subroutine is next called, execution continues at the point where it was last suspended. This means we will need to use an explicit variable for the text-pointer, which, by convention, we will call QS. Finally, we must ensure that the scheduler is informed of the reason for the current 'return' statement, whether the process is now suspended at a 'read C', at a 'write K' or at a 'write L' operation: it will not otherwise be able to deal correctly with the result of the subroutine call or to set the parameters correctly for the next call of the same subroutine.

The implemented subroutine, then, is simply the text of the process coded in a particular way: the structure of the process text, its control logic, has not been changed at all. By using the kind of coding described, we have implemented the process in a form which allows it to be activated and suspended, and hence to be scheduled, by means of the standard mechanisms of subroutine call and return.

3.10 THE SIGNIFICANCE OF IMPLEMENTATION TECHNIQUE

Some readers may feel that the outline given in the preceding section is far too sketchy, and that they would like much more detailed explanations, with illustrations of the coding discussed. These readers will find satisfaction in the later chapters of the book, where a much fuller discussion is given, with illustrative examples.

Other readers may feel that the topic of implementation is far too technical. Surely systems development should not be concerned with the minutiae of program coding?

Can't coding be left to the programmers, who are interested in these things, and not imposed willy nilly on systems analysts and designers?

Certainly, implementation is a technical matter: it concentrates attention on the machine, not on the user; it is about manipulating the specification to fit the hardware and software; it is about programs and subroutines, databases and segments, files and access methods; it is not about banking or sales order processing, controlling chemical plants or connecting telephone subscribers. To this extent the objection is justified. Readers whose interest lies solely with the user and the application may reasonably choose to skip the parts of this book which deal with implementation.

But implementation is an integral part of JSD, and so of this book. A satisfactory method must not only deliver a specification. It must also provide a negotiable path from that specification to an executable system; the value of a specification is greatly diminished if there is no systematic prescription for its implementation. So in presenting a development method we are obliged to show how the developer may implement what has been specified.

Another reason for dealing explicitly with implementation techniques in JSD and in this book is that we have relegated to the implementation stage many decisions which traditionally come much earlier in the development. So we need to demonstrate that these decisions have not been ignored or made harder. We hope, too, that by showing how they fit into the JSD development procedure we will show convincingly that it would be wrong to place them earlier. It should become apparent that many differences between one system and another, which at first sight are differences of specification, are really no more than differences between implementations.

SUMMARY OF CHAPTER 3

Much of what is often called 'design' is considered in JSD to belong to the implementation stage. In JSD, file design, the decomposition of the system into transaction modules and batch programs, and the decomposition of programs are all regarded as implementation tasks (3.1).

How is the specification to be related to its implementation? Testing is both expensive and inadequate. Correctness proofs seem inapplicable when the specification is long and detailed. It would be ideal if the specification could be directly executed on the computer, while at the same time being written in terms of the user's real world (3.2, 3.3).

A JSD specification is, in principle, directly executable. A microprocessor must be provided for each process, and other devices for process communication and input–output. This is an impractical requirement. We may hope to execute the specification on a single machine, shared among the various processes by an operating system which schedules execution of each process according to general rules (3.4, 3.5).

But a typical data processing system contains a very large number of processes, each of which uses only a very small amount of computer power over a very long elapsed execution time. A general-purpose operating system is ill-matched to such a requirement, being effectively unable to schedule such a set of processes (3.6).

A central theme of JSD implementation is that process scheduling may be determined when the system is built, rather than when it is run. Different scheduling choices give different implementations of the same specification (3.7).

To allow scheduling choices to be implemented when the system is built, it is necessary to transform the specification processes into a form which allows easy suspension and activation in conventional languages such as COBOL and Fortran. This basic transformation is called 'program inversion'. It is also necessary to transform the specification in other ways, and to design and write special-purpose scheduling programs. The results of these implementation activities are the familiar transaction modules, batch programs, and database records of a typical data processing system (3.8, 3.9).

Implementation is about computer technicalities, not about application problems. But it is an integral part of JSD, because a development method must provide a path from the specification to the implementation; also, many concerns which are traditionally viewed as design, or even specification, concerns, are firmly placed in the implementation stage in JSD (3.10).

4

JSD development procedure

4.1 DEVELOPMENT STEPS

The JSD development procedure is shown diagrammatically in Fig. 4.1. The diagram uses a notation which we will use in some of the development steps for rather different purposes and with much more precision than it is used here.

The diagram shows, following the principles discussed in earlier chapters, that the procedure consists of two major parts, develop specification and develop implementation, in that order. The first, in turn, consists of two ordered parts: specify model and specify functions. And so on.

The boxes at the lowest level of the diagram represent steps in the JSD development procedure. They are:

(1) Entity action step: in this step the developer defines the real world area of interest by listing the entities and actions with which the system will be concerned.

(2) Entity structure step: in this step the actions performed or suffered by each entity are arranged in their orderings by time. The orderings are represented by diagrams like that of Fig. 4.1.

(3) Initial model step: in this step, the description of reality, in terms of entities and actions, is realized in a process model and connections between the model and the real world.

(4) Function step: in this step, functions are specified to produce the outputs of the system, additional processes being added to the specification as necessary.

(5) System timing step: here, the developer considers some aspects of process scheduling which might affect the correctness or timeliness of the system's functional outputs.

(6) Implementation step: in this step, the developer considers what hardware and software is, or should be, provided for running the system, and applies the techniques of transformation and scheduling, along with techniques of database definition, to allow the system to be efficiently and conveniently run.

The individual steps of the procedure are illustrated in Sections 4.2–4.7, using a simplified version of the bank customer example which has been briefly discussed in the

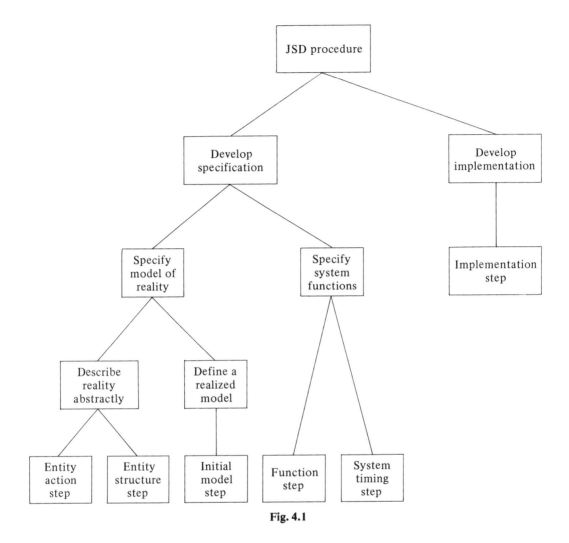

Fig. 4.1

preceding chapter. The remaining sections of this chapter discuss some general aspects of the procedure.

4.2   THE ENTITY ACTION STEP

The JSD method includes the development of a specification: it does not start from the point at which a specification is already written. So the starting point for the developer is often only a general idea of the purpose and subject matter of the system: the early steps of JSD are concerned to define and delimit this subject matter more closely.

In the entity action step, we begin to define the subject matter by describing the real world for the system in terms of entities and the actions they perform or suffer. The developer considers all the people, things, and organizations which might be taken to be entities, and all the events which might be taken to be actions; from these, a selection is made to give an initial list of entities and another initial list of actions. Broadly, there are two kinds of criterion to be applied in making the selection: the first kind is general, and applies to all JSD systems; the second kind is particular, and applies to the particular system being developed.

General criteria for actions include these:

—   An action must be regarded as taking place at a point in time, rather than extending over a period of time. Thus 'be in debt' would not be a permissible action, unless the real world timescale of the system were so long that the whole period of indebtedness could reasonably be regarded as an instantaneous event.
—   An action must take place in the real world outside the system, and must not merely be an action of the system itself. Thus 'issue error message' would not be a permissible action.
—   An action is regarded as atomic, and cannot be decomposed into subactions. Thus if 'withdraw money from checking account' is an action, and 'pay money into deposit account' is another action, there cannot also be a composite action 'transfer money from checking account to deposit account' consisting of the 'withdraw' and the 'pay in' actions occurring in sequence.

General criteria for entities include these:

—   An entity must perform or suffer actions, in a significant time-ordering. Thus 'date' and 'age' would not be permissible entities in any plausible system.
—   An entity must exist in the real world outside the system, and must not be merely a part of the system itself or a product of the system. Thus 'error report' would not be a permissible entity.
—   An entity must be capable of being regarded as an individual, and, if there is more than one entity of a type, of being uniquely named.

Subject to these general criteria, we are free to select any entities and actions which satisfy the particular criterion of the system being developed:

—   An entity or action is to be included in the list if the system will need to produce or use information about it.

In the very simple bank example, let us suppose that the developer selects only one entity type, CUSTOMER; and that the actions selected are INVEST, PAY-IN, WITHDRAW, and TERMINATE. Since CUSTOMER is the only entity, all the actions must be actions of CUSTOMER. These decisions are recorded by writing the lists explicitly:

Entities: CUSTOMER.
Actions: INVEST, PAY-IN, WITHDRAW, TERMINATE.

In addition to listing the actions, it is necessary to give an informal description of each action by which the name is associated with an understandable real world happening; along with the description the developer writes a tentative list of the attributes of the action. Thus:

> INVEST: Become a member of the scheme by making an initial investment.
>   Attributes: date, amount, name, address, age, . . .
> PAY-IN: Pay money into the scheme. Attributes: date, amount, . . .
> WITHDRAW: Take money out of the scheme. Attributes: date, amount, . . .
> TERMINATE: Cease membership of the scheme. Attributes: date, reason, . . .

The attribute lists of the actions will be extended in later development steps, particularly in the function step. No description is given of entities, beyond stating which actions each entity partakes in: an entity in JSD is fully described, at this development stage, by its actions.

The result of the entity action step is a highly abstract description of the real world. The developer has described the real world in terms of the listed entities and their actions: there are customers, and these are their actions. The system will, eventually, be capable of producing outputs which can be expressed in terms of this description. Almost more important than what has been included in the description is what has been left out: by leaving out 'employee' and 'manager' from the entity list, the developer has effectively decided that the system will not be able to produce information about the behavior of employees and managers; by leaving out 'change job' and 'move house' from the action list for CUSTOMER, he has decided that the system will not be able to produce information about the effect of these events on customers' participation in the bank's scheme.

We have spoken of these decisions as if they are made by the developer alone. But, of course, they are really made by the system's prospective users, with the developer's help. The entity and action lists form a glossary of terms that can later be used to specify functions of the system; they delimit the possible system functions by defining the words in which they can be expressed.

4.3   THE ENTITY STRUCTURE STEP

Because the actions of an entity are ordered in time, we need to express that ordering. Occasionally, we will find that an entity can perform (or suffer) any of its actions at any time: it is then enough to specify that the entity's behavior consists of performing its actions, one after another, in any order whatsoever. Almost always, however, there are ordering constraints. A boating session cannot end before it has begun; a customer of the bank cannot perform a terminate before a pay-in action.

In JSD, these constraints are expressed diagrammatically, in diagrams of the kind shown in Fig. 4.1. A suitable diagram for the bank customer is perhaps that given in Fig. 4.2. The exact meaning of this diagram is as follows:

—   The first action of a customer is invariably INVEST.

— Following the INVEST action, the customer performs a group of actions which we have called CUSTOMER BODY.

— Following completion of the group CUSTOMER BODY, the customer invariably performs the action TERMINATE.

— The group CUSTOMER BODY consists of zero or more occurrences of what we have called MOVEMENT.

— Each MOVEMENT is either a PAY-IN or a WITHDRAW action.

— Following a TERMINATE, no further action by the customer is possible.

The asterisk in the box named MOVEMENT and the circles in the boxes PAY-IN and WITHDRAW are an essential part of this diagrammatic notation. It is fully explained in Part II, and summarized in Appendix B, together with other notations used in JSD.

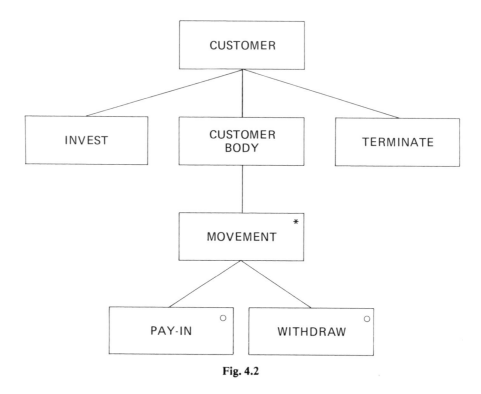

Fig. 4.2

The structure diagram constitutes a more exact specification of the behavior of a customer than the action list alone. Like the entity and action lists, it is to be determined by the developer and the system's users, working together, and its implications must be fully explored, understood, and agreed.

One implication of the diagram shown, which may be quite unacceptable to the bank, is that a customer can INVEST and TERMINATE once only. If the same person, after performing the TERMINATE action, returns later to the bank and re-enters the scheme by INVESTing again, then that person is now to be regarded as a new customer.

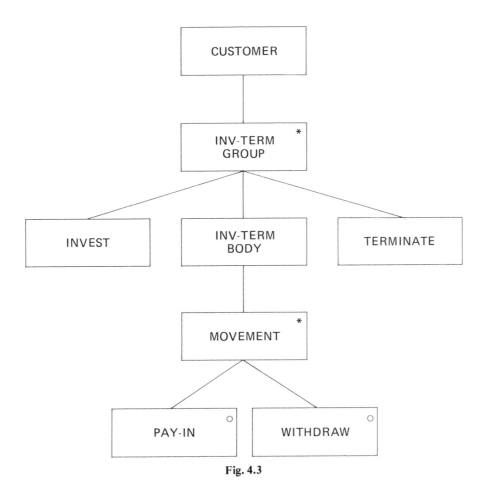

Fig. 4.3

The resulting system will not support such functions as carrying forward a credit rating from a TERMINATE to a subsequent INVEST by the same customer, or producing an exception report whenever a customer INVESTs more than twice. If, in fact, the bank does wish to regard each customer as being able to re-enter the scheme after TERMINATE and to retain the same identity, then the structure should be something like that shown in Fig. 4.3.

The output of the entity structure step is a set of structure diagrams showing the ordering of the actions of each entity. There are circumstances, discussed in Part II, under which the entity structure step may cause a reconsideration of the entity list, and an increase in the number of entity types.

The structure diagrams, like the entity and action lists and the action descriptions, form an integral part of the system specification. In some organizations, especially where users have in the past been subjected to the obscurities of logic flowcharts (D. Gries calls them 'flawcharts'), there may be an irrational prejudice in favor of purely narrative specification documents. The developer may then transcribe the diagrams into a narrative form to make them more palatable, but must take care to avoid introducing obscurity and imprecision. The diagrammatic notation is not hard to learn, and has the advantages of precision and immediacy of apprehension.

In the tiny example we are using to illustrate the development steps here, there is only one type of entity in the list and only one structure diagram. In a more realistic system specification there would be something between five and twenty structure diagrams produced in the entity structure step.

4.4   THE INITIAL MODEL STEP

The result of the entity action and entity structure steps is an abstract description of the real world in terms of sequential processes. The real world of the bank has been described by saying that there are customers, and that each customer performs certain actions in a certain order: in effect, each customer is represented in this specification as a sequential process, the structure of the process being given in the CUSTOMER diagram.

In the initial model step, the developer begins to specify the system itself by specifying a simulation of the real world. The basis of the simulation is very simple. For each sequential process in the real world—that is, for each customer of the bank—there will be a sequential process in the system, capable of being executed by a computer. The task in the initial model step is to state how the real-world process is to be connected to the model process, and to deal with any problems that arise because the connection is, inevitably, imperfect.

The standard form of connection is by data stream. That is, the real-world process produces a message for each action performed (or suffered), and the stream of these messages is input to the model process within the system. In the bank example, we may demand that the customer complete and sign a form for each action; these forms are eventually input, perhaps after some keypunching, to the process which models the customer. The arrangement is represented diagrammatically in a System Specification Diagram, or SSD (Fig. 4.4).

By convention, the suffix 0 indicates a real-world process, and the suffix 1 a model process. The diagram shows that the real-world customer, CUSTOMER-0, writes a data stream C which is input to the model process, CUSTOMER-1. The diagram does not show how many CUSTOMER-1 processes there are; but it does show that CUSTOMER-1 and CUSTOMER-0 processes are in one-to-one correspondence. There is one CUSTOMER-1 process in the system for each real-world customer.

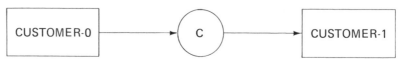

Fig. 4.4

Since there is a message in the data stream C for each action of the real-world customer, the model process can simulate the real-world process exactly. The developer specifies the model process by writing a structure text. The structure text is essentially a textual form of the structure diagram, but it includes operations to read the input data stream C, and it also includes conditions to direct the execution of the model process according to the input messages. The structure text of CUSTOMER-1 would be:

```
CUSTOMER-1 seq
  read C;
  INVEST; read C;
  CUSTOMER-BODY itr while (PAY-IN or WITHDRAW)
    MOVEMENT sel (PAY-IN)
      PAY-IN; read C;
    MOVEMENT alt (WITHDRAW)
      WITHDRAW; read C;
    MOVEMENT end
  CUSTOMER-BODY end
  TERMINATE;
CUSTOMER-1 end
```

The reader should compare this text with the first structure diagram for CUSTOMER given in Section 4.3 above. The notation used is fully explained in Part II, and is summarized in Appendix B, Section 2. It differs from conventional program notations in a number of respects; the most important is the use of names throughout the text, allowing it to be easily correlated with the associated structure diagram.

In this very simple example, the initial model step has been trivial. Difficulties and issues which have either not arisen or been ignored include these:

— The transmission of messages from the real-world process to the model process may be unreliable. Messages may be corrupted, transposed, or lost; spurious messages may be introduced. Eventually, an input subsystem must be provided to detect and, if possible, to repair these errors; the developer must specify at least a part of the input subsystem in the initial model step.

— It may be impossible, or impractical, to arrange for a stream of messages to be produced in the real world. A different form of process connection must then be used in place of data stream connection. This different form is state-vector connection. In the initial model step, where it is used to connect a level-0 to a level-1 process, it is regarded chiefly as a more awkward substitute for the preferable data stream connection. It is also used in the function step, which is discussed in the next section.

— An action in the action list may be impossible, or too expensive, to detect. For example, if we had decided that we were interested in how the bank's customers spend their money, we might have included SPEND as an action of customer. But we would not have been able to model these actions in the CUSTOMER-1 process. We would then have been forced to retrace our steps, and to eliminate SPEND from the action list and structure diagram.

— An action may be detectable, but not ascribable to a particular customer. For example, if we had decided that we were interested in visits made to the bank's premises by customers, we might have included VISIT as an action of customer. Turnstiles at the doors of the bank would allow each visit to be detected, but would not recognize whether the visitor was a customer, and, if so, which one.

— There may be difficulty in achieving fast enough transmission from the real-world process to the model process. The model always lags behind the real world, if only by some microseconds: even an on-line input message takes time to reach the model process. The developer may find difficulty in keeping the model sufficiently up to date to meet anticipated functional needs.

— In some cases a model process may obtain its input from another model process rather than directly from the real world. This happens when an action is common to two processes, performed by one and suffered by the other.

The chief outputs of the initial model step, apart from the statement of the connection paths, are the System Specification Diagram and the structures of the model processes. The developer should not normally need to discuss these documents directly with the system users, but only the changes they may require to the results of the entity action and entity structure steps. The connection paths always need discussion and agreement, because they constitute a major part of the interface between the system and the environment in which it will exist.

4.5   THE FUNCTION STEP

The model, or simulation, of the real world resulting from the first three steps of the JSD development procedure provides the basis on which the system functions are to be specified. In the function step the developer specifies the system functions in terms of the model. Broadly, a JSD function is specified in the form:

> When such-and-such a combination of events has occurred in the real world, the system should produce such-and-such outputs.

The model is adequate to support the function provided that the combination of real-world events is modelled by a combination of events within the system. The function specification therefore calls for the system to produce the required outputs when the specified combination of events occurs in the model. The developer examines each requirement for a function in this light, checking that the model is adequate for the purpose. In general, functional requirements based on a common model are highly mutually independent; the developer can therefore treat each function separately. This independence of functions is important both in the original development of the system, where it allows several people to work simultaneously on the function step, and in its maintenance during productive use, where it allows new functions to be added without interfering with the old ones.

Suppose that in our bank example we are required to produce an exception report on each overdraft. That is, a report should be produced whenever a customer performs a WITHDRAW action that leaves a negative balance in his account. This requirement must be restated in terms of the model, and can be restated as follows:

When a WITHDRAW action is performed, an exception report is to be produced if the cumulative amount of all actions performed so far by that customer is less than zero. The amount of INVEST and PAY-IN actions is considered to be positive, and the amount of WITHDRAW actions negative.

All the significant terms in this statement appear in the model, and the function can therefore be provided. Examination of the structure of CUSTOMER-1 shows that the necessary operations for producing the required report can be added directly to the text of that process. The SSD is elaborated in Fig. 4.5.

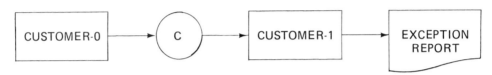

Fig. 4.5

Replacing the cumbersome phrase 'cumulative amount ...' by the more conventional word 'balance', the developer elaborates the text of the CUSTOMER-1 process, adding the balance variable and the operations which give it its successive values:

```
CUSTOMER-1 seq
  balance := 0;
  read C;
  INVEST seq
    balance := amount;
  INVEST end
  read C;
  CUSTOMER-BODY itr while (PAY-IN or WITHDRAW)
    MOVEMENT sel (PAY-IN)
      PAY-IN seq
        balance := balance + amount;
      PAY-IN end
      read C;
    MOVEMENT alt (WITHDRAW)
      WITHDRAW seq
        balance := balance − amount;
        P-EXC-REPORT sel (balance < 0)
          write 'overdrawn';
        P-EXC-REPORT end
      WITHDRAW end
      read C;
    MOVEMENT end
  CUSTOMER-BODY end
  TERMINATE;
CUSTOMER-1 end
```

Suppose now that a different function is required. Managers in the bank must be able to enquire about the balance of any particular customer. That is:

When an enquiry is input to the system, specifying a customer identifier, print the cumulative amount of all actions performed so far by the specified customer.

For this function we add a new process to the SSD (Fig. 4.6).

The connection between CUSTOMER-1 and ENQUIRY-FN is a state-vector connection: that is, the ENQUIRY-FN process directly inspects the local variables of the CUSTOMER-1 process. The diamond marked CV stands for the state-vector (the set of local variables) of the CUSTOMER-1 process. The double bar on the line from CUSTOMER-1 to CV indicates that the ENQUIRY-FN process, over the whole of its lifetime, inspects the state-vectors of many CUSTOMER-1 processes, although it will inspect only one for each ENQUIRY INPUT record.

The detailed specification of ENQUIRY-FN is very simple. Its structure text is:

```
ENQUIRY-FN seq
    read ENQUIRY-INPUT;
    ENQUIRY-FN-BODY itr
        ENQUIRY seq
            get state-vector of specified CUSTOMER-1;
            write 'balance is', balance;
        ENQUIRY end
        read ENQUIRY-INPUT;
    ENQUIRY-FN-BODY end
ENQUIRY-FN end
```

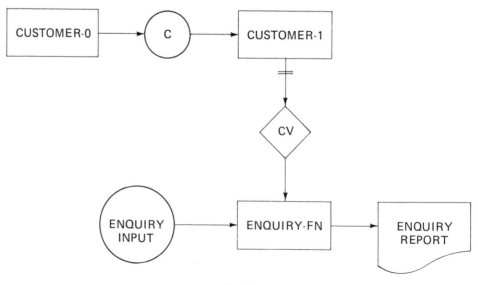

Fig. 4.6

The output of the function step is a specification of each of the required functions. This specification is documented in three ways:

— a restatement of the informal requirement in terms of the initial model;
— an elaboration of the initial model SSD, showing how the function is built into the model processes or is connected to them;
— structure text showing the detailed specification of the function.

For some functions, the first of these may be sufficient for communication between the developer and the system's users; for others the complete documentation may be needed, perhaps transcribed into a narrative form.

4.6 THE SYSTEM TIMING STEP

In the function step, the developer does not consider directly the question of timing as it affects function outputs. We have already observed that the model lags behind the real world because the messages from the real world must take some time to arrive at the system boundary. There may be further time lags introduced when the system is implemented: for example, if the bank system is implemented by monthly batch runs, the model will lag behind the real world by an additional time that will increase as the month progresses. Different parts of the system may be subject to different time lags; function processes, like model processes, may be implemented in a way which causes their execution to be delayed.

In the system timing step, the developer considers these potential delays, and determines, with the system's users, what delays are acceptable for the various parts of the system. The resulting decisions, informally documented, provide input to the implementation step; they constrain the implementation choices to those which will allow satisfactory response times and satisfactory time lags in the model.

For the bank system, the developer might determine the following timing requirements:

— exception reports for negative balances must be produced within one day of the WITHDRAW message arriving at the system boundary;
— enquiry reports must be produced within three seconds of the ENQUIRY INPUT message arriving at the system boundary;
— enquiry reports must be based on information (the customer balance) which is up to date at least to the close of business on the previous day.

Alternative possibilities for timing requirements include:

— enquiry reports must be produced within one day of the arrival of the ENQUIRY INPUT message;
— enquiry reports must be based on information which is up to date at the time of arrival of the ENQUIRY INPUT message;
— enquiry reports must be based on information which is up to date at least to five minutes before the production of the ENQUIRY REPORT.

In some systems, timing requirements will be even more informal than these examples. In a completely on-line data processing system, the requirements might be:

— terminal response time should be short enough for the operators to work comfortably;
— model and function processes should be delayed as little as is reasonably possible.

In other systems, the timing requirements may be very tight: a process control system is likely to be subject to stringent requirements on response time, necessary to ensure safety or the protection of valuable equipment.

Sometimes it will be necessary to specify very exact timing relationships among system processes. This can be done in JSD by introducing special synchronization processes into the SSD, connected by data streams to the processes which must be synchronized; the required timing relationships can then be specified exactly in the structure and text of the synchronization processes themselves.

4.7   THE IMPLEMENTATION STEP

In a typical data processing environment, the developer must consider many factors and ingredients in the implementation step. There will usually be a conventional programming language, such as PL/I or COBOL, a database management system, a database enquiry system, and a teleprocessing transaction monitor. There may be software packages for report writing, for generating screen-handling programs, and for tailoring standard batch program skeletons to particular specifications. It is not the purpose of JSD to guide the developer in the use of these facilities, but rather to concentrate on certain aspects of implementation which are arguably of prior, and fundamental, importance.

A JSD specification, which provides the input to the implementation step, is written in terms of a set of connected sequential processes. The SSD, or System Specification Diagram, shows what processes there are, how they are connected to one another, and the inputs and outputs at the system boundary. The detailed specification of each type of process is given in the form of a structure text. The number of processes is usually large: in the bank system, there is one ENQUIRY-FN process, and as many CUSTOMER-1 processes as there are real-world customers; so there are many hundreds or thousands of processes, if not more.

The primary task for the developer in the implementation step is to determine:

— how many real or virtual processors are to be used to execute the system;
— where there are fewer processors than processes (as there will always be in data processing systems), how the system processes are to be allocated to the available processors;
— where more than one process is allocated to a processor, how the time of that processor is to be shared among the allocated processes: that is, how the processes are to be scheduled on the processor.

For the bank system, there are many possible choices. For example, the system might be executed on two virtual processors, provided by two concurrent tasks running under a suitable operating system on a single hardware machine; one processor would execute the ENQUIRY-FN process, while the other would be shared among all the CUSTOMER-1 processes. In conventional parlance, we would say that the system is executed as an enquiry-handling task running concurrently with an updating task. Or the CUSTOMER-1 processes might be divided into several subsets, perhaps by geographical region, and a hardware processor provided for each subset, with an additional processor to handle the enquiries. Or the whole system might be run on a single hardware processor as a single task. We will here assume this last choice.

Because the whole system is to be executed as a single task, it is necessary to convert it from a set of sequential processes (as seen in the specification steps) to a single sequential process (as seen by the executing machine). First, the specification processes are transformed to bring them under the control of a single scheduling process:

— the ENQUIRY-FN process is transformed so that it is suspended (and may be reactivated) at each point at which it reads ENQUIRY-INPUT or writes ENQUIRY-REPORT;

— the CUSTOMER-1 process is similarly transformed to be suspended and reactivated at each point at which it reads C or writes EXCEPTION-REPORT;

— the state-vector of the CUSTOMER-1 process is separated from the executable text, so that there will be one state-vector for each real-world customer (the 'customer record'), but only one copy of the executable text.

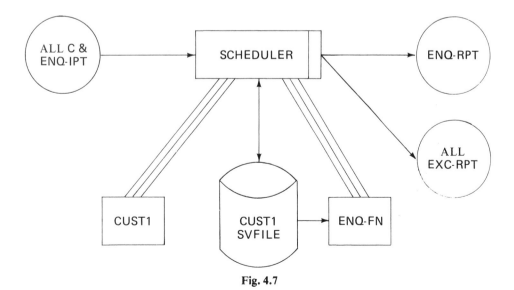

Fig. 4.7

The scheduling program, which is yet to be designed, reads all input and writes all output at the system boundary; it uses the transformed ENQUIRY-FN and CUSTOMER-1 processes as subroutines, and has access to the separated state-vectors of the CUSTOMER-1 processes. The resulting outline implementation is shown in a System Implementation Diagram or SID (Fig. 4.7).

The developer may now express decisions about the scheduling of the CUST1 and ENQ-FN processes in terms of the design of the SCHEDULER process, paying due regard to the constraints determined in the system timing step.

Suppose, first, that the following scheduling decisions are made:

—   as soon as a C message is input, the appropriate CUST1 process is to be activated; if it produces an EXC-RPT record, that record is to be printed immediately;

—   as soon as an ENQ-IPT message is input, the ENQ-FN process is to be activated and the resulting ENQ-RPT record is to be printed.

Then the structure of the SCHEDULER process is as shown in Fig. 4.8.

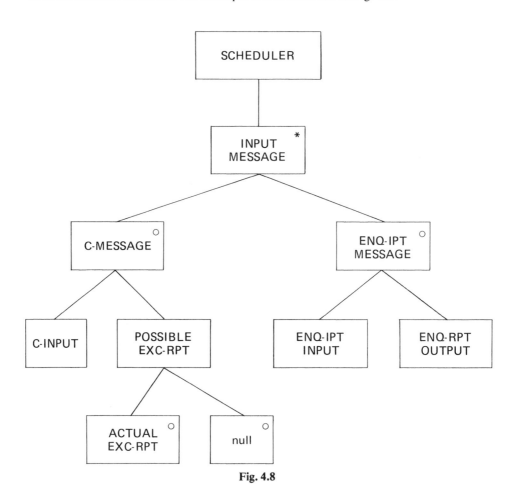

Fig. 4.8

The full detail of the SCHEDULER process would be shown in a structure text. Final implementation of the SCHEDULER process may be achieved, on a bare machine, by programming the SCHEDULER explicitly in an executable programming language; in a more typical environment, much of the SCHEDULER will be already provided in an on-line transaction-handler.

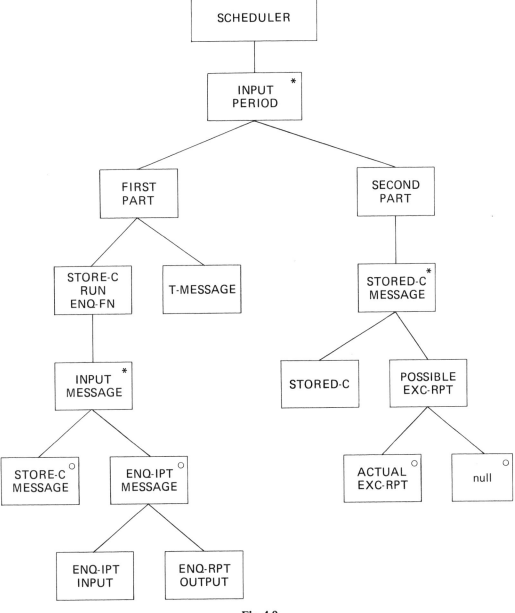

Fig. 4.9

Suppose, instead, that the developer makes quite different scheduling decisions:

— execution is to be divided into periods of one day, each period being marked by
the input of a special message type, T, to indicate its end;
— as soon as an ENQ-IPT message is input, the ENQ-FN is to be activated and the
resulting ENQ-RPT record is to be printed;
— C input messages are to be stored within the system, and the appropriate CUST1
processes activated only after a subsequent T message arrives; ENQ-RPT records
are to be printed immediately they are produced.

The structure of the SCHEDULER process would then be as shown in Fig. 4.9.

Again, the full detail of the SCHEDULER process would be shown in a structure
text. Final implementation of the process may be achieved by breaking it into three
parts:

(a) FIRST-PART; this is an on-line program which stores C input messages in a buffer
file and activates ENQUIRY-FN whenever an ENQ-IPT message is available;
(b) SECOND-PART; this is a batch program, which updates the customer master file
or database from the C input messages (transactions) stored in the buffer file by
FIRST-PART;
(c) the SCHEDULER and INPUT-PERIOD components; this part may be implemented
by a combination of instructions to the machine operator and job control statements, ensuring that FIRST-PART and SECOND-PART are run, in that order,
each day.

The essence of the JSD implementation step is that the system specification, embodied
in the SSD and process structures, is retained in the implementation. The System Implementation Diagram can be seen as a transformation of the System Specification
Diagram; the ENQUIRY-FN and CUST1 subroutines in the implementation are transformed versions of the corresponding processes in the specification. The only entirely
new component is the SCHEDULER process, whose design expresses explicitly those
decisions about process scheduling which have been consciously excluded from the
specification steps.

Documentation of the implementation step is not intended for communication with
the systems' users, but is purely technical.

4.8   ITERATIVE DEVELOPMENT

The JSD development steps are to be carried out in the order given in the preceding sections and in Fig. 4.1. The output of each step forms a part of the input to the next step;
the decisions made in each step define the context of the decisions for the following
steps.

In practice, development will not proceed entirely smoothly from step to step.
Some iteration will be necessary, in which the developer returns to an earlier step in the

light of what has been learnt in a later step. For example, in defining the structure for an entity, he may discover that a vital action has been left out in the previous step, without which no sensible structure can be drawn. In the initial model step, he may discover that a particular action cannot be reliably detected in the real world and so cannot be reliably modelled. In the function step, he may discover that the model is inadequate to support some part of the required function of the system, that the function cannot be specified in terms of the modelled actions and entities.

In all these cases, the developer must retrace his steps and reconsider what has been done earlier. To some extent, this retracing will be due simply to inexperience. In any system development procedure, the developer must make decisions at each step; these decisions will have consequences at later steps which an inexperienced developer may be unable to anticipate; he must then wait to be confronted by those consequences before he can recognize the error of the early decision. A more experienced developer might anticipate the consequences, and make the correct decision initially. But not always.

Although some iteration in development is inevitable, JSD aims to minimize it, by ensuring that:

— each development decision, whether in specification or in implementation, is made fully explicit;
— decisions are taken in the right order, so that the later decisions are not pre-empted by the earlier;
— easier, descriptive, decisions are taken before the harder, inventive, decisions.
— errors in decisions are detected as soon as possible, before consequential errors are made;
— decisions are, so far as possible, orthogonal—that is, they can be made independently of each other.

These methodological points are discussed in a retrospective chapter at the end of the book.

4.9 ONE IMPLEMENTATION STEP ONLY

Although the major division in the JSD procedure is that between specification and implementation, there are five steps for the former and only one for the latter.

This imbalance reflects the greater standardization of the specification stage. The order of the steps necessary to specify a system depends hardly at all on the particular specification. It would make little sense to define a realized model before determining a description of the world to be modelled; and we have already argued, at length, that decisions about the model of reality must precede decisions about system function. Implementation, by contrast, depends more heavily on particulars, both of the system to be implemented and of the hardware and software available for its execution. In one case, the crucial decision will be about response times for the most common transactions or inputs; in another, it will be about economy of data storage; in another, it will be about achieving a database design to allow a wide range of *ad hoc* enquiries. Usually, the crucial decision must be considered early, if not first.

The implementation step, therefore, will often consist in applying a repertoire of techniques in an order dictated by the needs of the particular system. These techniques will include:

— determining the number of processors required or available, and the allocation of specification processes to processors;

— transforming specification processes to allow explicit scheduling, and constructing special-purpose processes to schedule their execution;

— dismembering both specification and scheduling processes to allow convenient program loading and execution;

— dismembering and recombining process state-vectors into convenient database records;

— determining necessary access paths to database records according to the needs of function processes which inspect sets of state-vectors and to the patterns of process activation.

4.10   WHERE PROGRAMMING FITS IN

It may seem surprising to some readers that there is no step in the JSD development procedure clearly marked with the name 'programming'. Where, in JSD, is the programming done?

If programming means writing COBOL, PL/I, Pascal or Fortran statements, we may probably assign most of this activity to a fairly late part of the implementation step, much as expected. But programming means much more than this: above all, it means defining the exact order in which events are to occur within the system, the order in which elementary operations are to be executed.

Programming, in this larger sense, is diffused through several parts of JSD development. In the entity structure step, the developer specifies the order of actions for each entity in the real world, and this order is carried over into the initial realized model. The order in which the bank customer performs INVEST, WITHDRAW, PAY-IN, and TERMINATE actions becomes the order in which the customer model process performs the corresponding operations. Here, then, is a significant piece of programming being done at an early step in the system specification. In the function step it will be necessary to specify the structure of certain outputs, and the structures of the processes which produce them. Here, again, is programming work, although it may be appropriate to defer some detail until later. In the implementation step, the developer may make certain decisions about process scheduling and the structure of a special-purpose scheduling program—perhaps a conventional batch updating program; these decisions, too, are decisions about the order of events within the system, about the structure of a program.

It is inappropriate to bring together all these decisions and concerns into a single activity of programming, to be carried out at a single late stage of development. Certainly they are all dealing with the ordering of events within the system, but neither the events nor their orderings are in any useful sense the material of a single activity. In the design and programming of a batch updating and reporting program, if we assume the rather vague kind of specification that 'gives the programmer adequate scope and job satisfaction', all of the following considerations may arise:

— the order of retrieval and rewriting of master records (this is a matter of scheduling the processes whose state-vectors constitute the master records);

— treatment of transaction records in accordance with the previous contents of the master records they update (this is a perversely obscure way of dealing with the ordering of the actions for each entity);

— checking the ordering of transactions for each master record and rejecting misordered transactions (this is a concern of the input subsystem);

— production of report information before or after applying particular transactions (this is a matter of the connections between the model processes and the function process, and, perhaps, their relative scheduling);

— arranging the report information in the desired order (thus satisfying a part of the specification of the function process).

Each of these considerations should be dealt with at the appropriate step in the development. The retrieval of master records belongs in the implementation step; the treatment of transactions records in the entity structure step; checking the ordering of transactions in the initial model step; and producing and arranging the report information in the function step. There is no useful sense in which they should all be regarded as pertaining to a single activity of programming.

The important distinction in JSD is not between analysis and programming, but between specification and implementation. Specification concerns the user and the application, and it should be done by people whose interests lie in that direction. Implementation concerns the hardware and software, and should be done by people with a technical bent. Simplifying only a little, we may say that the first five steps of the JSD procedure are to be carried out by the user with the help of a user-oriented developer, while the last step is to be carried out by the machine with the help of a machine-oriented developer.

SUMMARY OF CHAPTER 4

The JSD development procedure has six steps: the entity action step; the entity structure step; the initial model step; the function step; the system timing step; and the implementation step (4.1).

The entity action step produces a list of entity types and a list of actions, and an informal description of each action. The entity structure step produces a diagrammatic statement of the ordering of actions for each entity type (4.2, 4.3).

In the initial model step, a sequential computer process is specified for each structure diagram, and also the connection between the process and the entity it models. An initial version is produced of the System Specification Diagram (SSD), showing how processes are connected (4.4).

In the function step, functions are specified as new processes added to the SSD, or as elaborations of model processes. New and elaborated process texts are produced, and elaborations of the SSD (4.5).

The system timing step is concerned with the delays which may be introduced in process scheduling, and their effect on the content and timeliness of system outputs. Constraints are specified on the absolute and relative scheduling of processes, in preparation for the implementation step (4.6).

In the implementation step, the developer determines how many real or virtual processors are to be used, and the allocation of processes to processors. The specification is transformed and special-purpose scheduling processes designed and written. The use of database and other available software is defined. A System Implementation Diagram (SID) is produced, showing in outline how the system has been transformed (4.7).

Inevitably, the development will require some iteration over the constituent steps. JSD aims to minimize this iteration (4.8).

The implementation step is less fully structured than the earlier specification stage, which contains five steps. This is because different systems will demand quite different emphases in implementation (4.9).

Unlike traditional approaches, JSD does not contain a single programming step. The traditional concerns of programming properly belong at various stages of system development (4.10).

PART II

JSD DEVELOPMENT STEPS

In this part of the book, each of the JSD development steps is discussed in detail. The discussion is illustrated by three application examples, which are introduced in the short Chapter 5. The following chapters deal with the development steps in the order of their execution, exploring the detailed considerations and questions relevant to each step.

Chapter 5 introduces the Widget Warehouse Company, the Hi-Ride Elevator Company, and the *Daily Racket* Competition. Each of these application examples is dealt with piecemeal in the following chapters, often in more than one version. The main results of the development steps for each example are gathered together in an Appendix.

Chapter 6 deals with the entity action step. Lists are made of entity and action types, and brief descriptions of actions, thus giving a preliminary determination of the scope of the real world to be modelled. Decisions in this step are highly tentative, but they are also highly independent of one another. The idea of an entity in JSD is very different from that of an entity in methods centering on database definition.

Chapter 7 deals with the entity structure step. Diagrams are drawn specifying the time-ordering of the entities' actions. There are limits to the expressive power of the diagrams, and it may be necessary to add notes specifying what cannot be specified diagrammatically. It may also be necessary to draw more than one diagram for an entity type, and this may lead to the recognition of further entities in addition to those listed in the previous step. The structures specify what can happen in the real world; system inputs contradicting this specification must be purged by the input subsystem.

Chapter 8 deals with the initial model step. A System Specification Diagram (SSD) is produced, showing the connections between the real world and the realized model: there is one model process for each entity structure diagram. There are two forms of process connection: data stream connection and state-vector connection. Other forms, such as interrupts, may be used in the implementation, but not in the specification. There may be some indeterminacy in the specification, due to state-vector connection and the merging of multiple input data streams to one process.

Chapter 9 deals with the function step. Adding functions to the specification is essentially a matter of adding function processes, although some function outputs can be produced directly by model processes. The SSD is elaborated for each function, showing the added processes and their connections to the model; for each added process, a full structural specification is produced. The same forms of process connection are used as in the initial model, and indeterminacy arises in the same way. Information flow is not only from the model to the function processes: interacting functions may feed information back to a model process. In JSD, each function can be specified independently of other functions.

Chapter 10 deals with the system timing step. This step forms a bridge between specification and implementation: the JSD specification leaves the implementor free to schedule the system process in various ways, and this freedom affects the timeliness (inevitably) and the content (where there is indeterminacy) of the system outputs; in the system timing step the developer documents the constraints that an adequate implementation must satisfy.

Chapter 11 deals with the implementation step. The central concern discussed is process scheduling: how to arrange a system for execution on a small number of processors—that is, smaller than the number of processes in the system. The specification processes are transformed to run under control of explicit scheduling processes. The transformations include inversion with respect to one or more data streams, separation of state-vectors, and dismembering of processes into parts which can be conveniently loaded and executed. The results of the JSD implementation step are usually conventional: on-line and batch programs, database records, reporting and updating programs. But the results are reached essentially by transforming the specification rather than by creating something entirely new.

5

Three applications

5.1 APPLICATION OUTLINES NOT SPECIFICATIONS

In this chapter the outlines of three system development applications are presented: the control of an elevator in a building; allocation of stock to orders placed by customers; and the management of a newspaper readers' competition. The applications have been chosen because they can be used to illustrate various points in JSD, not because they are realistic in scope or detail.

It is important to understand that what follows is in no sense a set of problem definitions or specifications. In JSD we develop a specification; we do not start from one. The developer is therefore free to create the specification, with the user's concurrence, and to make the many choices which that involves. So the outlines of the three applications are intended only to sketch the areas of interest in the vaguest possible way, indicating what kind of thing might be found by a study of those realities and of the users' needs.

We will use this freedom to invent or imagine many possible results of the developer's study of the application areas; on the user's behalf, we will give different answers to the same question at different times, according to our need to simplify or elaborate the specification, to illustrate this point or that.

In the chapters that follow, each of the three applications will be treated piecemeal. We will consider each application in each step of JSD development, sometimes contenting ourselves with a single specification for an application, sometimes looking at different versions.

5.2 THE WIDGET WAREHOUSE COMPANY

The Widget Warehouse Company is less specialized than its name suggests. In addition to widgets, they deal also in gadgets, fidgets, flanges, grommets, and many other products which their customers find indispensable.

The company's customers order these products from the company, often by telephone but sometimes by other means such as mail or personal visit to the company's warehouse. There is a company rule that separate orders are required for separate products. The customers are happy with this rule, because few customers have a use for more than one of the products: a dedicated user of widgets is unlikely to find a purpose for gadgets or flanges.

Customers sometimes amend their orders, changing the quantity or the requested delivery date. Occasionally a customer may cancel an order.

The company employs a clerk whose job is to deal with the customers and to allocate the available stock to outstanding orders. This clerk has access to information about the available stock of each product. He can telephone the warehouse to ask how much of any product is currently in the associated warehouse location. This enquiry is usually answered with reasonable reliability. A system is being built to control the warehouse inventory and to reorder from suppliers when necessary. Because the director responsible for dealing with suppliers refuses to talk to the director responsible for dealing with customers, there has been, and will be, little communication between the purchasing and the selling sides of the business. Inevitably, this is reflected in the current plan to build two largely independent systems for the two applications. We will be developing only the sales system, handling customer orders.

5.3   THE HI-RIDE ELEVATOR COMPANY

The Hi-Ride Elevator Company installs elevators in buildings. The elevators are to be used to carry people from one floor to another, in the conventional way.

The directors are rather old-fashioned, and are only just starting to think about computer control of their elevators. They have a lot of experience in manually controlled elevators and the electromechanical devices on which they depend. In particular, they have developed and refined over many years the sensors which detect the arrival of the elevator at a floor, and other similar devices.

The company also prides itself on the reliability of its motors, winding gear, and switchgear. The number of accidents suffered by Hi-Ride elevators has been remarkably small.

Because computer control of their elevators is a new thing, the directors feel that each installation should be individually designed and developed to meet the particular needs of the building and its users. They hope eventually to achieve some standardization, but not yet.

5.4   THE *DAILY RACKET* COMPETITION

To boost circulation, the *Daily Racket* plans to run a competition open to subscribing readers. Once a reader has become a subscriber, he may enter the competition as often as he wishes, sending in one or more entries on each occasion that the newspaper publishes details of the competition. Each entry must be accompanied by an entry fee. The competition is judged periodically, by a panel of television celebrities, and the best entries received since the preceding judgement are awarded prizes.

The competition is based on a set of twelve very small, indistinct and poorly printed photographs of fashion models wearing rather ugly clothes. An entry consists of a ranking of these photographs in order of elegance and chic, together with a verse expressing extravagant praise of the *Daily Racket* and its proprietor, Sir Cunning de Ville.

The same photographs appear each week, but the quality of the printing ensures that no one will notice this. There are 479 001 600 possible rankings, so the competition can continue for a long time on the present basis. In case of difficulty in the judging, the merits of different rankings are resolved by considering the accompanying verses.

Some hidden rules are operated, designed to simplify the task of the judging panel, who are not very clever. No competitor can win more than once; no more than one entry from each competitor is submitted for judging in any one session of the panel. Entries which cannot win because of these rules are not returned to the competitors; instead the accompanying fees are retained by the *Daily Racket*, and the entries are quietly ignored. The editor's decision is final.

Sir Cunning has grandiose plans to dispense with the panel of judges altogether, and even to install on-line terminals for customers to make their entries in drive-in booths. But there are a few difficulties in these plans, and he is willing to consider something less ambitious that might help with the administration of the competitions.

6

The entity action step

6.1 THE MODEL BOUNDARY

In the entity action step we state, as simply as possible, what the system is about. Because modelling must come before function, we look at the real world outside the system, and not at the system itself and what functions it should provide. Because we regard the dynamic aspects of the real world as most important, we pay attention to what is happening, to the actions that are performed and suffered and to the entities, the things or people, that perform or suffer them.

The result of the entity action step is a list of entities and a list of actions. Necessarily, the list is selective: we choose to include some entities and actions, and to leave others out. By selecting, we are drawing a boundary between what will be included in the model and what will not; this is called the model boundary. In drawing this boundary, we are also implicitly drawing a boundary around the functions the system will be able to support. In making our selections, we bear in mind, in the most general way, this effect on the system's functions; sometimes, when we are in doubt, we will examine the effect directly.

The defining characteristic of a JSD entity is that it has an ordered set of actions which we wish to model. Anticipating the later steps, as we have already done to some extent in the introductory chapters, we know that we will model the entity by a sequential process: as the entity goes through its history of actions, so the model process will go through its executable text, carrying out simulated actions. We will be able to obtain information about the progress of the real entity through its lifetime by enquiring about the progress of the sequential process through its text. If we need to know whether Jane White, bank customer, has yet performed any withdraw or pay-in actions, we can inspect the process which models her and ask whether it has yet executed a simulated withdraw or pay-in.

Conversely, if we want to obtain information about the progress of a set of real world actions, we must ensure that there is some sequential process in the model that we can refer to. If there is no such process, we may be able to devise some expedient to solve the problem; or we may not. As we saw in the boating lake system, an inadequate model may allow some functions to be provided quite easily, and others not at all. We are trying to be explicit about the description of the real world, and hence of the model, and hence of the possible functions of the system.

When we choose to omit an entity or action from our lists, because we decide that it is not the basis of any needed function, we will say that we are leaving it 'outside the model boundary'. This reason for omission is so common that we will denote it by an abbreviation: OMB (Outside the Model Boundary).

6.2   ENTITIES AND ACTIONS

In JSD, the ideas of entity and action are very closely associated: an action is always performed or suffered by one or more entities, and an entity is characterized by the actions which it performs or suffers, and their ordering in time.

In speaking of actions and entities, we must bear in mind the distinction between a type and its instances. When we speak of 'entity' we will sometimes mean an entity type, such as 'bank customer', and sometimes an entity instance, such as 'Jane Smith' or 'William Brown'. Similarly, when we speak of 'action', we will sometimes mean an action type, such as 'pay-in', and sometimes an action instance, such as 'the pay-in of this particular amount made by Jane Smith on this particular date'. The appropriate meaning will almost always be clear from the context; where it is not, we will use the words 'type' and 'instance' to make the necessary distinction.

A JSD action may be any event which:

— is regarded as taking place at a particular point in time, rather than persisting over a period of time; and
— takes place in the real world outside the system, and is not merely an action of the system itself; and
— is regarded as atomic, and not decomposable into subactions.

The first criterion distinguishes actions from states: in the entity action step we are never concerned with states. Suppose for example that we are developing a system to give information about an experiment in human behavior; the subject of central interest is human patterns of sleeping and waking. In the entity action step, we identify the human subjects as the entities. What are the actions? It would be wrong to list 'be asleep' and 'be awake' as actions, because they are definitely states, not actions. The appropriate actions would be 'fall asleep' and 'wake up', which can be considered to be events taking place at particular points in time. There might, of course, be severe difficulties in defining the occurrence of these actions in the real world, but these difficulties do not concern us here. Nor are we concerned with more elaborate possible descriptions, in which there might be actions such as 'begin to drowse', 'begin to wake up', in addition to the two mentioned above.

As always, when we are formulating a description, we are free to take different points of view. In particular, we may choose to treat as an action some occurrence which in reality occupies many minutes, hours, or even years. Thus we might consider 'have a sleep' as an action of our human experimental subject, or 'reign' as an action of a member of a royal family. But in doing so we must be aware that we are treating these as instantaneous events: it then becomes meaningless to ask 'when did she begin to have a sleep?', or 'when did he cease to reign?'. To choose an occurrence which occupies a period of time as a JSD action is to regard that period of time as a single instant.

A JSD action must take place in the real world, and not merely in the system itself. Events that are obviously actions of the computer are therefore excluded: 'print exception report' and 'display enquiry menu' are clear examples. But sometimes the distinction is harder to make, especially where there is an existing set of clerical procedures associated with the subject matter of the system being developed. Is the salaries department a part of the real world for the payroll system? Is an invoice a part of the real world for a billing system? If so, we would expect to have actions such as 'receive cash for distribution', and 'be sent to customer' in the lists for the payroll and billing systems. In general, it seems that errors of inclusion are more likely than errors of omission in this matter; the developer is more likely to err by including what should be left out than by omitting what should be included.

A JSD entity must:

— perform or suffer actions, in a significant time-ordering; and
— exist in the real world and not merely within the system; and
— be capable of being regarded as an individual, and, if there is more than one entity of a type, of being uniquely named.

The first criterion is the most important in distinguishing the meaning of 'entity' in JSD from its meaning in some other approaches to system development. A JSD entity is never an inert thing, without a recognizable pattern of behavior over time: we are necessarily interested in its history, in asking 'has it performed this action yet?', or 'how many times has it suffered that action?'. If such questions make no sense, we are not talking about a JSD entity. Once again, application of the criterion depends on our point of view, on the purpose for which we are making the abstract description of the real world. In a typical data processing system, we would not expect 'town' to be an entity: it may be a part of an address, which in turn is an attribute of some action (for example, 'request delivery'), but it has itself no actions. But in a system concerned with the economic and social patterns in a nation, we might expect to find that town is indeed an entity, with such actions as 'increase population by 1000', 'receive tax grant from central funds', and so on.

6.3   MAKING THE LISTS

To make the lists, we need to study the real world, keeping in mind the general purpose of the system. We can study the real world by interviewing users, by reading existing documents such as a feasibility study report, by looking at the world directly, and in any other way we can find. We would certainly want to look at the *Daily Racket*'s competition entry form, and the Widget Warehouse's printed terms of business; we might even, if we are bold, travel in one of the Hi-Ride Company's elevators. If there is an existing system, consisting of clerical and computer procedures with a similar or related function, we might study that too; but we must be careful to remember that we are interested in the real world outside the system, not in the system itself directly.

The greatest danger in the entity action step is the danger of jumping to conclusions without adequate thought or study. Because the output of the entity action step is small—a list of entity types, a list of action types, and a brief narrative explanation of each action type—we may be tempted to give it only a perfunctory treatment. But in this step we are laying the foundation of our model of reality, and we must take care. In traditional, functional, system development, the developer never makes an explicit model of reality. Instead, he starts with an implicit model, based on previous knowledge, intuition, and intelligent imagination, and adjusts it a little where it is evidently in conflict with the user's statement of some required function. It is not uncommon for the user's view of the real world, radically different from the developer's, to emerge as an unpleasant surprise at a stage where it is too late to do much about it. We want to avoid this failure.

One way is to make a comprehensive list of the nouns and verbs we encounter in our study of reality: each noun is a possible entity; each verb is a possible action. We then scrutinize each one, deciding explicitly whether it should be selected or rejected, and why. The idea, of course, is slightly playful. In English, almost every noun has associated verb forms,* and vice versa; sometimes an important entity may have no name, but be referred to by a circumlocutory phrase. A truly comprehensive list would be unmanageably long: most potential items can be eliminated immediately as being outside any conceivable model boundary. When the director of the Widget Warehouse Company tells us that 'the company is less specialized than its name suggests', we hardly want to write down 'suggest' as a possible action.

But this playful idea has a serious point. The output of the entity action step may be small and simple, but the input must be extensive and rich. We cannot afford to ignore possible clues to the user's view of reality; no shred of evidence can be discarded without at least a brief inspection.

The list of entities and actions will be much smaller than a comparable database definition. One reason is that the functional components of the system are excluded at this stage: they will be added later, in the function step. Another is that we are limiting our attention to entities and actions. We are not concerned with the attributes of entities, and we are concerned only in a very informal and incomplete way with the attributes of actions. Once we have determined the entities and actions, we can easily add attributes in later steps as we discover the need for them.

In addition to the lists themselves, we will write a brief informal narrative description of each action; its purpose is to tie the action name a little more closely to the real world. The full connection between the action name and the real world happening will be made in the initial model step. No description is written for entities: entities are defined by their actions.

Even when they are based on careful thought, the entity and action lists made in

---

* Brian Randell observes that 'in English, every noun can be verbed'.

this step are only tentative. As we will see later, both lists are likely to be heavily modified during the entity structure and initial model steps. The likely modifications include:

— rejecting an action in the entity structure step because it appears, after all, to belong to the system rather than to the real world;
— rejecting an action in the initial model step because it cannot be conveniently and economically detected and signalled to the model;
— adding an entity in the entity structure step because it is necessary for specifying the ordering of actions of an existing entity;
— adding an action in the initial model step because it is necessary for the interpretation of existing actions.

In our treatment of the entity action step, we will be making many choices that will need later modification.

6.4   *DAILY RACKET*: **ENTITIES LIST**

The purpose of the *Daily Racket* system is to help to administer the competitions. So we will certainly reject anything that is entirely irrelevant to this purpose, placing it outside the model boundary (OMB). We will also reject many things that are relevant, but do not satisfy our criteria for JSD entities.

To convey the full flavor of the real world study, we would need a novel, or at least a short story. We would describe the interviews with Sir Cunning de Ville, the competition manager, the editor, and other *Daily Racket* employees. We would record the conversations verbatim, and provide realistic replicas of the newspaper. But that would hardly be practical, nor would it be appropriate: we are not concerned in this book with the specific techniques of interviewing, of gathering evidence, but rather with the use the developer should make of the evidence gathered.

So we will start with a list of possible entities, and confine ourselves to discussing the reasons for rejecting or selecting each one. Where necessary, we will refer back to conversations that we suppose to have preceded the making of this list. Some of the items in the list raise general issues that deserve general discussion in a later section of this chapter; some can be disposed of more quickly in this section.

Here is the initial list, largely but not exclusively nouns taken from the *Daily Racket* application outline given in a previous chapter:

Circulation, competition, reader, subscriber, entry, fee, entries list, panel, television celebrity, prize, photograph, ranking, verse, proprietor, Sir Cunning de Ville, competitor, session, on-line terminal, prize list, journalist.

Circulation is rejected as being OMB. The competition is intended to boost circulation, so we might have modelled the upwards and downwards movements of circulation; but Sir Cunning explained that we should interpret the purpose of the system quite narrowly, limiting our attention to the competition itself.

Competition seems to be a general term, referring to the whole activity rather than to an identifiable grouping of entries and judgements. In fact, we were told, the competition runs continuously, to ensure that there is no moment when a reader might be inhibited from sending an entry (and, of course, the fee). We might conceivably want to regard the competition as an entity, but probably not. We reject it.

Reader is clearly relevant. A reader may become a subscriber, and enter the competition as often as he wishes. We are certain to be interested in the behavior of readers, and we select reader as one of the entities.

Subscriber seems also relevant. A subscriber is a reader who has performed the action of subscribing. We cannot want to select both reader and subscriber, for reasons discussed in a later section.

Entry seems clearly relevant, and clearly an entity. Its actions might be 'be submitted', 'be awarded a prize', and so on. We will return in a later section to some reasons why we might reject it, and the effect on system function.

Fee is certainly highly relevant but not really an entity. Its actions might be 'accompany an entry', 'be paid into the bank', and so on; but this is not a financial system, and certainly not one in which we are anxious to follow the history of individual fees. We reject it.

Entries list is an output to be produced by the system each week. Outputs of the system can never be entities.

Panel seems to be an entity. The panel meets, judges, awards prizes, and so on. We select it.

Television celebrity seems to be an entity for the same reasons as panel. We will return in a later section to the question whether we could, or should, select both of them.

Prize will not be an entity unless we distinguish individual prizes and model their histories—perhaps in actions such as 'be awarded', 'be mailed to winner', 'be returned in disgust'. We choose to place all of this OMB.

Photograph is relevant, but nonetheless OMB. We are not at all interested in the history of the photographs.

Ranking is certainly relevant. In the sense 'a particular choice of ranking sent with a particular entry', we reject it, for much the same reason as we rejected fee. We will return in a later section to some more general considerations.

Verse is rejected for the same reason as fee.

Proprietor is OMB. Sir Cunning has made it abundantly clear that the system is not to collect or disseminate information about his actions for any purpose whatsoever. He has good reason for his secrecy.

Sir Cunning de Ville is, of course, merely a synonym of proprietor, and so OMB.

Competitor seems relevant. A competitor is a subscriber who has entered at least once.

As mentioned above, we cannot want more than one of reader, subscriber, and competitor, for reasons discussed in a later section.

Session appears to be a grouping of the actions of the panel; it is a session of judging. We do not expect to find any actions of session that are not actions of panel, which we have already selected. We reject session.

On-line terminal is a part of the system itself, and so is to be rejected. This would be so even if it were a part of the system we are developing now, and not of Sir Cunning's grandiose plans that will probably never come to fruition. A system for which on-line terminal is a real world entity would surely be some kind of teleprocessing monitor, system performance monitor, or similar support software.

Prize list is rejected for the same reason as entries list: it is an output of the system.

Journalist is relevant, because journalists employed by the *Daily Racket* are not allowed to enter the competition. But we reject it, since we are not interested in the actions performed and suffered by journalists as such. We can, if we wish, later decide that one of the attributes of a reader is whether or not he is employed by the paper.

The resulting list, after removal of items we have definitely rejected, is:

READER, SUBSCRIBER, ENTRY, PANEL, TELEVISION CELEBRITY, COMPETITOR.

In the immediately following sections we discuss some of the general issues raised above, before returning to make an action list for the *Daily Racket* and a more fully refined entity list.

6.5 GENERALIZING AND CLASSIFYING ENTITIES

When we select and reject possible entities, we are making two different kinds of choice simultaneously. We are choosing which individual things and people should be described in our abstract description of the world, and also how they should be classified. We are choosing which entity instances we want to include, and also which entity types. The two choices coincide when there is only one instance of a type: in rejecting proprietor we rejected both the entity type 'proprietor' and the individual instance 'Sir Cunning de Ville'. The choices diverge when we know which instances we want to include, but we are not sure whether they should be instances of one type or two. In a system for a transport company, we know that we want to include all the company's load-carrying vehicles, but we are not sure whether we want the single type 'vehicle' or the two types 'truck' and 'pick-up'. In the *Daily Racket* system, we know, perhaps, that we want to include all readers, but we are not sure whether we want to classify them by the types 'reader', 'subscriber', and 'competitor'.

In JSD, the choice of entity types is limited by two considerations. First, an entity type is specified in terms of the possible actions performed or suffered by instances of the type, and by the ordering of those actions. In the bank example, the customer entity type was specified in terms of the actions invest, withdraw, pay-in, and terminate, and their ordering. Any entity whose actions are constrained to conform to that specification must be an instance of the entity type 'customer'. Conversely, any instance of the type must conform to the specification. Therefore, in the transport company system, there can be two entity types 'truck' and 'pick-up' only if they have some difference in the types or orderings of their actions. This might be true, for example, if we choose to model an action 'obtain transport department certificate' which is an action of truck but not of pick-up.

Second, we specify the whole lifetime of an entity, to the extent that its lifetime is within the model boundary. The lifetime of an employee in a payroll system is specified from the time of joining to the time of leaving, retiring, or perhaps dying. We do not specify only a week, a month, or a year for an employee, because that would be less than the whole lifetime; we do not specify birth, childhood, schooling, and adolescence, because they are outside the model boundary. The type of an entity instance is determined when it comes into existence in the model, and remains fixed throughout its lifetime. There is no notion in JSD of an entity instance changing its type during its lifetime, or at all. It was for this reason that we said in the previous section that we cannot want more than one of the types 'reader', 'subscriber', and 'competitor'. A subscriber is a reader who has performed the action of subscribing; a competitor is a subscriber who has performed the action of entering the competition. If we had both reader and subscriber as entity types, we would have instances which were initially of type 'reader', and later of type 'subscriber'; this cannot happen in a JSD system.

The solution in the *Daily Racket* case is obvious: if we are concerned with readers before they become subscribers, we will select the entity 'reader'; if not, we will select 'subscriber' or perhaps 'competitor'.

A harder case arises when one entity instance can play two roles that are separated in time. Suppose that in a system for a school we are led to specify two entity types: 'pupil' and 'teacher'. We then discover that some pupils, after leaving the school, later return as teachers. How should we describe this reality in JSD?

We must choose between two descriptions. In the first, we retain the two entity types unchanged. This means that we are placing outside the model boundary the fact that John Smith, teacher, is the same person as John Smith, the pupil who left some years ago. There are two distinct entity instances, with distinct identifiers in the system, and there will be no way of referring to them as one person. (Of course, this is not strictly true. We will be able to introduce an attribute of the teacher entity, indicating whether the teacher used to be a pupil, and, if so, what was the pupil's identifier; and we could introduce a corresponding attribute for pupil. This is the system-level equivalent of a program binary switch: a disreputable device to compensate for incorrect structure.)

In the second description, we replace the entity types 'pupil' and 'teacher' by the single type 'person'. The actions of the person entity will be the actions of both pupil and teacher entities, ordered to indicate that pupil actions must precede teacher actions for any instance, and that either pupil actions or teacher actions, or both, may be performed. With this description, each person is a single entity instance, and the complete lifetime of the person can span everything from arrival as a new pupil in the kindergarten class to retirement as the oldest teacher in the school.

The association between entity instances and roles is important in the entity structure step; we will discuss it further in the next chapter.

6.6   COLLECTIVE ENTITIES

Television celebrity and panel both seem to be possible entities. We may regard panel simply as a collective name for the celebrities employed at any particular time. The question arises whether the list should include only panel, only celebrity, or both.

Certainly we might well choose to include only panel. Our description of the world can simply omit the fact that the panel is composed of individual celebrities; we can consider the panel as a single entity, and treat such actions as judging and awarding prizes as actions of that entity. This is exactly what is meant by abstraction. The consequence of this abstraction would, of course, be that the system would not be able to provide information about the histories of the individual celebrities.

We might choose to include only the celebrities, omitting the panel. This would be right if we were interested in the behavior of each celebrity, and if we could model whatever is of interest in the judging in terms of actions of celebrities.

We might be forced to include both if we were interested in the behavior of individual celebrities, and there were actions that could be ascribed only to the panel. For example, the panel might decree in each judging session, for reasons we regard as being OMB, how many prizes are to be awarded. Such an action is clearly not an action of any individual celebrity; if the action is included in the action list, then panel must be included in the entity list.

6.7   GENERIC ENTITIES

We rejected ranking from the list, taking the word to mean 'a particular choice of ranking sent with a particular entry'. The same word could also mean 'one of the 479 001 600 possible rankings'. If we use the terms 'ranking-choice' and 'ranking-value' to refer to these different meanings, we may say that an instance of ranking-choice is a specific entity, while an instance of ranking-value is a generic entity.

A familiar example of the same distinction occurs with the word 'part' in manufacturing and inventory applications. The specific entity is a particular physical object—'this widget that I am holding in my hand'; the generic entity is the class of all objects with a particular part-number and description—'widgets'. In the manufacture of extremely expensive and technically critical products, such as aircraft engines, it is customary to model the particular physical objects as entity instances. The resulting system can then be used to trace each particular part in each particular engine, providing answers to questions such as these: 'to which particular engine was fan bearing

123/456/789 fitted as original equipment, and on what date?'; 'which fan bearings were machined on the same machine and on the same day as the fan bearing 123/456/789?'. In such a model, there are entity types 'fan bearing', 'forward engine mounting', 'inner fan shaft', and so on; each of these entity types has instances which are particular physical objects, such as 'fan bearing 123/456/789'. For less critical products, it is customary to model a single entity type 'part', whose instances are then the generic entities 'widget', 'gadget', and so on. No account is taken of the specific physical objects, and the resulting system is thus unable to provide such information as the date on which the widget supplied to customer 234 was received in the warehouse.

Just as in a manufacturing application we may be interested in the generic entity 'part', so in the *Daily Racket* we may be interested in the generic entity 'ranking-value'. Sir Cunning de Ville may well want to know whether the panel has been foolish enough to award a prize for a ranking-value that has been chosen by many competitors; he may even want them to give first prize to a ranking-value that has been chosen by no competitor at all, thus ensuring that no first prize need be awarded; he may want them to avoid giving a prize to the same ranking-value more than once. To support the provision of the relevant information, we would need to model the history of a ranking-value, with actions such as 'be chosen in an entry', 'be selected for first prize', and so on.

However, we discover that such functions will not be required, and we will reject the generic as well as the specific entity.

6.8   ENTITIES, FUNCTIONS AND COSTS

In the *Daily Racket* list, we considered whether entry should be an entity. It might have actions such as 'be submitted', 'be awarded a prize', 'be received from reader', and so on. If we include entry in the entity list, we will be able to support such functions as the following enquiries: has entry E been submitted yet? how many entries have been received from readers but not yet submitted? which entries have been awarded prizes more than two weeks after being received from the reader? These are all functions about the history of entries, and they can be easily provided on the basis of a model in which entries are included as entities. If entries are not entities, the possibility of providing these functions is left largely to chance; some may be surprisingly easy, some may be entirely impossible.

Even if a possible entity type seems relevant, and the functions that could be based on it seem desirable, the developer must take account of the cost of including an entity type in the abstract description. Broadly, the cost is made up of two parts: the cost of developing and maintaining the system, and the cost of running it. Without being able to put any firm estimate on the development and maintenance cost of adding another entity type to the description, we might guess that it is roughly proportional to the inverse of the number of entity types already included: to add a second entity type might double the cost, while to add an eleventh might increase the cost by ten per cent. The added running costs will depend on the number of instances of the type, and the number of actions of each instance.

The fee for an entry in the *Daily Racket* competition is very small, and we might reasonably judge that it is not sensible to model individual entries in the system. In the same way, the developers of banking systems decide not to model the individual checks as entity instances. Notice that this decision does not preclude the possibility of giving each entry a unique identifier, and making this identifier an attribute of every action associated with the entry. It will then be possible to answer certain questions about entries by a combination of functional outputs and manual analysis of these and other documents that exist in the *Daily Racket* office but have been ignored in the specification and running of the system.

6.9   *DAILY RACKET*: **ACTION LIST**

Rejecting entry from the entities list, we reduce the list finally to no more than two items:

    READER
    PANEL

We may find later, especially at the entity structure step, that this list needs revision or expansion. There is little scope for contraction.

We turn now to selecting an action list. Obviously the two lists are intimately associated; we were unable to discuss the selection of entities without some consideration of the actions we thought they might have. Now we are concerned to be more precise about the actions of the entities we have selected.

Treating the actions much as we treated the entities, we will begin with an initial list taken largely, but not exclusively, from the application outline:

    Subscribe, enter, send entry, judge, receive entry, award prize, meet, submit, return, ignore, win.

Subscribe is evidently an action of READER. We select it.

Enter is also an action of READER, and is selected.

Send entry appears to be an action of READER. To regard it as different from the action ENTER would involve us in modelling the post office. We decide against this, and reject it.

Judge occurs in the context 'the competition is judged periodically', where it refers to a whole group of entries, not to a single entry. We are probably going to be interested in it as an action by the panel referring to a single entry, and on that basis we select it.

Receive entry might be an action of the panel: the panel receives an entry for judging. It might be an action of the *Daily Racket* mail room, which receives entries from readers by post. We are certainly not interested in this latter action: we already have the action ENTER for READER, and we do not plan to model the *Daily Racket* mail room. We would want to select the former action, the action of the panel, only if we intend to produce reports on whether they have judged every entry they actually received. More likely, we will provide a list of the entries due to be judged, which will be based on the model of the readers; we will then assume that this list is received by the panel, and we need not therefore model the action receive entry.

Award prize is selected, as an action of PANEL. It seems that we do not need the action JUDGE, which we selected above.

Meet is selected, as an action of PANEL. The panel meets periodically to perform its judging.

Submit means to submit an entry to the panel for judging. We might view it as an action of READER, different from the action ENTER, because the hidden rules operate to ensure that not every entry is submitted. However, operating the rules will be a function of the system, and submission will thus be an action of the system, not of the reader.

Return appears in the context 'entries . . . are not returned'. Since this is an invariable rule, we need not consider this action further. We consider briefly whether to select its complementary action: if entries are not returned, they are presumably kept, so perhaps keep is an action. But we reject this also.

Ignore appears in the context 'entries which cannot win . . . are quietly ignored'. It is not clear whether ignore is an action of the panel: the application outline tells us that surplus entries (more than one entry in a session for a reader) are not submitted for judging, but it does not state the same about entries from competitors who have already won. Perhaps the panel is required to ignore further entries from winning competitors. We intend to provide the list of entries to be judged, so we will take ignore to be a function of the system rather than an action of PANEL.

Win seems clearly an action of READER. The question arises whether the win action of READER is the same as the AWARD PRIZE action of PANEL. If it is the same action, we should reject it as an action of READER: the effect of an award on a reader will be according to the rules operated by the system. If it is not the same action, perhaps because the editor can give prizes which are nothing to do with the panel's awards, we should keep it. This proves not to be the case, and we reject it.

Here is the action list as it now stands:

```
READER:   SUBSCRIBE, ENTER;
 PANEL:   AWARD, MEET.
```

The name of the action award prize has been abbreviated to the single word AWARD.

6.10 *DAILY RACKET*: **ACTION DESCRIPTIONS**

It is not enough to list the names of entities and actions; names are liable to different interpretations by different people. We will therefore write a brief, informal, narrative description of each action, and list some of the attributes it may have. These descriptions and attribute lists may provide a starting point for entries in a data dictionary. In this book we will not discuss documentation in detail, but limit our attention to those aspects that seem of greatest importance.

Descriptions of *Daily Racket* actions might be:

SUBSCRIBE: become a regular customer by paying for a year's copies of the paper; action of READER. Attributes: date, name, address, . . .

ENTER: make an entry in the competition and send it to the *Daily Racket*; action of READER. Attributes: ranking, fee, verse, . . .

AWARD: award a prize to an entry; action of PANEL. Attributes: ranking, verse, prize-type, . . .

MEET: come together, usually about once a week, to receive and judge entries; action of PANEL. Attributes: date, . . .

The descriptions, like the names, are liable to different interpretations by different people; but perhaps a little less so. The attribute lists are the merest hints of what the action attributes might be. We do not write descriptions of entities. An entity is specified in terms of its actions, and its attributes are derived from the attributes of its actions, either directly or indirectly. Thus, for example, we might eventually decide that the attribute 'date of becoming a subscriber' is an important attribute of READER for the purposes of some function: this attribute is directly derived from the date attribute of the action SUBSCRIBE. We might decide that 'total fees paid' is an important attribute of READER: this would be derived from the fee attribute of the ENTER action by an embedded function which added the fee for each ENTER action to the required total.

6.11 WIDGET WAREHOUSE: ENTITIES AND ACTIONS

Our purpose in the initial system for the Widget Warehouse is to handle the allocation of product stock to orders. We are not yet sure what automation, if any, will be possible: the staff of the warehouse have assured us that the decisions they make in allocating stock to orders are so complex and so subtle that we cannot hope to automate them.

However, we can certainly set about modelling what happens in this complex and subtle real world. After some study, we produce the following entity and action lists:

Entities: CUSTOMER, CLERK, ORDER, PRODUCT
Actions: PLACE, AMEND, CANCEL, DELAY, ALLOCATE, DELIVER.

Here are the action descriptions:

PLACE: convey an order to the company for allocation and delivery. Action of CUSTOMER and ORDER.
Attributes: product-id, quantity, requested date, . . .

AMEND: change the quantity or requested date of an order; product-id cannot be changed. Action of CUSTOMER and ORDER.
Attributes: code (new quantity or new requested date), quantity or date, . . .

CANCEL: cancel an order. Action of CUSTOMER and ORDER.
Attributes: . . .

DELAY: delay an order because stock is not available for it to be allocated. Action of CLERK and ORDER.
Attributes: . . .

ALLOCATE: allocate product stock to an order. Action of CLERK, ORDER, and PRODUCT.
Attributes: quantity, . . .

DELIVER: deliver ordered product to a customer. Action of CUSTOMER, ORDER, and PRODUCT.
Attributes: date, quantity, . . .

As always, the result of the entity action step is very tentative. We have made a first rough statement of the model boundary: for example, we consciously excluded the reordering of products from suppliers and also the picking of stock from the warehouse for delivery; but we have chosen to include the clerks. The entity and action lists will be reconsidered in the entity structure step, and perhaps again in the initial model and function steps.

In the Widget Warehouse lists, we have some common actions: indeed, all actions are common to at least two entities. In the *Daily Racket*, we had no common actions, although the possibility was mentioned. Common actions are discussed in the next section.

6.12 COMMON ACTIONS

An action may be common to two entities in the sense that it is a single event in which they both partake. If two motor vehicles collide, that is a single event, and both vehicles have performed the action collide. If a customer of the Widget Warehouse cancels an order, the order is cancelled, and the cancellation is a single event. The car collision is an action common to two entities of the same type; the order cancellation is common to entities of different types.

The decision to regard an action as common is a modelling decision, a decision about how we choose to describe the real world. Within broad limits, we are free to make the decision either way; especially, we are free to describe two actions as distinct even when they are unmistakably a single event in the real world. We simply choose to omit their common identity from our description. For example, a claims system for an insurance company might reasonably treat the collision as two distinct actions, one for each vehicle. (The system would not then be able to provide such functions as 'list all collisions in which both vehicles were insured by the company'; at least, not without some good luck and some *ad hoc* cunning.)

In some cases, as in the vehicle collision, a common action has the same significance to both parties: both have performed the action collide. In others, one entity performs, and the other suffers, the action: the customer performs, and the order suffers, the cancellation. Where we can, we will use the same name for the common action whichever entity we are considering. So, we will name the action CANCEL, and it will be an action both of the customer and of the order entity. Sometimes it will be essential to distinguish the roles of the entities in the common action by giving different names. In a system modelling a biochemical experiment, we might list cell as an entity, and destroy as an action; one cell can destroy another. Clearly, there must be two names for the common action destroy, distinguishing the roles of the destroyer and the destroyed cell. We might therefore specify actions destroy and die; these would be common actions, each event consisting of one entity performing the destroy, and the other entity the die action.

Often, it will be wrong to treat two actions as common because careful study shows the actions to be distinct in the real world. Consider the *Daily Racket* specification, in which we chose to treat PANEL's action AWARD as distinct from READER's action WIN, and PANEL's action RECEIVE ENTRY as distinct from READER's action SUBMIT. We did so because a PANEL AWARD might be overruled by the editor, and so never become a READER WIN; and a READER SUBMIT might be lost by a staff member and so never become a PANEL RECEIVE. Similarly, we might reconsider our decision to make DELIVER an action common to ORDER, CUSTOMER and PRODUCT, in the Widget Warehouse specification. Perhaps a more careful study would define the CUSTOMER action as actual receipt of the delivered goods, and the PRODUCT action as removal from the warehouse. Clearly, goods may be removed from the warehouse that are not, for various reasons, then delivered to the customer who has ordered them. It is not the separation in time that matters here so much as the uncertainty of the connection between the two actions. It is always wrong to treat two actions as common if, in the real world, one may occur without the other: we would then be making a description of the real world which is untrue, or can be made true only by some desperate fictions.

Sometimes a careful analysis of common actions will provide the resolution of conflicts between one user's view of reality and another's. Suppose, for example, that in the Widget Warehouse we were concerned not only with allocation of stock to orders but also with the accounts receivable. In the early stages of the study, the developer might find that the word 'sold' is used in both contexts, but with rather different meanings. In stock allocation, stock is said to be 'sold' to a customer when it is allocated to his order; in the accounts department, when a pink slip is received from the sales office. The developer might reasonably decide either:

—   that there is no action associated with the word 'sold' that is an action both of the order and of the account; or

—   that there is a common action, which might perhaps be the signature by the customer of a goods-received note.

In the first case, the model of reality would impose no consistency between the orders and the accounts for a customer; the resulting system might then provide a function output which reported and analyzed apparent discrepancies between the goods ordered and the goods accounted for. In the second case, the common action, perhaps called 'receive goods', would appear in both the model of an order and the model of an account; since it is a common action, any discrepancy would be due to a failure in the specification or the running of the computer system.

6.13   HI-RIDE ELEVATOR: ENTITIES AND ACTIONS—1

The Hi-Ride Elevator Company is installing elevators in a small building of six floors. There will be two elevators, each serving all the floors. At each floor, except the top floor, there is a button which users can press to summon an elevator to take them upwards; at each floor, except the ground floor, there is a similar button for downwards travel. Inside each elevator there are six buttons marked with the floor numbers. There is a pair of doors at each floor, and another pair on each elevator. The elevators are raised and lowered by cables which are wound and unwound by motors positioned above the top floor. At each floor, in each elevator shaft, there is one of the company's famous sensors, operated by a small wheel attached to the elevator: when the elevator is within 15 cm of the home position at that floor, the sensor is depressed by the wheel, and closes an electrical switch. Other, different, sensors are provided which sense whether the various pairs of doors are in the fully open or fully closed position.

The company's engineers are highly skeptical of the idea of computer control of the elevators, and have convinced the directors that computer control should be limited. The computer system will schedule the travel of the elevators according to the users' requests for service, and will produce commands for the motors and the lights which are associated with the buttons. In the usual way, when a button is pressed, the associated light must be turned on. The motor commands are these:

START: causes the motor to start.
STOP: causes the motor to stop.
UP: sets the motor polarity for upwards travel.
DOWN: sets the motor polarity for downwards travel.

The light commands are simply:

ON: turns the light on.
OFF: turns the light off.

The company's engineers will, as in previous installations, use their traditional skills to control the doors, and to ensure that elevators stop at the home position of a floor (provided that the STOP command has been issued when the elevator is within 15 cm of the home position). We will need to discuss some details with them, especially how the control of the doors is related to the behavior of other parts of the system, but we defer that discussion for the time being.

Our first attempt at listing entities and actions gives:

Entities: USER, ELEVATOR
Actions: USER: PRESS-UP(i),   PRESS-DOWN(j),   PRESS-EL(k),   GET-IN,
                    GET-OUT.
            ELEVATOR: START-UP,   START-DOWN,   HALT,   ARRIVE(m),
                        LEAVE(n), WAIT(p).

The letters in parentheses indicate floor numbers: thus PRESS-UP(i) means to press the upwards travel request button at floor(i); WAIT(p) means to wait at floor(p); and so on. The actions START-UP, START-DOWN and HALT are actions of the elevator, as shown, and are not the commands which the system must issue to the motors.

We have, correctly, omitted the motors from the entity list, and the motor commands from the action list. Issuing the motor commands is a function of the system we are developing, not actions in our real world. The motors themselves are not a part of our real world unless we intend to monitor their behavior, to report on it, or to use information about it for the system functions. The company's engineers would never allow us to monitor the behavior of their motors, which they assert to be completely reliable. We do not require information about the motors for the system's functions, but about the elevators: we want to know when the elevator arrives at a floor, not when the motor is in a certain position.

However, having avoided that error, we have committed others. We should not have included 'wait' as an action of elevator, because it does not satisfy the requirement that it should be regarded as instantaneous, taking place at a point in time rather than extending over a period. By any reasonable interpretation, to wait is to be in a particular state, not to perform a particular action—at least, in the context of the present discussion. If we ask 'when did the elevator wait?', we would expect an answer like 'between 12.15 and 12.18', not like 'at 12.17 exactly'. So we should exclude 'wait' from the action list. Notice that this does not preclude functions that might be expressed in terms of 'if the elevator is waiting, and ...', because we can reword them in terms of the other actions: 'if the last action of the elevator was HALT (or ARRIVE(m), and ...'.

Inclusion of the wait action was not the only error. Another error has been made, which in principle might not be revealed until a later step. But in practice it should be recognized at this step, and we discuss it in the next section, before returning to correct our lists.

6.14 UNDETECTABLE ENTITIES AND EVENTS

After the entity action and entity structure steps, we will specify the initial model in the following step. There, we will require to connect the real world to a set of sequential processes which model the entities of our abstract description; we will require to find some way of signalling to those processes the actions performed and suffered by the entities. If we do not take care at the earlier steps, we may find that these connections cannot be made.

We listed actions 'get-in' and 'get-out' for the user entity. We would discover at the initial model step, if we had not found out earlier, that these actions by a user simply cannot be detected. The Hi-Ride Elevator Company's elevators are not equipped with photo-electric devices to sense whether there is an obstruction between the doors; nor are they equipped with dropping floors which sense whether there is any load in the elevator. So we have no way of detecting the actions 'get-in' and 'get-out'. We might decide that these actions are so important that it is worth while to provide the necessary equipment for their detection, and, perhaps, to impose some necessary obligations on users of the elevators. For example, we might install an additional button inside the elevator which each user must press on entering, and another on each floor which each user must press on leaving the elevator. But merely to state such a requirement is to demonstrate that it would not be acceptable. The actions 'get-in' and 'get-out' must therefore be removed from our list.

There is a similar problem in the entity list. Suppose we have reduced the user actions to PRESS-UP(i), PRESS-DOWN(j), and PRESS-EL(k). These actions are certainly detectable if we have any way of connecting the buttons to the system, as we must have if we are to build a system at all. However, we need also to detect which user has performed each action, so that the signal indicating the occurrence of the action can be transmitted to the process that models that user. This, again, cannot be done with the existing hardware. We would need to issue each user with a key or a card, and insist that instead of pressing a button the user insert his card into a device which has replaced the button; the device could then signal to the system both the performance of the action and the identity of the user who has performed it. Once more, the necessary arrangement would not be acceptable. We are forced to the conclusion that we must remove 'user' from the entity list.

This is an unwelcome conclusion. It is made bearable only by our familiarity with elevator systems which are limited in this way. In a typical system, a mischievous user can press all the buttons inside the elevator; the other users must then tolerate the annoyance of the elevator stopping at every floor whether or not anyone wants to get in or out at that floor. A user might press the button for travel to the top floor, and then get out before that floor is reached; the elevator will travel to the top floor regardless of the absence of the user who requested the journey.

6.15   HI-RIDE ELEVATOR: ENTITIES AND ACTIONS—2

Having determined that user cannot be included as an entity type, we must find some reasonable substitute. There is really no alternative to BUTTON: the various buttons provided at the floors and in the elevators must be entities of the system.

There are several instances of BUTTON: in each of the two elevators there are six floor buttons; at each of the five lower floors there is an up button; and at each of the five upper floors there is a down button. We may imagine that these buttons are named: E11–E16 and E21–E26 are the buttons in the elevators; U1–U5 are the up buttons; and D2–D6 are the down buttons.

For any one button, there is only one action type: PRESS. The history of every button consists merely in being pressed some number of times. The action we had pre-

viously named PRESS-UP(3) when it was an action of a user is now simply named
PRESS when it is an action of BUTTON; the same action type, PRESS, is the sole
action type of every button entity. There is therefore no difference between the behavior
of one button and the behavior of another, and we require only a single entity type
BUTTON; every button, whether E14 or U3, is an instance of this entity type.

The entity and action list now looks like this:

Entities: BUTTON, ELEVATOR
Actions: BUTTON: PRESS
            ELEVATOR: START-UP,   START-DOWN,   HALT,   ARRIVE(m),
            LEAVE(n).

The actions for the elevator entity are still not quite right. The proposed actions 'start-
up', 'start-down', and 'halt' are probably undetectable, given the electromechanical
equipment provided by the company's engineers. We discuss the matter with them, and
they tell us that these actions can be detected by the sensors positioned at the floors.

We are not satisfied. We can detect when an elevator arrives at a floor and when it
leaves, by the opening and closing of the sensor switch. But we cannot detect whether it
leaves the floor travelling in an upwards direction or in a downwards direction. Nor can
we detect when the elevator stops: it might be oscillating up and down within 15 cm of
the home position at a floor, keeping the sensor switch closed all the time. We ask
whether more elaborate sensing equipment might be used: for example, the engineers
might install inertia sensors on the elevators themselves. We are told that the company's
existing devices have always proved entirely adequate in the past. We creep quietly
away, and remove the apparently undetectable actions from our list. We are willing to
do this, rather than insisting on more elaborate sensing equipment, because it seems
likely that the necessary functions can be provided on the basis of the other actions
alone. Some evidence in support of this view is the contemptuous remark made by one
of the engineers: 'if you can't control the elevator with your computer, perhaps we
ought to install one of our standard relay controllers'.

The complete list is now:

Entities: BUTTON, ELEVATOR
Actions: BUTTON: PRESS
            ELEVATOR: ARRIVE(m), LEAVE(n).

Here are the action descriptions:

PRESS: be depressed and released once; action of BUTTON.
           Attributes: . . .
ARRIVE(m):   arrive at floor(m), either from above or from below; action of
           ELEVATOR.
           Attributes: floor-number, . . .
LEAVE(n):   leave floor(n), either upwards or downwards; action of ELEVATOR.
           Attributes: floor-number, . . .

SUMMARY OF CHAPTER 6

In the entity action step we draw a conceptual boundary around the aspects of the real world which are to be modelled by listing the entities and their actions. This model boundary is implicitly a boundary around the functions that the system will be able to support (6.1).

Actions are atomic and instantaneous; entities perform and suffer actions in a significant time-ordering. We may expect entities to be mentioned as nouns, and actions as verbs, in the users' accounts of their real world. We are not concerned with objects and events within the system itself, but only in the real world. There will be many fewer JSD entities than database entities for the same application (6.2, 6.3).

The *Daily Racket* entities list raises some general issues. A JSD entity instance is of the same type throughout its life; so there is no possibility of an individual person or thing being first an instance of one type and then an instance of another (6.4, 6.5).

We should include in the list a collective entity and its members only if there are actions pertaining to one and not to the other (6.6).

An entity type may be such that its instances are generic, in the sense of representing a class of objects; thus 'widget' may be an instance of the entity type 'part', and represent the class of all particular, individual, widgets (6.7).

The cost of system development and maintenance, and also of running the system, must be taken into account in deciding whether to include a possible entity in the list. The value of the functions made feasible by its inclusion may not justify the cost (6.8).

A brief narrative description of each action, together with a tentative and incomplete list of its attributes, must be given in the entity action step. Entity attributes will eventually be derived from action attributes (6.9, 6.10).

The Widget Warehouse list is straightforward, but contains common actions. An action is common to two or more entities if it is a single event in which they both necessarily partake. Some conflicts between different views of reality may be resolved by careful consideration of common actions (6.11, 6.12).

The Hi-Ride Elevator list raises questions of the detectability of actions and their correct ascription to entities. These considerations would arise in the initial model step if not recognized in the entity action step, but an experienced developer would anticipate them here (6.13–15).

7

The entity structure step

7.1 ACTION ORDERING IN TIME

In the entity structure step the developer specifies how the actions of each entity are ordered in time. In general, the ordering is not entirely fixed: we cannot usually predict exactly what will happen next. If an order has been placed with the Widget Warehouse Company, we cannot say whether the next action for that order will be amend, cancel, allocate, or delay: any of these might happen next, following the place action. However, the ordering is constrained to follow certain patterns. We do know that after an order is placed it cannot be placed again; and it cannot be delivered without an allocate action intervening between the place and the deliver actions. It is these patterns of constraints that we specify in the entity structure step.

The specification is made in the form of structure diagrams, using a notation familiar to practitioners of JSP program design. The diagrams allow us to express the three classical constructs of structured programming: sequence, selection, and iteration. There is an equivalent textual notation, which we will use in later steps, translating from the diagrammatic to the textual form.

Although we are using notations which, to some readers, are familiar from programming, it must always be remembered that we are describing the real world, not the programs which make up the system. Nor are we describing the structure of a database, nor the structure of the system itself. We are simply describing the order in which each entity performs or suffers the actions in which it participates. As we will see later, when we discuss the implementation step, one of the large benefits of the kind of model we build in JSD is the comparative ease with which we can transform it into a set of runnable programs; it is not an accident that we describe the ordering of real world actions in constructs that are also used in programming.

We might hope that a single structure diagram will suffice for each entity listed in the entity action step. But specifying ordering constraints is a little more complex than this. We will find that a single entity may require more than one diagram, and that the additional diagrams suggest entity types that should perhaps have appeared in the original list.

A fundamental requirement in specifying entity structures is to span the whole lifetime of the real world entity, and not only a part of it. In some countries, employment legislation requires that a person who leaves an organization and is later re-employed must be differently treated from one who is employed for the first time. Clearly, the lifetime of an employee must be able to span more than one period of employment. In a telephone switching system, the lifetime of a call may be thought to begin when the caller picks up the handset and to end when both parties replace their handsets; but a conference call may involve more than two parties, and may continue after all the original participants have rung off. In a telephone billing system, a subscriber may have more than one line, and a line may remain installed in a house when one subscriber moves out and another moves in. In all of these cases there are significant specification choices to be made about entity lifetimes.

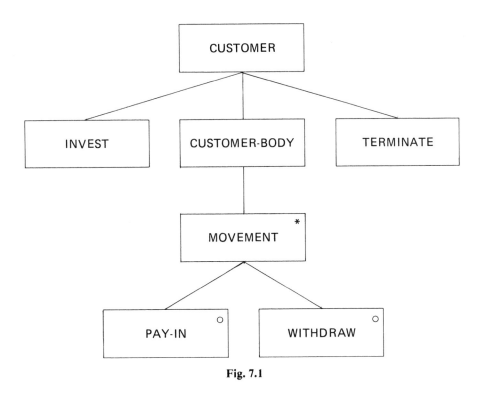

Fig. 7.1

The temptation to specify only a part of the lifetime of an entity is particularly strong when the developer pays premature attention to implementation questions. For example, in a payroll system, employees may be paid weekly; it seems clear that some weekly batch programs will be needed, and hence that the developer should consider what can happen to an employee in any one week. This is entirely wrong. By specifying a structure whose name is, perhaps, EMPLOYEE-WEEK, the developer implicitly declares that there is no sequential connection between one employee-week and another, contrary to the obvious modelling and functional requirements. Since it will be necessary to provide functions such as paying an employee for a vacation which spans three weeks, or computing pay for an employee who becomes sick in the middle of one week and returns to work in another week, the developer will be forced to patch the specification, making obscure connections between one weekly run and another. The result will be a rash of what are sometimes referred to as system design errors, contrasted with programming errors; such errors will certainly be difficult to detect and repair, and will manifest themselves at a late stage of development when detection and repair will be most expensive.

7.2   STRUCTURE DIAGRAMS

Figure 7.1 provides an example of a structure diagram. It shows the ordering of the actions of the bank customer, discussed in earlier chapters. The diagram, like all JSD structure diagrams, is a tree. The box marked CUSTOMER is called the root of the tree; the boxes marked INVEST, PAY-IN, WITHDRAW, and TERMINATE are called the leaves of the tree. If you stand on your head, or perhaps stand the picture on its head, you can see why the diagram is called a tree. The essential characteristic of a tree is that there is one, and only one, path from the root to any leaf: the path from the root to PAY-IN is CUSTOMER, CUSTOMER-BODY, MOVEMENT, PAY-IN. So Fig. 7.2 is not a tree diagram—there are two paths from the root to the leaf E: A, B, E; and A, C, E.

In the diagrams drawn in the entity structure step, every leaf must be an action (with one very minor qualification which we will come to later). So the actions of CUSTOMER, namely INVEST, PAY-IN, WITHDRAW, and TERMINATE, are all leaves of the tree.

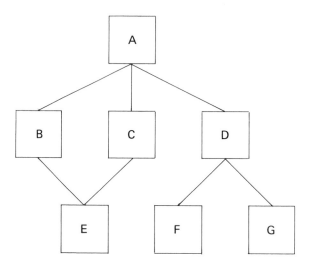

Fig. 7.2

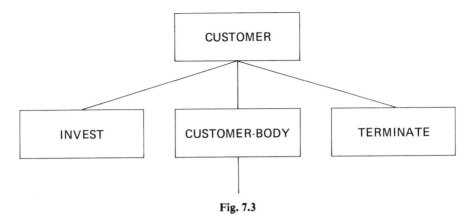

Fig. 7.3

The tree shows how the actions are ordered. Each box which is not a leaf has one or more boxes at the next level down, directly connected to it; these are called its children, and it is called their parent. So the children of CUSTOMER are INVEST, CUSTOMER-BODY, and TERMINATE; and the parent of TERMINATE is CUSTOMER. By marking the upper right corner of the children with asterisk, circle, or neither, we indicate whether the parent is an iteration, a selection, or a sequence, respectively. Any box in the diagram which is not an action must be one of these three. Action boxes are sometimes called elementary. The children of a parent are sometimes called its parts.

7.3   SEQUENCE

A sequence is indicated by leaving its child boxes unmarked. In the CUSTOMER diagram, CUSTOMER itself is a sequence (Fig. 7.3). The meaning of a sequence is that for each instance of the sequence itself, one instance of each child occurs in order from left to right in the diagram. So for each CUSTOMER, INVEST occurs once, then CUSTOMER-BODY occurs once, then TERMINATE occurs once. There is no possibility of any child of a sequence being omitted, or occurring more than once, in any occurrence of the sequence.

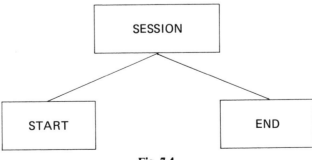

Fig. 7.4

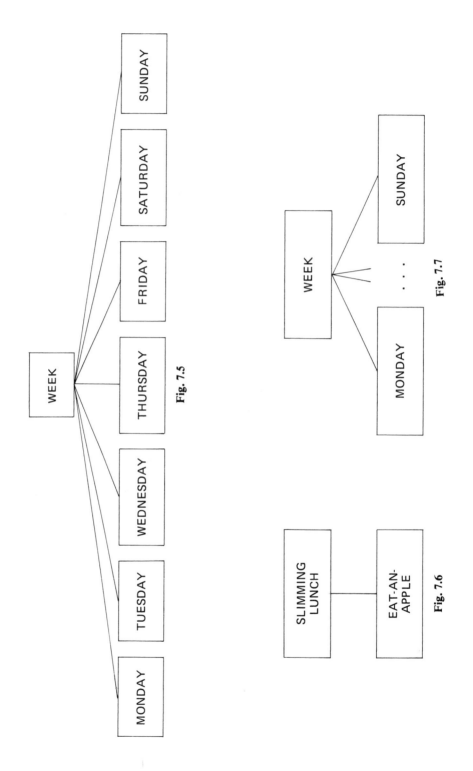

Fig. 7.5

Fig. 7.7

Fig. 7.6

A sequence can have any number of children. A session of boating on the boating lake might be described as in Fig. 7.4, and a week as in Fig. 7.5. Sometimes, but not often, it will be appropriate to describe a sequence with one child only, as in Fig. 7.6.

Clearly, in specifying a sequence it is necessary to enumerate every part of the sequence. There is no notation in JSD such as that shown in Fig. 7.7. The number of children, and their names, must be explicitly fixed in the specification of the sequence. Where the number of children is not known at the time the specification is written, it may be appropriate to use an iteration rather than a sequence.

7.4   ITERATION

An iteration is indicated by marking the child box with an asterisk in the upper right corner. There is always one child box for an iteration. In the CUSTOMER diagram, CUSTOMER-BODY is an iteration (Fig. 7.8). The meaning of an iteration is that for each instance of the iteration itself, the child occurs zero or more times. So for each CUSTOMER-BODY there are zero or more occurrences of MOVEMENT.

The occurrences of the part of an iteration are sequentially ordered: that is, one MOVEMENT is completed before the next is started. There is no concept, within one structure diagram, of concurrent or parallel events.

The number of occurrences of the part of an iteration may be limited. We might describe a month as in Fig. 7.9. The number of DAYs in a MONTH is always more than 27 and less than 32. We do not show these limits in JSD structure diagrams. There is no conclusive reason why we should not, and some people like to show them; it is simply a matter of what to include and what to leave out in a particular notation. Our practice is to append notes to diagrams where necessary, keeping the content of the notes out of the diagrams themselves. There are theoretical restrictions on what can be shown explicitly in a structure diagram of the kind we use, as we will see later. Inability to show the number of occurrences of an iterated part is far from the only such restriction.

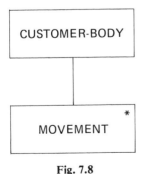

Fig. 7.8

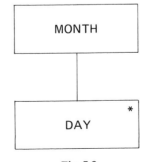

Fig. 7.9

7.5   SELECTION

A selection is indicated by marking each child box by a small circle in the upper right of the box. In the CUSTOMER diagram, MOVEMENT is a selection (Fig. 7.10). The meaning of a selection is that for each instance of the selection itself, one instance occurs of one of the children. So for each MOVEMENT, there is either one PAY-IN occurrence or one WITHDRAW occurrence: it is not possible for neither of them to occur, nor for both to occur, in one instance of MOVEMENT.

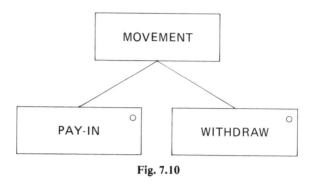

Fig. 7.10

A selection, like a sequence, can have many children. We might describe the result of a student's examination as in Fig. 7.11. Unlike a sequence, a selection cannot have only one child, unless it is intended as a joke (Fig. 7.12). The joke is, of course, that you can select, but there is only one possible outcome of your selection. JSD, unlike the manufacture of automobiles, is a highly serious affair, and selections of one part only are not allowed. (In JSP, a selection diagram showing only one child is sometimes used to indicate that there is a second, null, child (see following paragraph); but this usage is now obsolete.)

In some selections, one of the children is null, or empty, representing the absence of any action. For example, a slimmer might compensate for the days on which he eats a

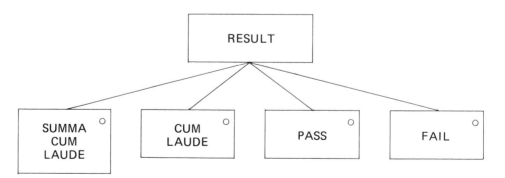

Fig. 7.11

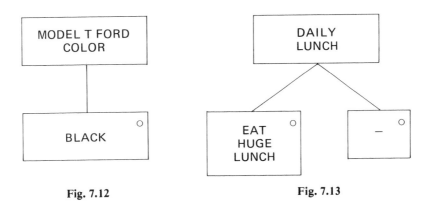

Fig. 7.12   Fig. 7.13

huge lunch by days on which he eats no lunch at all (Fig. 7.13). The box with a dash means 'nothing': the DAILY LUNCH is a selection of EAT HUGE LUNCH or nothing. The null, or empty, box can occur only as a leaf of the tree, for obvious reasons. For reasons only slightly less obvious, it can occur only as a part of a selection, never as a part of a sequence or iteration.

The parts of a selection are unordered. The two structures in Fig. 7.14 are in all respects equivalent. We may choose to draw either, arbitrarily, with identical meaning.

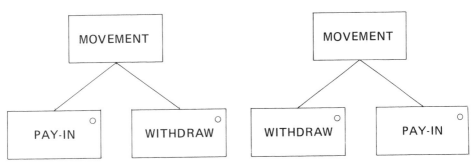

Fig. 7.14

7.6   HI-RIDE ELEVATOR: ENTITY STRUCTURES

We listed two entities: BUTTON and ELEVATOR. There is only one action for BUTTON, and that is PRESS. Each button may be pressed any number of times during the whole lifetime of the system (Fig. 7.15). We have no need of additional notes for this diagram: it is possible for a button to be pressed zero times, and there is no upper limit on the number of times it may be pressed.

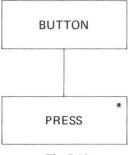

Fig. 7.15

There are two actions for ELEVATOR: ARRIVE(m) and LEAVE(n). We might consider the structure shown in Fig. 7.16, but this structure does not constrain the possible orderings of elevator actions tightly enough. It allows the elevator to perform actions in the order:

```
. . .
ARRIVE(i)
ARRIVE(j)
ARRIVE(k)
. . .
```

We know this cannot happen. After the elevator arrives at a floor, its next action must be to leave that floor. In fact, the ARRIVE and LEAVE actions must alternate. We might then consider the structure in Fig. 7.17, which we may read 'the (behavior of the)

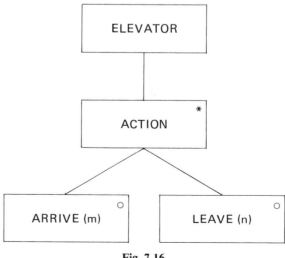

Fig. 7.16

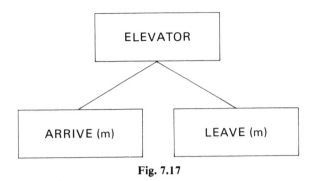

Fig. 7.17

elevator is a sequence; first it arrives at a floor, then it leaves that same floor'. But this is still wrong. We are describing the whole lifetime of the entity, and clearly the whole lifetime of the elevator consists of more than one arrive and one leave action. Much better is Fig. 7.18, which is nearly correct. We still have not considered where the elevator begins its life. Figure 7.18 suggests that it begins life somewhere between two floors, because its very first action must be to arrive at a floor. This could conceivably be true, if the installation instructions for a Hi-Ride elevator require that the system be started with the elevator positioned between floors. More realistically, we expect the elevator to be installed at the ground floor, so we obtain the structure shown in Fig. 7.19.

The appearance of the same letter, m, in the boxes FLOOR(m), ARRIVE(m), and LEAVE(m) indicates that in any one instance of the sequence FLOOR(m), the value of (m) must be the same in both the ARRIVE and the LEAVE part. There are further constraints which cannot be shown in the diagram, but must be stated explicitly in an accompanying note. These constraints are:

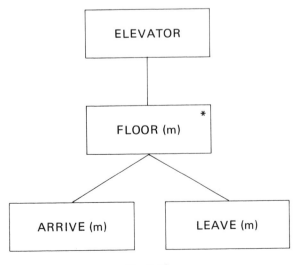

Fig. 7.18

— the value of (m) must always be in the range 1 to 6 inclusive;
— for the first instance of FLOOR(m), the value of (m) must be 1 or 2;
— in any two successive instances of FLOOR(m), the values of (m) must be identical, or must differ by 1.

These constraints on the value of (m) are, of course, the physical constraints on the elevator travel imposed by the shaft in which it moves. The diagram shows that LEAVE and ARRIVE actions must alternate; the accompanying note states that after leaving FLOOR(m), the elevator must next arrive at FLOOR(m + 1), at FLOOR(m − 1), or FLOOR(m). The elevator cannot skip floors. Notice that we are stating what the elevator can do, not what we would like it to do: we have allowed for the possibility that it stops between floors, reverses direction, and returns to the floor it has just left, although no doubt that would not be desirable behavior.

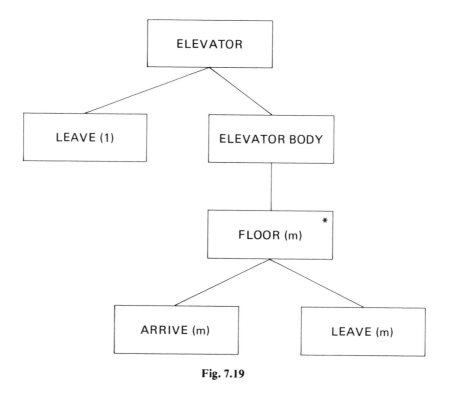

Fig. 7.19

7.7   ERRORS AND FALSEHOODS

In our structure for ELEVATOR, augmented by our notes on the possible values of the floor number, (m), we have specified an ordering of the actions of the real elevators in the real world. Eventually, in later steps of the development, we will connect the real elevators to the processes which model them in the system; messages will, somehow, be input, signalling that the elevator has arrived at FLOOR(3), has now left FLOOR(3), and so on. The question arises: what if the ordering of the input messages is inconsistent with the structure we have specified? what if the message that the elevator has left FLOOR(3) is followed by a message that it has arrived at FLOOR(5)?

Essentially, our reaction to that sequence of messages must be to reply 'it cannot be true'. We have specified, and we are committed to our specification, that after leaving FLOOR(3) the next action of the elevator can only be one of:

—   arrive at FLOOR(3)
—   arrive at FLOOR(2)
—   arrive at FLOOR(4).

There must be some falsehood in the sequence of input messages: perhaps the elevator has in fact arrived at FLOOR(4) (wrongly signalled as FLOOR(5)); perhaps an intervening arrival and departure at FLOOR(4) have wrongly gone unsignalled; perhaps something quite different has happened. But certainly the elevator cannot have arrived at FLOOR(5) immediately after leaving FLOOR(3).

If we could make the assumption (which we cannot) that input messages are always true, and never distorted in any way, we would simply ignore the possibility of such a sequence of messages. It makes no more sense, in the Hi-Ride Elevator system, to consider how the system should respond to such behavior than it makes, in the boating lake system, to ask 'how much time is assigned to a session of boating which ends before it begins?'. There is no point in elaborating the structure of ELEVATOR to accommodate the deviant behavior.

But the assumption that input messages are always true and undistorted is a large one, and cannot be made. That is one reason why an input subsystem must be interposed between the real world and the model that we will build in the next step. This role of the input subsystem is pictured in Fig. 7.20. The input subsystem receives input messages, possibly distorted, from the real world; it detects and repairs some, at least, of the falsehoods and distortions, and passes on to the model sequences of input messages that are plausible in the sense of conforming to the description of the real world given in the system specification. The model need not therefore accommodate inputs that do not conform: they are precluded by the input subsystem.

The input subsystem is discussed in Chapter 12. In many applications, especially in data processing, it will be enough to ensure that inputs are plausible, and that some means is provided of compensating for false inputs that escape detection in the input subsystem. But in the case of a system to control elevators, we might feel that more stringent safety requirements are appropriate: detection of any error in the input should be regarded as evidence that the electromechanical equipment has broken down, and that emergency measures must be taken. We might then specify a function:

when the equipment breaks down, the system must STOP the motor, apply the override brake to the elevator, and ring the alarm bell.

Clearly this function can be provided only if 'break down' is an action in the abstract

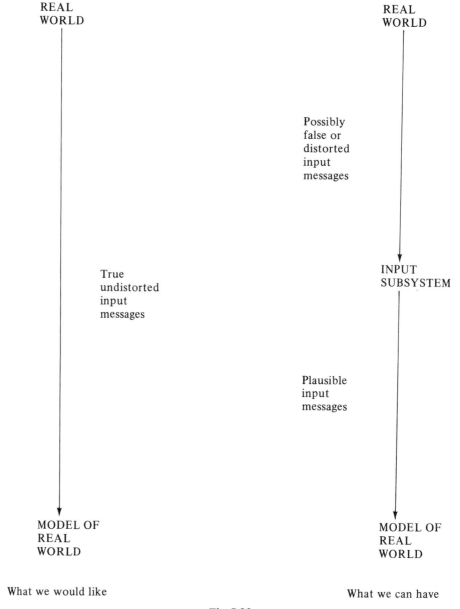

Fig. 7.20

description of the real world and hence is modelled in the system. We would then need to add this action to our list, and to elaborate the elevator structure to contain it. In the specification of the input subsystem we would determine how the occurrence of the action 'break down' is to be detected.

7.8 *DAILY RACKET*: **ENTITY STRUCTURES**

We listed PANEL and READER as entities. The actions of PANEL are AWARD and MEET; the actions of READER are SUBSCRIBE and ENTER.

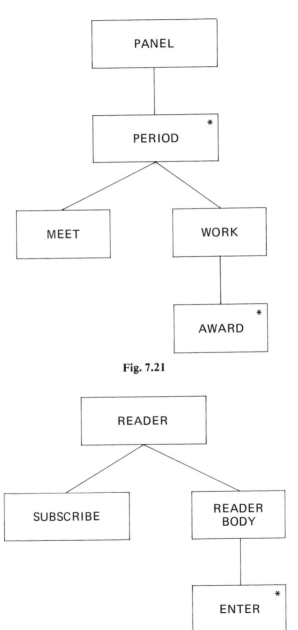

Fig. 7.21

Fig. 7.22

The structures are straightforward (Figs. 7.21, 7.22). The structure for READER seems a little too simple. We have shown the reader as subscribing only once; apparently the subscription is valid for eternity. When we discuss this point with the user, we discover that this is indeed true: Sir Cunning is unwilling to turn away any potential provider of fees, and the requirement for the initial subscription is no more than an attempt to give the competition a false air of exclusivity.

7.9   MINIMAL STRUCTURES

In drawing entity structures we are concerned to specify the constraints on the possible orderings of actions in the real world. The structures must be sufficient, with any necessary additional notes, to express these constraints, but should not be elaborated to serve other purposes. In particular, they should not be drawn with functional requirements in mind.

Suppose that we are specifying the life of a book in a lending library, and that we have listed three actions: BUY, USE, and BIND. The BUY action is performed when the book is initially purchased; the USE action is performed when the book is lent to a library member (we assume that it is always subsequently returned); the BIND action is performed when the book is bound or rebound to strengthen its fabric. We specify the structure of BOOK as in Fig. 7.23.

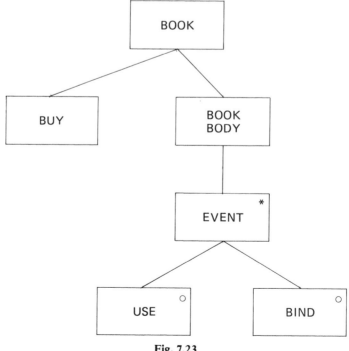

Fig. 7.23

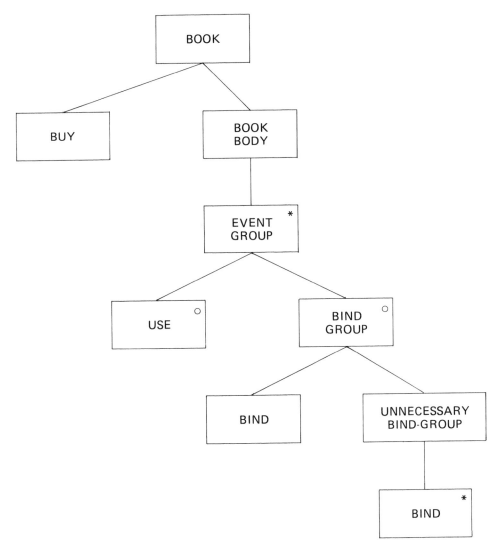

Fig. 7.24

Assuming a simple specification, this structure expresses the ordering constraints exactly: the first action in BOOK's lifetime is always the action BUY; subsequently there can be any number of USE and BIND actions. Among the possible histories are all of these:

BUY, USE, USE, USE;
BUY, BIND, USE, USE, BIND;
BUY, BIND, BIND;

and an infinity of others. When we consider the expected functions of the system, we reflect that the library manager said something about cutting down the number of rebindings being done: he has a suspicion that the bookbinder is the librarian's cousin, and that some books are being rebound unnecessarily. He will therefore probably be very interested in a report telling him how many times a book has been bound without an intervening USE action since the previous BIND action. This function can be provided directly by redrawing the structure of BOOK as in Fig. 7.24. Each BIND action in the UNNECESSARY BIND-GROUP should be reported.

But we should not draw this more elaborate structure now, in the entity structure step; if it is needed, it belongs to the function step. It adds nothing to the first structure in constraining the possible ordering of actions: any history which fits the first structure fits the second also, and vice versa. We therefore draw the simpler, first, structure in the entity structure step.

7.10   MARSUPIAL ENTITIES

A marsupial animal is one which spends the first part of its existence in its mother's pouch, like a kangaroo. Later it emerges to lead a life of its own. During the development procedure, some entities may do likewise. At first they seem, in the entity action step, to have no separate existence of their own; they are merely a part of some other entity. Later, in the entity structure step, they emerge as entities in their own right.

Suppose, in the bank customer system, we have just agreed that the lifetime of a CUSTOMER can span more than one INVEST action, and have drawn the amended structure shown in Fig. 7.25. We now point out to the user that the CUSTOMER can be engaged in only one INV-TERM-GROUP at one time; the first TERMINATE action must occur before the second INVEST. 'Oh, no', says the user, 'we would certainly allow a second invest to happen before the first terminate. We would simply start a new account for the same customer.' Evidently, what we have been calling INV-TERM-GROUP is what the bank calls 'account'. The required ordering of actions for a CUSTOMER is exactly the ordering given above, except that more than one INV-TERM-GROUP (or account) may run concurrently for one CUSTOMER.

There is no way to show concurrency in a single structure diagram. To express what we now know about the ordering of the customer's actions, we must draw one diagram for CUSTOMER (Fig. 7.26) and another for ACCOUNT (Fig. 7.27).

For one CUSTOMER, there may be several ACCOUNTS. The CUSTOMER structure shows that the four different types of CUSTOMER action can occur in any order: INVEST can follow WITHDRAW, TERMINATE can be followed by PAY-IN. The ordering constraint for actions referring to a single ACCOUNT is shown in the ACCOUNT structure, and is already familiar. Technically, we say that the CUSTOMER structure is an interleaving of the ACCOUNT structures. (Readers who know JSP program design will recognize what is there known as an interleaving clash or multi-threading clash.)

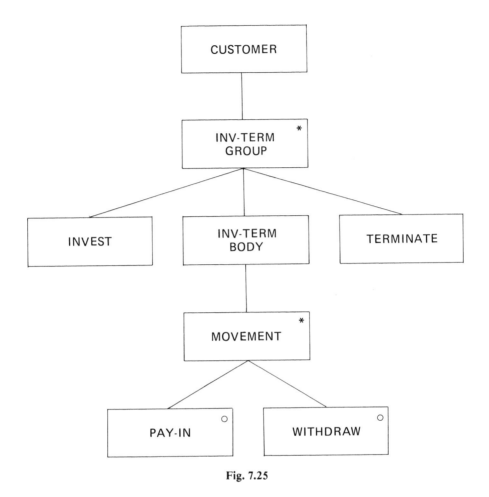

Fig. 7.25

It might appear that we can, in fact, specify some ordering constraints in the CUSTOMER structure. For example, the first action of a CUSTOMER must be an INVEST; the second action must either be an INVEST for another ACCOUNT, or else a PAY-IN, WITHDRAW, or TERMINATE for the first ACCOUNT; the third action must be .... But almost at once the structure becomes hopelessly complicated: we specify the ordering easily by having a separate structure for each ACCOUNT, leaving the CUSTOMER structure as shown.

We have now arrived at the point of recognizing two entities, CUSTOMER and ACCOUNT, with common actions. We might have reached this point much earlier, in the entity action step; indeed, in a realistic development of a banking application, we could hardly have avoided doing so.

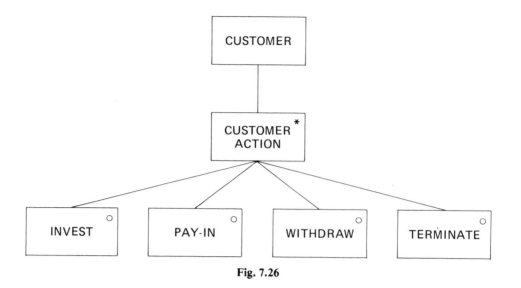

Fig. 7.26

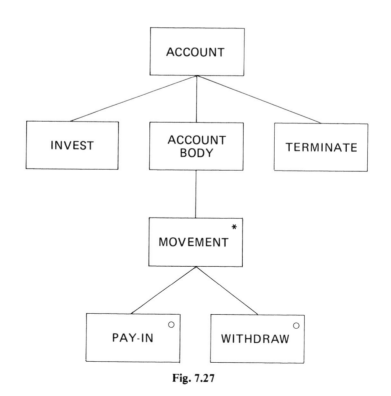

Fig. 7.27

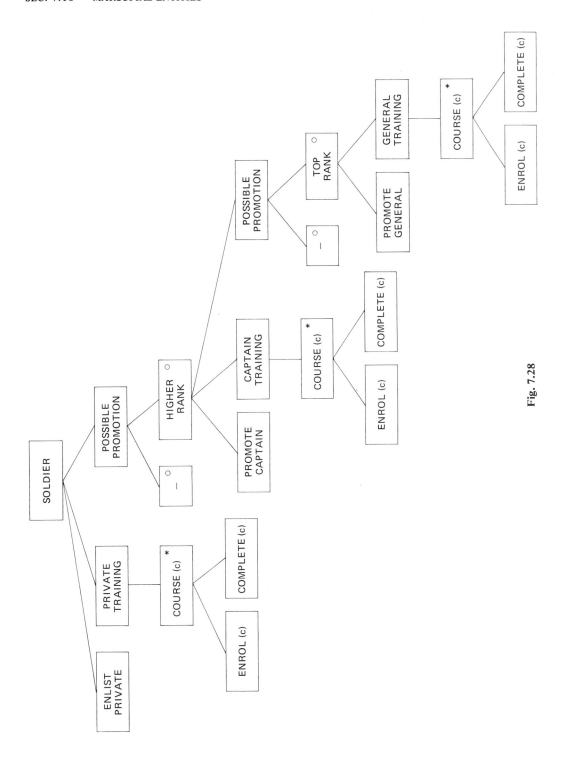

Fig. 7.28

7.11   ENTITIES, STRUCTURES AND ROLES

In the bank system specification we concluded that CUSTOMER and ACCOUNT were distinct entities. So long as a customer was limited to running one account at a time, the ACCOUNT entity could lie hidden in the CUSTOMER structure, concealed by its pseudonym INV-TERM-GROUP; as soon as concurrent accounts were permitted, we were forced to treat the INV-TERM-GROUP component as an entity in its own right, with its own identifier and its own structure tree. The technical considerations of the interleaving clash harmonized happily with the modelling considerations to give the new entity type.

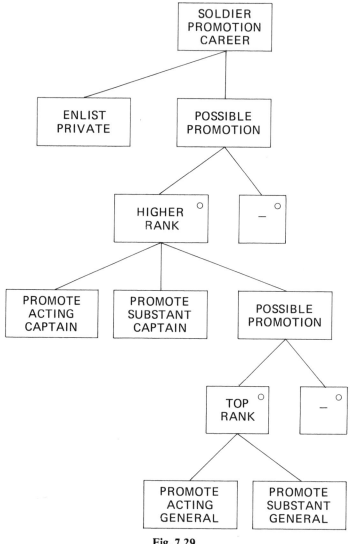

Fig. 7.29

Sometimes we will find that a different kind of structure clash is present, leading to the identification of different roles of a single entity rather than to different entity types.

The Ruritanian army has only three ranks: private, captain, and general. Every soldier is enlisted as a private, and may be promoted to captain and then to general; some soldiers are never promoted, and some are promoted only to captain. The army lays great emphasis on training, and every soldier is enrolled in a succession of training courses, completing each one before being enrolled in the next. Promotions take place only between courses.

The ordering of soldier actions is shown in Fig. 7.28, the structure of SOLDIER. Showing this to our user, with a modest degree of self-congratulation, we learn that there have been some changes in the army even while we were working on our description:

—   Each promotion takes place in two stages; first, promotion to acting rank, then promotion to substantive rank. These two stages are separated in time, but the substantive promotion is inevitable once the acting promotion has been made.

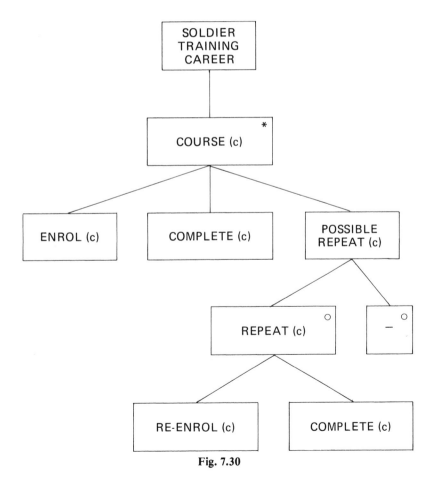

Fig. 7.30

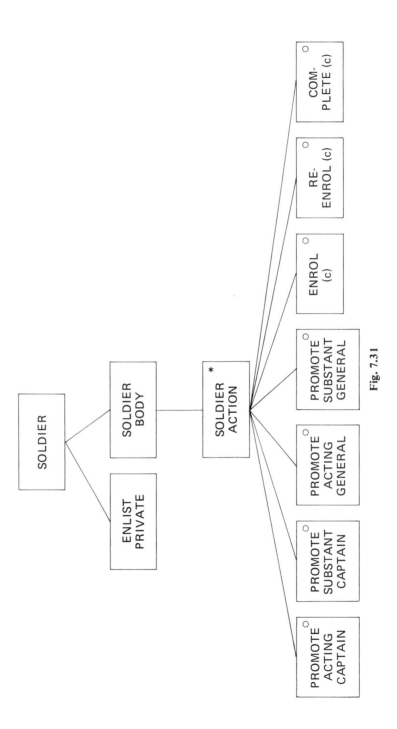

Fig. 7.31

— Sometimes a soldier, on completing a course, is judged not to have reached the required standard. He is then re-enrolled in the same course, and completes it again. The required standard is always reached on the second completion.

— Promotion, both acting and substantive, can occur at any time, not only between courses.

The reader should experiment with the elaboration of Fig. 7.28 to accommodate the new facts. It will soon become apparent that the elaborated structure is extremely difficult to draw, perhaps impossible, and obscure to the point of unintelligibility. The difficulty is that the soldier is pursuing two careers simultaneously: his training career and his promotion career. With the simpler specification of Fig. 7.28, these careers were conveniently coordinated; with the new specification they are hopelessly entangled. We can resolve the difficulty by drawing two separate structures, one for each career. They are as shown in Figs. 7.29 and 7.30. We may retain a structure of soldier (Fig. 7.31).

The three structures describe the action ordering of a single entity, SOLDIER, with a single identifier. The two career structures have common actions with the SOLDIER structure.

7.12   PREMATURE TERMINATION

The meaning of a sequence in a structure is that for each instance of the sequence itself one instance of each of its parts occurs, in order from left to right in the diagram. So, for example, a Ruritanian soldier who achieves top rank eventually performs the sequence shown in Fig. 7.32.

Since the Ruritanian army wisely avoids the battlefield, no soldier is ever killed in active service. However, nature is not to be denied, and it can happen that an acting general is carried to an early grave by natural causes. In such a case, we might think to elaborate the structure as in Fig. 7.33. This seems preferable to maintaining a fiction of posthumous substantive promotions. We should also consider the same possibility of premature death of an acting captain, perhaps making a rather large change this time to the structure.

As we consider more complex structures, the difficulty of elaboration to allow for premature termination becomes more severe, perhaps almost insurmountable. (Again, the reader should experiment with the elaboration of Figs. 7.29 and 7.30 to show the possible occurrence of NATURAL DEATH at any point in those structures.) We might therefore consider introducing another structure (Fig. 7.34).

We might make RETIREMENT a common action to all three structures, placing it at the end of SOLDIER PROMOTION CAREER and of SOLDIER TRAINING CAREER. But this approach does not achieve our aim of showing that the PROMOTION CAREER can be prematurely terminated. The standard solution is to use the rather special kind of structure shown in Fig. 7.35.

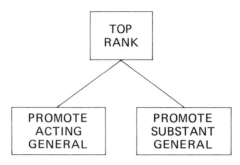

Fig. 7.32

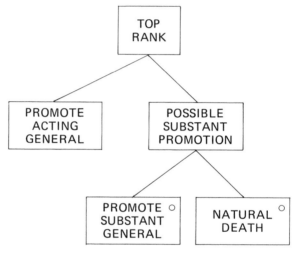

Fig. 7.33

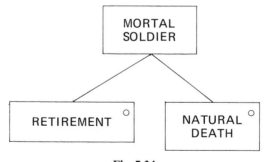

Fig. 7.34

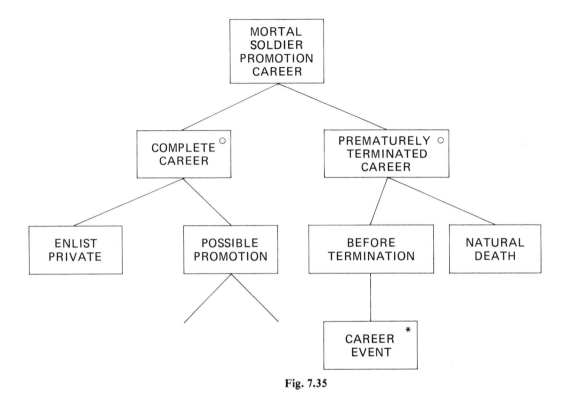

Fig. 7.35

The structure of COMPLETE CAREER, not shown here in full, is the structure of SOLDIER PROMOTION CAREER shown in Fig. 7.29. The PREMATURELY TER-MINATED CAREER is one which ends in natural death; BEFORE TERMINATION is simply an iteration of career events, avoiding the need to spell out all the possible versions of prematurely terminated structures (which is the very thing that we are unable to do). This 'unstructured' description of BEFORE TERMINATION is one of the special features of this kind of structure. The other special feature, which makes the first acceptable, is that we must proceed on the assumption that a soldier's CAREER will be COMPLETE rather than PREMATURELY TERMINATED: this assumption will be proved false if NATURAL DEATH occurs during the soldier's CAREER.

In the initial model step, discussed in the next chapter, we will deal with some of the questions arising from structures of this kind. These questions, and their answers, will already be familiar to those readers who are practitioners of JSP program design: they concern the technique of backtracking as a method of handling recognition (or parsing) difficulties. Here we are interested only in the specification of the structure diagram, and, by that means, specification of the action ordering for an entity type.

7.13   WIDGET WAREHOUSE: ENTITY STRUCTURES—1

We listed four entities for the Widget Warehouse model: CUSTOMER, CLERK, ORDER, and PRODUCT. The actions are:

      CUSTOMER: PLACE, AMEND, CANCEL, DELIVER;
         CLERK: DELAY, ALLOCATE;
         ORDER: PLACE, AMEND, CANCEL, DELIVER, DELAY, ALLOCATE;
       PRODUCT: ALLOCATE, DELIVER.

The structure of CUSTOMER exhibits an interleaving clash, with a marsupial entity CUS-ORDER (Fig. 7.36).

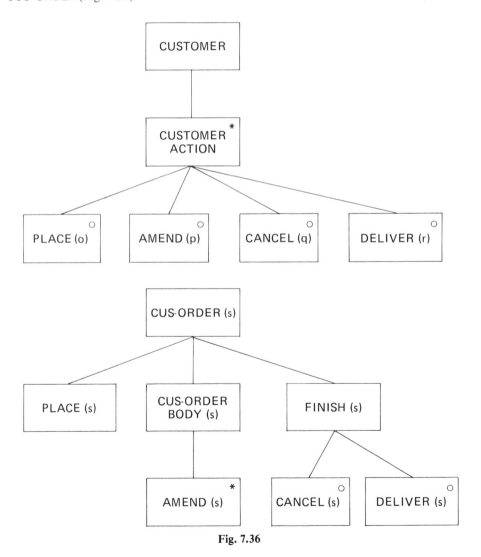

Fig. 7.36

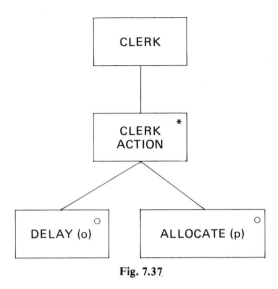

Fig. 7.37

For any CUSTOMER, the instances of CUS-ORDER are arbitrarily interleaved. The letters in parentheses stand for the identifier of the order with which each action is associated. The structure of CLERK is similar (Fig. 7.37). For any CLERK, the instances of CLK-ORDER are arbitrarily interleaved (Fig. 7.38).

The reader should not lose sight of the fact that these early JSD steps are developing a specification, not solving a given problem. What has been expressed in these diagrams may be right or wrong: only a particular user in a particular context can say which. We have specified that once a customer has PLACEd an order, he must

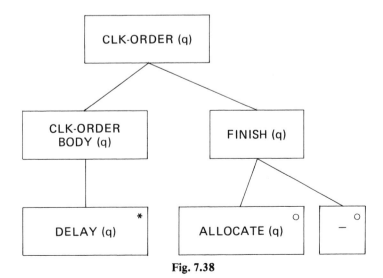

Fig. 7.38

eventually either CANCEL it or perform the DELIVER action (perhaps, sign a goods-received note): there is no possibility, for example, of the order being cancelled by the CLERK, or lapsing after a certain period. We have specified that a CLERK may perform an ALLOCATE action at the end of an order's life, or a null action (i.e., no action): it is not necessary, for example, that the CLERK should confirm acceptance by the company of a CUSTOMER's cancellation. It would be a normal part of JSD development for the developer to find, when discussing the entity structures with the user, that they revealed a need for further action types that had been wrongly omitted at the previous step.

The entity ORDER is essentially a composite of the two marsupial entities CUS-ORDER and CLK-ORDER (Fig. 7.39).

This composition of structures raises some general questions, which are discussed in the next section.

The PRODUCT entity can have no structure other than that shown in Fig. 7.40. The ordering constraint on the ALLOCATE and DELIVER actions is specified in the structure of the entity ORDER. It would be wrong to show the structure of PRODUCT as in Fig. 7.41, because this wrongly implies that ALLOCATE and DELIVER actions must alternate for a PRODUCT. The correct constraint is that the number of DELIVER actions performed cannot exceed the number of ALLOCATE actions performed.

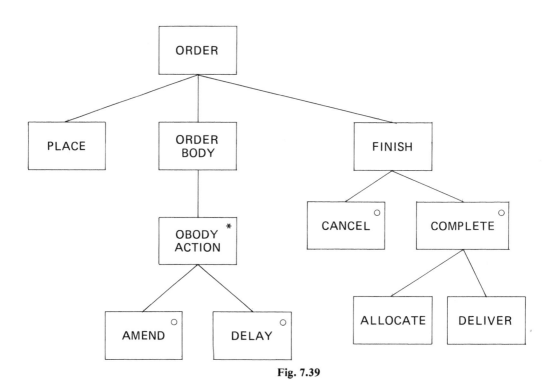

Fig. 7.39

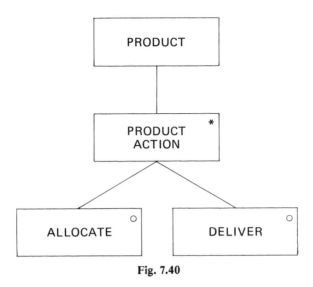

Fig. 7.40

The DELIVER action is common to PRODUCT and to CUSTOMER and ORDER. It was described as 'deliver ordered product to customer'. Looking at the PRODUCT entity structure, it is hard to see much sense in this. The DELIVER action, as described, means little from the point of view of the product entity.

We consider whether to define a new action ISSUE to replace the action DELIVER in the PRODUCT structure. To ISSUE a product is to take an ordered quantity out of the warehouse location. It is not the same action as DELIVER; an ISSUE action can

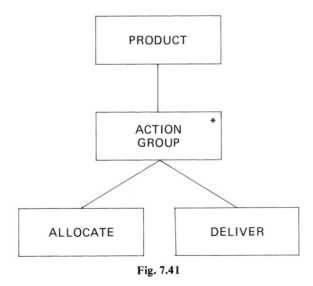

Fig. 7.41

occur without the issued product being delivered to any customer. But now we are straying outside our model boundary. We are beginning to model the inventory in the warehouse, which belongs to the world of the purchasing and inventory system, not to our own assigned reality.

What kind of model, then, do we want of PRODUCT? Really, none. The useful model of PRODUCT is the model accessible to the clerk when he telephones the warehouse; it answers the question 'how much of this product is available for me to allocate?'. If we retain the CLERK as an entity, and make no attempt to automate the clerical activity of delaying and allocating orders, we can leave the PRODUCT entity out of our model.

7.14 CHECKING A COMPOSITE STRUCTURE

The composite structure ORDER is an interleaving of the CUS-ORDER and CLK-ORDER structures. To check that the composition has been carried out correctly, we must satisfy ourselves:

— that no possible instance of ORDER infringes the constraints on the sequencing of PLACE, AMEND, CANCEL and DELIVER actions imposed by CUS-ORDER, or the constraints on the sequencing of DELAY and ALLOCATE actions imposed by CLK-ORDER; and

— that any constraint imposed by ORDER on the way in which CUS-ORDER and CLK-ORDER may be interleaved is a true constraint in the real world.

We check the first condition for each of CUS-ORDER and CLK-ORDER in turn as follows:

(1) Replace by null (—) those leaves of ORDER which are not leaves of the relevant interleaved structure.

(2) Apply successively any of a set of permissible operations to the result, until the relevant interleaved structure is obtained.

Taking CUS-ORDER to be the relevant interleaved structure, we carry out (1), obtaining the structure of Fig. 7.42.

For (2), the permissible operations are those which do not change the constraints on the ordering of the leaves of the structure. They include:

(a) removing a null leaf which is a part of a sequence;

(b) removing a null leaf which is a part of a selection which itself is the part of an iteration;

(c) replacing a selection of one part by its part;

(d) replacing a sequence of one part by its part;

(e) removing one of two identical parts of a selection;

(f) removing one of two identical iterations which are consecutive parts of a sequence;

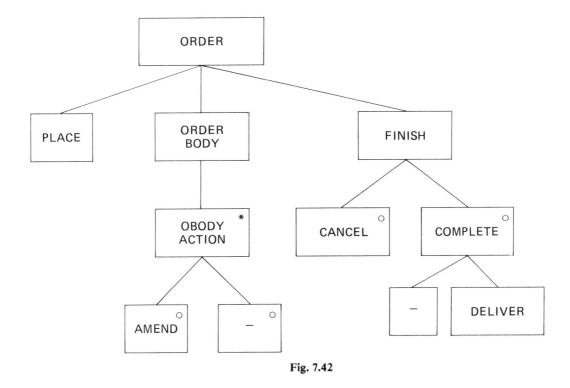

Fig. 7.42

(g)   reducing two levels of iteration to one: that is, replacing B by C where A is an iteration of B and B is an iteration of C.*

Applying (a) and (d) to COMPLETE, and (b) and (c) to OBODY ACTION, we obtain the structure of Fig. 7.43 which is identical, except for the naming of non-elementary components, to CUS-ORDER.

Now taking CLK-ORDER to be the relevant interleaved structure, we carry out (1) and obtain Fig. 7.44.

Applying (a) to ORDER, (a) and (d) to COMPLETE, and (b) and (c) to OBODY ACTION, we obtain Fig. 7.45, which is identical, except for the naming of non-elementary components and the (arbitrary) ordering of the parts of the selection FINISH, to CLK-ORDER.

We have now checked that the first of the two conditions is satisfied. This is a formal check, and is carried out purely by examining and manipulating the structure diagrams: it does not involve the system user in any way. The second condition, by contrast, is a matter of checking the specification against the real world facts, and involves the user immediately. The structure of ORDER specifies:

---

*   These are examples of transformations of regular expressions, preserving equivalence. See Chapter 4 of M. Minsky, *Computation: Finite and Infinite Machines*, Prentice-Hall.

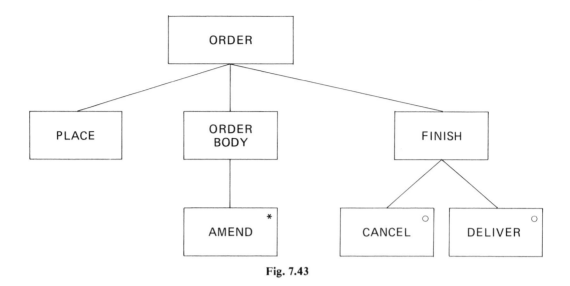

Fig. 7.43

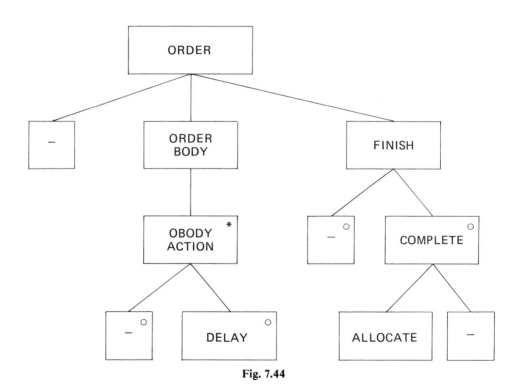

Fig. 7.44

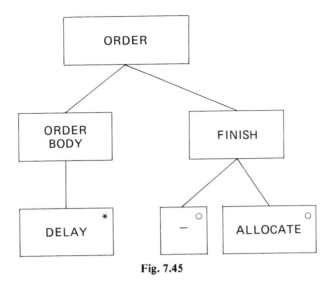

Fig. 7.45

— that nothing can happen to an order before it is placed by the customer—in particular, that the clerk can perform no action before the order is placed;
— that the customer cannot amend or cancel the order once it has been allocated by the clerk;
— that the clerk cannot delay or allocate the order once it has been cancelled by the customer.

Input messages purporting to indicate events not conforming to this specification would be rejected by the input subsystem as falsehoods. Bearing in mind that the customers and the clerks may have only imperfect and outdated information about each other's behavior in the real world, the developer and the user may well conclude that the specification of ORDER is too tightly constrained. We will return to this point and reconsider the specification in the next chapter.

7.15 WIDGET WAREHOUSE: ENTITY STRUCTURES—2

In a realistic system, we would surely intend to automate the allocation and delay of orders. Automation would mean that the DELAY and ALLOCATE actions of the clerk would become part of the system function. The clerk would cease to be an entity in the model. Because the DELAY and ALLOCATE actions would now be part of the system function, they disappear from the ORDER structure, which then becomes identical to the marsupial CUS-ORDER (Fig. 7.46). The CUSTOMER entity is unaffected, unless automation of the order allocation requires different behavior on the customer's part.

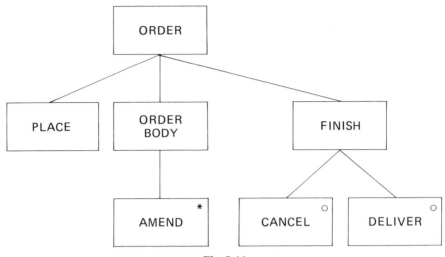

Fig. 7.46

If we automate the clerk's activity, we will need to model the PRODUCT entity. The real world product is clearly in the warehouse; but we will be required, for good technical and economic reasons (as well as some bad political reasons) to obtain our information about products from the purchasing and inventory control system. For us, therefore, that system will be the real world: we cannot include anything in our model that is not in that system, and we can abstract, ignoring things and aspects of that system, when we make our description of the PRODUCT entity. The entity we will call PRODUCT is actually the product stock record in that system.

After some investigation, we discover that we can model the behavior of PRODUCT by a single action:

AVAIL: a quantity of the product is stated to be available for allocation to orders.
          Attributes: quantity, . . .

The AVAIL action is not cumulative. If AVAIL 55 occurs at 10 a.m., our system allocates 30 at 10.30 a.m., and then AVAIL 40 occurs at 11 a.m., the quantity available

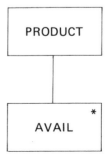

Fig. 7.47

for allocation immediately after 11 a.m. is 40, not 40 + (55 – 30). Our model of product answers the question: 'taking account of everything, how much is available now?' Keeping account of the availability is a problem for the inventory system, not for us. Of course, in the inventory system itself the model of PRODUCT is much more complex. There are issues and receipts, purchases and stock wastages. The system must take account of allocations made by our system, for which we will no doubt have to provide some output in the function step. Our simple description in terms of AVAIL actions abstracts from those complexities, which themselves are an abstract description of the yet more complex real world of the warehouse.

The structure of PRODUCT is as shown in Fig. 7.47.

SUMMARY OF CHAPTER 7

In the entity structure step we specify the ordering of the actions of each entity in structure diagrams composed of sequence, iteration, and selection components. The whole life span of each entity must be specified, not only a part of it (7.1).

Structure diagrams are trees. The parts of a sequence occur once each, in order from left to right, for each occurrence of the sequence. An iteration has one part, which occurs zero or more times for each occurrence of the iteration. A selection has two or more parts, of which exactly one occurs once for each occurrence of the selection (7.2–5).

The expressive power of structure diagrams is limited. We need to add notes to the structure of elevator in the Hi-Ride Elevator system to show that the elevator cannot skip floors (7.6).

The entity structures describe what can happen in the real world. Any input appearing to contradict the ordering specified by a structure must be false or distorted in some way. One purpose of the input subsystem will be to detect and repair these falsehoods. For certain highly critical applications we may regard false input as signalling the occurrence of an emergency in the real world (7.7).

The *Daily Racket* entity structures are very straightforward (7.8).

Entity structures specified in this step must not be elaborated to anticipate functional requirements: they must be, in some sense, minimal structures to express the real world constraints (7.9).

A single diagram cannot express concurrency. For example, if a bank customer can operate several accounts concurrently, and there are constraints on the ordering of events for each account, the behavior of a customer cannot be shown in one diagram. It is necessary to extract the ACCOUNT entity from the structure of CUSTOMER. Entities recognized in this way in this step are called marsupial entities; they are associated with interleaving clashes in JSP structures (7.10).

Another form of concurrency appears when one entity plays several roles, and the ordering constraints of the roles cannot be combined in one structure. It is then necessary to specify a separate structure for each role (7.11).

Curtailment, or premature termination, of an entity's life is difficult to express in structure diagrams. A special kind of selection is needed (7.12).

In a non-automated version of the Widget Warehouse system the entities CUSTOMER and CLERK both have marsupial entities associated with ORDER. The ORDER entity is a composition of these marsupial entities, specifying how the actions of the customer and of the clerk on one order are interleaved. No model is needed for the entity PRODUCT in this non-automated version of the system (7.13).

A composite structure, such as ORDER, can be checked for its formal correctness (that is, not infringing the constraints imposed by its constituent structures) and its specification correctness (that is, not imposing untrue constraints on the interleaving of its constituent structures) (7.14).

An automated version of the Widget Warehouse system would not model the CLERK's behavior (naturally). It would need a model of PRODUCT, which is taken from another system (7.15).

8

Initial model step

8.1 LEVEL-0 AND LEVEL-1

In the entity action and entity structure steps we have made an abstract description of the real world in terms of entities, the actions they perform and suffer, and the ordering of those actions. In the initial model step we will begin to build our system by specifying a set of sequential processes which model the real world entities and their behavior. Where there is an entity structure in the abstract description, there will be a sequential process in the model.

To ensure that the behavior of the model correctly reflects the events in the real world, we will need to connect the model processes, directly or indirectly, to the real world. Our abstract descriptions can themselves be regarded as specifications of sequential processes: we have described the *Daily Racket* reader as a sequential process by drawing the structure diagram of READER. So we can regard the task of connecting the model processes to the real world as one of connecting sequential processes together. We will refer to the real world processes as level-0 processes, and to the model processes as level-1 processes. For convenience and brevity we will often refer to the real *Daily Racket* reader as READER-0, and to the process which models the reader within the system as READER-1.

Once connected to the real world, the sequential processes of the model are, in principle, executable computer programs. We cannot execute them directly on a typical mainframe configuration, because they tend to have awkward characteristics: there are far too many of them, and they have very long execution times. In the implementation step, we will apply some transformations to make them more amenable to execution on the available hardware and software. In the earlier steps, we can think of their execution more abstractly, without reference to supporting hardware or software. Readers who find it hard to think in this way can instead imagine each model process running on its own, dedicated, microprocessor, with appropriate devices to connect it to the real world

121   and to other microprocessors.

Although we will talk in terms of computer implementation, we are not excluding the possibility of manual procedures to implement all or part of the system. Some aspects of manual implementation will be discussed later in the book. Readers who feel more comfortable discussing system specifications in terms of manual procedures will find a resting place in Section 8.12, where the JSD ideas of process connection are restated in human terms: in place of a set of microprocessors we visualize an office occupied by clerical workers following carefully specified procedures; in place of the technicalities of process connection we have the rules for communication between clerical workers.

8.2   STRUCTURE TEXT

For many purposes we will need a textual notation to specify sequential processes, in addition to the diagrams we have used so far. The basis of the textual notation is simply a transcription of the diagrammatic form. On that basis we can later add some elements, such as executable operations and condition tests, which do not fit easily into the diagrams; we can also, in the implementation step, derive program code in languages like PL/I, Pascal, or COBOL, very directly from the structure text.

In the previous chapter we discussed the structure of a book in a lending library (Fig. 8.1).

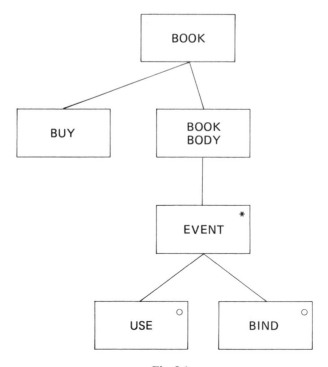

Fig. 8.1

Here is the equivalent structure text:

```
BOOK seq
   BUY;
   BOOK-BODY itr
      EVENT sel
         USE;
      EVENT alt
         BIND;
      EVENT end
   BOOK-BODY end
BOOK end
```

As can be easily inferred from this example, the rules for writing structure text are very straightforward. The leaves of the diagram are represented by their names, terminated by semi-colons. A sequence node X is represented by

```
X seq
   . . .
   . . .
X end
```

with the parts of the sequence represented, in order, between the beginning and end of the text of the sequence. An iteration node Y is represented by

```
Y itr
   . . .
Y end
```

with the single part of the iteration represented between the beginning and end of the text of the iteration. A selection of two parts, Z, is represented by:

```
Z sel
   . . .
Z alt
   . . .
Z end
```

in which the first part of the selection is represented immediately following the beginning of the selection, and the second part following the word **alt** (alternative). A selection of three parts (Fig. 8.2) is represented by

```
P sel
   Q;
P alt
   R;
P alt
   S;
P end
```

with the obvious extension for selections of four or more parts.

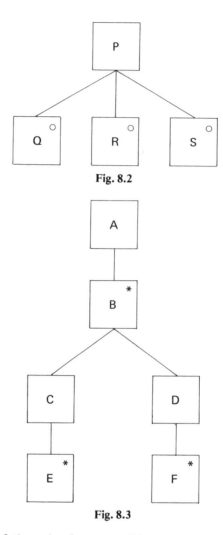

Fig. 8.2

Fig. 8.3

One relaxation of the rules for transcribing structures from diagrammatic to textual form is permitted, in the case of a sequence which is not the root of the structure: in this case, it is permissible to omit the textual indications of the sequence construct. So, for example, the structure diagram shown in Fig. 8.3 may be transcribed as:

```
A itr
  C itr
    E;
  C end
  D itr
    F;
  D end
A end
```

omitting the textual indications of the sequence B.

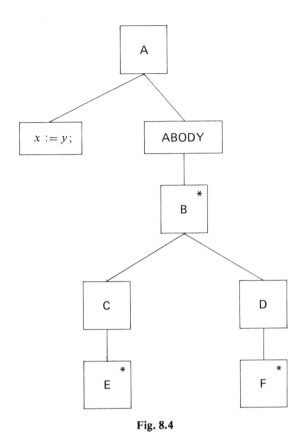

Fig. 8.4

When we come to add elementary components to a structure (for example, operations in the initial model and later steps), we may need to elaborate the structure a little to preserve its formal correctness. For instance, if we wish to add the operation '$x := y$;' at the beginning of the structure A above, we will need to respecify the structure as in Fig. 8.4, or in some similar way, to ensure that we still have a structure in which every component is either a sequence, an iteration, a selection, or an elementary component.

When we come to write conditions in structure text, as we will later in this chapter, we will write a condition against the header of an iteration:

   Y **itr while** (*condition*-Z)
     . . .
   Y **end**

The meaning of the condition is the conventional meaning in programming languages: the iteration continues so long as *condition*-Z is true. *Condition*-Z is therefore the condition under which a (further) instance of the iterated part is present. For a selection, we will write a condition against the header of each part of the selection:

```
P sel (condition-Q)
   Q;
P alt (condition-R)
   R;
P alt (condition-S)
   S;
P end
```

Condition-Q, *condition*-R, and *condition*-S are the conditions under which the parts Q, R, and S are present respectively.

By writing a condition for the last part we do not mean to imply that there is a hidden fourth alternative. We mean only to document the fact that, according to our specification, one of the three conditions shown must be true in any instance of the selection P. This usage is different from the conventional usage in programming languages, where, for example,

```
if condition-Q then Q
elseif condition-R then R
elseif condition-S then S
endif
```

implies a null part of the selection, to be chosen when none of *condition*-Q, *condition*-R, and *condition*-S is true. There is no such implication in the structure text.

A difference between the diagrammatic and the text form of a selection is that the parts of the text form are considered to be ordered, while in the diagrammatic form they are unordered. Thus, in the selection P shown above, the part Q is taken to be present when both *condition*-Q and *condition*-R are true; the part R is taken to be present only if *condition*-R is true and *condition*-Q is false. The part S is taken to be present only when *condition*-Q and *condition*-R are both false: in that case, *condition*-S must be true (in an instance of P).

In certain cases, the truth of the condition on the last part of a selection is logically implied by the falsity of all of the conditions on the earlier parts. Thus, for example, in the selection:

```
P sel (x < y)
   . . .
P alt (x > y)
   . . .
P alt (x = y)
   . . .
P end
```

$x = y$ is necessarily true if both $x < y$ and $x > y$ are false. In such a case, the condition on the last part may be written in the form (**else**):

P **sel** $(x < y)$
 . . .
P **alt** $(x > y)$
 . . .
P **alt** (**else**)
 . . .
P **end**

8.3   PROCESS CONNECTION

In the initial model and function steps of JSD there are two ways, and only two ways, of connecting processes together: data stream connection and state-vector connection. In data stream connection, one process writes a sequential data stream, consisting of an ordered set of messages or records; the other process reads this stream. In state-vector connection, one process directly inspects the state-vector—that is, the internal local variables—of the other process. We will use these forms of connection both to connect the model processes to the real world and to connect model and function processes within the system. Later, in the implementation step, the developer is free to use other forms of connection, such as interrupts, where appropriate or necessary; but they must then be seen as correct implementations of the specified data stream or state-vector connections.

We need to be able to represent connections among several processes, showing which processes are directly connected and in what way. For this purpose we use a diagram which we call a System Specification Diagram or SSD. In the SSD, data stream connection is shown like this:

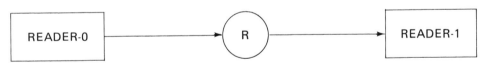

The rectangles in an SSD represent sequential processes, in this case READER-0 and READER-1. Circles represent data streams, in this case the data stream named R. The arrows show the direction in which information is moving, in the obvious way. READER-0 writes the data stream R, which is read by READER-1.

State-vector connection is shown like this:

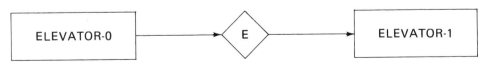

Again the rectangles represent processes. The diamond shows that the connection is by state-vector inspection: ELEVATOR-1 inspects the state vector of ELEVATOR-0.

The connections shown above are one-to-one: there is exactly one process on each side of the connection. Sometimes a connection is many-to-one; we represent the multiplicity by placing a double bar on the arrow on the side of the many processes. So the SSD

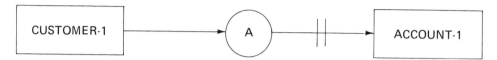

means that there are many ACCOUNT-1 processes connected to one CUSTOMER-1 process. The multiplicity is to be interpreted as follows:

— over the whole lifetime of a CUSTOMER-1 process, it may be connected to any number (including zero) of ACCOUNT-1 processes; and
— at any time, a CUSTOMER-1 process may be connected to zero, one, or more ACCOUNT-1 processes.

No distinction is made in the SSD between this general case and the more restricted case in which a CUSTOMER-1 process may not be connected to more than one ACCOUNT-1 process at any one time.

With the same interpretation of multiplicity, many-to-many connections are also permitted in the SSD:

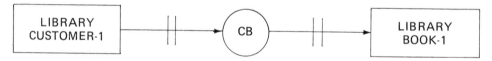

means that each LIBRARY-CUSTOMER-1 process is connected to many LIBRARY-BOOK-1 processes, and vice versa.

Multiplicity shown by double bars in the SSD is always purely relative to the connection. For example, the SSD

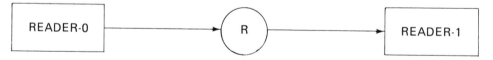

tells us nothing about how many READER-0s there are; it tells us only that there is one READER-0 connected to each READER-1, and vice versa. To show absolute multiplicity, we could write upper and lower limits against each box representing a process:

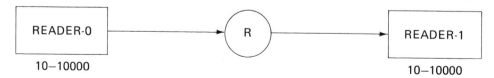

but we will not usually do so. Absolute multiplicity is not of much importance until the implementation step.

We will explore the characteristics of data stream and state-vector connection, and their use in the initial model step, in the sections that follow. Some aspects will be discussed later when we come to the function step.

8.4 DATA STREAM CONNECTION

In this section we will look at the general characteristics of data stream connection between two processes; then, in the next section, we will consider data stream connection between the real world and the model.

Suppose that we have a sequential process P, whose structure diagram and text are as shown in Fig. 8.5. We are not concerned here with the question: what drives P? Nor with the question: how does P decide whether to perform A, B, C, or D? We are simply assuming that P does behave as specified, performing the actions A, B, C, and D in the order shown. (This assumption, in fact, is the assumption we must make about all level-0 processes.)

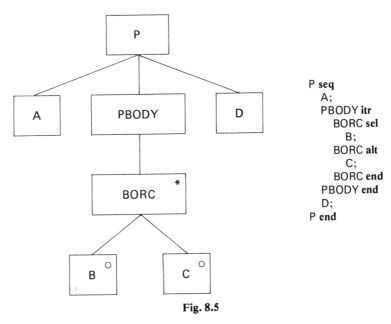

P seq
    A;
    PBODY itr
        BORC sel
            B;
        BORC alt
            C;
        BORC end
    PBODY end
    D;
P end

Fig. 8.5

Suppose now that we wish to construct another process Q to model the behavior of P in some way. Initially, we will suppose that Q is to model the behavior of P exactly: that is, Q is to perform actions QA, QB, QC, and QD in the same order as P performs A, B, C, and D respectively. We will connect P and Q by a data stream DS:

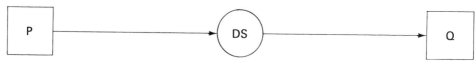

We will arrange that each action of P is signalled to Q by a record of DS: action A is signalled by record RA, and so on. These records must be written by P when the signalled actions are performed:

    P **seq**
        A; *write* RA *to* DS;
        PBODY **itr**
            BORC **sel**
                B; *write* RB *to* DS;
            BORC **alt**
                C; *write* RC *to* DS;
            BORC **end**
        PBODY **end**
        D; *write* RD *to* DS;
    P **end**

Since Q is to model the behavior of P exactly, it must have the same structure. Q's behavior could be described very informally: 'wait for a signal to arrive from P, in the form of a record of DS, and, when it does arrive, perform the corresponding action within the structure of Q'. This behavior is achieved by appropriate 'read DS' operations and conditions, added to the text of Q. The 'read DS' operations wait for the signals from P, and receive them when they arrive; the conditions guide Q through its structure (Fig. 8.6).

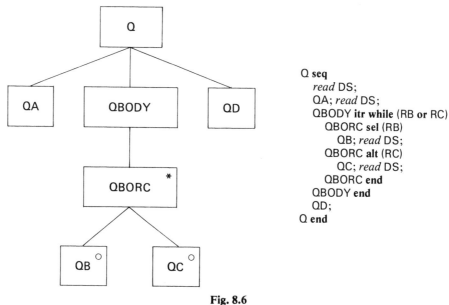

Q **seq**
    read DS;
    QA; *read* DS;
    QBODY **itr while** (RB or RC)
        QBORC **sel** (RB)
            QB; *read* DS;
        QBORC **alt** (RC)
            QC; *read* DS;
        QBORC **end**
    QBODY **end**
    QD;
Q **end**

Fig. 8.6

The 'read DS' operations have been allocated systematically in the text of Q, according to a 'read ahead' rule. This rule reflects the requirement that Q must wait for and receive each message of DS before it can determine which action is to be executed. That is why each action in Q is followed, rather than preceded, by a *read* operation, and there is an initial read operation at the beginning of Q. If we wish, we can remove the read operations appearing in the parts of BORC, and replace them by a single read operation at the end of BORC. We can also eliminate the slight anomaly of the absence of a read operation after QD, by introducing a 'close DS' operation in P to write an end-of-stream marker record. These technical matters will be important in the implementation step, but we will lay them aside for the moment.

The data stream connection between P and Q, like all data stream connections in JSP specifications, is considered to be buffered. Nothing is specified about the speed of transmission of records from P to Q; also, P can write any number of records of DS in advance of their being read by Q. The buffering is strictly first-in–first-out: no reordering of records can take place in the buffer, and no record can get lost there.

The characteristics of this data stream connection are the following:

—   The initiative lies with P to determine the content and order of the records of DS. We can deduce these by considering the behavior of P alone, without considering Q at all.

—   Q is forced to read every record written by P. There is no mechanism by which Q can choose to skip records of DS, or to read them in a different order from their order of writing by P.

—   If, for any reason, execution of Q is slowed down or stops temporarily, records of DS wait in the buffer until Q continues execution and reads them. There is no mechanism by which they wither away, or are read by some other process, or are overwritten by later records.

—   If execution of Q reaches a read DS operation, and there is no record available in the buffer (because Q has already read all the records which P has so far written), Q is said to be blocked. Execution of Q cannot continue until a record becomes available and the read DS operation can be completed.

—   Because the data stream is buffered, P is not blocked when it reaches a write operation, irrespective of the number of records previously read by Q. The buffer is considered to be of unlimited capacity; the write operation in P is completed by the addition of the written record to the buffer, and P continues execution.

Summarizing the effect of these characteristics, we can say that Q behaves in a way determined by P, but lags behind P by some indeterminate and possibly varying number of records of DS. How far Q lags behind P will depend on the relative speeds of the processors on which they run, and on the speed with which the buffer can make a written record available for reading. But it is only the amount by which Q lags behind P that is affected by these speed considerations: the content of DS, and the resulting behavior of Q, remains entirely unaffected, whatever the speeds of the processors or the buffer operation.

We have been supposing that we want Q to model the behavior of P exactly; so P and Q have the same structure, and there is a record of DS for each action of P. But data stream connection permits other relationships between P and Q. One obvious possibility is that Q may model only a subset of P's actions. Suppose, for example, that we want Q to model only the actions B and D. Then:

— in P we place write operations only for actions B and D; actions A and C will have no associated write operation in the text of P;
— the structure of Q may be as shown in Fig. 8.7.

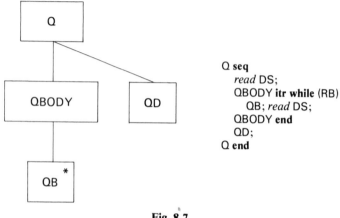

Q **seq**
    read DS;
    QBODY **itr while** (RB)
        QB; *read* DS;
    QBODY **end**
    QD;
Q **end**

Fig. 8.7

Another possibility is that P may write only a summary of its behavior to DS, signalling, for example, the A action and a count of the B actions. P would then be

```
P seq
    A; write RA to DS; count := 0;
    PBODY itr
        BORC sel
            B; count := count + 1;
        BORC alt
            C;
    PBODY end
    write count to DS;
    D;
P end
```

and the structure of Q would be as shown in Fig. 8.8. Yet another possibility is that Q may model all the actions of P, but in a more elaborate structure. For example, the structure of Q might distinguish the three cases:

— no B or C action is performed;
— the first action following A is a B;
— the first action following A is a C.

The structure of Q would then be as shown in Fig. 8.9.

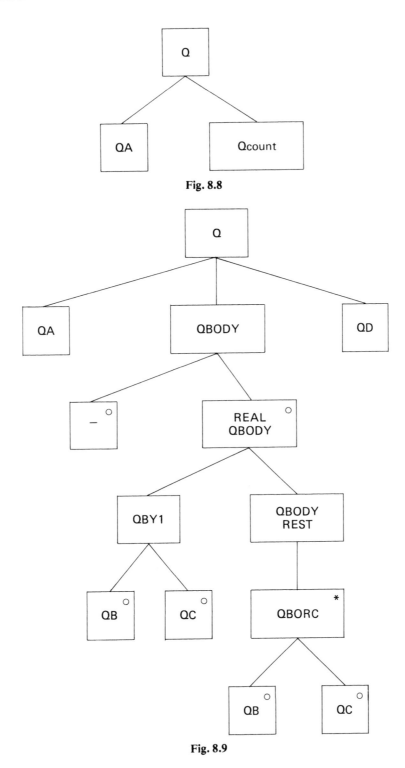

Fig. 8.8

Fig. 8.9

Subset, summary, and elaborated relationships like these will be important in the function step. In the initial model step we will always be concerned to make the reading process model the writing process exactly.

8.5   *DAILY RACKET*: **INITIAL MODEL—1**

The entity structures for the *Daily Racket*, specified in the preceding chapter, are illustrated in Fig. 8.10. We can regard these structures as specifying real world sequential processes PANEL-O and READER-O. In the initial model step, we wish to construct processes PANEL-1 and READER-1 which will model the real world processes exactly. We need to connect PANEL-O to PANEL-1, and READER-O to READER-1, and we will use data stream connections to do so. The complete SSD is as shown in Fig. 8.11. Just as before, we must embed *write* P operations in the real world process PANEL-O, and *write* R operations in the real world process READER-O, and place appropriate *read* P and *read* R operations in PANEL-1 and READER-1.

Where the real world entity is a machine, it may be obvious what is meant by embedding write operations in it; it is perhaps less obvious when the real world entity is a human being or a group of human beings. What we mean is that when each action of

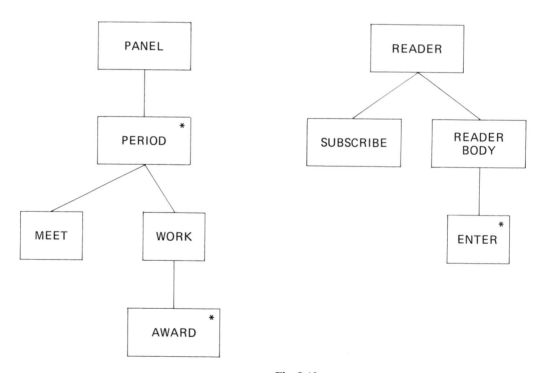

Fig. 8.10

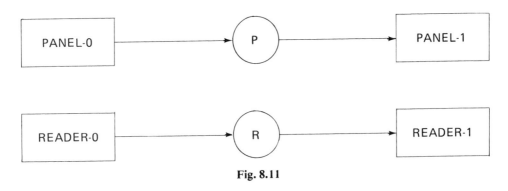

Fig. 8.11

the entity is performed a message must be sent to the model processes, either by the
entity himself or by some device or person on his behalf. So, for READER-0 we provide
the readers of the *Daily Racket* with a subscription form and an entry form, and instructions to complete these forms and send them to the paper's offices. Looking forward to

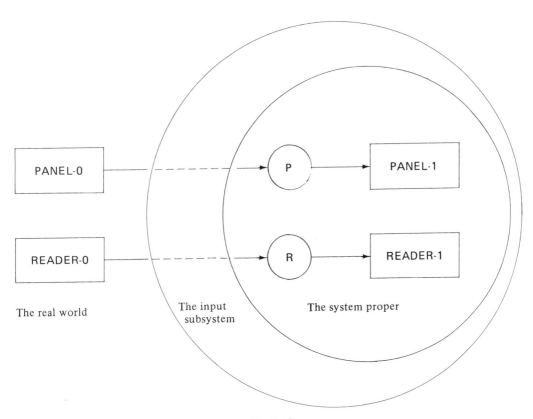

Fig. 8.12

the realization of Sir Cunning's hopes and ambitions, we might imagine an on-line terminal at every street corner, at which readers could key-in their subscription and entry actions at any hour of the day or night. For the panel of celebrities, it would no doubt be politically wise to provide some kind of assistant who would undertake the obligation of writing MEET and AWARD records to be read by PANEL-1; he might write the data on forms, or key it in on-line.

The data streams P and R are regarded as buffered, like the data stream DS of the previous section. In general, some time will elapse between the real world action and the arrival of the corresponding input record, especially if there are postal and similar delays. Even when input is on-line, there is still some delay, if only the delay due to the internal operation of the terminal control program, and the transmission of electrical pulses.

We are less certain, especially if the postal system or some data preparation activity is involved, that the records input to the level-1 processes will be the same records that are written by the level-0 processes, and in the same order. If records become garbled or misordered, we would like to restore their original content and ordering if we can. This is one of the purposes of the input subsystem. For the moment, we will assume that a satisfactory input subsystem is interposed between PANEL-0 and the data stream P, and between READER-0 and the data stream R, as indicated in Fig. 8.12. We will return to the subject of the input subsystem in some detail in Part III.

Ignoring the complexities of the input subsystem, we may regard the connections between PANEL-0 and READER-0 and the processes that model them as ordinary data

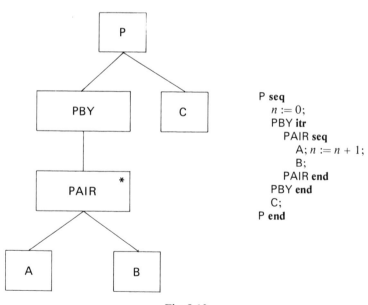

Fig. 8.13

stream connections. The behavior of the model processes is determined by the behavior of the real world entities; the model processes lag behind the real world entities by an indeterminate amount depending on the speeds of the processes and of the buffers that connect them.

It may seem surprising that there is no connection in the SSD between the PANEL and the READER processes. But there are no common actions, and therefore no reason for connection. We may expect to make some indirect connections later, in the function step, when we specify functions which are based both on the READER-1 and on the PANEL-1 model. Where there are common actions, we may expect to see connections among the processes of the SSD in the initial model step.

8.6   STATE-VECTOR CONNECTION

As we did for data stream connection, we will first consider state-vector connection in general, and then turn to its use in connecting model processes to the real world.

Suppose that we have a simple process P, with the structure diagram and text as shown in Fig. 8.13. As before, we will not be concerned with questions about P's execution, but will simply assume that it behaves as specified. We have introduced the variable n, with associated operations, into the text of P; n is a count of the completed A actions, and we will suppose that its purpose is related to some function of the system.

Suppose now that we have another process Q, whose structure need not concern us yet. Q is connected to P by state-vector connection:

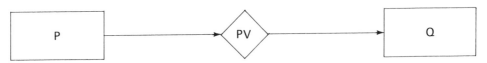

The connection is that Q executes operations which directly inspect the state-vector of P: that is, P's local variables and text-pointer. We will write this operation in the form:

getsv PV;

one or more of these operations will appear in the text of Q. The result of a *getsv* PV operation in Q is that the state-vector of P is placed in a record area directly accessible to Q. In the case of P as shown above, the contents of the state-vector of P will be the variable n and the text-pointer of P. The value of n indicates how many A actions have been completed, and the value of the text-pointer indicates where in its text P has currently reached.

The characteristics of state-vector connection are very different from those of data stream connection:

— The initiative in the communication lies entirely with Q. There is no operation in P to cause its state-vector to be inspected by Q.

— The *getsv* operations executed by Q are determined entirely by Q itself. P's state-vector will take a succession of values determined by the structure of P, but these values will not affect Q except to the extent that Q executes *getsv* operations.

— If execution of Q is slowed or stopped temporarily, the current values of P's state-vector, that might have been obtained by *getsv* operations, are lost.

— The *getsv* operation does not cause blocking of Q or of P.

The most important effect of these characteristics is that the succession of values of P's state-vector obtained by the *getsv* operations in Q will depend on the relative speeds of execution of the processes. Suppose, for example, that P runs at a certain speed SP, and that Q runs at a speed $SQ1$; and that the succession of values of n obtained by the *getsv* operations in Q is then:

$$0, 2, 7, 23, 23, 67, 89, \ldots$$

If, instead, Q runs at a different speed $SQ2$, while P runs at its original speed SP, the succession of values of n may be quite different:

$$4, 13, 20, 36, 67, 92, \ldots$$

The behavior of Q, then, in so far as it is affected by the values of n, will depend on the relative speeds of the processes. These speeds will be determined by the implementation, not by the specification, of the system. We will be particularly concerned with this point when we come to use state-vector connection for some of the functions of the system.

8.7   STATE-VECTOR VALUES

We have placed no restriction on the times at which Q can inspect the state-vector of P: Q is never blocked by a *getsv* PV operation, nor is P. But we need to specify the treatment of state-vectors a little more precisely than this, to ensure that the value obtained always represents a meaningful state of the process.

Suppose that the processor on which P executes implements the operation $n := n + 1$ by the following sequence of machine operations:

load register X *from n;*
store the value 1 *in n;*
add register X *to n;*

This is certainly rather perverse, but quite possible as code generated by a poorly designed compiler. Obviously, if the *getsv* operation occurs between the store and add operations, the value of n obtained will be 1. We must ensure that this cannot happen.

It will not be enough simply to obtain better compilers: with a slightly more complex example we can see that the problem is not so easily avoided. Suppose, for example, that P not only counts the A actions in the variable n, but also accumulates an attribute of A (say, 'amount') in another variable *tot*. P will then contain:

A; $n := n + 1$; *tot* := *tot* + *amount*;

  . . .

Whatever the generated code, it is clearly possible for the *getsv* operation to occur between the incrementing of *n* and the incrementing of *tot*. The combination of values of *n* and *tot* will then be meaningless. This is, of course, a microscopic version of the 'database consistency' problem: how to ensure that information taken from two records of a database is self-consistent if there are currently executing transactions which update first one, and then the other, record?

We choose to impose the following restriction. The values of the state-vector of a process P, obtainable by *getsv* operations executed by other processes, are the values at those points in P's execution where:

— P has just reached a *read* operation on a data stream; or
— P has just reached a *write* operation on a data stream; or
— P has just reached a *getsv* operation referring to some other process.

This restriction need not cause blocking of either P or Q. A possible, though clumsy, implementation would be to keep two versions of the state-vector: one public, obtainable by *getsv* operations, and one private to P; the public version would be replaced by the private version immediately before each *read*, *write*, and *getsv* operation in P, the replacement operation itself being a single indivisible operation at the machine code level.

One consequence of this restriction is that the possible values of the text-pointer, as obtained by *getsv* operations, are limited: the text-pointer can indicate only those points in the text at which *read*, *write*, and *getsv* operations appear.

8.8   HI-RIDE ELEVATOR: INITIAL MODEL

As a general rule, we prefer to connect a level-1 process to the corresponding level-0 entity by data stream connection; it is then easy, without considering execution speeds, to ensure that the model process exactly reflects the behavior of the level-0 entity. Sometimes, however, we are forced by practical limitations in the real world to use state-vector connection.

Our description of the elevators is shown in Fig. 8.14. The only mechanism provided for connecting the real elevators to their model processes is the set of sensors. For each elevator, there is a sensor at each floor which closes an electrical switch when the elevator is within 15 cm of its home position at that floor. The Hi-Ride Company's engineers tell us that they can easily arrange for these switches to be directly accessible to the computers: for each elevator we can regard the 6 switches as a set of 6 bits, a bit being set to 1 when the corresponding switch is closed, and otherwise to 0.

For the moment, we can ignore much of the implementation detail of this arrangement. What concerns us is this:

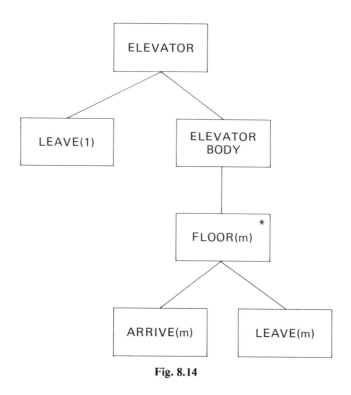

Fig. 8.14

— there is a state-vector of each elevator, which we can access by a *getsv* operation;
— the values of the state-vector can be named as follows:

AT1, AT2, . . . , AT6:   the elevator is at floor(1), floor(2), . . . , floor(6);
          NAT: the elevator is not at any floor;

— a *getsv* operation can be executed at any time, and will obtain one of the values
    AT1, AT2, . . . , AT6, NAT.

We will connect each ELEVATOR-1 to its corresponding ELEVATOR-0 by state-vector
connection:

We require ELEVATOR-1 to model exactly the behavior of ELEVATOR-0, as shown in
Fig. 8.14. We must therefore ensure that ELEVATOR-1 executes the *getsv* EV operation
sufficiently often for no action of ELEVATOR-0 to pass undetected. Now, ELEVATOR-1
has little or nothing to do except to execute *getsv* EV operations; and the speed of any
imaginable dedicated microprocessor is enough for, say, 10 000 *getsv* operations per

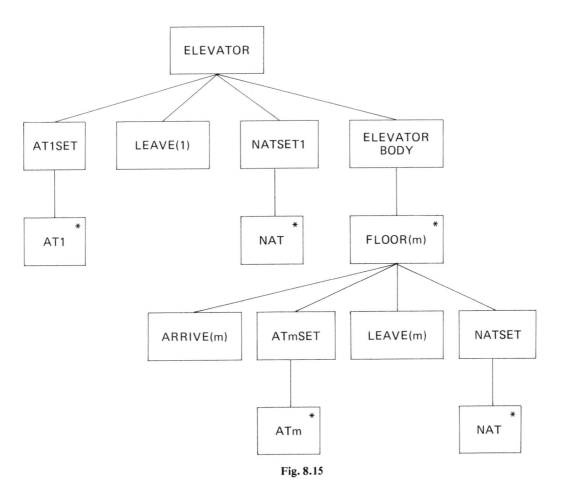

Fig. 8.15

second; and the speed of the real world ELEVATOR-O is, say, 0.5 metres per second; so we have no problem here. Indeed, each value of the state-vector of ELEVATOR-O will be obtained many times before it is replaced by the next value.

We can show the states (that is, the values of the state-vector) of ELEVATOR by adding them to its structure diagram. (We would not do this normally in development: we are doing it here only to help the explanation.) Since each state may be obtained many times, we will show iteration components (Fig. 8.15).

We may now treat the connection as if it were a data stream connection, with ELEVATOR-O writing a record of the stream for each of the AT1, NAT, and ATm components; the *getsv* EV operation in ELEVATOR-1 can be treated like the read operation on a data stream. The resulting structure for ELEVATOR-1 is shown below, with operations to set a local variable, *m*, to indicate the current floor number:

```
ELEVATOR-1 seq
  m := 1; getsv EV;
  AT1SET itr while (AT1)
    getsv EV;
  AT1SET end
  LEAVE(1);
  NATSET1 itr while (NAT)
    getsv EV;
  NATSET1 end
  ELEVATOR-BODY itr
    FLOOR-M seq
      m := j where EV = ATj;
      ARRIVE(m);
      ATMSET itr while  (ATm)
        getsv EV;
      ATMSET end
      LEAVE(m);
      NATSET itr while (NAT)
        getsv EV;
      NATSET end
    FLOOR-M end
  ELEVATOR-BODY end
ELEVATOR-1 end
```

By assiduous execution of *getsv* EV operations, ELEVATOR-1 succeeds in modelling exactly the behavior of ELEVATOR-0. The correctness of the modelling depends crucially on ELEVATOR-1 executing fast enough in relation to ELEVATOR-0.

Turning our attention to the buttons, we have a very simple structure (Fig. 8.16).

If the company's engineers are feeling exceptionally helpful and resourceful, we will be able to persuade them that their buttons should emit a pulse when pressed; we will then send this pulse down a wire to the model process, and we will have a simple data stream connection:

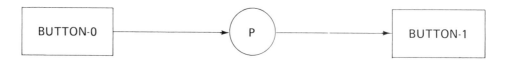

More likely, they will insist that the buttons are merely switches, biased in the open position and closed when fully depressed. If so, we are back in the state-vector connection business:

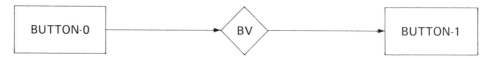

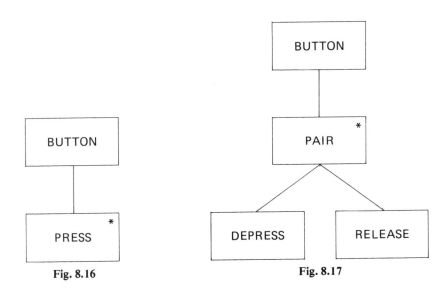

Fig. 8.16   Fig. 8.17

This time our description of the real world is not quite good enough. If we regard the action PRESS as atomic and indivisible, then BUTTON-0 has only one detectable state: it is always in the state of 'having been pressed zero or more times', since the atomic PRESS action is instantaneous and cannot give rise to any intermediate state such as 'being pressed at this moment'. The necessary elaboration of our description of BUTTON is obvious (Fig. 8.17).

Showing the states of BUTTON-0 as we did for ELEVATOR-0, we have the situation shown in Fig. 8.18.

The rest is straightforward, giving the structure text:

```
BUTTON-1 seq
  getsv BV;
  OPENSET1 itr while (OPEN)
    getsv BV;
  OPENSET1 end
  BUTTON-BODY itr
    PAIR seq
      DEPRESS;
      CLOSEDSET itr while (CLOSED)
        getsv BV;
      CLOSEDSET end
      RELEASE;
      OPENSET itr while (OPEN)
        getsv BV;
      OPENSET end
    PAIR end
  BUTTON-BODY end
BUTTON-1 end
```

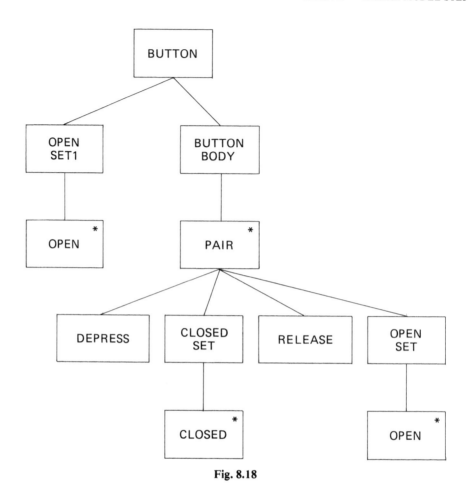

Fig. 8.18

8.9   DATA STRUCTURES

When two processes are connected by a data stream, and the data stream does not contain a record for each action in the writing process, it is sometimes useful to describe the structure of the data stream separately from the structures of the connected processes. Sometimes, too, when state-vector connection is used in the way we have used it for the initial model of the Hi-Ride Elevator system, it is useful to regard the succession of state-vector values as if it were a stream of records, and to describe its structure explicitly.

The structure diagram notation which we have been using for process structures may be used to describe such data structures; the leaves of the tree will be records rather than actions, but the meaning of the notation is otherwise unchanged. We might, for example, describe the stream of BV values passing between BUTTON-0 and BUTTON-1 by Fig. 8.19.

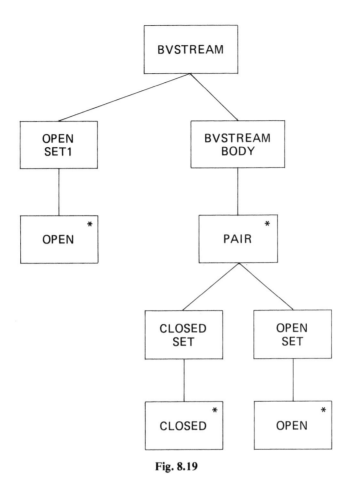

Fig. 8.19

Not surprisingly, there is an obvious relationship between the structure of the data passing into or out of a process and the structure of the process itself. Where a data stream connects two processes, it embodies an abstract description of both of them; the fact that one data stream can thus embody a description of two processes shows clearly that their behavior must be coordinated to the extent that it is described in the data stream.

8.10 *DAILY RACKET*: **INITIAL MODEL—2**

Our model for the PANEL in the *Daily Racket* system is as shown in Fig. 8.20. Looking forward to the function step, we can imagine that we might want to provide the function: 'at the end of each session, produce a report showing the number of awards made'.

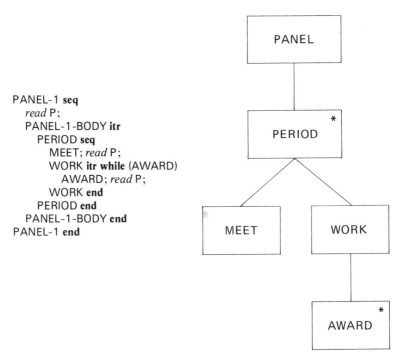

```
PANEL-1 seq
   read P;
   PANEL-1-BODY itr
      PERIOD seq
         MEET; read P;
         WORK itr while (AWARD)
            AWARD; read P;
         WORK end
      PERIOD end
   PANEL-1-BODY end
PANEL-1 end
```

Fig. 8.20

This seems to be quite straightforward. We can easily arrange to count the AWARD actions, and, following the end of the WORK, to print out the value of this count.

The printout, however, will not be made until the PANEL MEETs for the next session. The PANEL-1 process will be blocked at the *read* P operation following the last AWARD, and cannot continue execution until the next input record of P becomes available. The difficulty arises because in our description of the real world panel, and hence in our model, we have no action corresponding to the dispersal of the panel at the end of a session; according to our description, therefore, AWARD actions can be made at any time before the next MEET action. We can correct this deficiency by introducing an action DISPERSE (Fig. 8.21). Often, we will not be able to anticipate a deficiency in the model in this way, and must wait until it becomes apparent in the function step.

8.11   WIDGET WAREHOUSE: INITIAL MODEL—1

We considered two versions of the specification for the Widget Warehouse system: in one, the entities were CUSTOMER, CLERK, and ORDER; in the other, automated, version, they were CUSTOMER, ORDER, and PRODUCT. In this section we will look only at the initial model for the automated version, deferring the other version to a later section.

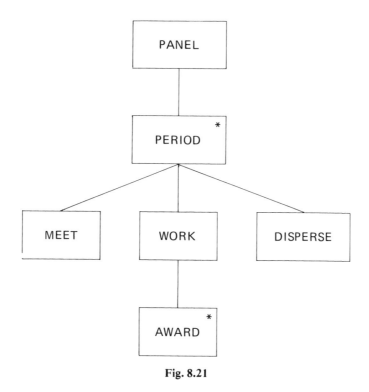

Fig. 8.21

In the automated system, the entities are CUSTOMER, ORDER, and PRODUCT. Looking first at PRODUCT, we have the structure shown in Fig. 8.22. Although for us the PRODUCT is a real world entity, it is in fact the product stock record in the purchasing and inventory control system. The AVAIL action represents the completion of that system's computations based on receipts into inventory and wastage and issues from inventory, giving a quantity of the product available for allocation by our system.

Fig. 8.22

If we are permitted to embed a suitable write operation in the other system, we can use a data stream connection:

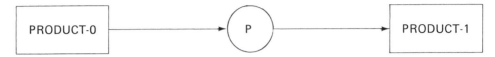

It may be, however, that we are permitted merely to access the product stock record by what must be regarded as a *getsv* operation:

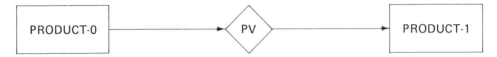

In this case, we will have to work a little harder. The difficulty is that two successive *getsv* operations might be executed which obtain the same value of the state of PRODUCT-0, that is, of the quantity available for allocation. We do not then know whether the identity of the two states is due to the chance occurrence of two successive AVAIL actions giving the same quantity, or to the absence of an intervening AVAIL between the two *getsv* operations.

There are two immediate solutions to this difficulty. One is to elaborate our description of PRODUCT-0, much as we did for BUTTON-0 (Fig. 8.23). Successive AVAILs are now distinguished not by their values but by the intervention of an UNAVAIL action. The UNAVAIL action occurs at any point in the execution of the purchasing and inventory system, which is known to alternate with the point at which we have defined the AVAIL action. Such a point in a batch system would be the point at which the batch computation is begun for the particular PRODUCT; effectively, the UNAVAIL action locks the product stock record against access while it is being updated.

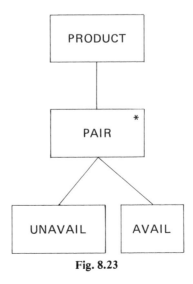

Fig. 8.23

Another solution is to require that the AVAIL action is associated with some serial identification, such as a date stamp if the action can occur only once per day. This date stamp, along with the quantity, is a part of the state of PRODUCT-0. The succession of state-vectors in PV, regarded as a data stream, would then have the structure shown in Fig. 8.24.

By grouping, according to date stamp, the successive values which it finds in the PRODUCT-0 state-vector, PRODUCT-1 is able to ensure that the AVAIL action has occurred at least once in each instance of the component AVAILABILITY-AT-DATEi. It has the structure:

```
PRODUCT-1 seq
  getsv PV;
  PRODUCT-1-BODY itr
    AVAILABILITY-AT-DATE-I seq
      AVAIL; i := j (where PV = DATEj);
      getsv PV;
      AVDATE-BODY itr while (DATEi)
        getsv PV;
      AVDATE-BODY end
    AVAILABILITY-AT-DATE-I end
  PRODUCT-1-BODY end
PRODUCT-1 end
```

The advantage of this solution is that PRODUCT-1 need inspect the state of PRODUCT-0 only occasionally: nothing depends on detecting every AVAIL action that occurs in PRODUCT-0. The first solution, with the two actions AVAIL and UNAVAIL, requires that an UNAVAIL action must not go undetected if any use is to be made of the quantity made available by the following AVAIL. We would therefore be obliged to implement our system in such a way that the PRODUCT-1 processes, at least, are running while the other system is executing its batch computation.

The two remaining entities in the automated system are CUSTOMER and ORDER. Evidently we will use data stream connection for CUSTOMER:

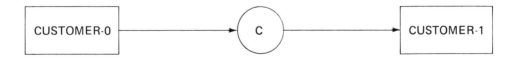

ORDER in the automated system is a marsupial of CUSTOMER, so we must use the same input, somehow, to connect it to the real world. The appropriate configuration reflects the relationship between CUSTOMER and ORDER:

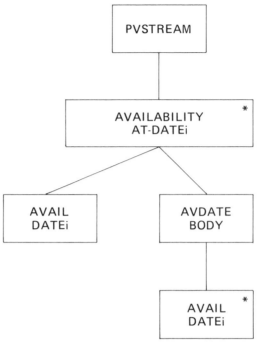

Fig. 8.24

As indicated by the double bars on the arrow from CO to ORDER-1, there are many ORDER-1 processes connected to each CUSTOMER-1 process. The operations in CUSTOMER-1 which write the records of the data stream CO specify the identifier of the ORDER-1 process for which it is destined. The CUSTOMER-1 process is:

```
CUSTOMER-1 seq
  read C;
  CUSTOMER-1-BODY itr
    CUSTOMER-ACTION sel (PLACE(i))
      PLACE; write PLACE to CO(i); read C;
    CUSTOMER-ACTION alt (AMEND(j))
      AMEND; write AMEND to CO(j)); read C;
    CUSTOMER-ACTION alt (CANCEL(k))
      CANCEL; write CANCEL to CO(k); read C;
    CUSTOMER-ACTION alt (DELIVER(l))
      DELIVER; write DELIVER to CO(l); read C;
    CUSTOMER-ACTION end
  CUSTOMER-1-BODY end
CUSTOMER-1 end
```

The ORDER process is:

```
ORDER-1 seq
  read CO;
  PLACE; read CO;
  ORDER-1-BODY itr while (AMEND)
    AMEND; read CO;
  ORDER-1-BODY end
  FINISH sel (CANCEL)
    CANCEL; read CO;
  FINISH alt (DELIVER)
    DELIVER; read CO;
  FINISH end
ORDER-1 end
```

No identifier is necessary in the read operations in ORDER-1: each instance of the ORDER-1 process can read only those records of CO which belong to it.

8.12   A RESTATEMENT IN MANUAL TERMS

Some readers, especially those who are ill at ease with technicalities, may feel that specifications are better discussed in human terms than in terms of reading and writing data streams, state-vectors, *getsv* operations, buffers, and the like. We can readily imagine that the system is to be entirely manual, and we can restate the preceding contents of this chapter in terms of manual procedures.

Let us suppose that we have available an indefinitely large number of clerical workers. (We will refer to them as 'workers' rather than as 'clerks', to avoid confusion with the clerk of the Widget Warehouse system.) Each worker is to do the job of one sequential process: so we will assign one worker to model the behavior of one reader of the *Daily Racket*, one worker to model the behavior of one customer of the Widget Warehouse Company, and so on. Of course, this will mean that a very large number of workers is needed: the *Daily Racket* will require at least as many workers as it has readers. We see immediately that Sir Cunning de Ville would never tolerate such a scheme, because it is insanely expensive. So in the implementation step, later in the development, we will devise arrangements which will allow one worker to do the jobs of many. But in the specification steps, we are resolved to assume that each worker does only one job, and to postpone the complexities of sharing one worker's time among many jobs until we have determined exactly what modelling and functional jobs are to be done.

In Section 8.5 we specified the initial model for the *Daily Racket* system. Each READER-0 is connected by a data stream R to a READER-1 model process. The entity structure for READER-0 is shown in Fig. 8.25.

Here is the procedure to be followed by the worker assigned to the job of modelling reader John Smith:

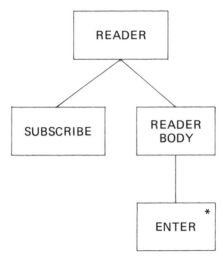

Fig. 8.25

(a)   Your job is to model the reader John Smith. You will receive messages from John Smith, telling you what actions he has performed. These messages will arrive in your in-tray; they may be delayed, but they will not be misordered or distorted. You are to follow the rules given in (b) exactly. You have a piece of paper on which you are to note any counts, totals, or other variables you are required to calculate. In particular, you must make sure that when you are waiting for a message to arrive in your in-tray, you write down on the paper the line number of the place you have reached in the rules (b): this is called the current value of your text-pointer.

(b)   1   First, wait for a message.
       2   When a message arrives, it will be a SUBSCRIBE message. Do that action.
       3   Wait for a message.
       4   When a message arrives, you are beginning the part of your job called READER-BODY. Here it is:
       5   For each arriving message:
            5.1   The message will be an ENTER message. Do that action.
            5.2   Wait for a message.

The piece of paper, is, of course, the worker's state-vector. At this stage of development, the instructions 'Do that action' are null in this procedure: there is nothing for the worker to do with the messages. We may possibly specify something to do when the messages arrive, and at other points in the procedure, later in the development. The worker's procedure never terminates, because the entity structure for READER-O has no terminating action.

   In Section 8.11 we specified the initial model for the automated system for the Widget Warehouse. Here is the procedure to be followed by the worker assigned to the job of modelling product Widget (corresponding to the structure text shown for PRODUCT-1):

(a)   Your job is to model the product Widget. You are able to look at the Widget
       product record in the purchasing and inventory control system, as often as you
       like. You are to follow the rules given in (b) exactly. You have a piece of paper on
       which you are to note any counts, totals, or other variables you are required to
       calculate. In particular, you must make sure that when you go to look at the
       Widget product record, you write down on the paper the line number of the place
       you have reached in the rules (b): this is called the current value of your text-
       pointer.

(b)   1   First look at the product record.
       2   You are now beginning the part of your job called PRODUCT-1-BODY. Here
            it is:
       3   Do the following repeatedly:
            3.1   Take the date from the product record and write it on your paper as the
                   value of the variable *i*.
            3.2   Look at the product record. You are now beginning the part of your job
                   called AVDATE-BODY. Here it is:
            3.3   Do the following repeatedly, so long as the date in the product record
                   (that is, the date you saw when you last looked at it) is the same as *i*:
                   3.3.1   Look at the product record.

The instruction 'look at the product record' is, of course, the *getsv* PV operation. The
piece of paper used by the worker is the state-vector of PRODUCT-1, not of
PRODUCT-0.

    In Section 8.10 we also specified the initial model processes for customers and
orders. Here, omitting the preambles, are the procedures to be followed by a worker
assigned to modelling a customer and by a worker assigned to modelling an order:

—   customer worker:
(b)   1   First, wait for a message.
       2   When a message arrives, you are beginning the part of your job called
            CUSTOMER-1-BODY. Here it is:
       3   Do the following repeatedly:
            3.1   Do one of the following, according to the message that has arrived:
                   3.1.1   For a PLACE(i) message:
                            3.1.1.1   Do that action.
                            3.1.1.2   Send a copy to the worker who is modelling order *i*, by
                                       office internal mail.
                            3.1.1.3   Wait for a message.
                   3.1.2   For an AMEND(j) message:
                            · · ·
                            · · ·
                            3.1.4.2   Send a copy to the worker who is modelling order 1,
                                       by office internal mail.
                            3.1.4.3   Wait for a message.

—   order worker:
(b)   1   First, wait for a message.
       2   When a message arrives, it will be a PLACE message. Do that action.

3   Wait for a message.

4   When a message arrives, you are beginning the part of your job called ORDER-1-BODY. Here it is:

5   For each arriving AMEND message:

     5.1   The message will be an AMEND message. Do that action.

     5.2   Wait for a message.

6   When a message arrives, you are beginning the part of your job called FINISH. Here it is:

7   Do one of the following, according to the message type:

     7.1   For a CANCEL message:

          7.1.1   Do that action.

          7.1.2   Wait for a message.

     7.2   For a DELIVER message:

          7.2.1   Do that action.

          7.2.2   Wait for a message.

The language we have used to express these clerical procedures for the workers is very informal. It relies heavily on the hierarchical numbering scheme for the rules, and on the indentation of the text, to show the structure. It is also somewhat more cumbersome than straightforward structure text.

The general discussions in earlier sections about data stream and state-vector connection between processes are no less important in the context of communication between clerical workers. Data stream connection corresponds to communication by sending and receiving messages. For example, the worker who models a Widget Warehouse customer sends messages to the workers who model the orders of that customer, as stipulated in rules 3.1.1.2, ..., 3.1.4.2. In Section 8.4 we discussed the characteristics of JSD data stream connection. Here are their implications for these workers:

— The initiative lies with the customer worker to send messages; the order worker cannot demand or request a message, but can only wait for one to arrive.

— The order worker is not allowed to ignore any messages, or to receive them in an order different from the order in which they were sent.

— If the order worker takes a break, or goes on vacation, the messages simply lie in his in-tray until he restarts work.

— The order worker is said to be blocked when he is waiting for a message and there is none in his in-tray.

— Because the internal mail service is always ready to accept messages for transmission, and there is no limit to the capacity of a worker's in-tray, the customer worker is never blocked when sending a message: he can always send the message and immediately carry on with whatever has to be done next, even if the order worker's in-tray contains many messages that have not yet been dealt with.

For state-vector connection between workers, we need to imagine one worker strolling over to the desk of another to inspect the piece of paper he is using. The implications of the characteristics discussed in Section 8.6 for these workers are:

— The initiative lies with the inspecting worker; the inspected worker cannot request or demand that his paper be looked at.
— The inspecting worker will not be affected by what the inspected worker does, except to the extent that he chooses to look at his paper.
— If the inspecting worker takes a break, or goes on vacation, he will never see what the inspected worker does while he is away.
— The act of inspection does not cause significant delay either to the inspecting or to the inspected worker.

The discussion in Section 8.7, about state-vector values, deals with such questions as: what happens if you inspect a worker's paper while he is writing on it? how can you make sure that what you see will make sense? The answer given there was that you will always see the paper as it is when the inspected worker is waiting for a message, sending a message, or looking at another worker's paper: so you will never see it in course of being changed.

8.13 MULTIPLE INPUTS TO ONE PROCESS

We have not yet considered cases where one process has more than one input data stream—or, in manual terms, where one worker has more than one in-tray. Some special issues arise in these cases, and we consider them in this section and the next.

Suppose, in the bank example, two customers have a joint account, and that our initial model is as shown in Fig. 8.26. We will suppose, for simplicity, that the only actions are pay-in and withdraw; both Jack and Lucy can perform these actions, and they affect the balance on the account in the obvious way. Our interest in this section will center on the ACCT-1 process, which has the two input data streams JA and LA. In some sense, the ACCT-1 process must merge its two input streams, and we will examine the various ways in which this merging can properly take place.

First, let us make a very large assumption: that the pattern of activity on the account is fixed. Jack and Lucy both PAY-IN their salaries, at the beginning of the month; and each withdraws an amount for spending money three or so days later. The

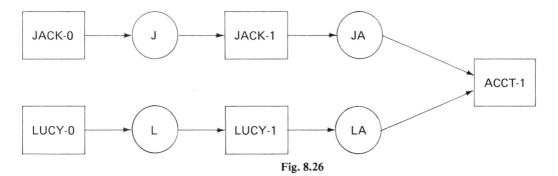

Fig. 8.26

timing of the PAY-IN and WITHDRAW actions in the real world is always exact, and always satisfies the structure shown in Fig. 8.27.

Then the structure text for ACCT-1 is:

```
ACCT-1 itr
  MONTH seq
    read JA; JACK-PAY-IN;
    read LA; LUCY-PAY-IN;
    read JA; JACK-WITHDRAW;
    read LA; LUCY-WITHDRAW;
  MONTH end
ACCT-1 end
```

Notice that the ACCT-1 process may be waiting for a JA record to arrive at a time when an LA record is already available: this may happen because of any combination of the following reasons:

— The J stream transmits records slower than the L stream (Jack transacts his bank business at an out-of-town branch).

— The JACK-1 process runs slower than the LUCY-1 process (the dedicated microprocessor is slower, or the worker assigned to model Jack is lazier, or taking a break).

— The JA stream transmits records slower than the LA stream (the internal office mailman doesn't like visiting the Jack worker so often, because his desk is on the top floor).

Nonetheless, in spite of the ready availability of the LA record, the ACCT-1 process happily waits for the JA record, which is certainly signalling the next real world event. Nothing will be gained, and something lost, by taking the records in the 'wrong' order.

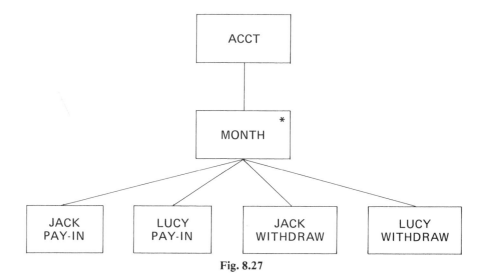

Fig. 8.27

We will call this kind of treatment of multiple input streams a 'fixed merge'. The messages from the streams are merged according to fixed rules determined when the system is specified. No decisions need be made in ACCT-1 at run time.

Now let us relinquish our assumption of a fixed pattern, and suppose that Jack and Lucy can perform their PAY-IN and WITHDRAW actions in any order whatsoever, but each of them can perform at most one action on any one day. To help keep the actions in ACCT-1 in their real-world order, the PAY-IN and WITHDRAW messages carry date stamps. Now how are we to specify ACCT-1 so that it will take its input messages in the right order?

One view of the structure of ACCT-1, ignoring the distinction between PAY-IN and WITHDRAW actions, is as shown in Fig. 8.28. On any active date, there is either an action by Jack only, or an action by both (Jack's is regarded as following Lucy's), or an action by Lucy only. The structure text for ACCT-1, showing the placing of read operations, is:

```
ACCT-1 seq
    read JA; read LA;
    ACCT-1-BODY itr
        ACTIVE-DATE seq
            date := min (Jack-date, Lucy-date);
            ACTIVE-DATE-BODY sel (Jack-date = date ≠ Lucy-date)
                JACK-action; read JA;
            ACTIVE-DATE-BODY alt (Jack-date = date = Lucy-date)
                JACK-AND-LUCY-ACTION seq
                    LUCY-action; read LA;
                    JACK-action; read JA;
                JACK-AND-LUCY-ACTION end
            ACTIVE-DATE-BODY alt (Jack-date ≠ date = Lucy-date)
                LUCY-action; read LA;
            ACTIVE-DATE-BODY end
        ACTIVE-DATE end
    ACCT-1-BODY end
ACCT-1 end
```

The expression *min (Jack-date, Lucy-date)* means the smaller of the two date-stamps, Jack-date and Lucy-date. The *read* JA and *read* LA operations have been allocated in the structure in accordance with the 'read-ahead' rule: clearly, it is necessary to wait for a record to become available in both JA and LA before determining which is the next active date, and whether a Jack-action, a Lucy-action, or both have occurred on that date.

We will call this kind of treatment of multiple input streams a 'data merge'. The messages from the streams are merged according to their data contents—in this case, the date stamps. The behavior of a data merge, like that of a fixed merge, is quite independent of the speeds of the processes and buffers: that is, the actions performed in ACCT-1 will not be in any way affected by the absolute or relative speeds of the processes JACK-1 and LUCY-1 or by the buffering of J, L, JA, and LA.

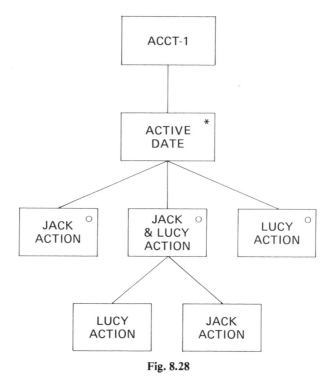

Fig. 8.28

However, a data merge suffers from a serious disadvantage. The inevitable use of the 'read-ahead' rule for allocating read operations means that ACCT-1 is always blocked unless both a JA and an LA record are available. So if Jack's first action is dated 5 JAN 1982, and Lucy's first action is dated 21 DEC 1982, ACCT-1 will be blocked until at least 21 DEC 1982: in manual terms, the ACCT-1 worker cannot know that the next active date is 5 JAN 1982 until there is a record in the LA in-tray showing that Lucy's next action is dated no earlier than 5 JAN 1982. In general, a period of inactivity in one data stream prevents a data merge from dealing with the available records of other streams. Since there is no definite limit to the length of a possible period of inactivity (Lucy may stop using the joint account altogether), the data merge process may be indefinitely blocked.

This indefinite blocking can be prevented by ensuring that special marker records are inserted into each data stream at fixed intervals. For example, if we arrange that each bank customer performs a special action (perhaps a 'confirmation of continued custom') as his very last action in each calendar month, then the maximum blocking period of ACCT-1 will be reduced to about one month. (More realistically, we might abandon the date stamps on the real world actions, and cause the processes JACK-1 and LUCY-1 to insert daily marker records in JA and LA: but this scheme, properly viewed, merely shifts the merging problem back from ACCT-1 to JACK-1 and LUCY-1.) We will call this kind of modified data merge a 'periodic data merge'. It gives rise to a synchronous system, in which each marker record is like a clock pulse, allowing its reading process to progress to the next time interval. At a gross level, batch data processing systems can be regarded as synchronous systems; when the time for the batch run arrives, each process is brought up to date. We will see in some detail how this may be handled in the implementation step in JSD.

Finally, we may consider a quite different kind of solution: we will allow ACCT-1 to test its input streams JA and LA, to determine whether a record is available for reading. We will denote the outcome of the test by the condition 'empty' or 'not empty' with obvious meaning. The kind of scheme that results is called a 'rough merge': the roughness is due to a dependence on factors—the speeds of processes and of record transmission in buffers—which are left indeterminate until the implementation step. We will discuss rough merge in some detail in the next section: its indeterminacy distinguishes it sharply from the fixed merge, data merge, and periodic data merge.

8.14   ROUGH MERGE

Continuing with our joint bank account example, we may specify a rough merge version of ACCT-1 as:

ACCT-1 **itr**
   POSSIBLE-RECORD **sel** (LA *not empty*)
     read LA; *LUCY-action*;
   POSSIBLE-RECORD **alt** (JA *not empty*)
     read JA; *JACK-action*;
   POSSIBLE-RECORD **alt** (LA *and* JA *both empty*)
     (*no action*)
   POSSIBLE-RECORD **end**
ACCT-1 **end**

Suppose that Jack and Lucy perform actions in the real world on these dates in the same year:
   Jack: 7 JAN, 12 JAN, 13 JAN, . . .
   Lucy: 9 JAN, 10 JAN, 14 JAN, . . .

Without considering the speeds of the processes and of the J, L, JA, and LA buffers, can we say anything about the order in which ACCT-1 will deal with these actions? No, we cannot. It may be that the JACK-1 process is very slow and the LUCY-1 process is very fast, and ACCT-1 receives all Lucy's actions before any of Jack's; or the opposite may be true. It may be that the ACCT-1 process itself has a period of very slow execution (the ACCT-1 worker is on vacation) in the first half of January: when it starts to go faster, in the second half of January, all six messages shown are available and ACCT-1 will then deal with all of Lucy's messages before any of Jack's, because it has the property that it will always deal with an available Lucy message in preference to an available Jack message (the reader should verify that this is so by examining the text given of ACCT-1).

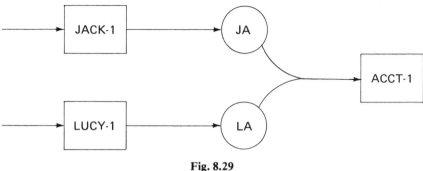

Fig. 8.29

We may characterize this last property by saying that the merge is 'not fair': it favors Lucy at the expense of Jack. We can do nothing in the specification of ACCT-1 itself about the relative speeds with which messages will arrive in the streams JA and LA. But we might hope that the merge would be fair, in the sense that a message that arrives first will be dealt with first. For example, we might specify ACCT-1 as:

```
ACCT-1 itr
    POSSIBLE-JA-RECORD sel (JA not empty)
        read JA; JACK-action;
    POSSIBLE-JA-RECORD alt (JA empty)
        (no action)
    POSSIBLE-JA-RECORD end
    POSSIBLE-LA-RECORD sel (LA not empty)
        read LA; LUCY-action;
    POSSIBLE-LA-RECORD alt (LA empty)
        (no action)
    POSSIBLE-LA-RECORD end
ACCT-1 end
```

This is certainly better, but it is still not perfect. The execution of ACCT-1 text, even in the absence of input records, must take some time. It is possible that immediately after JA is found to be empty a JA record arrives, followed after a very small time interval by an LA record: by the time ACCT-1 has reached the test of LA, both records have arrived, and the LA record is dealt with before the JA record, although it arrived slightly later. Try as we will, we cannot make the rough merge perfectly fair. There will always be some residual indeterminacy in addition to the indeterminacy arising from the unknown speeds of the other parts of the system.

The best we can do is to assume that the unfairness, which we cannot altogether eliminate, will be small: the speed of execution of the merging process is high, and the frequency of arrival of input records is low; the records will almost always be dealt with in the 'right' order, and the wrong order will be taken only when records arrive nearly simultaneously. These assumptions, of course, depend heavily on the eventual implementation of the system: we are, in fact, assuming that the implementation itself will be 'fair'.

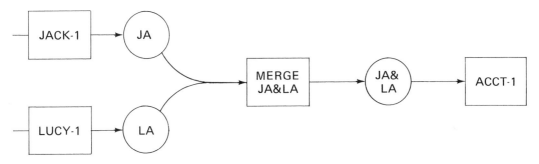

Fig. 8.30

It will be useful to indicate in the SSD where there are rough merges in the specification. We will show a rough merge of two or more data streams by joining their arrows on the side of the process which merges them. So, if ACCT-1 rough merges its input streams LA and JA, we will show it as in Fig. 8.29.

In the text of the merging process we will use operations of the form '*read*JA&LA', referring to the merged input streams as if they were a single stream. Unless we specify otherwise, it is to be assumed that the rough merge is adequately fair in some reasonable sense. Sometime we will need to be explicit about the exact rules for a rough merge, favoring one stream over another in certain circumstances. We will then need to show a separate rough merge process, whose only purpose is to rough merge the inputs for another process. No special notation is used here, but we can try to choose suggestive or informative names (Fig. 8.30).

Where there is a many-to-one connection, with many processes writing and one reading, as in:

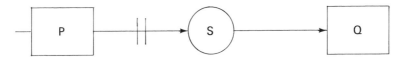

it is to be assumed, unless stated otherwise, that the many output streams of the processes P are rough merged to give a single input stream S for the process Q.

8.15 WIDGET WAREHOUSE: INITIAL MODEL—2

The version without automation has entities CUSTOMER, CLERK, and ORDER. We discussed these entities and their structures in the preceding chapter. ORDER is essentially a composite of the two marsupial entities CUS-ORDER and CLK-ORDER: in other words, what happens to the ORDER is a composite of what the CLERK does to it and what the CUSTOMER does to it. The structure of ORDER has been specified as in Fig. 8.31, in which the actions of CUSTOMER are PLACE, AMEND, CANCEL, and DELIVER; the actions of CLERK are DELAY and ALLOCATE.

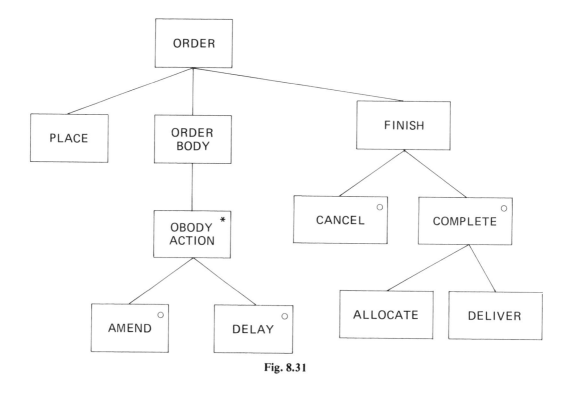

Fig. 8.31

The process ORDER-1 must merge its two input streams CO and KO, and we need to consider what form of merge is appropriate (Fig. 8.32). Clearly we cannot have a simple fixed merge. In both ORDER-BODY and FINISH, we see that the next input (in chronological order) might come from either CO or KO; after PLACE, we cannot predict whether the next action will be AMEND or CANCEL in CO, or DELAY or ALLOCATE in KO. We can observe in passing that the first input record is always PLACE, from CO, and that after ALLOCATE the next record must always be DELIVER, from CO.

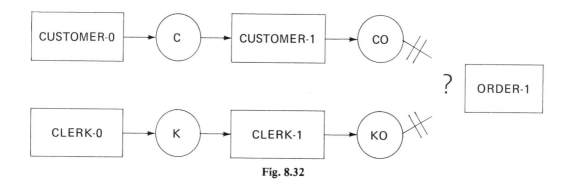

Fig. 8.32

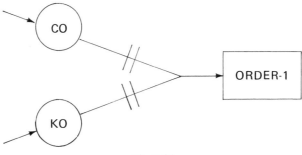

Fig. 8.33

A simple data merge is also impossible. If we date stamp each record of C and K, and hence of CO and KO, ORDER-1 could be specified as a data merge. But the result would be absurd. ORDER-1 would be unable to model any action by the customer until a later action had been performed by the clerk, and vice versa. So if the real world sequence of actions were PLACE, AMEND, ALLOCATE, DELIVER, the ORDER-1 process would not catch up with the PLACE and AMEND until the ALLOCATE occurred; then it would not catch up with the ALLOCATE until the DELIVER occurred; and it would never catch up with the DELIVER, unless the KO input stream contained an end-of-stream marker with an appropriate date stamp.

(It is worth noting that if we did ensure that there was an end-of-stream marker in CO and in KO, the model of the order would not be entirely useless: it could provide historical information which would become available after the order has been finished.)

A periodic data merge is certainly possible. We might choose a period of a day, thus committing ourselves to a system that could not sensibly be on-line; or we might choose a period of a second, thus committing ourselves to a very expensive synchronous system. Any such commitment would be premature, and we reject this choice.

We therefore find ourselves choosing a rough merge. ORDER-1 will rough merge its input streams CO and KO; we complete the SSD accordingly (Fig. 8.33).

The consequence of choosing the rough merge is, as always, that we must consider the possibility of misordering. One approach is to regard the detection and rejection of misordered input as a function of the input subsystem, and that would be quite reasonable. We will return to this viewpoint when we discuss the input subsystem later in the book. Here we will consider the problem on the following assumptions:

—   The system will provide output information to both the clerk and the customer, with some variable time delay which may be different for the two of them.
—   The clerk and the customer will each behave correctly on the basis of his own past actions and the information now available to him.

A structure reflecting these assumptions, and the rough merge of the input streams of ORDER-1, is shown in Fig. 8.34. The components whose names include the word LATE are actions or sets of actions which would not have been performed had the appropriate output information been available earlier. The structure embodies the assumption, made in the entity structure step, that the customer is not allowed to amend or cancel the

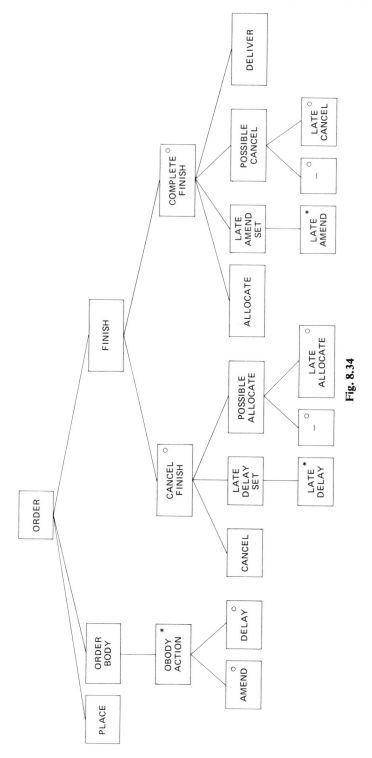

Fig. 8.34

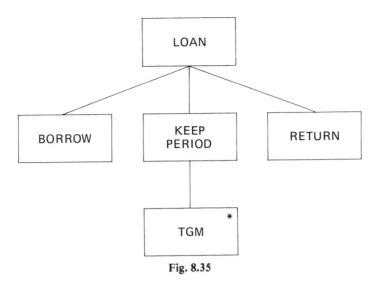

Fig. 8.35

order after allocation by the clerk. The Widget Warehouse operates very simple and very stringent rules of business. The disallowed actions are LATE AMEND and LATE CANCEL.

The structure text for ORDER-1 presents no difficulties. The rough merged input streams are read by the operation '*read* CO&KO'; it will be necessary to read ahead on the merged input stream CO&KO.

8.16 TIME GRAIN MARKERS

In the process models we are specifying, the passage of time in the real world is marked only by the occurrence of actions, signalled to the model by records in input streams. Between one action and the next, a process is blocked, waiting for input; nothing is happening in the model, because nothing is happening in the real world. There is no global clock, causing each model process to count off the seconds, hours, or days that elapse between consecutive actions of the modelled entity.

Sometimes we will want to model an action type which consists of doing nothing for some period of time, or of failing to do a certain action within a certain time limit. For example, a loan of a library book might have the actions BORROW and RETURN; but we might want to model a third action 'let one day pass without RETURNing'. Or an employee might have the action CLOCK-ON, but we might want also to model the action 'fail to CLOCK-ON within the stipulated time limits'. We could, in principle, regard such actions as being different from other actions only in causing a little more difficulty in detection and signalling to the model. However, we will usually prefer to recognize that the arrival of a particular point in time may itself be treated as significant to a model process, and to provide appropriate input accordingly. Such inputs are called Time Grain Markers, or TGMs.

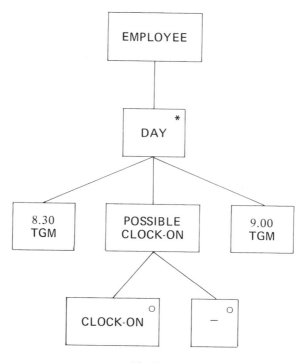

Fig. 8.36

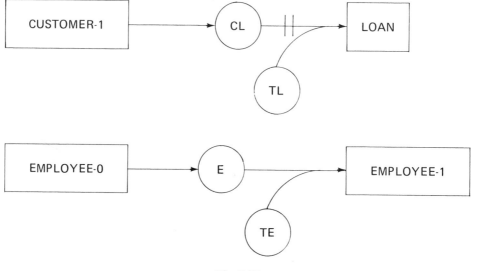

Fig. 8.37

In the case of the library book, we might specify the structure shown in Fig. 8.35, where each TGM signals the arrival of midnight (a time at which the library is closed).

In the case of the employee, we might specify that clocking-on should happen only between 8.30 and 9.00. Outside that time the device used for clocking-on is switched off and cannot be used: employees who arrive before 8.30 must wait to clock-on, and those who arrive after 9.00 are deemed, ruthlessly, to have been absent for the whole day (Fig. 8.36).

TGMs are considered to appear in data streams called TGM streams. They will almost always require to be rough merged with other input to a process (Fig. 8.37).

The rough merge corresponds often to a rough merge in the real world: an employee arriving exactly at 9.00 may find the manager with his hand on the switch. Attempts to avoid the real world rough merge may take the form of limiting business hours, by closing the library between 5.00 pm and 9.00 am; but the problem is merely moved, not avoided. The customer with a book to return is, if anything, even more angry when he finds the doors being closed in his face.

Sometimes it will be appropriate to show explicitly a CLOCK process writing a TGM stream; this will not, in general, be one process for the whole model. We will return later to the subject of such CLOCK processes.

8.17 PROCESS CREATION AND DELETION

We have been discussing the model as if the number of entity instances were fixed. No processes are created during the lifetime of the system, and none die. Obviously, this is not so. There will be new readers for the *Daily Racket*, and new customers and orders for the Widget Warehouse.

For each entity type, the developer must decide where to place responsibility for creating new entities of that type. In some systems, the number of entities may be regarded as fixed; any change to the number is outside the operation of the system itself, and must be achieved by a change to the specification and the consequent changes to the implementation. In the Hi-Ride Elevator system, for example, we may regard the number of elevators and buttons as being fixed for the lifetime of the system: we do not include in the system specification any arrangements for the addition of further floors to the building or of further elevators.

For some entities, the developer must arrange for the creation of new instances, but not within the system itself. There is no process in the *Daily Racket* system that could possibly be charged with the responsibility of creating new instances of the READER entity: certainly not any existing reader, and certainly not the panel of celebrities. The same is true of customers in the Widget Warehouse system. New entities of these types must be created outside the system, and added to it. Their creation is much like the creation of a new elevator in the Hi-Ride Elevator system, except that it will occur frequently enough to require a much more convenient implementation. These are the entities which in a network database are regarded as being members of sets 'owned by the system'. Creation of new instances of these entity types is a matter for the implementation, rather than for the specification, of the system.

Marsupial entities, by contrast, may be created by their parent entities. In the Widget Warehouse system, it is appropriate for new instances of the ORDER-1 process to be created by the CUSTOMER-1 process, probably when the PLACE action is performed. The text of the CUSTOMER-1 process may be:

```
CUSTOMER-1 seq
  read C;
  CUSTOMER-1-BODY itr
    CUSTOMER-ACTION sel (PLACE(i))
      create ORDER-1 (i) (where PLACE (i));
      PLACE; write PLACE to CO(i); read C;
    CUSTOMER-ACTION alt (AMEND (j))
      . . .
```

A newly created entity instance is assumed to be immediately connected into the SSD. Once the ORDER-1 process has been created by CUSTOMER-1, it can communicate both with the CUSTOMER-1 process and with the CLERK-1 process, as shown in the SSD.

Process deletion is always regarded as an implementation matter in JSD. Processes do not delete themselves, nor can they be deleted by other processes of the system. The purpose of process deletion is to free the resources occupied by the process, so that they may be used by a newly created process. A process may be deleted only when no further communication will take place between it and other processes; this point is not, in general, well defined. Some processes have no defined end to their text. For example, the ORDER process whose structure is shown in Fig. 8.34 may be CANCELled by the customer; unless the clerk then makes the (permissible) error and ALLOCATEs the order, the process will never reach the end of its text. Even where a process does, unmistakably, reach the end of its text, there is no guarantee that another process will not inspect its state-vector.

SUMMARY OF CHAPTER 8

The entity structure step produces an abstract description of the real world; the initial model step produces a realized model of that real world, ready for the addition of system functions. Our description in entity structures is, in effect, a description in sequential processes: connecting the reality to its model is therefore a matter of connecting sequential processes. We distinguish the reality from its model by referring to them as level-0 and level-1 respectively (8.1).

We will need a textual notation for structures. Structure text is basically a transcribed form of structure diagram, but there are some differences. We can readily insert operations into text, and show conditions on iteration and selection parts. In diagrams, selections are unordered, but they are ordered in text (8.2).

Process connection may be by data stream or by state-vector connection. We show connections in a System Specification Diagram (SSD). Process connection of either kind may be one-to-one, one-to-many, many-to-one, or many-to-many (8.3).

Data stream connection is by writing and reading messages. One data stream connects only two processes. The connection is considered to be buffered, so the writing process is never blocked; the reading process may lag behind the writing process by an indefinite number of records. This form of connection is appropriate to the connections between the real and model panel, and between the real and model readers, in the *Daily Racket* system (8.4, 8.5).

State-vector connection is direct inspection by one process of the state-vector of another process; that is, of its local variables. The connection is unbuffered, and does not cause blocking of either process. The result of a state-vector inspection (a *getsv* operation) depends on the relative speeds of the two processes involved. This is not the case for data stream connection. We require an implementation which ensures that the state-vector values obtained are always meaningful and self-consistent (8.6, 8.7).

We need to use state-vector connection in the Hi-Ride Elevator system, in effect to simulate the data stream connection which is preferable in the initial model. The model processes are in 'busy loops', repeatedly examining the states of the real entities to detect the occurrence of actions. It may sometimes be helpful to describe a set of successive state-vector values (or a data stream) by a structure diagram or text (8.8, 8.9).

The *Daily Racket* initial model requires the introduction of a new action (DISPERSE) of the panel, in anticipation of a difficulty that would otherwise arise at the function step. Without this new action, the panel model process could not be brought up to date with the end of a judging period until the beginning of the next period (8.10).

The initial model for the automated version of the Widget Warehouse system contains processes for each customer, each order, and each product. The first two are connected in the model, because they have common actions. The product process specification needs some care to ensure that it is able to model the availability of stock as computed by the purchasing and inventory system (8.11).

The discussion of process connection may be restated in terms of an imaginary manual system. Each process is a clerical worker, communicating with others by an internal mail system with in-trays and out-trays (data stream connection), and by looking at their working papers (state-vector connection). Process structure texts may be rewritten informally as clerical procedures (8.12).

Multiple inputs to one process require careful specification of the rules for determining which input is to be taken next. The determination may be made by fixed rules (fixed merge), or in accordance with the content of the messages (data merge), or in accordance with the availability of messages in the different streams (rough merge). Rough merge introduces indeterminacy: process behavior depends on relative speeds of system processes and buffers. In general, we assume that a rough merge is reasonably, but not completely, 'fair' (8.13).

The non-automated version of the Widget Warehouse system needs a rough merge of customer and clerk actions. We must therefore elaborate the structure of the order process, which merges the customer and clerk actions, to accommodate the possible resequencing that may result (8.15).

In some models we may need to introduce Time Grain Markers (TGMs) to indicate the arrival of particular points in real world time. TGMs are usually to be rough merged with other data stream messages (8.16).

Processes in JSD may be created by other processes or by means to be specified in the implementation step. Process deletion is always an implementation concern: the purpose of deleting a process is to free its resources for use by other processes (8.17).

9

The function step

9.1   ADDING FUNCTION TO THE MODEL

The result of the initial model step is a System Specification Diagram or SSD, showing the system as composed of model processes, connected to the real world entities which they model. For each process we also have a structure diagram and text. At this point, there are no outputs from the system, and the inputs are solely messages which signal the occurrence of events in the real world to the system so that they can be appropriately simulated in the model.

The purpose of the function step is to provide system outputs. Most systems are required to support several functions, of which some are specified when the system is originally developed and others later, after the system has come into operational use. One of the important advantages of the JSD development method is that each function is based on the model and so can be specified largely in isolation from other functions. The general form of a functional requirement may be stated as:

> In the combination of circumstances C, produce outputs O computed from data D.

Simplifying outrageously, we may say that the addition of a function to the system requires the addition of a function process F, of which there may be one or more instances (Fig. 9.1).

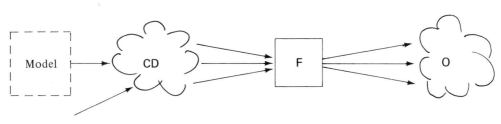

171   **Fig. 9.1**

The outputs of the function process may be produced on printers, terminal screens, disks or tapes (for transportation to another system), command lines to devices outside the system, or in any other appropriate way. The inputs CD inform F that the combination of circumstances C has arisen, and provide the data D necessary to compute the outputs. These inputs will be largely, but not exclusively, derived from the model processes. Different statements of the circumstances C and the data D will lead to different connections of the function process into the SSD.

One of the simplest forms of C and D is 'whenever a model process M has performed a certain combination of actions, report their cumulative effect'. This leads to the arrangement:

F is connected to M by a data stream MF, in which M signals its performance of the relevant actions and the attributes of each. F computes the cumulative effect and reports it. The lifetime of F is, in general, the same as the lifetime of M: the specified circumstances C may arise many times in the course of M's lifetime, and the function F produces some output whenever they arise. If there are many instances of M, there will be many instances of F. Sometimes, the statement of C is so simple, and the computation of the cumulative effect is so straightforward, that all the operations of F can be embedded directly in the structure of M:

In such a case, we call F a 'simple embedded function'.

Sometimes, C is in the form 'on request', or 'at the end of each week': that is, the circumstances C do not depend on the model but on some extraneous occurrence. If we arrange to signal each extraneous occurrence by a TGM or request record in a data stream R, we have the arrangement shown in Fig. 9.2.

M might, for example, model a bank account. F produces statements of the account, on request, showing all the actions that have been performed since the previous

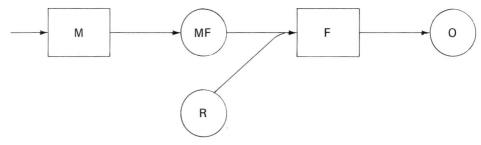

Fig. 9.2

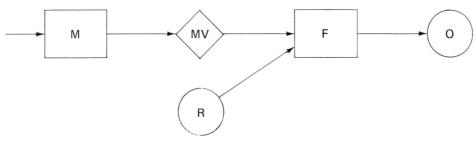

Fig. 9.3

time a statement was produced. The data stream MF contains a message for each action that is to appear on the statements. F rough merges its input streams MF and R; there is therefore some indeterminacy in the function output O.

Sometimes, the output produced by F for each input record of R is essentially no more than the values of a small number of variables. For instance, instead of a bank statement F might produce only a note of the current balance on the account. If the values of the reported variables are unaffected by the production of function output (an example of a variable that is *not* unaffected would be 'the number of actions performed since the last report was produced'), they may be computed directly by the model process M and form a part of its state-vector. F would then be connected to M by state-vector connection; the indeterminacy of the rough merge is replaced by the indeterminacy of the state-vector connection (Fig. 9.3). In such a case, we call F a 'simple imposed function'. The computed variables are sometimes called 'attributes' of M.

Sometimes, a function process needs to obtain information from many model processes. For example, the function stated as 'on request, list all withdrawals exceeding $100 that have occurred since the previous request' would require the arrangement shown in Fig. 9.4.

The function stated as 'on request, list all current balances exceeding $1000' would require the arrangement shown in Fig. 9.5. F inspects the state-vectors of model processes M. In the function step we can specify the particular set of state-vectors to be inspected (those with balances exceeding $1000) and the order in which they should be visited (in this case, any order is acceptable); this part of the function specification is an input to the design, in the implementation step, of the access paths to be provided in the database.

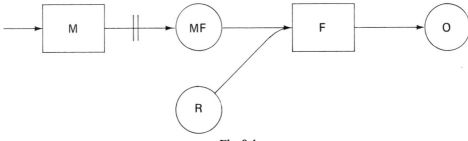

Fig. 9.4

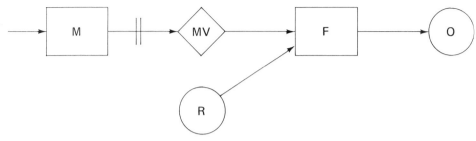

Fig. 9.5

In all the cases we have discussed so far, the information flow is only from the model to the function process, never in the opposite direction. More accurately, we may say that any information flowing from function processes to model processes must cross the system boundary as function output, pass through a part of the real world which is not described in the abstract specification of reality, and cross the system boundary again as input to the model processes. For example, the list of current balances exceeding $1000 might go to the bank's department of customer relations and crazy gifts: they choose one customer from the list at random, and send that customer a congratulatory letter and a check as a money prize: the customer, they hope, will immediately pay-in that check to his account, thus creating an input to the model process which results, however indirectly, from the original output list.

When we are interested in automation, rather than in information alone, we would like to make the feedback of information from the function to the model much more direct, and bring it within the system boundary. The function process can easily choose a customer at random, and we arrive at an arrangement like that shown in Fig. 9.6.

The data stream MI is the original model input to the process M; the data stream FM contains messages signalling the award of a prize check and its enforced, automated, pay-in. The customer would receive some notification, no doubt; but he would not receive a check and so would not have the opportunity to invest his prize elsewhere.

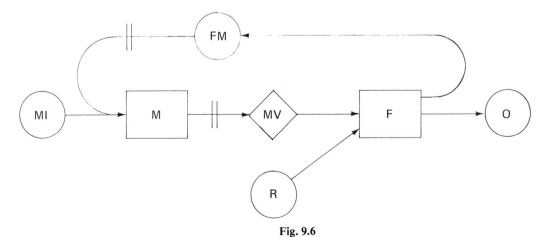

Fig. 9.6

We call F an 'interactive function', because it interacts with the model. The pattern of connections between F and the M processes is characteristic of interactive functions: the function inspects the state-vector of the model process and writes a data stream which the model process rough merges with its other data stream input. (As we will see when we consider detailed examples of interactive functions, later in this chapter, we would not in practice elaborate the model process M itself; we would prefer instead to create another level of model process to interact with the function process, leaving the original model process M structurally intact.)

The various arrangements discussed above for connecting function processes into the system may be combined in many different ways. One function may require more than one function process; one function process may be connected to more than one type of model process, or to another function process; a function may be an interacting function with respect to one part of the model, and a simple imposed function with respect to another part. Determining what function processes are needed, and how they should be connected into the SSD, is, of course, only one aspect of the work to be done in the function step. It is also necessary to specify the structure of each function process and any elaborations of connected model processes.

In this chapter we will discuss various functions for the three applications: the Widget Warehouse, the Hi-Ride Elevator, and the *Daily Racket*. For the most part, we will discuss each function in isolation, starting afresh from the model. We will introduce the functions in an order suited to exposition rather than to the likely priorities of a user; so we will often discuss some small and rather marginal function before considering the function which serves the central purpose of the system. As in earlier chapters, the discussion of illustrative examples will be interspersed with discussion of more general points.

In discussing the examples, we will usually show the full text of function processes, but omit the detailed steps of their derivation where this is a matter of straightforward JSP program design and the correctness of the text given is reasonably obvious. Sometimes we will explore the derivation in a little more detail, especially when there is a structure clash between the input and output data structures of a process. For the purpose of expounding JSD this seems the best compromise between obscurity and tedium. Readers who would like a full explanation of the JSP program design method may find it in M. A. Jackson, *Principles of Program Design*, Academic Press, or in Leif Ingevaldsson, *JSP: A Practical Method of Program Design*, Studentlitteratur.

9.2 SOME GENERAL CONSIDERATIONS

The specification of functions requires a degree of invention on the part of the developer and of the users with whom he works. Often there will be more than one way of providing a particular function, and the developer is faced with a choice among legitimate alternatives. Some general considerations are briefly discussed in this section, before we embark on the application examples. Some of these considerations are firm JSD rules, excluding certain possibilities altogether; others will help to guide the choice among alternative JSD solutions.

A firm rule in JSD is that functions are always specified as processes with long lifetimes, and never as procedures. We never specify a weekly report function, for example, by specifying a procedure to be executed each week; instead we specify a sequential process whose output is the set of all weekly reports produced in the lifetime of the system. Processes are more powerful than procedures in this context. If we specify a weekly procedure, we will find it difficult and cumbersome to specify any relationships among the reports, such as cumulative totals, or running comparisons; by specifying a process we leave open the opportunity, and we make available the mechanism, for specifying any desired relationships over the whole life of the process. If, in the end, a procedure would have been adequate, we can readily transform the process into a procedure in the implementation step.

Another firm rule is a limitation on the extent to which model processes may be elaborated for functional purposes. A model process may be elaborated by the introduction of variables, and of elementary operations; it should not be elaborated structurally in any way. (Strictly, the elaboration of the bank customer process in Section 4.5 was impermissible because it introduced the selection component which conditionally produced the overdraft report.) If structural elaboration is required, a new model process must be specified, connected to the original model process by a data stream. We will refer to such new model processes as 'level-2' processes: to make a more elaborate structure for CUSTOMER-1, we introduce CUSTOMER-2:

Subject to the firm rule about structural elaboration of model processes, variables may be freely introduced into model processes, along with the operations necessary to maintain their values. In particular, the state-vector of a model process may be elaborated in whatever way is convenient for function processes inspecting it. The most

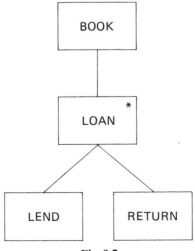

Fig. 9.7

important case concerns the process text-pointer: it will almost invariably be wrong to allow a function process to examine the value of the model process' text-pointer directly. For example, the model of a library book might be as shown in Fig. 9.7. The text-pointer of the BOOK process will have one of these values when the state-vector is inspected:

a — waiting for the first action: that is, at a *read* operation at the beginning of the process text;

b — in the middle of a LOAN: that is, at a *read* operation after LEND;

c — at the end of a LOAN: that is, at a *read* operation after RETURN.

The inspecting process could determine whether the book is out on loan by examining the value of the text-pointer: the value *b* indicates that the book is out on loan, while the values *a* and *c* indicate that it is not. But allowing such examination will make the function process too heavily dependent on the actual text of the BOOK process. We prefer to introduce a variable *out*, and to set its value by operations added to the model process (Fig. 9.8). The variable *out*, with values *yes* and *no*, may now be regarded as an attribute of BOOK.

The developer choosing whether to use state-vector or data stream connection between the model and a function process should be guided by a consideration of the initiative in the communication. If the function process requires to take the initiative in obtaining input, state-vector connection is appropriate; but if the initiative must lie with the model, data stream connection is appropriate. A heavy sleeper who needs to be

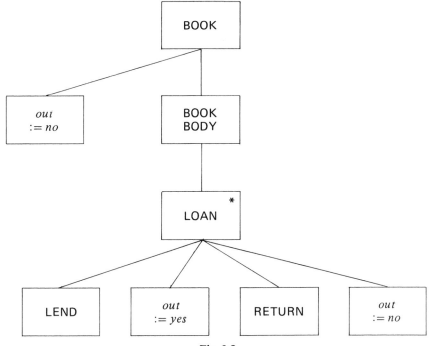

Fig. 9.8

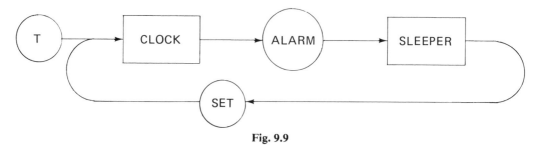

Fig. 9.9

woken in the morning uses an alarm clock: the sound of the alarm is a data stream message, written at the initiative of the clock which provides a model of time. A light sleeper who wants to know the time whenever he wakes in the night uses a clock with a luminous dial: his looking at the dial is a state-vector inspection, in which the initiative is his. (It is fortunate that both features are available in clocks: if only the luminous dial were available, the heavy sleeper would need to sit up all night, continually looking at his clock; if only the alarm were available, the light sleeper would have to set his alarm to go off every five minutes, like a chiming clock.)

Sometimes the initiative cannot be assigned so easily. The heavy sleeper must allow the initiative to his clock when he wants to be woken in the morning; but he must also be able to shut off the alarm in the evening (if he has a 12-hour clock) and on holidays. A data stream cannot be shut off by the reading process, in the sense that records written cannot be ignored or skipped; but two-way communication can allow the sleeper to affect the behavior of his clock (Fig. 9.9).

The CLOCK process writes a message on the ALARM data stream only when it's 7 o'clock and the last message in the SET data stream was 'ring' rather than 'silent'.

9.3   HI-RIDE ELEVATOR: FUNCTION 1 (EMBEDDED)

Conforming to standard practice, our user introduces a new functional requirement during the system development. There is a display panel inside each elevator, showing the floor numbers 1–6; each number can be illuminated from behind, the illumination being turned on and off by the commands:

DON (e, f):   turns on the light for floor f in elevator e;
DOFF (e, f):   turns off the light for floor f in elevator e.

We are required to issue the appropriate commands from our system. The light for floor f in elevator e should be turned on, we are told, when the elevator arrives at that floor, and should be turned off when the elevator arrives at a different floor. Checking our initial model, we see that we have a process which models each elevator, and we have an action ARRIVE(m); so it looks as if there will be no difficulty in providing the requested function.

The ELEVATOR-1 process structure is shown in Appendix E, and the reader should refer to it before reading on. From an examination of that process, it is clear that a simple embedded function can produce the required output. We go back to the user to clarify what output is required in the parts of the structure preceding ELEVATOR-BODY: we learn that the light for floor 1 should be turned on, and all others turned off, at the beginning of the process execution, and the light for floor 1 should then be turned off in the obvious place.

We document this function by adding an output symbol to the SSD and the appropriate executable operations to the structure of ELEVATOR-1. The SSD becomes that shown in Fig. 9.10.

The addition of operations to the structure of a model process may be specified in diagrammatic or text form:

— in text form, we simply insert the operations directly into the structure text;
— in diagrammatic form, we list the required operations, assign an identifying number to each one, and add these identifiers to the diagram.

In this book, for purposes of exposition we will sometimes do one and sometimes the other. Here we add the operations to the text:

```
ELEVATOR-1 seq
  d := 2;
  DOFFSET itr while d ⩽ 6
    DOFF (e,d); d := d + 1;
  DOFFSET end
  DON (e,1);
  m := 1; getsv EV;
  . . .
  NATSET1 end
  DOFF (e,1);
  ELEVATOR-BODY itr
    FLOOR-M seq
      m := j where EV = ATj;
      DON (e,m);
      ARRIVE(m);

      . . .
      NATSET end
      DOFF (e,m);
    FLOOR-M end
  ELEVATOR-BODY end
ELEVATOR-1 end
```

There is, of course, one instance of ELEVATOR-1 for each real world elevator. The value of e in the DON and DOFF operations is fixed for each ELEVATOR-1 process; another way of regarding this fact is to observe that each ELEVATOR-1 process has its own output device for the function output.

We have been slightly clever about the placing of the DOFF operations: by placing them at the end of the FLOOR-M component, we have been able to use the value of the floor number, m. We should always be suspicious of cleverness in system development:

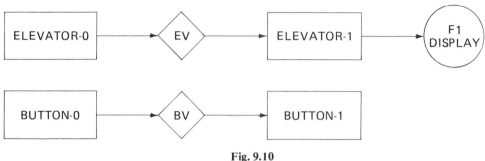

Fig. 9.10

it is often a sign that we have specified not what we mean, but something else which we hope will be equivalent. In this case, we are relying on the fact that when NATSET ends it can only be because the elevator has now arrived at another floor. After a short struggle with our conscience we decide that this piece of cleverness is acceptable; we may regret it if we are asked to ensure that the light for one floor is not turned off until the light for the succeeding floor has been turned on.

9.4 *DAILY RACKET*: **FUNCTION 1 (EMBEDDED)**

We are required to acknowledge each entry. The acknowledgement should contain details of the entry and the reader's name and address.

Again, this is a simple embedded function. The operation *write acknowledgement* can be placed in the structure of READER-1 at the point where the ENTER action occurs; the entry details are taken from the input record of the data stream R, and the name and address are taken from the stored attributes of the SUBSCRIBE action. If we have not previously done so, we must add a local variable for the name and address and an operation to store its value. Name and address are now an attribute of READER. The SSD is as shown in Fig. 9.11.

We are assuming that a separate output device is available for each READER-1 process, hence that there is a separate output stream F1 ACKNTS for each reader. Obviously, this assumption is unrealistic from an implementation point of view, and we

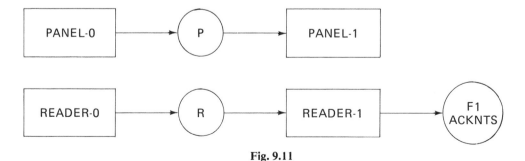

Fig. 9.11

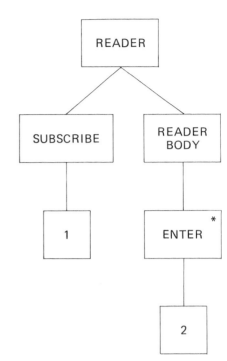

1   Store name & address in n-and-a;

2   Write entry details and n-and-a;

Fig. 9.12

will need to reconsider it in the implementation step; but now, in the function step, there is no reason not to make the assumption, since nothing in the function specification requires us to gather together outputs from many readers.

The output stream F1 ACKNTS contains all the acknowledgements written during the whole lifetime of the reader; each one is output when the ENTER action is simulated by READER-1. We are paying no attention to the print format of an acknowledgement; at the function step it is enough to satisfy ourselves that the required information is output in each record of F1 ACKNTS.

Adding the necessary operations to the structure diagram we have Fig. 9.12.

9.5   *DAILY RACKET*: **FUNCTION 2**

Sir Cunning, who likes to keep an eye on the cash, has asked us to provide him with a weekly report on the number of entries made by readers. The report is no more than three lines:

WEEK *nnn* ENTRIES REPORT

ENTRIES THIS WEEK—*eeee*
TOTAL ENTRIES SO FAR—*fffff*

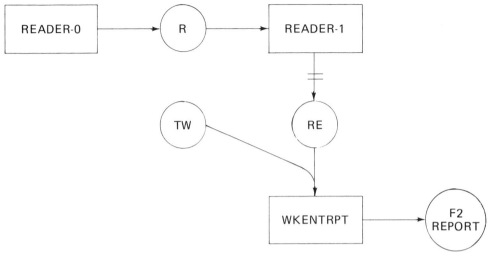

Fig. 9.13

We ask about the week number shown in the heading line, and we learn that it should start at 001 and simply increase by 1 each week.

Clearly, this cannot be a simple embedded function: there is no process in the model which could produce the required output, since each READER-1 process models the behavior of exactly one real world reader. So we will certainly need to add a

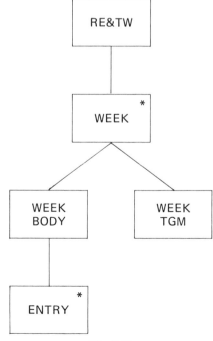

Fig. 9.14

function process: let us call it WKENTRPT. Each READER-1 process must write a data stream to be read by WKENTRPT, there being one record in this stream for each ENTER action. WKENTRPT requires a TGM input stream to indicate the arrival of the point in time at which a week's output is to be produced. The SSD is thus as shown in Fig. 9.13.

There is one WKENTRPT process in the system, receiving RE input from every READER-1 process. This RE input is rough merged as between one READER-1 process and another, and also rough merged with the TW stream of weekly TGMs. Without making any assumptions about the relative speeds of the processes involved, we can draw a data structure diagram of the merged stream RE&TW (Fig. 9.14).

Each ENTRY record need be no more than a unary digit: not even one bit is needed, since the information contained in the record is simply the occurrence of an ENTRY action in READER-1. The structure of F2-REPORT is as shown in Fig. 9.15.

After completing the derivation of the process text we obtain the result:

```
WKENTRPT seq
  wk := 1; sofar := 0; read RE&TW;
  WKENTRPT-BODY itr
    WEEK seq
      thiswk := 0;
      WEEK-BODY itr while (ENTRY)
        ENTRY seq
          thiswk := thiswk + 1; sofar := sofar + 1;
          read RE&TW;
        ENTRY end
      WEEK-BODY end
      WEEK-TGM seq
        print headline;
        print detail lines;
        read RE&TW;
      WEEK-TGM end
      wk := wk + 1;
    WEEK end
  WKENTRPT-BODY end
WKENTRPT end
```

As its text shows clearly, this process runs for ever, producing one set of heading and detail lines each time a weekly TGM appears in the merged RE&TW input stream. The local variables *wk* and *sofar* are initialized at the beginning of the process execution, and updated at the appropriate points during execution: they keep their updated values from week to week.

The rough merge of the multiple RE streams is of no consequence: the output of WKENTRPT is not in any way dependent on the relative ordering between one READER-1 output stream RE and another. The rough merge between the RE streams and the TW stream, by contrast, does have consequences for the output of WKENTRPT: the count of entries this week in the first detail line of the F2 REPORT will be affected directly by the way the rough merge operates. If the rough merge tends to favor the TW stream, then an ENTRY record appearing in RE at the end of the week may fail to be

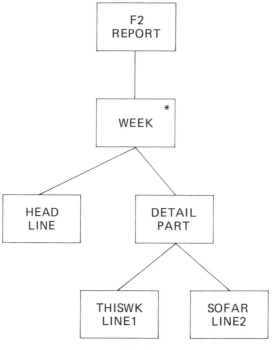

Fig. 9.15

included in that week's report, and will be included in the following week. So the exact output of WKENTRPT is, to some extent, dependent on the relative speeds of the READER-1 and WKENTRPT processes and on the buffering of the RE and TW data streams.

However, this is not a disadvantage. We want the exact output of each WEEK in F2-REPORT to remain indeterminate in this way, because full determinacy would be spurious, based on the characteristics of the implementation of the system rather than on its specification. At first sight, the indeterminacy may seem intolerable to some readers: we are accustomed to system specifications which have at least the appearance of determinacy. But on looking more deeply we observe that:

— the indeterminacy affects only the partitioning into weeks; the cumulative total in the second detail line of the report is not affected cumulatively, and the error becomes, week by week, a smaller fraction of this cumulative total;

— the partitioning into weeks is not significant in the model, or in the real world on which it is based; the week is only a convenient period for Sir Cunning to wait before he can next gloat over his receipts;

— the indeterminacy introduced by the buffering of R through the postal system is far greater than the indeterminacy of the rough merge of RE with TW.

It will often be so. Data processing systems typically produce periodic reports according to time periods which have no significance in the real world. Everyone is familiar with the monthly bank statement for a checking account: we happily accept the indeterminacy at the end of the month, where we cannot be sure whether the cheque drawn on the 29th will appear in the statement or not; what we do want is to be certain that nothing is lost in the crack between one month and the next, that if the cheque drawn on the 29th does not appear this month, then it will certainly appear next month. Similar considerations apply to almost every periodic report in a data processing system.

Where indeterminacy in a specification is genuinely intolerable, we will need to ensure, in the function step or later in the system timing step, that it is controlled within acceptable limits or even removed altogether. There are various ways of doing so, which we will discuss later in this and the next chapter.

9.6   WIDGET WAREHOUSE: FUNCTIONS 1 AND 2 (LEVEL-2)

The initial model of the system for the Widget Warehouse was discussed in Section 8.15; Appendix D gives the structure of the ORDER-1 process, with actions PLACE, AMEND, CANCEL, and DELIVER performed by the customer, and DELAY and ALLOCATE performed by the clerk.

The sales manager has become worried by what he thinks may be excessive AMENDing activity on the part of some customers. He asks the developer to provide two functions:

— F1: an exception report for any order which is AMENDed more than once without an intervening DELAY; and

— F2: an exception report for any order which is AMENDed more than twice in a week.

Clearly, these functions are concerned with orders. In the structure of ORDER-1 there are AMEND and LATE AMEND actions, and both are relevant. LATE DELAY cannot be relevant, because it can never be followed by AMEND or LATE AMEND. Remembering that the input streams to ORDER-1 are rough merged, we mention to the manager that both F1 and F2 output will be affected by the rough merge, which in turn is affected by the fact that the customer may AMEND an order in ignorance of the clerk's most recent activity. Exploring this point with him, we agree that it can be ignored: the F1 and F2 reports will be incomplete, but will not contain wrong information, so we can go ahead.

We consider whether these might be simple embedded functions, but it is soon apparent that they are not: the structure of ORDER-1 does not contain appropriate components for allocation of the *write* F1-REPORT or *write* F2-REPORT operations. The required structures for these operations are something like those illustrated in Fig. 9.16.

These structures are quite incompatible with the structure of ORDER-1. We must therefore add function processes having these structures to the SSD; each will be a level-2 model of the order entity. Two process types will be needed, because the structures of F1-ORDER and F2-ORDER are mutually incompatible (there is a boundary clash between GROUP and WEEK). Each function process must be connected to its associated ORDER-1 process by a data stream, since the initiative clearly lies with the

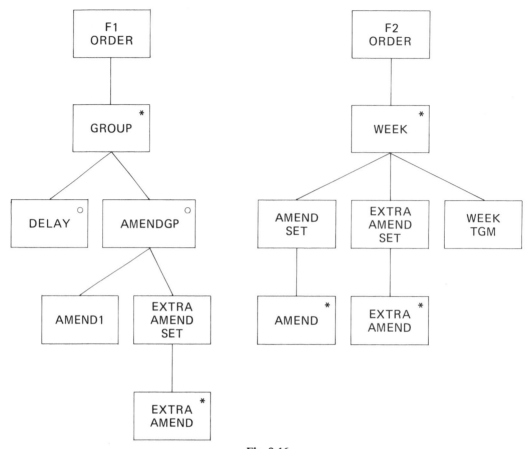

Fig. 9.16

performance of AMEND and DELAY actions in the order. The process for F2 will also require an input data stream of weekly TGMs. The necessary elaboration of the SSD is as shown in Fig. 9.17.

In ORDER-1 we place operations to write:

— a record for each DELAY, AMEND, and LATE AMEND to OF1; and
— a record for each AMEND and LATE AMEND to OF2.

TW is a TGM stream of WEEK TGMs, one TGM appearing each week; TW is rough merged with OF2 to give OF2&TW input to F2-ORDER-2. There is an F1-ORDER-2 and an F2-ORDER-2 process for each ORDER-1; we are assuming a separate output device for each of these processes.

We have not yet specified the functions adequately. We must check whether each report is to be produced for every EXTRA AMEND or not. The manager tells us that this is what he wants, and gives us some further information about print format. The rest is straightforward. The structure text of F2-ORDER-2 is:

```
F2-ORDER-2 seq
  read OF2&TW;
  F2-ORDER-2-BODY itr
    WEEK seq
      amendcount := 0;
      AMEND-SET itr while (AMEND & amendcount < 2)
        amendcount := amendcount + 1; read OF2&TW;
      AMEND-SET end
      EXTRA-AMEND-SET itr while (AMEND)
        print F2 exception report;
        read OF2&TW;
      EXTRA-AMEND-SET end
      WEEK-TGM seq
        read OF2&TW;
      WEEK-TGM end
    WEEK end
  F2-ORDER-2-BODY end
F2-ORDER-2 end
```

The structure text of F1-ORDER-2 is equally simple, and is not shown here.

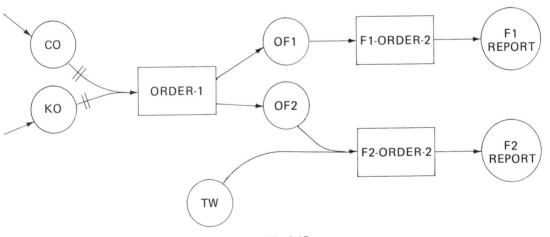

Fig. 9.17

9.7 *DAILY RACKET:* **FUNCTION 3 (IMPOSED)**

The competition manager wants to be able to enquire about the number of entries made by any reader. He is willing to enter the reader-id, and would like to receive in return a count of all entries made so far by that reader.

This is a simple imposed function. We need to elaborate the READER-1 process by adding a suitable count variable and the operations to update it, and to add to the SSD a function process RDRENQS; this process has an input stream of enquiries entered by the manager; it executes appropriate *getsv* operations; and it produces an output stream of the required responses. Omitting the parts of the SSD which are unaffected, we get Fig. 9.18.

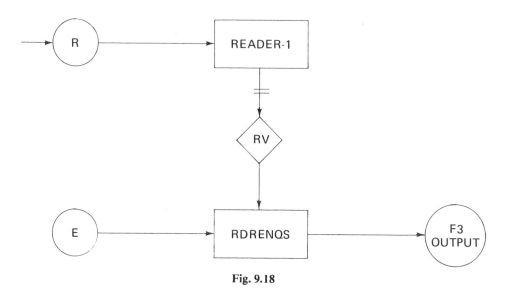

Fig. 9.18

The structure text of RDRENQS is no more than:

RDRENQS **itr**
  ENQUIRY **seq**
    read E;
    getsv RV (*reader-id in* E);
    write F3 *response*;
  ENQUIRY **end**
RDRENQS **end**

It may seem otiose to specify a process as simple as this, when we might instead have regarded the function as an executable procedure. The procedure can be executed whenever the manager chooses to invoke it, and each execution handles one ENQUIRY; there would be no connection of any kind between one invocation and another. But we have already discussed, in Section 9.2, why we do not use procedures in JSD specifications. If the enquiry function can be implemented as a procedure, we will easily transform the RDRENQS process into an ENQUIRY procedure at the implementation step.

9.8   ACCESS PATHS IN IMPOSED FUNCTIONS

Imposed functions will often be far more complex than the very simple function discussed in the preceding section. For each enquiry input record, it may be necessary to access many state-vectors of different entity types; it may be necessary to access the state-vectors in a certain order, and to access them selectively. In the Widget Warehouse System, for example, we may wish to provide the following functions:

— list all the orders for a specified product;
— list all the customers who have orders that have been placed but not yet allocated for a certain product;
— list all the customers who have orders for any of the products for which a certain customer has an order;
— determine whether there is any product currently ordered by more than ten customers, and, if so, list the orders for all such products.

In some implementation environments we may be able to leave such functions to be handled by general-purpose database query software. Indeed, the main thrust of much database software and almost all query languages is directed to precisely this end. In other environments, we will need to deal with the problems explicitly in the function step; even where suitable software is provided, we may want to make some analysis of the database accessing that will be needed in order to choose an efficient implementation of the database.

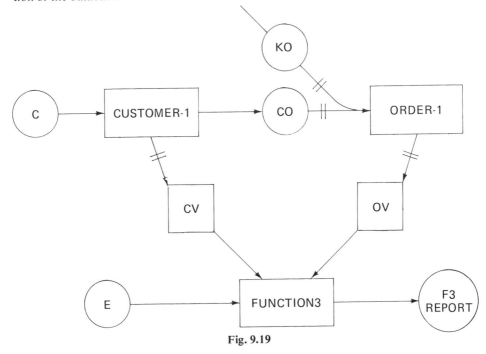

Fig. 9.19

In the function step in JSD, we can determine the access paths that will be needed by specified functions. These are not the only access paths that will be needed: later, in the implementation step, we will see that running the model processes will also require database access; but for now we are concerned only with access by function processes.

In specifying the functions of this kind, we will find it useful to draw data structure diagrams representing the access paths to the database. Previously, in Section 8.9, we looked briefly at the use of structure diagrams to represent the succession of state-vector values obtained by successive *getsv* operations on the same state-vector; here, we will be concerned with the use of *getsv* operations to obtain successively the state-vectors of different processes.

The approach we will take is to structure the function process specification on the assumption that the database contains only those state-vectors needed by the process, and in the order best suited to the needs of the process. Separately, we may draw any data structures necessary to specify the ordering and selection of state-vectors; these data structures will provide information needed for efficient organization of the database in the implementation step.

9.9   WIDGET WAREHOUSE: FUNCTION 3 (IMPOSED)

The sales manager has asked us to provide the following function: for a specified product-id, list the names of all customers who have outstanding orders for that product, and, against the name of each such customer, the total quantity outstanding. An order is outstanding if it has been placed but not yet allocated or cancelled.

How should this function be specified? We might perhaps specify one process instance for each product-id; but it is probably more appropriate to specify a single process instance to deal with all the enquiries for all the products. The initiative must clearly come from the manager's enquiry, which will be a message in an input data stream to the process. The process will need to inspect the current state of orders, and, assuming that the customer's name is an attribute of CUSTOMER-1, the current state of the customer processes also. So the elaboration of the SSD will be as shown in Fig. 9.19.

Fig. 9.20

We can readily introduce into the process ORDER-1 a variable *outstanding*; to this variable we assign the value *yes* when the PLACE action occurs, and the value *no* at the very beginning of the process text and at the end of the ORDER BODY. The FUNCTION3 process must obtain state-vectors of CUSTOMER-1 and ORDER-1 in an order which permits the required output to be produced. The gross structure of FUNCTION3 is as shown in Fig. 9.20; that is, it must deal successively with the products specified in the input records of the enquiry stream, E. Within each instance of PRODUCT(E) we have some latitude in choosing the order of obtaining state-vectors: we may obtain the customer state-vector either before or after the associated order state-vectors. Taking the former choice, we have Fig. 9.21.

What has been assumed here about the accessibility of state-vectors is the following:

— given a product-id E, it is possible to obtain successively all the customer state-vectors for those customers who have at least one outstanding order for the product E, and

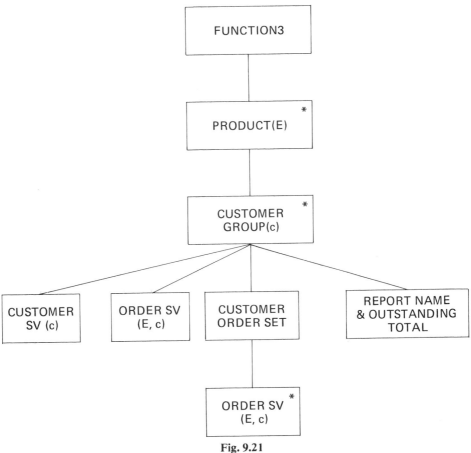

Fig. 9.21

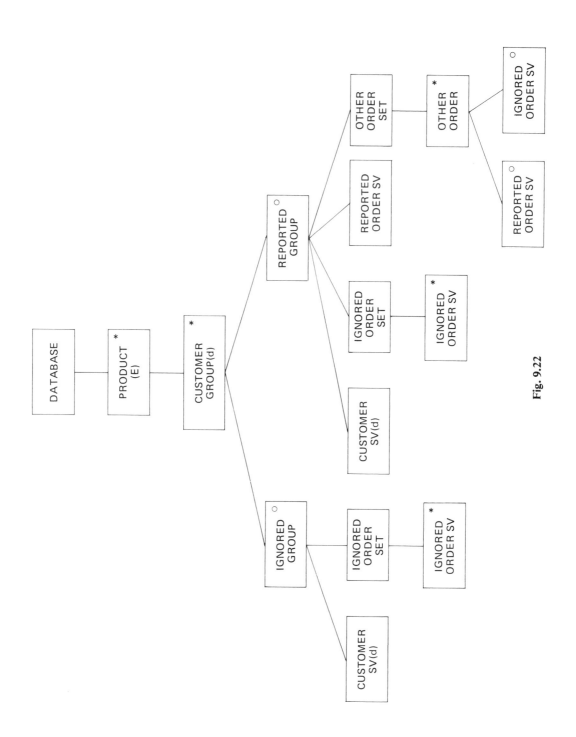

Fig. 9.22

— given a state-vector of a customer c, who has at least one outstanding order for product E, it is possible to obtain successively all the outstanding orders of that customer for that product.

To this diagram we must add notes to specify that each of the order state-vectors has the value *yes* for its variable *outstanding*, has been placed by customer c, and is an order for product E.

In the implementation step, it may be necessary to impose a more elaborate structure on the database than is shown above. If, for example, the database implementation allows the following accesses:

— given a product-id, it is possible to obtain the state-vector of that product directly; and
— given the state-vector of a product, it is possible to obtain successively all the state-vectors of customers who have ordered that product; and
— given the state-vector of a customer, it is possible to obtain successively all the state-vectors of orders placed by that customer;

then the structure imposed on the database for FUNCTION3 may be as shown in Fig. 9.22, in which an IGNORED ORDER is either not for PRODUCT(E) or is not outstanding; a REPORTED ORDER is outstanding, and is for PRODUCT(E). Only REPORTED GROUPs in this structure are CUSTOMER GROUPs in the FUNCTION3 process structure; only REPORTED ORDER SVs are ORDER SVs. A REPORTED GROUP is one which has at least one REPORTED ORDER.

9.10 RESTRUCTURING FOR OUTPUT

It is not always to be expected that the input to a function process, whether in data stream or in state-vector form, will be available in the ordering needed for the output. Sometimes, therefore, a function process will require to restructure its inputs in some way. Here are some examples:

— The Widget Warehouse manager wants a weekly list of all orders placed during the week, sorted by product-id. If we choose a state-vector connection between the order processes and the listing function process, we may assume that the order state-vectors can be obtained in sorted sequence by product-id. But if the connection is by data stream, there will be a rough merge in the function process, which will be forced to accept the messages from order processes in whatever sequence they arrive:

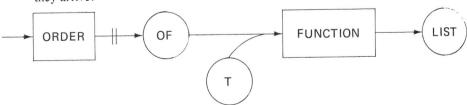

This will not be the sorted sequence required for the list.

— The *Daily Racket* panel must be provided with a list of all entries made by readers since the last judging session, sorted by ranking. Here, only data stream connection is possible; the initiative lies with the reader to inform the function process of each entry made. Again, there is a rough merge in the function process.

— The *Daily Racket* panel awards must be listed when the panel disperses at the end of each session; the list is to be in ascending sequence by reader-id. Restructuring will be necessary unless the panel are thoughtful enough to make their awards strictly in the required sequence.

— The Widget Warehouse manager wants a picking list of all orders allocated during the day, sorted by warehouse location of the product and, in a separate list, by customer delivery location.

Specification of these processes introduces no special problem. But the developer must be aware that the output of such a process will often be unavailable until the whole of an input group has been read or obtained. The Widget Warehouse picking list cannot be produced piecemeal: the first line cannot be printed until the last allocation for the day has been made.

9.11   HI-RIDE ELEVATOR: MAJOR FUNCTIONS—1

The major functions of the system are to control the movement of the elevators and to turn on and off the lights associated with the various call buttons. We need to specify these functions: that is, we need to invent, or to be told by the user, the rules according to which the system issues the appropriate commands to the elevator motors and to the button lights.

We will begin our discussion of the major functions by making some sweeping simplifications:

— there is only one elevator, not two;

— the elevator is to make continual journeys from the ground floor to the top floor and back again, irrespective of the users' requests for service;

— the elevator will stop at the ground floor and the top floor, and at any intermediate floor where there is a request for service;

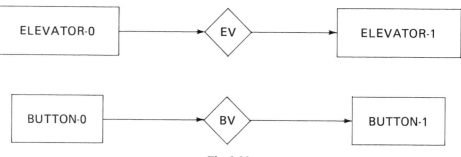

Fig. 9.23

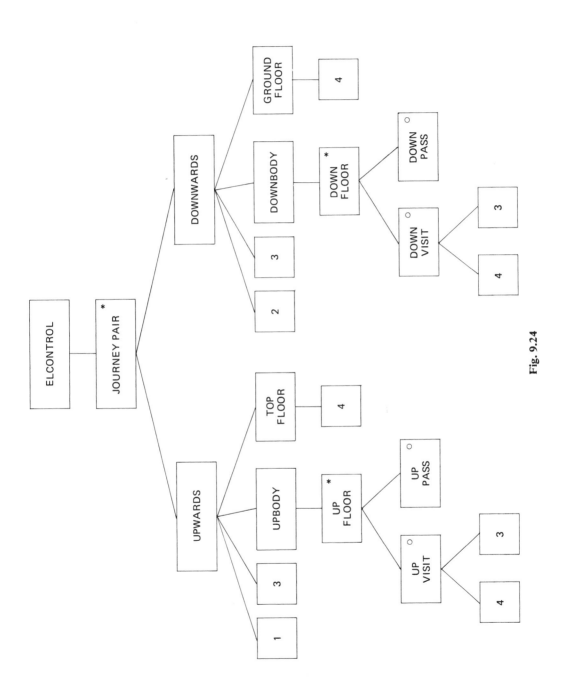

Fig. 9.24

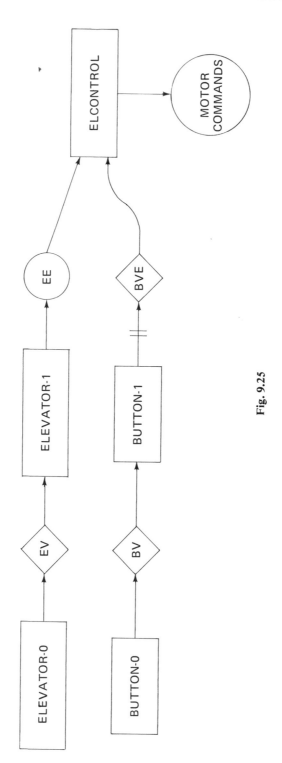

Fig. 9.25

— the mechanical arrangement of the elevators and doors is such that if the system issues a STOP command to the motor, followed immediately by a START command, there will be a suitable intervening delay while the doors open, stay open for a few seconds, and close.

In later sections we will remove these simplifications, specifying the functions more realistically.

Our initial model, developed in Section 8.8, is shown in Fig. 9.23. The actions of ELEVATOR are ARRIVE(m) and LEAVE(m), and the actions of BUTTON are DEPRESS and RELEASE. There is one elevator, according to our simplification. There are 16 buttons: E11 through E16 are buttons inside the elevators; U1 through U5 are the up buttons on floors 1 through 5; D2 through D6 are the down buttons on floors 2 through 6.

The pattern of motor commands to be issued is shown in Fig. 9.24. The commands are:

1   UP (set motor polarity upwards)
2   DOWN (set motor polarity downwards)
3   START (start motor)
4   STOP (stop motor).

Evidently, the ELEVATOR-1 process cannot accommodate this pattern without structural change. Production of the motor commands can therefore not be an embedded function, but will require an additional function process, ELCONTROL. This process must be connected to ELEVATOR-1 and to the BUTTON-1 processes, because the function statement inevitably includes something like:

> ... When the elevator arrives at a floor, and ... button has been pressed, ... the STOP command is to be issued, and ....

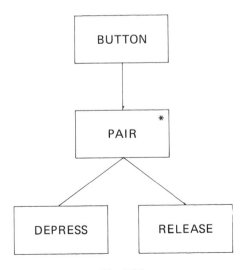

Fig. 9.26

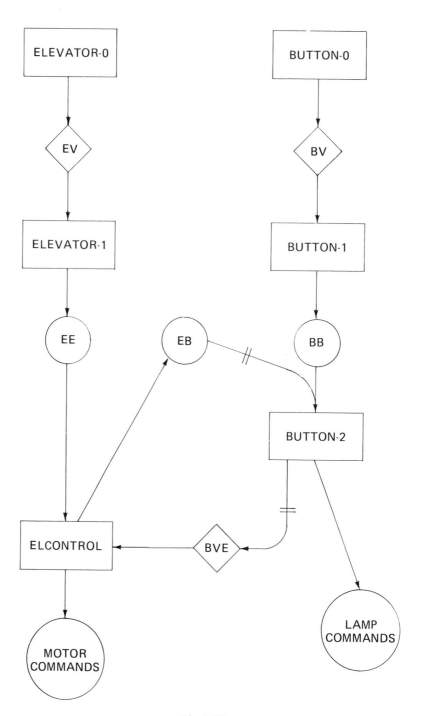

Fig. 9.27

Connection between ELCONTROL and ELEVATOR-1 must be by data stream: ELCONTROL must wait on the action of the elevator. At first sight, it may appear that data stream connection is required also to the BUTTON processes, because ELCONTROL does in some sense wait on the action of the buttons. However, ELCONTROL is interested in a summary of the button actions rather than in their individual occurrences, and it is interested only in particular buttons at particular times. So state-vector connection is appropriate (Fig. 9.25).

The data stream EE must certainly contain a record for each ARRIVE(m) action, to allow ELCONTROL to issue STOP commands at the right time; we leave aside for now the question whether it should also contain LEAVE(m) actions.

More significantly, we must consider what information ELCONTROL can obtain from the state-vectors of the BUTTON-1 processes. BUTTON-1 models the actions of BUTTON-0 as in Fig. 9.26.

The questions which ELCONTROL can answer by inspecting the state-vector of BUTTON-1 are:

—   has the button ever been DEPRESSed? and, if so,
—   was the last action DEPRESS or RELEASE?

Clearly, this is not adequate. The question to be answered is:

—   has the button been DEPRESSed since the associated floor was last serviced?

We therefore require a model of the buttons whose behavior is affected by the function process ELCONTROL, when the elevator visits the floor associated with the button. This model will be a new, level-2, process BUTTON-2 for each button. ELCONTROL will inspect the state-vector of BUTTON-2, and will write a data stream to each BUTTON-2 process, each record signalling a visit to the associated floor. Figure 9.27 shows the resulting SSD, with the addition of the lamp control outputs from the BUTTON-2 processes. ELCONTROL is an interacting function with respect to BUTTON-2.

BUTTON-2 rough merges its data stream inputs EB and BB. The EB stream is an iteration of VISIT records; the BB stream is an iteration of REQUEST records. The merged stream EB&BB has the structure shown in Fig. 9.28.

The EXTRA VISIT SET is present in the structure for two reasons. The first is that specification of the process ELCONTROL will be simpler if it can write a VISIT record to an EB stream when a floor is visited, irrespective of whether the associated button has been pressed (remember that there are buttons both outside and inside the elevator). The second reason is that the rough merge, combined with the state-vector inspection, leads to some indeterminacy. It is possible, at least in theory, for ELCONTROL to find that a request is outstanding, write a VISIT record, inspect the state-vector again before the VISIT record has been read, find the state unchanged, and write another VISIT record. There could thus be successive VISIT records without an intervening REQUEST.

More generally, we can observe that the structure of EB&BB places no constraint on the ordering of REQUEST and VISIT records: any ordered set of an unlimited number of REQUEST and VISIT records can be described by the structure given.

To complete the specification of the BUTTON-2 process we must add a variable to indicate whether a request is outstanding, together with the operations to update that

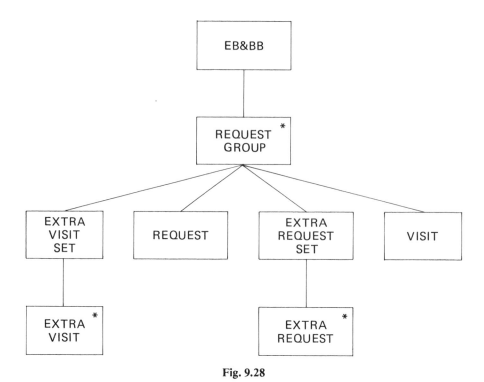

Fig. 9.28

variable; and we must embed the operations to write the lamp commands. The resulting text of BUTTON-2 is:

```
BUTTON-2 seq
  outstanding := no; OFF lamp; read EB&BB;
  BUTTON-2-BODY itr
    REQUEST-GROUP seq
      EXTRA-VISIT-SET itr while (VISIT)
        read EB&BB;
      EXTRA-VISIT-SET end
      REQUEST seq
        outstanding := yes; ON lamp; read EB&BB;
      REQUEST end
      EXTRA-REQUEST-SET itr while (REQUEST)
        read EB&BB;
      EXTRA-REQUEST-SET end
      VISIT seq
        outstanding := no; OFF lamp; read EB&BB;
      VISIT end
    REQUEST-GROUP end
  BUTTON-2-BODY end
BUTTON-2 end
```

The REQUEST records of the data stream BB are written by operations embedded in BUTTON-1, executed once for each DEPRESS/RELEASE pair of actions.

We have yet to specify the contents of the data stream EE. It is required as input to ELCONTROL in order to synchronize the behavior of ELCONTROL with the behavior of the real elevator. Certainly ELCONTROL must wait for the record ARRIVE(m) in EE before issuing the command STOP, if the elevator is to be stopped at FLOOR(m). Can there be any need for LEAVE(m) records also? LEAVE(m) records will be useful only if we wish to postpone as late as possible the inspection of the state-vectors of button processes, and find ourselves unable to postpone it as late as the ARRIVE(m) record. This would happen if we find that there is not enough time, after reading an ARRIVE(m) record of EE, to inspect two state-vectors, select the option of visiting FLOOR(m), and issue the STOP command to the motor: the STOP command would be too late to stop the elevator at FLOOR(m). We might then decide to inspect the state-vectors as soon as the LEAVE record appears, giving plenty of time to select the visit option and to issue the STOP command. By using the LEAVE record we delay slightly the inspection of button state-vectors, and so give a slightly better service to the elevator's users.

We are inescapably involved here with implementation questions. Eventually we satisfy ourselves that our system implementation will be entirely electronic, with no disk accessing, and that there will be no danger in postponing all the ELCONTROL activity for a floor until the ARRIVE record has been read. We do not therefore need any LEAVE records in EE.

The text of ELCONTROL is:

```
ELCONTROL itr
  JOURNEY-PAIR seq
    UPWARDS seq
      UP;
      flr := 1; write VISIT to EB (Uflr);
               write VISIT to EB (Eflr);
      START;
      flr := flr + 1;
      UPBODY itr while ( flr ≤ 5)
        UP-FLOOR seq
          read EE; getsv BVE (Uflr); getsv BVE (Eflr);
          UP-FLOOR-BODY sel (outstanding (Uflr) or
                                outstanding (Eflr))
            UP-VISIT seq
              STOP; write VISIT to  EB (Uflr);
                    write VISIT to EB (Eflr);
              START;
            UP-VISIT end
          UP-FLOOR-BODY alt (else)
          UP-FLOOR-BODY end
          flr := flr + 1;
        UP-FLOOR end
      UPBODY end
```

```
                TOP-FLOOR seq
                  read EE; STOP;
                  write VISIT to EB (Eflr);
                TOP-FLOOR end
            UPWARDS end
            DOWNWARDS seq
              DOWN; write VISIT to EB (Dflr);
              START; flr := flr − 1;
              DOWNBODY itr while ( flr ⩾ 2)
                DOWN-FLOOR seq
                  read EE; getsv BVE (Dflr); getsv BVE (Eflr);
                  DOWN-FLOOR-BODY sel (outstanding (Dflr) or
                                              outstanding (Eflr))
                    DOWN-VISIT seq
                      STOP; write VISIT to EB (Dflr);
                            write VISIT to EB (Eflr);
                      START;
                    DOWN-VISIT end
                  DOWN-FLOOR-BODY alt (else)
                  DOWN-FLOOR-BODY end
                  flr := flr − 1;
                DOWN-FLOOR end
              DOWNBODY end
              GROUND-FLOOR seq
                read EE;
                STOP;
              GROUND-FLOOR end
            DOWNWARDS end
          JOURNEY-PAIR end
        ELCONTROL end
```

The BUTTON-2 processes are referred to in the *getsv* BVE and *write to* EB operations, and in the tests for the condition *outstanding*. The notation Eflr means 'the button inside the elevator for the floor whose number is *flr*'; and the notations Dflr and Uflr refer similarly to the buttons located on the floors for downward and upward travel requests.

Neither the VISIT records of the EB data streams nor the ARRIVE records of the EE data stream need have any data content; in both cases the required message is conveyed adequately by the mere presence of the record. It would be possible to verify that the ARRIVE records correspond as expected to the current value of the variable *flr*: each read EE operation should read an ARRIVE(flr) record, unless the elevator, the motor, or the sensors have failed. But, in this version at least, we are placing full confidence in the traditional skills of the Hi-Ride Company's mechanical engineers.

9.12 A LITTLE LIGHT BACKTRACKING

In the next section we will specify a more realistic version of ELCONTROL which will provide a better service to users of the elevator. That will not be a very difficult task, but we will need a little backtracking technique to tackle it properly. The full motivation for the backtracking technique will appear when we tackle the task itself; in this section we will explain some elements of the technique using simple illustrations relevant to the task.

Suppose that we want to improve our existing version of the ELCONTROL process by causing the elevator to wait at the ground floor until a request arrives. Then we will have the gross structure shown in Fig. 9.29. In the WAIT AT GROUND part of the sequence, ELCONTROL will scan the states of the BUTTON-2 processes repeatedly until it finds that one has an outstanding request. A reasonable structure for this is shown in Fig. 9.30.

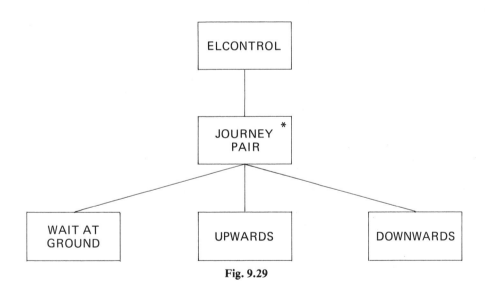

Fig. 9.29

We need to be able to terminate the WAIT AT GROUND component as soon as any outstanding request is detected. To do so, we must be able to jump out of the top-level iteration; this jump is a restricted kind of GO TO statement, and in JSP and JSD it is written in the form of a **quit** statement, specifying the name of a structure component and sometimes also a condition. The structure text for WAIT AT GROUND is:

```
WAIT-AT-GROUND itr
  COMPLETE-SCAN seq
    i := 2;
    SCAN-OF-2-THRU-5 itr while (i ⩽ 5)
      SCAN-MIDDLE-FLOOR-I seq
        getsv BVE (Ui);
WAIT-AT-GROUND quit (outstanding (Ui));
        getsv BVE (Ei);
WAIT-AT-GROUND quit (outstanding (Ei));
        getsv BVE (Di);
WAIT-AT-GROUND quit (outstanding (Di));
        i := i + 1;
      SCAN-MIDDLE-FLOOR-I end
    SCAN-OF-2-THRU-5 end
    getsv BVE (E6);
WAIT-AT-GROUND quit (outstanding (E6));
    getsv BVE (D6);
WAIT-AT-GROUND quit (outstanding (D6));
  COMPLETE-SCAN end
WAIT-AT-GROUND end
```

The assumption specified in the structure without the **quit** statements is that WAIT AT GROUND would be a perpetual iteration, never terminating, and that each part would be a COMPLETE SCAN as specified. The **quit** statements appear at the points in the structure where that assumption may be proved wrong.

The use of backtracking **quit** statements may give rise to what we call side-effects. At the end of the WAIT AT GROUND component execution, there will, in general, have been a partial execution of COMPLETE SCAN and, possibly, a partial execution of SCAN MIDDLE FLOORi; the state of ELCONTROL is not, therefore, quite what it seems from the structure diagram. In the present case, it is easy to see that this does not matter at all.

Quit statements can also appear in selections of exactly two parts; they are not permitted in selections of more than two parts. We then write the selection structure text in the form:

```
X posit (some assumption)
  · · ·
X quit (some condition disproving the assumption);
  · · ·
X quit (some condition disproving the assumption);
  · · ·
X admit (the assumption was wrong)
  · · ·
X end
```

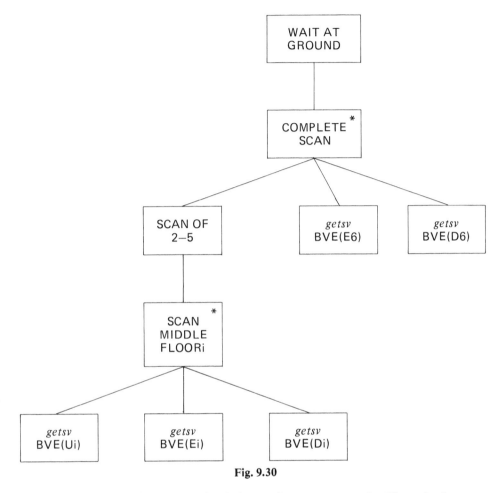

Fig. 9.30

The conditions on the **posit** and **admit** are for comment only. The selection part introduced by the structure node **posit** is the part which is assumed to apply; the part introduced by the node **admit** is the part which applies if the assumption proves wrong; as in iteration, the **quit** statements appear at the points where the assumption may be proved wrong.

Suppose that we want a selection of two parts; the first part applies if there is no outstanding request on any of the buttons E2 through E6, and the second part applies otherwise. The required structure diagram for scanning the state-vectors is shown in Fig. 9.31. Here we have shown explicitly the specified results of the *getsv* operations. If the assumption that there is no request is true, then all the state-vectors obtained in NO REQUEST SET will have the value *not outstanding*; if the assumption is wrong, then in the first part of the scan the state-vectors obtained will have that value but then one will be obtained with the value *outstanding*. The structure text, at first sight, is:

```
SELECTION posit (there are no outstanding requests)
  NO-REQUEST-SET set
    i := 2;
    NO-REQUEST-BODY itr while (i ⩽ 6)
      getsv BVE (Ei);
SELECTION quit (outstanding (Ei));
      i := i + 1;
    NO-REQUEST-BODY end
  NO-REQUEST-SET end
SELECTION admit (there is an outstanding request)
  SOME-REQUEST-SET seq
    i := 2;
    FIRST-PART-OF-SCAN itr
      getsv BVE (Ei);
    FIRST-PART-OF-SCAN quit (outstanding (Ei));
      i := i + 1;
    FIRST-PART-OF-SCAN end
    getsv BVE (Ei);
  SOME-REQUEST-SET end
SELECTION end
```

There is a lot of text here that is not needed, because of side-effects. Looking first at the **admit** part, we see that the *getsv* operation at the end of SOME REQUEST SET is not needed: that state-vector has already been obtained by the *getsv* operation in FIRST PART OF SCAN which caused the jump out of that component. Then, looking at both parts of the selection, we see that the remainder of SOME REQUEST SET is not needed either: it has all been already executed as a result of NO REQUEST SET and the jump out of that component. So the final structure text, with the addition of two comments, is:

```
SELECTION posit (there are no outstanding requests)
  NO-REQUEST-SET seq
    i := 2;
    NO-REQUEST-BODY itr while (i ⩽ 6)
      getsv BVE (Ei);
SELECTION quit (outstanding (Ei));
      i := i + 1;
    NO-REQUEST-BODY end
  NO-REQUEST-SET end
  {there is no outstanding request, definitely}
SELECTION admit
  {there is an outstanding request in Ei}
SELECTION end
```

In this case, the side-effects were helpful; when the jump out of NO REQUEST SET takes place, everything that was needed in SOME REQUEST SET has already been

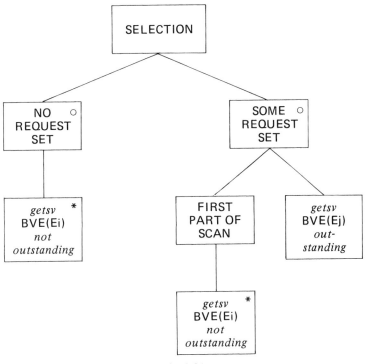

Fig. 9.31

done. There are cases where the side-effects are harmful, and these need very careful treatment; but they do not concern us here.

The essence of backtracking is that some decision has to be made for which the evidence is not available at the right time. We would have liked to write:

WAIT-AT-GROUND **itr while** (no outstanding request)

. . .

WAIT-AT-GROUND **end**

and:

SELECTION **sel** (no outstanding request)

. . .

SELECTION **alt** (at least one outstanding request)

. . .

SELECTION **end**

but the evidence for the conditions was not there at the time the conditions had to be evaluated. So we had to proceed by making an assumption, and abandoning, or quitting, it when it proved wrong.

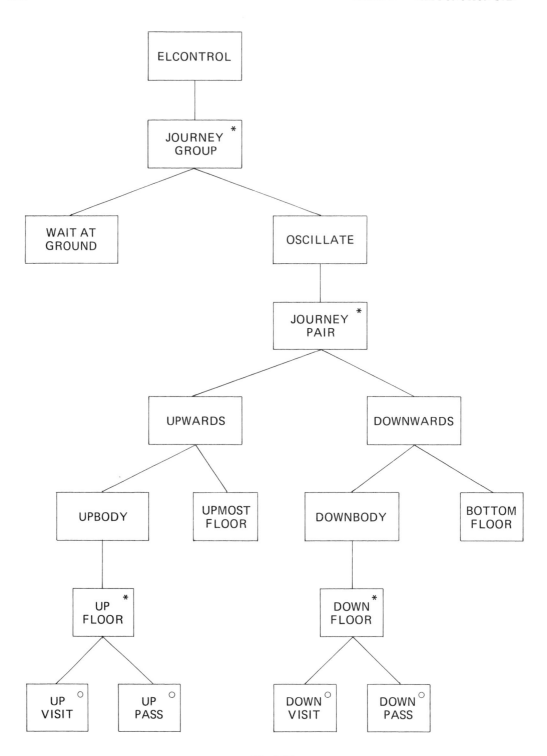

Fig. 9.32

9.13   HI-RIDE ELEVATOR: MAJOR FUNCTIONS—2

A more realistic scheme for controlling the movement of the elevator would be:

— the elevator waits at the ground floor when there are no outstanding requests;

— when travelling, the elevator reverses direction from upwards to downwards when there are no outstanding requests for floors above the floor it has currently reached; it reverses direction from downwards to upwards when there are no outstanding requests for floors below the floor it has currently reached and there is at least one outstanding request for a floor above it, or it has reached the ground.

The structure of ELCONTROL for this scheme is outlined in Fig. 9.32.

UPMOST FLOOR is the highest floor reached in an upwards journey, and BOTTOM FLOOR the lowest floor reached in a downwards journey. The last JOURNEY PAIR in an instance of OSCILLATE is that in which BOTTOM FLOOR is the ground floor for the first time in that OSCILLATE.

Writing summary conditions in the **quit** statements, rather than showing the detailed structure of *getsv* operations, we have the structure text:

```
ELCONTROL itr
  JOURNEY-GROUP seq
    WAIT-AT-GROUND itr
    WAIT-AT-GROUND quit (some outstanding request);
    WAIT-AT-GROUND end
    flr := 1;
    OSCILLATE itr
      JOURNEY-PAIR seq
        UPWARDS seq
          UP; write VISIT to EB (Uflr);
              write VISIT to EB (Eflr);
          START;
          flr := flr + 1;
          UPBODY itr
            UP-FLOOR seq
            read EE;
          UPBODY quit (no reason to go higher);
              getsv BVE (Uflr); getsv BVE (Eflr);
              UP-FLOOR-BODY sel (outstanding (Uflr) or
                                       outstanding (Eflr))
                UP-VISIT seq
                  STOP; write VISIT to EB (Uflr);
                        write VISIT to EB (Eflr);
                  START;
                UP-VISIT end
              UP-FLOOR-BODY alt (else)
              UP-FLOOR-BODY end
              flr := flr + 1;
            UP-FLOOR end
          UPBODY end
```

```
                        UPMOST-FLOOR seq
                            {read EE not needed}
                          STOP; write VISIT to EB (Eflr);
                        UPMOST-FLOOR end
                    UPWARDS end
                    DOWNWARDS seq
                      DOWN;
                      write VISIT to EB (Dflr);
                      START;
                      flr := flr − 1;
                      DOWNBODY itr
                        DOWN-FLOOR seq
                          read EE;
                        DOWNBODY quit (no reason to go lower);
                          getsv BVE (Dflr); getsv BVE (Eflr);
                          DOWN-FLOOR-BODY sel (outstanding (Dflr) or
                                                        outstanding (Eflr))
                            DOWN-VISIT seq
                              STOP; write VISIT to EB (Dflr);
                                      write VISIT to EB (Eflr);
                              START;
                            DOWN-VISIT end
                          DOWN-FLOOR-BODY alt (else)
                          DOWN-FLOOR-BODY end
                          flr := flr − 1;
                        DOWN-FLOOR end
                      DOWNBODY end
                      BOTTOM-FLOOR seq
                          {read EE not needed}
                          STOP; write VISIT to EB (Eflr);
                    OSCILLATE quit (flr = 1);
                        BOTTOM-FLOOR end
                    DOWNWARDS end
                  JOURNEY-PAIR end
                OSCILLATE end
              JOURNEY-GROUP end
          ELCONTROL end
```

The backtracking in this structure text is unavoidable. The UPMOST-FLOOR is different from an UP-FLOOR, if only because the elevator always stops at the UPMOST-FLOOR. But the difference cannot be detected until after execution of the *read* EE operation, since it is not until then that we inspect the button state-vectors. We are therefore compelled to make the assumption that the next floor is an UP-FLOOR, and, after arrival, be prepared to abandon our assumption if it is proved wrong. Exactly similar considerations apply to BOTTOM-FLOOR and DOWN-FLOOR.

The *read* EE operations are not needed in UPMOST-FLOOR and in BOTTOM-

FLOOR because of the side-effects of the preceding **quit** statements jumping out of UPBODY and DOWNBODY respectively.

We have already seen, in the preceding section, the detailed structure of WAIT-AT-GROUND. The **quit** statements for UPBODY and DOWNBODY require some care. We want to jump out of UPBODY if:

— $flr = 6$: this must certainly then be the UPMOST-FLOOR; or
— $flr \neq 6$ and (Uflr not *outstanding*) and (nothing outstanding for any higher floor).

Notice that if Uflr is *outstanding*, we must not jump out of UPBODY. If we do, it will be impossible to summon the elevator from a lower floor, enter, and request it to travel to a higher floor, unless there happens to be a previous request outstanding for a higher floor. The effect of the arrangement we are now specifying is that when the elevator is summoned by an upwards floor button it will always continue up for at least one floor even if no further request is made. Our specification for the jump out of UPBODY is:

```
        UB-JUMP seq
UPBODY quit ( flr = 6);
        UB-OUTSTANDING posit (nothing outstanding for Uflr etc.)
          getsv BVE (Uflr);
        UB-OUTSTANDING quit (outstanding (Uflr));
          getsv BVE (D6);
        UB-OUTSTANDING quit (outstanding (D6));
          getsv BVE (E6);
        UB-OUTSTANDING quit (outstanding (E6));
          higher := flr + 1;
          UB-OUTSTANDING BODY itr while (higher ⩽ 5)
            getsv BVE (Uhigher);
        UB-OUTSTANDING quit (outstanding (Uhigher));
            getsv BVE (Dhigher);
        UB-OUTSTANDING quit (outstanding (Dhigher));
            getsv BVE (Ehigher);
        UB-OUTSTANDING quit (outstanding (Ehigher));
            higher := higher + 1;
          UB-OUTSTANDING-BODY end
    UPBODY quit
        UB-OUTSTANDING admit (something was outstanding)
        UB-OUTSTANDING end
        UB-JUMP end
```

We want to jump out of DOWNBODY if:

— $flr = 1$: this must certainly then be the BOTTOM-FLOOR; or
— $flr \neq 1$ and (Dflr not outstanding) and (nothing outstanding for any lower floor) and (something outstanding for a higher floor).

The second part of the condition is more complex than for the jump out of UPBODY; this is because a positive reason is needed for reversing direction rather than continuing on to the ground floor and ending this JOURNEY GROUP. The detailed specification is left as an entertainment for the reader.

Some readers may feel, not for the first time in this book, that we are immersing ourselves in programming instead of sticking to the higher-level considerations of system development. We do not agree with this view. 'Higher-level' is often a euphemism for 'vague': without the 'lower-level' detail we cannot be sure that the 'higher-level' decisions are right. This is why JSD is not a top-down method. In JSD we separate various concerns in the various development steps; and we can also separate the specification of one function from others based on the same model, much as we can separate the behavior of one entity from the behavior of others. But we do not aim to separate the decision to connect a function process into the SSD from the specification of the detail of that process. By considering the function process in detail now, we are giving ourselves the first opportunity of discovering whether:

—   the function can be unambiguously specified to satisfy the user's requirements;
—   the right set of function processes has been added to the SSD;
—   the function processes have been correctly connected to the model and to each other;
—   the model is adequate to support the specified function.

More generally, we are concerned in JSD with systems in which the ordering of events and actions is a central aspect of the real world and of functions specified on it: we must not regard that ordering as a trivial or unimportant detail.

9.14   HI-RIDE ELEVATOR: MAJOR FUNCTIONS—3

One of our simplifying assumptions has been that there is only one elevator. For an installation with two or more elevators, we will need to make some changes to our system specification.

The SSD shown in Fig. 9.27 is now certainly inadequate; we need at least to modify it to show that the relation between elevator and button is now many-to-many (Fig. 9.33).

There is one ELCONTROL process for each ELEVATOR-1, rather than a single ELCONTROL to control both elevators. The ELCONTROL structure for each elevator will be something like the structure shown in Section 9.11 or in Section 9.13: two such structures cannot be interleaved into a single process structure. There is some limitation on this many-to-many relationship: the buttons E1–E6 for each elevator are connected only to the ELCONTROL process for the elevator in which they are situated. We may therefore wish to show two types of button: elevator buttons and floor buttons. This would be a simple elaboration of the SSD, requiring no change to the specifications of the button processes, and we will not illustrate it explicitly here. As before, the input streams to the BUTTON-2 processes are rough merged; now, for the floor buttons, the rough merge includes the implicit rough merge of the multiple EB input streams from the ELCONTROL processes.

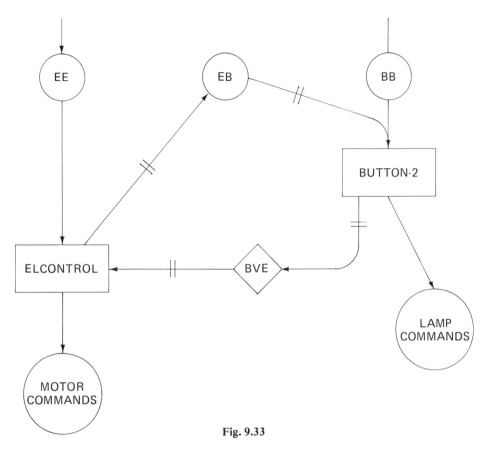

Fig. 9.33

We might choose to leave our specification as it is now. The elevators operate independently; each elevator services the requests made on its own elevator buttons, and any requests it detects on the floor buttons. However, in some circumstances the resulting service will be both expensive and bad. Suppose that in a period of relatively low demand both elevators are waiting at the ground floor. A request is made on the top floor button. Both elevators will detect this request, and both will set off on an upwards journey to service it. If their speeds are approximately the same, and no other request is made at any middle floor, both will travel all the way to the top floor. This is wasteful. If, while they are travelling upwards, a request is made on the ground floor, that request will not be serviced until one of the elevators has made its fruitless journey to the top and back again. This is bad service.

It is desirable, therefore, to introduce some arrangement for avoiding such behavior. One possible arrangement is to switch off one of the elevators manually during periods of low demand. During periods of high demand we may hope that there will be very little waste, since there will usually be several requests outstanding. As in periods of low demand, the elevators will be racing to service those requests, but their journeys will not be fruitless. The different incidence of requests made on the elevator buttons will avoid the synchronization which appeared to be a prime cause of the waste.

Switching off elevators manually is an unattractive solution; we would prefer to tackle the problem differently, specifying our system so that the elevators will behave in a more desirable way. A good solution to the problem would require expertise in an area of mathematical analysis: we would need to study the distribution of service requests and many other aspects of the real world. This area is not the subject of this book, nor is it the direct concern of the system developer; the necessary study and analysis should be done by an appropriate expert. For our present purposes we will be satisfied to consider a possible solution that relies on intuition for the mathematics.

The basic idea of the solution is that an ELCONTROL process can issue a promise to service requests from certain floor buttons. For example, if an elevator is at the ground floor, and a request is made from inside the elevator to travel to floor 4, then the ELCONTROL process for that elevator can promise to service requests for upward travel made on the buttons at floors 2 and 3. Similarly, if it is at floor 6, and a request is made for it to travel to floor 2, its ELCONTROL process can promise to service requests for downward travel made at floors 5, 4, and 3. In deciding whether to service floor button requests which would extend an UPWARDS or DOWNWARDS part of a JOURNEY PAIR, the ELCONTROL process can then ignore requests for which the other elevator has made a promise of service. A promise can be fulfilled either by the elevator on whose behalf it was made or by the other elevator if it happens to reach that floor.

Postponing specification of the rules for making promises, we can see that some structure such as that shown in Fig. 9.34 is needed for each floor button. It will not be

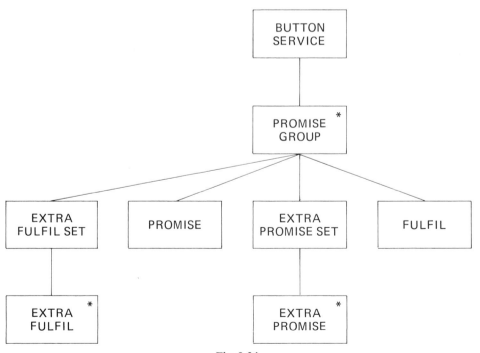

Fig. 9.34

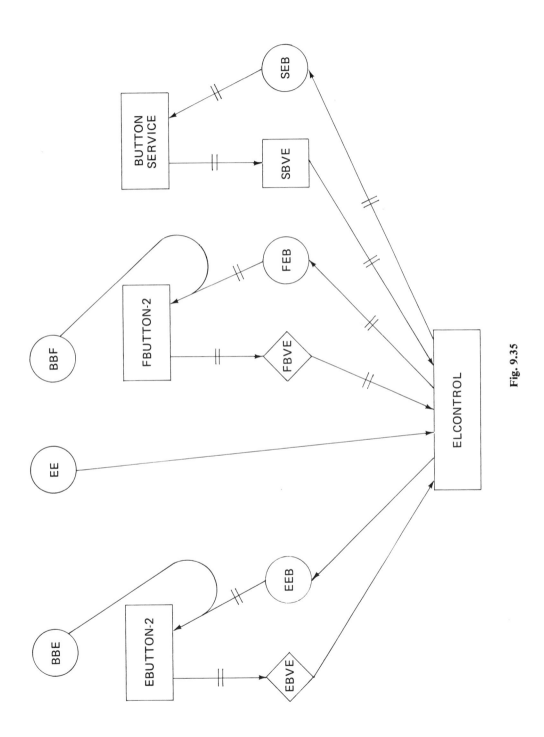

Fig. 9.35

easy to combine this structure with the structure of BUTTON-2 discussed in Section 9.11. A complete PROMISE GROUP can occur without any REQUEST being made; a REQUEST can be followed by a VISIT without any intervening PROMISE. We decide therefore to add BUTTON SERVICE as a separate process type to the SSD. Separating the floor buttons from the elevator buttons, and showing only the button and elevator control processes, we have the partial SSD shown in Fig. 9.35.

The BUTTON SERVICE processes rough merge their SEB input streams; each PROMISE record contains the id of the elevator for which the promise is issued. The EXTRA PROMISE SET and EXTRA FULFIL SET are needed for the same reason as the EXTRA VISIT SET and EXTRA REQUEST SET in the button processes: that is, to simplify the ELCONTROL processes and to take proper account of the rough merge of the input. BUTTON SERVICE maintains a local variable *prom*, which has the value of the id of the elevator for which the PROMISE was issued; we assume that the values of the elevator-ids are assigned so that *prom* = 0 indicates the absence of a promise. The structure text of BUTTON SERVICE is:

```
BUTTON-SERVICE seq
  prom := 0; read SEB&SEB;
  BUTTON-SERVICE-BODY itr
    PROMISE-GROUP seq
      EXTRA-FULFIL-SET itr while (FULFIL)
        read SEB&SEB;
      EXTRA-FULFIL-SET end
      PROMISE seq
        prom := elevator-id of PROMISE;
        read SEB&SEB;
      PROMISE end
      EXTRA-PROMISE-SET itr while (PROMISE)
        read SEB&SEB;
      EXTRA-PROMISE-SET end
      FULFIL seq
        prom := 0;
        read SEB&SEB;
      FULFIL end
    PROMISE-GROUP end
  BUTTON-SERVICE-BODY end
BUTTON-SERVICE end
```

We must now consider the rules to be applied in ELCONTROL to govern the writing of PROMISE and FULFIL records to the SEB data stream and to govern the conditions under which ELCONTROL may ignore an outstanding request.

The rules for writing FULFIL records are obvious. ELCONTROL writes a FULFIL record for a floor button whenever it writes a VISIT record for that button; in addition, it writes a record to the upwards button when it passes an UP-FLOOR, and to the downwards button when it passes a DOWN-FLOOR.

An outstanding request is never ignored by an elevator which is at the requesting floor and travelling in the right direction. The selection conditions on UP-FLOOR-BODY and DOWN-FLOOR-BODY are therefore unaffected. The time to ignore an outstanding request is when it would initiate or extend elevator travel, and a promise for that request has already been issued by the other elevator. The affected components of ELCONTROL are WAIT-AT-GROUND, UB-JUMP (the expansion of the jump out of UP-FLOOR-BODY), and DB-JUMP (the expansion of the jump out of DOWN-FLOOR-BODY). In each of these, requests on floor buttons other than the current floor are ignored if a promise has already been issued by the other elevator. Thus, for example, the text

> *getsv* BVE (Uhigher);
> UB-OUTSTANDING **quit** (*outstanding* (Uhigher));

is replaced by

> *getsv* FBVE (Uhigher); *getsv* SBVE (Uhigher);
> UB-OUTSTANDING **quit** (*outstanding* (Uhigher) **and**
> $\qquad$ (*prom* = 0 **or** *prom* = *this-el-id*));

The writing of PROMISE records to SEB is executed following each of WAIT-AT-GROUND, UB-JUMP, and DB-JUMP. We have to decide whether to issue promises for both directions of travel, or only for the current or imminent direction. For example, following WAIT-AT-GROUND, ELCONTROL may initiate an OSCILLATE because it has detected, and not ignored, a downwards request on floor 5; we have to decide whether to issue promises only for upwards travel requests on floors 1–4, or also for downwards requests on those floors. Clearly a promise must be issued for the downwards request on floor 5, in either case. Since our whole purpose is to reduce the amount of unnecessary elevator travel, we decide to issue the maximum set of promises. Thus, after each of the components WAIT-AT-GROUND, UB-JUMP, and DB-JUMP, we calculate the floor number of the most distant non-ignored request in the direction of current or imminent travel; we then issue promises for all floor button requests at floors between the current floor and that most distant floor, inclusive.

It is not clear that this is a good strategy. If both elevators are waiting at the ground floor, and one then issues both upwards and downwards promises for every floor, a user waiting to go down from floor 2 will have an unnecessarily long wait for service: he will have to wait until the elevator which issued the promises has travelled to the top floor and back to floor 2, although the other elevator is idle during this time. In this book it would not be appropriate to embark on the mathematical analysis (we have already decided against that course), but it is worth pointing out that the system we have specified might serve as the basis for a simulation study. We would need to do the following:

— modify the BUTTON-1 processes so that instead of inspecting the state-vectors of the real buttons they generated statistically suitable patterns of records in the BB data streams;

— modify the ELEVATOR-1 processes so that instead of inspecting the state-vectors of the real elevators they accepted the motor commands produced by ELCONTROL as input and produced, with suitable time lags, ARRIVE(m) records in the EE data streams;

— add one or more function processes to produce whatever analysis of the system behavior is desired.

Simulation of this kind can certainly help to clarify obscure consequences of development decisions, and to allow the developer to experiment with alternative specifications.

However, we have not yet reached the point where either simulation or mathematical analysis is necessary: we can still examine the behavior of our system further by considering the process connections and what they imply.

9.15   SOME INDETERMINACY IN FUNCTION

State-vector connection and rough merging introduce some indeterminacy or looseness into our specification. We rely on an implicit assumption that the eventual implementation will keep this looseness to tolerable levels, that the rough merge will be reasonably fair.

Returning to the SSD shown in Fig. 9.27, we can see what will happen if a rough merge is unreasonably unfair. Suppose that the single elevator travels to floor 4 in response to a request on its elevator button E4. The ELCONTROL process writes a VISIT record to EB for the appropriate floor button on floor 4, and eventually issues the command for the motor to START, causing the elevator to leave the floor. Just as the elevator leaves, a request is made on the floor button, causing a REQUEST record to be written to BB for the BUTTON-2 process. If the rough merge of BB with EB is very unfair, this request record may appear in the merged stream EB&BB before the VISIT record; the request will then appear to have been satisfied, although in fact it was made after the elevator had already begun to leave. From the point of view of the user making the request, the sequence of events is this:

— the user arrives just as the doors are closing, and presses the button in the hope that it will cause the doors to open again;
— the lamp beside the button goes on for a moment, and then goes out again;
— the elevator leaves without the user having been able to get in.

Connoisseurs of elevator behavior will recognize the scenario. They will also recognize the value of the lamp: when the lamp goes out, the user realizes that his request has failed in some way, and presses the button again immediately. Eventually the elevator returns to service this new request.

If the merge is ridiculously unfair, the effect visible to the user will be even more frustrating. Apparently ordinary requests, made when there is no sign of the elevator's presence, will sometimes be treated in the same kind of way: the lamp goes on when the button is pressed, and after a short interval it goes out again without the elevator having come. Advanced connoisseurs of elevator behavior will recognize this scenario too.

This aspect of indeterminacy is considered in the system timing step of JSD development, and we discuss it in the next chapter. For the moment we will set it aside, and turn to another feature of our specification which may prove unsatisfactory in the case of the system with two or more elevators.

9.16   STATE-VECTORS AND MUTUAL EXCLUSION

The pattern of behavior we specified for ELCONTROL, in the parts of its structure associated with WAIT-AT-GROUND, UB-JUMP, and DB-JUMP, was essentially:

(a)   inspect the state-vectors of many button and button service processes;

(b)   jump according to the service requirement detected;

(c)   if service is required, promise service to many button service processes.

Suppose that both elevators are waiting at the ground floor, and a request is made on an upper floor. Then, we hope, only one ELCONTROL process will respond to this request: it detects the request, jumps, and promises service, all before the other ELCONTROL process detects the request. This can happen because there is no synchronization of the COMPLETE SCAN components in the two processes: one is obtaining the state-vector of U5 while the other is obtaining the state-vector of D2; by the time that the second process obtains the state-vector of U5, the first process has already issued its promise to service U5; the second process will then ignore the request on U5.

But the outcome may be quite different. It may be that both processes detect the request before either has had time to issue a promise. They will then both issue promises, of which only one will be effective, and will both set off to service the request. If there is no other request, one of the elevators, whose promise was not effective, will get no further than floor 2: it will determine, in UB-JUMP, that there is no reason to go higher, and will return to the ground floor. Perhaps we can tolerate this behavior, but more probably not.

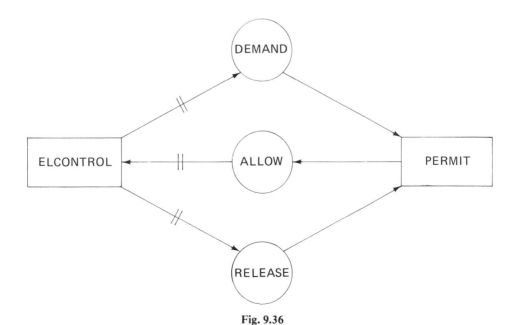

Fig. 9.36

The difficulty can be viewed, and solutions considered, at more than one level. We might decide that we will be satisfied if the bad outcome, where both elevators set off to service the same request, happens only very rarely. This could be achieved by arranging for part (a) of the pattern to be executed very slowly and part (c) very quickly; it would then be highly probable that whichever ELCONTROL process first detected the request would have time to issue its promise before the second process came to inspect the state-vector. Another approach would be to ensure that only one ELCONTROL process could be executing its pattern (a), (b), (c), at any one time: execution of the pattern in the two processes would be mutually exclusive. This approach could guarantee that the bad outcome would never happen.

Mutual exclusion can be specified by introducing a process PERMIT, connected to the ELCONTROL processes by data stream connection. Since we want only one ELCONTROL process to be executing (a), (b), and (c) at one time, we certainly want only one instance of PERMIT (Fig. 9.36). The pattern in each ELCONTROL process would be:

> X **seq**
>   *write* DEMAND;
>   *read* ALLOW;
>   (a), (b), (c);
>   *write* RELEASE;
> X **end**

The multiple DEMAND input streams are rough merged in PERMIT; the RELEASE streams are not. The structure of PERMIT is:

> PERMIT **itr**
>   ONE-PERMISSION **seq**
>   *read* DEMAND;
>   *write* ALLOW (e), *where* DEMAND *was from* ELCONTROL (e);
>   *read* RELEASE (e);
>   ONE-PERMISSION **end**
> PERMIT **end**

Clearly, only one ELCONTROL can be executing (a), (b), (c), at any one time. Having written a DEMAND, ELCONTROL is blocked until the corresponding ALLOW record becomes available.

This is not a complete solution. The mutual exclusion problem is still present at the lower level. It is possible that one ELCONTROL process will promise service to a particular button in its part (c); the process then writes its RELEASE record, and the other ELCONTROL process reads its ALLOW record and begins its part (a). It then gets the state-vector of the button to which the other process has promised service, but the PROMISE record has not yet been read by the button process. To avoid this possibility, we need to replace the state-vector connection between ELCONTROL and the button processes by a tighter synchronization. We need to ensure that there can be no interleaving of pairs of the following sequences of events:

(d)   ELCONTROLi obtains the state-vector of BUTTON-SERVICEj;

(e)   ELCONTROLi writes a PROMISE record to BUTTON-SERVICEj, or indicates positively that it is not doing so (e.g., by writing a NO-PROMISE record);

(f)   BUTTON-SERVICEj reads the PROMISE or NO-PROMISE record written by ELCONTROLi, and updates its state-vector.

The necessary SSD arrangement is much the same as the connection between ELCONTROL and PERMIT, although there are many BUTTON-SERVICE processes and only one PERMIT process (Fig. 9.37). ELCONTROL writes an INSPECT record when it requires to inspect the state-vector of BUTTON SERVICE; BUTTON SERVICE rough merges its INSPECT input streams. For each INSPECT, BUTTON SERVICE writes an appropriate STATE record, and ELCONTROL, having examined the record, writes a REPLY which may be a PROMISE or a NO-PROMISE record. The BUTTON SERVICE process reads the REPLY and updates *prom* before reading the next INSPECT record.

The penalty for tightening up process connection in this way is that there will be less concurrency in the system. Only one ELCONTROL process can be communicating with the button processes at any one time: the other, or others, must wait their turn. In the Hi-Ride Elevator system, we must consider whether the resulting delay to the ELCONTROL processes endangers their ability to respond quickly enough to the ARRIVE(m) records from ELEVATOR-1 processes. We would certainly not want to run the risk that an elevator might have gone too far by the time the STOP command is issued. This consideration might force us to bring forward the decisions embodied in UB-JUMP and DB-JUMP, making them while the elevator is stationary at the preceding floor rather than postponing them until it arrives at the floor itself.

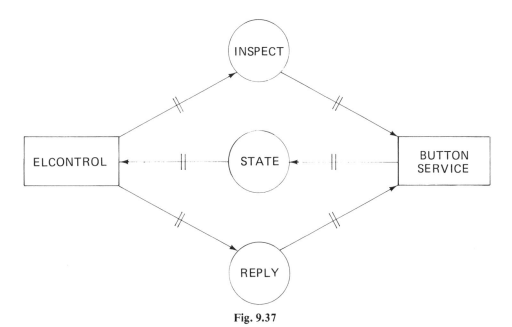

Fig. 9.37

9.17   DELAY TIMING

If the Hi-Ride Company's mechanical engineers are less helpful than we have been assuming them to be, we may require to specify a minimum delay between production of a STOP command to the motor and production of the following START command.

At first sight, it might appear that we need only provide an input stream of TGMs to ELCONTROL. After issuing a STOP, the ELCONTROL process would then count off enough TGMs to ensure the required delay. But this is a poor solution, or no solution at all, for these reasons:

— The TGM records in the input stream would appear continually, whether they were wanted or not. The structure of ELCONTROL would therefore have to be such that the TGMs were read in every part of the structure, and were read very soon after they became available. If TGMs are allowed to accumulate in the input stream buffer, their value as timing indicators is frustrated: for example, if there are 10 TGMs in the buffer, counting off a delay of 10 periods would take much less time than it should.

— If ELCONTROL has any input stream which is not rough merged with the TGM stream, it is not possible for ELCONTROL to read TGMs while it is blocked waiting for that input stream. This would be true, for example, if we made use of the mutual exclusion technique discussed in the preceding section: while ELCONTROL is blocked waiting for a STATE record from the BUTTON SERVICE process, or an ALLOW record from PERMIT, it cannot at the same time be reading TGMs.

Broadly, there are two solutions which provide timing delay within ELCONTROL itself. The first is to provide a CLOCK process, driven by a TGM stream, whose state ELCONTROL inspects when it needs to (Fig. 9.38). The issuing of a STOP command in ELCONTROL may then be:

STOP;
getsv CVE; *stoptime* := *CVEtime*;

The issuing of a START command is preceded by a waiting loop:

getsv CVE;
START-WAIT-LOOP **itr while** (*CVEtime* ⩽ (*stoptime* + *minimum delay*))
   getsv CVE;
START-WAIT-LOOP **end**
START;

The CLOCK process itself is simply:

CLOCK **itr**
   read STGM;
   CVEtime := *TGMtime*;
CLOCK **end**

In this solution, the CLOCK process is available to any process of the system. The second solution provides a timing process dedicated to one ELCONTROL process

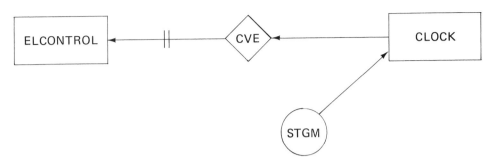

Fig. 9.38

(Fig. 9.39). Each record in the BEGIN data stream is a demand from ELCONTROL to begin a timing period; CLOCK rough merges the BEGIN stream with the STGM stream, and writes an END record when the timing period is completed. The issuing of a STOP command in ELCONTROL is then:

STOP; *write* BEGIN *to* CLOCK;

and the issuing of a START command is:

read END; START;

The CLOCK process is:

```
CLOCK itr
   read BEGIN&STGM;
   CLOCK-GROUP sel (TGM)
   CLOCK-GROUP alt (BEGIN)
     count := min;
     DELAY-BODY itr while (count > 0)
        read BEGIN&STGM;
       count := count − 1;
     DELAY-BODY end
     write END;
   CLOCK-GROUP end
CLOCK end
```

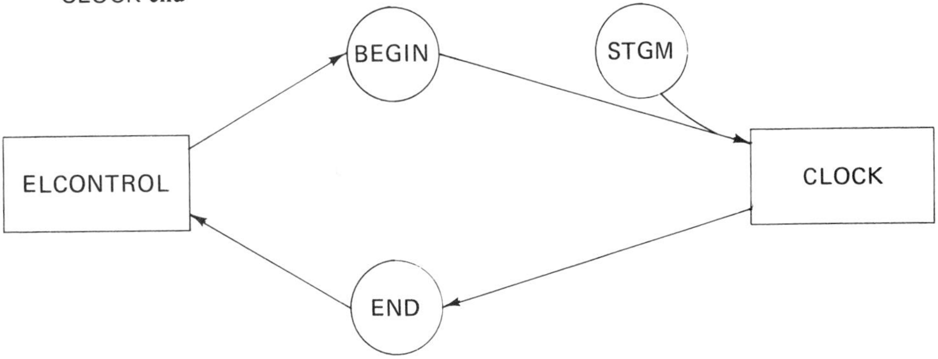

Fig. 9.39

The CLOCK process is dedicated to one ELCONTROL process, and is specified on the assumption that only one delay can be in progress at one time. So when a BEGIN record is read from the rough merged input stream BEGIN&STGM, all following records must be TGMs until after the writing of the corresponding END record.

The advantage of this second solution is that it avoids the 'busy wait' of the first solution. In JSD specifications, this is not really a genuine advantage, since we are imagining that each process has its own processor; there is nothing the ELCONTROL processor can do instead of the 'busy waiting'. The apparent disadvantage of the second solution is that a CLOCK process is needed for each ELCONTROL process. This is inescapable if timing delay in one ELCONTROL process can overlap timing delay in the other.

9.18   WIDGET WAREHOUSE: MAJOR FUNCTIONS—1

We are to specify a function for automatic allocation of stock to outstanding orders. A list is to be produced showing the allocations made and also any delays of orders that cannot be allocated because there is insufficient stock available.

The initial model for the automated version was discussed in Section 8.11 (Fig. 9.40). The clerk does not appear in the model. The purpose of the automation is to replace his activity by the execution of a function process or processes.

Evidently, we will need to have some function process which we may call ALLOCR, which performs the allocation and delay actions previously performed by the clerk. Some immediate questions arise:

— how many ALLOCR processes are there?
— how is an ALLOCR process connected to the ORDER and PRODUCT and, perhaps, CUSTOMER processes?
— what exactly does an ALLOCR process do?
— when does an ALLOCR process do whatever it does?

After some discussion with the manager, we determine that the policy for allocation is to be as follows:

(a)   From the allocation point of view, there is no interchangeability of products: an order for widgets can be satisfied only by widgets.

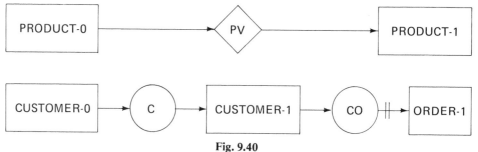

Fig. 9.40

(b) If an order is delayed in one allocation, it must receive a higher priority in the next allocation, to reduce the likelihood of a further delay.

(c) The priority of an order is not affected by what happens to other orders placed by the same customer. An order for gadgets is not given a higher priority because the same customer's order for fidgets has been delayed.

(d) Allocation is to be performed daily, after the completion of the stock file updating by the purchasing and inventory control system.

From these rather vague stipulations it is clear that we need one allocator process for each product. The allocator process must be connected to the PRODUCT-1 process, from which it can obtain information about the availability of stock. It must also be connected interactively to an ORDER-2 process, but there is no reason for it to be connected to CUSTOMER-1 processes. The SSD, with some assumptions about the exact forms of connection, is shown in Fig. 9.41.

Each record of the TA input stream to the ALLOCR process signals that allocation is required for the product handled by that ALLOCR. We have assumed state-vector connection between the ALLOCR and PRODUCT-1 processes, and between the

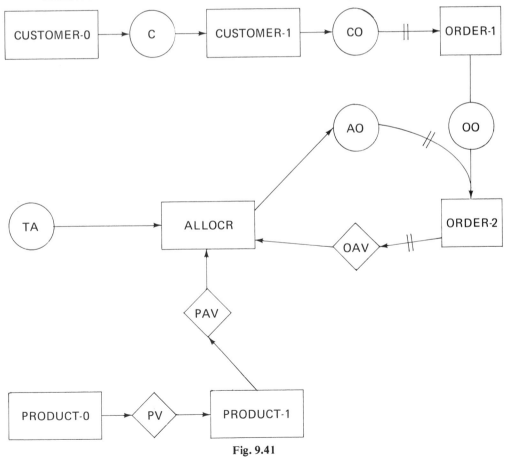

Fig. 9.41

ALLOCR and ORDER-2 processes. The AO data stream contains DELAY and
ALLOCATE records, and is rough merged with the OO data stream for ORDER-2; this
rough merge gives rise to the same structure for ORDER-2 as shown in Appendix D for
ORDER-1.

The detailed structure of ALLOCR will reflect our specification of the allocation
function. Figure 9.42 shows a possible outline structure. When a TA TGM is read,
ALLOCR obtains the state-vector of PRODUCT-1 to determine what stock is available
for allocation. It then obtains the state-vectors of ORDER-2 processes for the product
which are currently due for allocation; first the state-vectors of delayed orders, and then
those of other orders, are obtained. There may be further constraints on the structure of
AGROUP BODY: for example, it may be decided to access state-vectors in descending
order by quantity ordered, within the two groups. The structure of AGROUP BODY,
with the associated notes detailing all the constraints not shown explicitly in the
structure diagram, defines an access path to ORDER-2 state-vectors which will be
important for the database design in the implementation step.

The structure text for ALLOCR is:

```
ALLOCR itr
  AGROUP seq
    read TA;
    getsv PAV; available := quantity in PAV;
    AGROUP-BODY seq
      getsv OAV;
      DELAY-GROUP itr while (DELAYED)
        DELAY-ORDER sel (requested ⩽ available)
          available := available – requested;
          write ALLOCATE to AO (OAV);
        DELAY-ORDER alt (else)
          write DELAY to AO (OAV);
        DELAY-ORDER end
        getsv OAV;
      DELAY-GROUP end
      NORMAL-GROUP itr while (not end-of-OAVs)
        NORMAL-ORDER sel (requested ⩽ available)
          available := available – requested;
          write ALLOCATE to AO (OAV);
        NORMAL-ORDER alt (else)
          write DELAY to AO (OAV);
        NORMAL-ORDER end
        getsv OAV;
      NORMAL-GROUP end
    AGROUP-BODY end
  AGROUP end
ALLOCR end
```

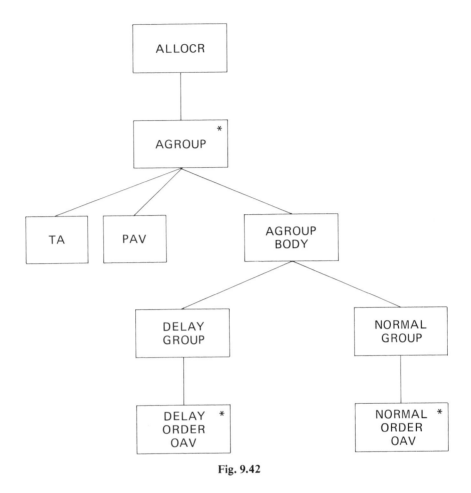

Fig. 9.42

The separation of DELAYed and NORMAL orders is not strictly necessary in ALLOCR as shown above; since the treatment of both groups is the same, they could be regarded as a single group from the point of view of ALLOCR. The structure of the access path, however, must be shown explicitly in some structure diagram produced at this stage.

The looseness of the connection between ALLOCR and ORDER-2 allows, in principle, the following sequence of events:

— ALLOCR obtains the state-vector of the order, and writes an ALLOCATE record to AO;

— before the ALLOCATE record is read by ORDER-2, a CANCEL record is read;

— the ALLOCATE record is therefore a LATE ALLOCATE in the structure shown in Appendix D for ORDER.

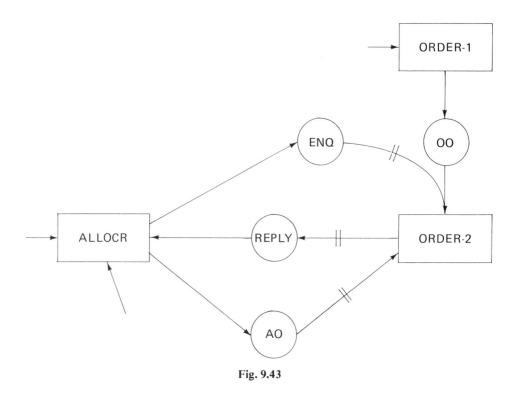

Fig. 9.43

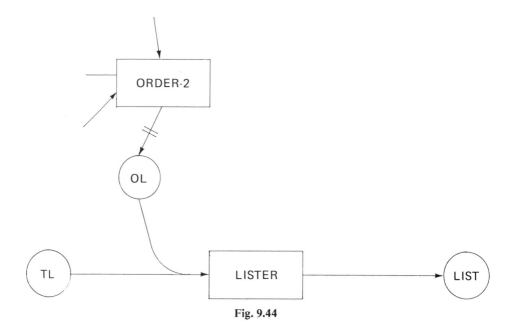

Fig. 9.44

The result of this sequence of events is that stock allocated to the cancelled order will not in fact be delivered to the customer, but is now unavailable for allocation to any other order. We may be willing to accept this possibility if it occurs only infrequently. We may choose to rely on our expectation that allocation will be performed only during times when input from customers is not accepted. We may decide to tighten the connection, as we discussed in the case of the Hi-Ride Elevator system, replacing the state-vector connection OAV by data stream connections. If we make this last choice, the connections will be as shown in Fig. 9.43. The ALLOCR process writes an enquiry record in ENQ, asking what is the quantity requested for allocation. ORDER-2 rough merges the ENQ streams with its OO stream. On reading an ENQ record, it writes a REPLY and then waits for an ALLOCATE or DELAY record in the AO stream. It is thus impossible for an OO record to be read between the ENQ and the AO record; the structure in Appendix D can therefore be simplified by removal of the LATE DELAY SET and POSSIBLE ALLOCATE components.

Notice that the AGROUP-BODY structure in ALLOCR becomes a structure of data

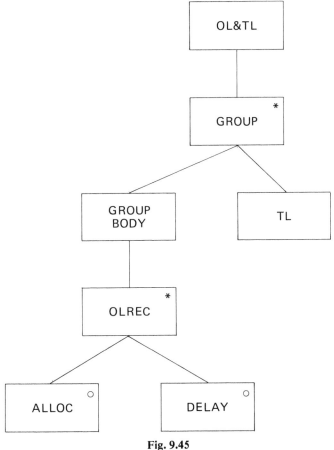

Fig. 9.45

stream rather than state-vector connections. It will, of course, still be important in the implementation step when we consider database design.

The list of allocations and delays presents no new difficulty, but we must determine what its contents should be. The main point to consider is whether it is a list of actions taken by the ALLOCR or a list of actions suffered by the ORDERs. This difference becomes significant when we use the loose connection between the ALLOCR and the ORDER processes, tolerating the possibility that an ALLOCATE or DELAY action by the ALLOCR will prove to be a LATE ALLOCATE or LATE DELAY action for the ORDER. Clearly, if the list is a list of ALLOCR actions, it may be produced by operations embedded in the ALLOCR process; in that case the list will contain effectively the

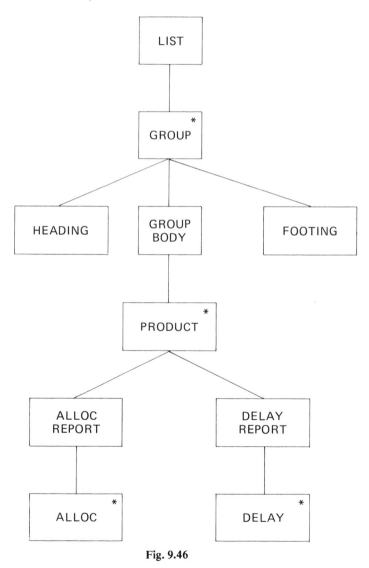

Fig. 9.46

ALLOCATE and DELAY records written by ALLOCR to the AO data streams, with no distinction made (or possible) between ALLOCATE and LATE ALLOCATE or between DELAY and LATE DELAY actions. If the distinction is needed, the list must be produced by operations embedded in the ORDER-2 processes.

If the list is to be in a particular sequence—perhaps in ascending order by product-id—we must add a function process to the system to perform the necessary restructuring of output. This process will require an input stream of TGMs to indicate when a further instalment of the list is needed. The resulting SSD would include the structure shown in Fig. 9.44.

The LISTER process rough merges its inputs OL and TL. The structure of the merged input stream OL&TL is shown in Fig. 9.45. The structure of LIST is perhaps as shown in Fig. 9.46.

There is a standard form of structure clash between the structures of OL&TL and LIST: it is an ordering clash. Within each GROUP the ALLOC and DELAY records are differently ordered, although the GROUPs correspond perfectly. The OL&TL input for one GROUP must therefore be read before GROUP BODY for that GROUP in LIST can be started.

9.19   WIDGET WAREHOUSE: MAJOR FUNCTIONS—2

We have been assuming that allocation will be performed only once each day, after the stock file is updated by the other system. We were therefore able to use a very simple connection between the ALLOCR and PRODUCT-1 processes. We assumed that when a TA record is read by ALLOCR, the following *getsv* PAV operation will obtain a state-vector of PRODUCT-1 showing a fresh quantity of stock available for allocation.

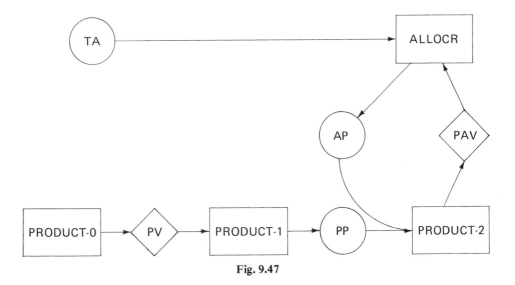

Fig. 9.47

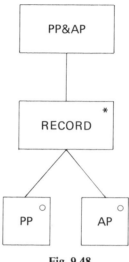

Fig. 9.48

We are now required to permit allocation to be performed on demand for individual products. It is therefore possible for more than one allocation to intervene between one AVAIL action of PRODUCT-1 and the next. The connection between ALLOCR and PRODUCT-1 must take account of this. We may specify ALLOCR as an interacting function with respect to the PRODUCT model process (Fig. 9.47).

PRODUCT-2 is connected to PRODUCT-1 by a data stream PP, each record of which indicates a fresh availability of stock. This data stream PP is rough merged with the stream AP, each record of which indicates the total amount allocated by ALLOCR in one instance of AGROUP. As before, ALLOCR obtains the state-vector of PRODUCT before beginning an allocation group. The structure of PRODUCT-2 is based on the structure of the merged stream PP&AP (Fig. 9.48).

The structure text of PRODUCT-2 is:

```
PRODUCT-2 seq
   quantity := 0;
   read PP&AP;
   PRODUCT-2-BODY itr
      PRODUCT-2-RECORD sel (PP record)
         quantity := quantity in PP record;
      PRODUCT-2-RECORD alt (AP record)
         quantity := quantity-allocated;
      PRODUCT-2-RECORD end
      read PP&AP;
   PRODUCT-2-BODY end
PRODUCT-2 end
```

The separation of PRODUCT-2 from ALLOCR essentially allows the consumption of available product (by the ALLOCR) and its replenishment (by the arrival of PP records) to proceed independently. If the number of outstanding orders for a product is likely to be large, then the time taken by the ALLOCR to deal with one TA record will be correspondingly large: it may then be right for the ALLOCR to be specified so that it obtains the PRODUCT-2 state-vector and writes an AP record for each order allocated.

There is a potentially dangerous indeterminacy in the connection between the ALLOCR and PRODUCT-2 processes: it is possible for successive *getsv* PAV operations in ALLOCR to occur so close together that the AP record written by ALLOCR between these operations has not been read by PRODUCT-2 in time to update its variable quantity for the second *getsv*. ALLOCR would then be able, following the second *getsv* operation, to allocate more stock than is in fact available. Another, less dangerous, possibility is that PRODUCT-2 may favor PP in its rough merge: an AP record that should have been deducted from the availability in one PP record may then be deducted instead from the next. If these indeterminacies are regarded as serious (the decision will depend on likely implementation characteristics in relation to likely frequency and timing of TA and PP records), a tighter synchronization between ALLOCR and PRODUCT-2 could be specified.

9.20 *DAILY RACKET*: **MAJOR FUNCTIONS—1**

Sir Cunning has asked us—and Sir Cunning's requests are not easily refused—to provide the following functions:

— a list of entries to be judged by the panel in each session, ensuring that there is no more than one entry from any reader and no entry from a reader who has already won a prize;
— a report on the activity of the panel, showing in particular whether they have awarded a prize to any reader who had no entry in the list (Sir Cunning combines a suspicious nature with his other qualities).

To provide these functions we will certainly need a function process to gather the entries from the readers for inclusion in the list, and a model process for reader which takes account of prize wins. Looking first at the READER process, we require the SSD shown in Fig. 9.49, where the WF data stream contains information about whether an entry by

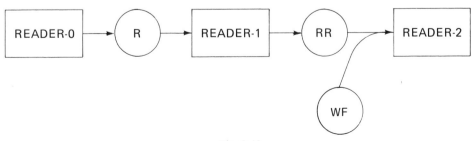

Fig. 9.49

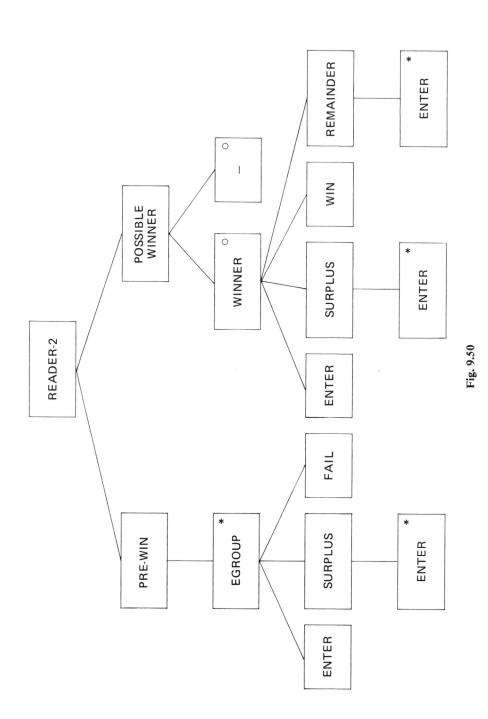

Fig. 9.50

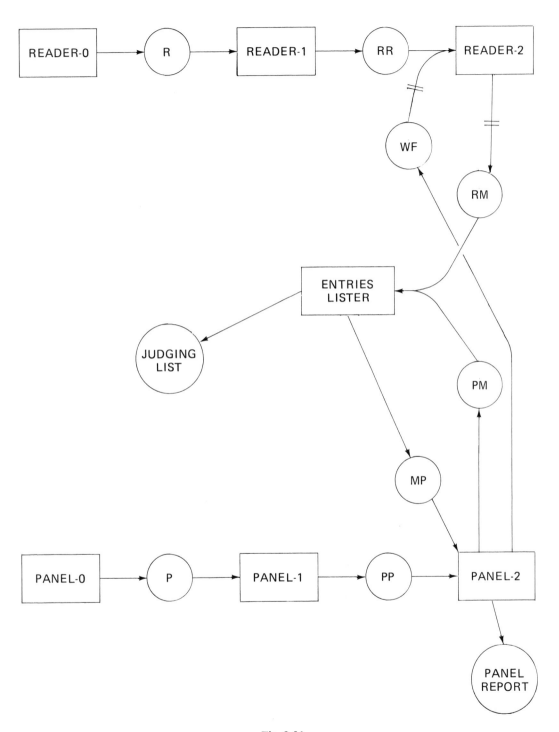

Fig. 9.51

the reader which has been included in the list has or has not won a prize. The structure of READER-2 may be as in Fig. 9.50.

The FAIL records in WF are introduced because we anticipate the need for a positive indication that an ENTER has been judged but not awarded a prize: compare the NO-PROMISE record in the REPLY stream between ELCONTROL and BUTTON-SERVICE in Section 9.16. The data stream RR contains only ENTER records; the SUBSCRIBE record in R is not written to RR. Only the first ENTER in each EGROUP is written to the list for judging; the ENTERs in SURPLUS and in REMAINDER are ignored. The data streams WF and RR are rough merged; but we are assuming, and will later need to ensure, that a FAIL or WIN record can appear in WF only after an ENTER has occurred in EGROUP. The iteration PRE-WIN is terminated by a **quit** when a WIN record appears. The ENTER and SURPLUS parts of WINNER will not be needed in the structure text, because of side-effects of the partially executed EGROUP which was ended by the WIN.

The complete SSD may be as in Fig. 9.51. PANEL-2 is a model of the panel which takes account of the entries submitted by readers. Its input stream PP is a copy of the stream P, signalling the MEET, AWARD, and DISPERSE actions of the panel. The input stream MP is a copy of the JUDGING LIST. It has the structure shown in Fig. 9.52.

Informally, the behavior of PANEL-2 is as follows. When the panel meets, PANEL-2 receives the SESSION SUBLIST and the AWARD records; it writes the PANEL REPORT, and also a WIN or FAIL record in WF for each SUBMITted entry. (We have not yet determined how the report is constructed, or how the AWARD and SUBMIT records are brought together.) The output stream PM contains a record for each MEET action of the panel.

The ENTRIES LISTER receives entries from the READER-2 processes in the input stream RM. These are output to the JUDGING LIST and to the MP stream, and each sublist is ended when a MEET record is received in the rough merged input RM&PM. The structure text of ENTRIES LISTER is:

```
ENTRIES-LISTER seq
   read RM&PM;
   ENTRIES-LISTER-BODY itr
      SUBLIST seq
         SUBLIST-BODY itr while (ENTER)
            write ENTER to JUDGING LIST;
            write ENTER to MP;
            read RM&PM;
         SUBLIST-BODY end
         PANEL-MEETS seq
            write SUBLIST-END to JUDGING-LIST;
            write SUBLIST-END to MP;
            read RM&PM;
         PANEL-MEETS end
      SUBLIST end
   ENTRIES-LISTER-BODY end
ENTRIES-LISTER end
```

The structure text of READER-2 is:

```
READER-2 seq
  read RR&WF;
  PRE-WIN itr
    EGROUP seq
      write ENTER to RM;
      read RR&WF;
      SURPLUS itr while (ENTER)
        read RR&WF;
      SURPLUS end
    PRE-WIN quit (WIN);
      read RR&WF;
    EGROUP end
  PRE-WIN end
  POSSIBLE-WINNER sel (not end-of-RR&WF input)
    WINNER seq
      {ENTER and SURPLUS not needed}
      read RR&WF;
      REMAINDER itr while (not end-of-RR&WF input)
        read RR&WF;
      REMAINDER end
    WINNER end
  POSSIBLE-WINNER alt (end-of-RR&WF input)
  POSSIBLE-WINNER end
READER-2 end
```

In the specification of READER-2 we have assumed that the entry to be submitted for judging, by being written to the RM output stream, is the first ENTER in EGROUP rather than some other ENTER. We might have been required to submit the last entry before the panel next meets, or the entry with the lowest ranking value, or the entry satisfying some other criterion. This would have made the specification considerably more difficult. By taking the first entry, we have been able to ignore the panel sessions entirely in READER-2. We may describe the behavior of READER-2 informally as follows. The first ENTER is submitted for judging in the next session. It may be submitted for that session, or it may be too late, depending on the specification of the ENTRIES LISTER. After READER-2 has made the submission, it ignores all subsequent entries until the result of the submitted entry is known to be WIN or FAIL. When a FAIL result is received, the very next ENTER is submitted, and again READER-2 waits for the result, ignoring subsequent entries until the result is received. A WIN result causes all subsequent entries to be ignored. If the ENTRIES LISTER is very perverse, it may delay a submitted entry indefinitely; this will merely cause READER-2 to continue ignoring entries, while it waits for the indefinitely postponed result. READER-2 relies on the behavior of other processes in the system only to the extent that it requires a WIN or FAIL to appear in RR&WF only after READER-2 has submitted an entry for which a WIN or FAIL has not previously been received.

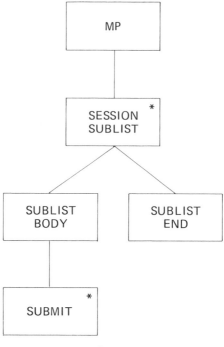

Fig. 9.52

9.21 *DAILY RACKET*: **MAJOR FUNCTIONS—2**

We still have to consider the specification of PANEL-2, the process which models the panel's behavior, including its treatment of submitted entries which are not awarded prizes.

We may be in a position to constrain the real world panel in the order of its consideration of the submitted entries in the judging list. For example, we might arrange that the judging list is displayed on a video terminal in the panel's meeting room; as each entry is displayed, the panel decides whether or not to award a prize to that entry, and indicates its decision by pressing a function key on the terminal. Pressing the key to indicate an award causes an AWARD record to be created in the P input stream. When all the entries have been considered and judged in this way, the DISPERSE key is pressed to signal the end of the session.

If the panel conducts its judging in this computer-assisted way, we can be quite sure that the AWARD records in P and in PP are the same order as the SUBMIT records in the JUDGING LIST and in MP. Sir Cunning's suspicions that the panel might award a prize to a reader who has not submitted an entry would, of course, be entirely unfounded: they would have no means of doing so. The structure of PANEL-2 would then be composed from the data stream structures in the simplest JSP manner, with no structure clash. This structure is shown in Fig. 9.53, omitting the PANEL REPORT. The

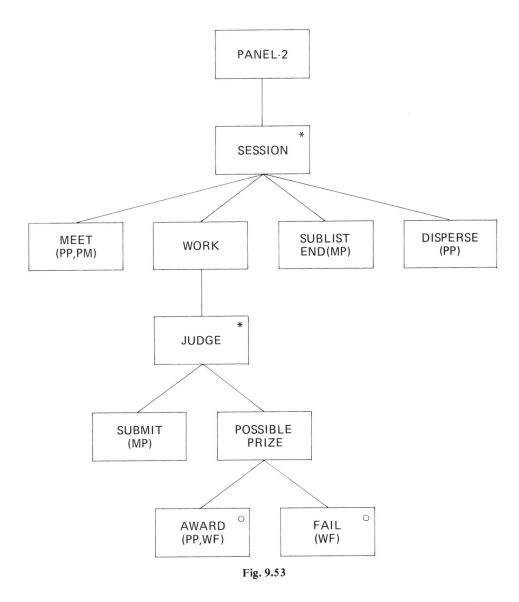

Fig. 9.53

AWARD and FAIL output records are written to the WF stream with the identifier of the reader which appeared in the preceding SUBMIT record. It is this identifier which allows SUBMIT and AWARD records to be associated: there can be only one SUBMIT from any reader because that is guaranteed by the specification of the READER-2 process.

If we cannot constrain the real world panel, we are laboring under the disadvantage of knowing nothing of the order in which they do their judging. There is then an ordering clash between the AWARD contents of PP and the SUBMIT contents of MP in each session. Since we are no longer attempting to model the order within one session of the panel's actions, we may reasonably choose the most convenient way of

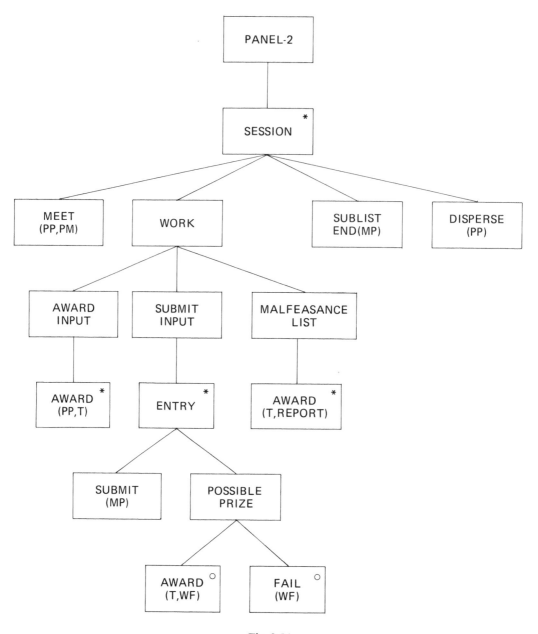

Fig. 9.54

bringing the AWARD and SUBMIT records together. There are relatively few AWARDs; we may therefore store the AWARDs in a table, and access them by reader-id as the SUBMIT records are read. Any AWARD unaccounted for when the SUBMIT records are exhausted is either an error due to the input subsystem or an attempt at malfeasance by the panel. The structure of PANEL-2 would then be as in Fig. 9.54. The annotation

(T) refers to the table in which AWARD records are stored. The AWARD records corresponding to SUBMIT records are marked in the table; the MALFEASANCE LIST contains those AWARDs remaining unmarked.

9.22 ATTRIBUTES

From time to time in this and previous chapters we have referred to attributes of entities and of actions. Our chief purpose in making these references has been to allay fears that a central topic in some approaches to database design might pass without comment.

Attributes are a vexed topic, raising a variety of awkward questions. If 'shoe size' is an attribute of 'person', can 'size' also be an attribute of 'shoe'? If 'subscribing' is an attribute of 'reader', is 'has submitted an entry but not yet received the result' also an attribute of 'reader'? Is 'located inside elevator 2' an attribute of 'button'? Is 'between floors' an attribute of 'elevator'? Is 'husband's date of birth' an attribute of 'woman'? William Kent, in *Data and Reality*, published by North Holland, writes:

> But as common as the term 'attribute' may be, I don't know what it means. The fact that I've been using the term is totally irrelevant.

Attribute is not a JSD term, so we are not concerned to answer the general question 'what is an attribute?' We are concerned, in this section, to discuss briefly the origins, updating, and use of local variables in processes.

The local variables of a process become available to other processes only by state-vector inspection. In Section 8.7 we mentioned the restriction which applies to state-vector inspection: the value obtained by a *getsv* operation is always the value at a point in the text at which a *read*, *write*, or *getsv* operation appears. We can always, therefore, associate a state-vector value, and hence a value of any local variable of a process, with a particular node, usually a leaf, of its structure.

The one local variable which must appear in every state-vector is the process text pointer, indicating where the process has reached in executing its text. The text pointer provides the answer to questions of the forms 'what was the last action?', and 'has such-and-such happened yet?' For example, in the Widget Warehouse automated system, the ALLOCR process needs to obtain the state-vectors of ORDER-2 processes which are DELAYed. The question whether a particular ORDER is DELAYed is to be answered in terms of the text pointer of the process which models it. Assuming the structure of ORDER given in Appendix D, we have:

```
ORDER seq
    read AO&OO; _ _ _ _ _ _ _ _ _ _ _ _ (1)
    PLACE; read AO&OO; _ _ _ _ _ _ _ _ (2)
    ORDER-BODY itr while (AMEND or DELAY)
        OBODY-ACTION sel (AMEND)
            AMEND; read AO&OO;  _ _ _ _ _ (3)
        OBODY-ACTION alt (DELAY)
            DELAY; read AO&OO; ._ _ _ _ _ _ (4)
    . . .
```

The order is delayed if its text pointer, when the state-vector is obtained, points to the *read* AO&OO operation immediately following the action DELAY; the process is then blocked, waiting for the next event following a DELAY. If we consider the values of the text pointer to be numbered sequentially in the text, from beginning to end, then 'this order is delayed' is equivalent to 'the text pointer of this ORDER process has the value 4'.

It will always be convenient and preferable to introduce a local variable purely for the purpose of making the text pointer value more directly intelligible and less dependent on the whole of the process structure. The variable 'outstanding', which we introduced into the BUTTON process in the Hi-Ride Elevator system, was of this kind: instead of using the condition '*text-pointer* (Uflr) = *x or y or z*', the ELCONTROL process was able to use the much more convenient condition '*outstanding* (Uflr)'.

Some local variables arise from the need to compute values for specific function output. For example, the variable *amendcount* for a Widget Warehouse order arose from the need to produce the output for Function 2. Its value indicates whether the order has been amended 0, 1, or more times in the current week. Similarly, the CLOCK process described in Section 9.17 contains a variable *count*; when the associated elevator is stationary at a floor, the value of this variable is the number of time units still to elapse before the earliest time at which the elevator can start again.

Significantly, these variables are specialized in their meaning and use. Variables of more general utility arise from the provision of enquiry functions. The RDRENQS function specified in Section 9.7 requires a count variable in READER-1 whose value is the number of entries made by the reader since becoming a subscriber. Clearly, it is possible, and commonplace, to anticipate general categories of enquiry function, and hence to provide many local variables of general utility.

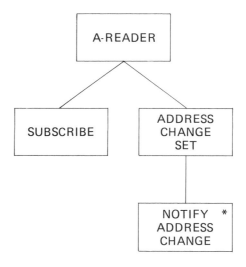

Fig. 9.55

All of the variables discussed so far are associated with the execution of the process text, modelling the actions performed and suffered by the corresponding real world entity. We may also need to introduce variables which become part of the process state-vector but are not associated with execution of its text, and are not updated by the entity's actions. These variables may be needed for various purposes. The name and address of a *Daily Racket* reader is needed so that the entry acknowledgement can be correctly addressed for the mail. The date of birth of an employee may be needed for government reports or because pay rates depend on age. Such variables are characterized by the fact that the changes in their values are outside the model boundary, and are not coordinated with the entity actions. For example, if a *Daily Racket* reader changes address, we would probably decide not to discuss the question whether the entry acknowledgement should be sent to the address from which the entry was made or to the address at which the reader is now resident. In effect, we are regarding the reader as having an additional structure which we have chosen not to show explicitly (Fig. 9.55).

The first value of the attribute ADDRESS is an attribute of the SUBSCRIBE action, common to READER and to A-READER. Later actions of A-READER are entirely uncoordinated with those of READER. The process A-READER will usually degenerate in the implementation into no more than a local variable of READER, because there are no functions dependent on the value of its text-pointer and no connections to it except for inspections of its only other local variable, ADDRESS.

If this rather high-handed approach to the reader's address is not acceptable, we must go back to the earliest specification steps and treat NOTIFY ADDRESS CHANGE as an explicit action of READER; the ordering of this new action in relation to other actions must be carefully considered, and we can then specify functions which take account of this ordering.

It must not be supposed that everything which might be called an attribute of an entity will appear as a local variable of that entity's model process. For example, 'having made a promise to service a particular button' might be called an attribute of an elevator, but we would look in vain for any local variable in ELEVATOR or ELCONTROL corresponding to this attribute. In this case, we might find a relevant variable in the BUTTON process, but even that might not be possible.

Summarizing, we may say that in JSD we are not concerned with entity attributes, but with local variables of the sequential processes which model entities. These local variables arise in the specification from different sources:

— the text-pointer is implicit in the level-1 process structure;
— a more convenient form of the text-pointer may be made for each distinct purpose that it serves for connected function processes;
— attributes of the most recent instance of an action type may be held as local variables;
— summaries of past actions may be computed for purposes of connected function processes.

Questions that might otherwise be phrased in terms of entity attributes are instead to be phrased in terms of process local variables.

SUMMARY OF CHAPTER 9

Functions are added to the system in the form of function processes. Function processes receive inputs from the model processes and, in some cases, from extraneous data streams. Different forms of connection are suitable to different function specifications. Sometimes information flows from a function to a model process (9.1).

Functions are always processes, with long lifetimes. Model processes may not be structurally elaborated; instead, a new, level-2, model is made. Model text-pointers are not directly inspected. The initiative in communication is a strong guide to choosing between data stream and state-vector connection (9.2).

Simple embedded functions produce output directly by operations in model processes, with no separate function process (9.3, 9.4).

Where outputs are gathered from model processes for periodic reporting, the function process may rough merge its inputs. The resulting indeterminacy in the output is fully acceptable (9.5).

Two simple functions for the Widget Warehouse system require level-2 models of the ORDERs (9.6).

Even a simple imposed function, inspecting model processes' state-vectors, must be a process, not a procedure. In the function step, we assume that any necessary access paths to state-vectors are available; in the implementation step we may later need to take a different view. Even assuming access paths to state-vectors, a function process may need to restructure its model input to produce its specified outputs (9.7–9.10).

In the Hi-Ride Elevator system, controlling the elevator, even in a very simple way, is an interacting function. A level-2 BUTTON model is required to take account of output from the function process which issues commands to the elevator motor (9.11).

A more realistic way of controlling the elevator requires the developer to use backtracking technique in the specification. **Quit** statements jump out of structure components: they are a limited form of GO TO statement (9.12, 9.13).

Aiming to provide a better service to users of the elevators, the developer is led to consider mathematical analysis of the real world, but this is not a part of JSD. A JSD system can be used for statistical simulation with very little change (9.14).

Various other topics arise in the Hi-Ride Elevator system. Rough merging causes a familiar indeterminacy; questions of mutual exclusion occur in specifying state-vector inspection; treatment of delay timing leads naturally to the introduction of local or global clock processes (9.15–17).

Automatic allocation of stock to orders, in the Widget Warehouse system, requires an interacting function process, ALLOCR, for each product, which interacts with a level-2 model of each order for that product. Some indeterminacy in the interaction can be removed by a tighter synchronization using data stream connection in place of state-vector connection. If allocation can be performed on demand, it is necessary to introduce a level-2 model of PRODUCT, with which the ALLOCR process interacts (9.18, 9.19).

Generating lists of *Daily Racket* entries and reports on the judging panel's activities are the major functions for this system. The chief new feature in this specification is that a level-2 model of the judging panel is made which performs the same actions as the real world panel but not necessarily in the same order (9.20, 9.21).

Attributes of entities are not considered directly in JSD development. Instead, we are concerned with local variables of processes. These local variables may be derived from the process text-pointer, from action attributes, or from summaries of action attributes; for the most part, they are specified to meet functional requirements (9.22).

10

The system timing step

10.1 TIMING AND THE SPECIFICATION

The system timing step is interposed between the function and implementation steps. In the system timing step the developer considers, or reconsiders, the timing constraints which must be satisfied by the implementation if the system is to do what is required. These constraints are collected together and documented before the implementation step is begun. In some cases, they will lead to a change in the specification or to a more exact specification of some rough merges.

Timing constraints may include such requirements as these:

— certain system outputs must be produced within a limited time following the arrival of the inputs from which they are derived;
— level-1 processes which are connected to their level-0 real world entities by state-vector connection must execute *getsv* operations with a certain minimum frequency;
— model processes whose state-vectors are inspected by function processes must be sufficiently up to date when their state-vectors are obtained;
— model processes whose state-vectors are inspected by processes of the input subsystem must be sufficiently up to date;
— TGM records must be read within a certain time after they are written;
— certain pairs of processes in which the output of one is rough merged with other input streams by the other must be more tightly synchronized than is already specified.

As presented here, the documentation of timing constraints is entirely informal in most cases. In one case, discussed in detail in this chapter, the constraint is expressed as a change to the specification; but for the most part, the result of the timing step is a set of informal notes to be referred to during the implementation step.

10.2 IMPLEMENTATION FREEDOM

A JSD specification says nothing explicit about the speed of execution of the system. In principle, we can imagine each process of the system executing at an arbitrary varying speed. This speed can even be reduced to zero for some periods, although we are assuming that over a long period the average speed of each process will be sufficient to allow it to keep up with the real world events.

In Section 9.6 we specified two functions of the Widget Warehouse system. The relevant part of the SSD for the function F1 is shown in Fig. 10.1. The F1 REPORT contains a message for each occasion on which the order is amended for the second or further time without any delay action having intervened. The data stream OF1 which connects the two processes ORDER-1 and F1-ORDER-2 contains a record for each delay and each amend action of the order. We may imagine that the ORDER-1 process runs continuously, stopping only when blocked waiting for input, but that the F1-ORDER-2 process runs spasmodically, its speed rising above zero only for a period of a few seconds every week. Or we may imagine that both processes run continuously; or that both run spasmodically.

The freedom to imagine these different patterns of process speed is an important freedom for the implementation step. What we have called spasmodic running is essentially the pattern that results from a batch implementation. If we run the ORDER-1 process on-line and the F1-ORDER-2 process in a weekly batch run, we will have implemented continuous running for the one and spasmodic running for the other. If we run them both on-line, we will have implemented continuous running for both.

This implementation freedom reflects the nature of our specification. By using buffered data streams in the specification, we have been able to avoid over-specifying the execution characteristics of the system. But it may be that we have slightly under-specified, by omitting to say anything about the urgency of the F1 REPORT. We correct this omission in the system timing step. After consultation with the user, we ma describe the additional constraint in any suitable way. For example, we may say that each message of the F1 REPORT must be output no later than one day after the amendment which caused it is received at the system boundary. This is, of course, a constraint on the speeds of both processes, ORDER-1 and F1-ORDER-2, and on the buffering of all four data streams.

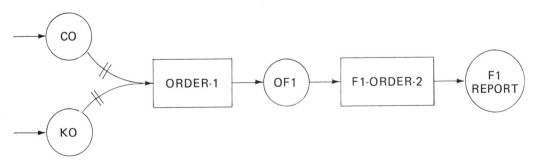

Fig. 10.1

There is still a considerable implementation freedom left to us. We can still choose to run both processes on-line, to run ORDER-1 on-line and F1-ORDER-2 in a daily evening batch run, to run both processes in two daily batch runs, morning and evening, or any of a large number of other possibilities. But we have certainly excluded those implementations which run either of the processes in a weekly batch, since such implementations could not satisfy the timing constraints.

10.3   STATE-VECTOR CONNECTION TO LEVEL-0

In Section 8.8 we specified an initial model for the Hi-Ride Elevator system in which state-vector connection was used, perforce, between the buttons and the processes which model them:

The actions of BUTTON-0 are DEPRESS and RELEASE, with obvious meaning; the values of the state-vector of BUTTON-0 are OPEN (initially, and following a RELEASE) and CLOSED (following a DEPRESS).

BUTTON-1 must inspect the state-vector of BUTTON-0 sufficiently frequently for the connection to be satisfactory. We can estimate the sufficient frequency by considering the length of time for which BUTTON-0 remains in each state. Suppose that we determine that we expect the user of the button to hold it down for not less than 20 milliseconds; if the button is depressed and released more quickly than this, we do not promise that the actions will be detected by BUTTON-1. It is therefore necessary for BUTTON-1 to inspect the state-vector of BUTTON-0 at least once in every 20 milliseconds, and BUTTON-1 must run fast enough for this to be done.

We chose to consider the requirement for detecting the DEPRESS action, which gives rise to the CLOSED state, rather than the RELEASE action, which gives rise to the OPEN state. This was because our experience of pressing buttons tells us that the CLOSED state is likely to persist for a much shorter time than the OPEN state. Strictly, we should consider all the actions to which they give rise, and base the frequency of state-vector inspection on the state of shortest duration.

In addition to requiring that no DEPRESS action should go undetected by BUTTON-1, we may also be interested in the time that can elapse between the real world action taking place and its detection in the model. If we consider that the DEPRESS action takes place at the moment when the state changes from OPEN to CLOSED, we can say that the action will be detected within 20 milliseconds at most. Thus, if BUTTON-1 writes an output data stream containing one record for each detected DEPRESS action, we can say that the record will be written within $20 + x$ milliseconds of the action occurring, where x milliseconds is the time elapsing between detection of the DEPRESS and writing of the record. This is of little importance in the present example, but the Hi-Ride Elevator system furnishes another example in which it matters greatly.

10.4   A MORE DEMANDING EXAMPLE

Part of the SSD for the Hi-Ride Elevator system with the major functions added is shown in Fig. 10.2. The state-vector connection between ELEVATOR-0 and ELEVATOR-1 is provided by inspection of the sensors at each floor. When the elevator comes within 15 centimeters of its home position at a floor, the associated sensor changes state from NAT to AT; in this way, ELEVATOR-1 detects the actions ARRIVE and LEAVE of ELEVATOR-0.

The elevator travels at a speed of 0.5 meters per second; it will therefore reach the home position in 0.3 seconds after the sensor changes state to AT. If the elevator is to stop at the floor, the following things must all happen within this time:

— ELEVATOR-1 must detect that the elevator has arrived;
— the ARRIVE record in EE must be written and read;
— ELCONTROL must execute various *getsv* and *write* operations on BVE and EB;
— ELCONTROL must write STOP to MOTOR COMMANDS;
— the motor must receive the STOP command and stop soon enough to allow the elevator to decelerate to rest at the home position.

ELEVATOR-1 must inspect the state of the sensors often enough to ensure that its contribution to the total delay is acceptably small. Clearly, the required frequency cannot be determined without considering all the components of the delay; clearly, too, it must be very much higher than is needed purely for detection of the ARRIVE action.

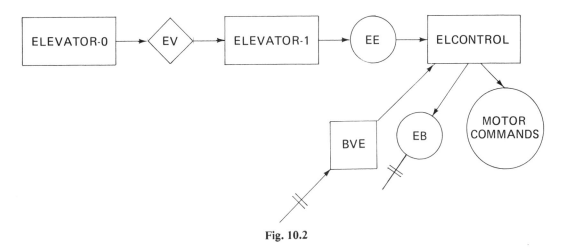

Fig. 10.2

10.5   HOW UP TO DATE IS THE MODEL?

An *ad hoc* enquiry process is usually connected to the model processes by state-vector connection. Figure 10.3 shows the SSD of a system with bank customers, accounts, and an enquiry function process.

Enquiry inputs can arrive for the function process ENQRY at any time between 9 a.m. and 5 p.m. The following connected questions arise:

— how soon is the output of the enquiry needed?
— how up to date must the information be?

There are many possible answers to these questions:

— the output is needed immediately (say, within 2 seconds) and the information must be up to date at least to a point 3 seconds before the enquiry was made;
— the output is needed immediately, and the information must be up to date at least to 5 p.m. on the previous day;
— the output is not needed until 9 a.m. on the following day, and the information must be up to date at least to a point 3 seconds before the enquiry was made and no further;
— the output is not needed until 9 a.m. on the following day, and the information must be up to date to 5 p.m. on the day the enquiry was made;
— the output is needed immediately; the customer information must be up to date to a point 3 seconds before the enquiry was made, but the account information need only be up to date to 5 p.m. on the previous day.

The answers given will constrain the running requirements of all three process types.

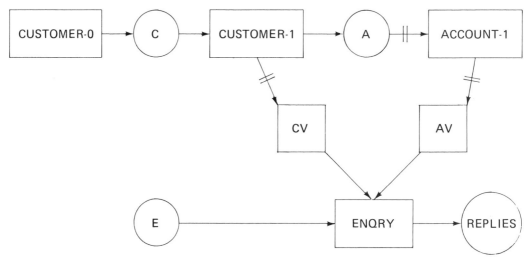

Fig. 10.3

10.6 TIMING AND ROUGH MERGES

In discussing and using rough merges we have often had occasion to appeal to the assumption that the merge is reasonably fair. The validity of this assumption does not depend solely on the algorithm of the merge program; it depends also on the speeds of process execution, in a more dramatic way than one might at first suspect.

Part of the initial model for the Widget Warehouse system was as shown in Fig. 10.4. The ORDER-1 process rough merges its input streams CO and KO. The purpose of

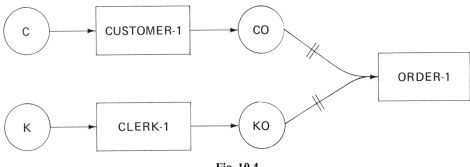

Fig. 10.4

the rough merge is that ORDER-1 should receive the records of CO and KO in the order in which they are produced by CUSTOMER-1 and CLERK-1. In Section 8.14 we looked at two algorithms for rough merging, and concluded that the second was fairer than the first. Broadly, the second consisted of looking at each data stream in turn, and taking a record from it if one is available.

Consider now what would happen if CUSTOMER-1 and CLERK-1 are run continuously, and ORDER-1 is run in a daily batch run each evening. It might be, in a day of fast and furious activity, that the customer performed two actions very early in the morning for a particular order, and the clerk performed one action late in the afternoon. Then the effect of our 'fairer' rough merge algorithm would be either:

> clerk action, customer action (1), customer action (2);

or:

> customer action (1), clerk action, customer action (2);

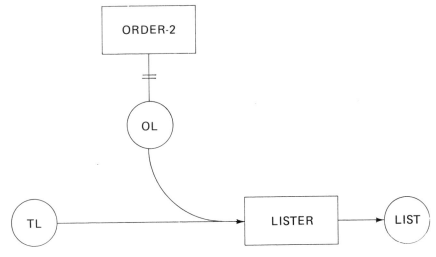

Fig. 10.5

depending on whether the CO or the KO stream is looked at first. Under no circumstances would the actions be taken in their true real world ordering.

Where there are rough merges in the specification, we expect to take some trouble to ensure that the system can tolerate a large measure of unfairness. In the structure of ORDER-1, for example, we specified that actions could occur in almost any ordering. We insisted that PLACE must come first, but allowed for any subsequent merging, however unfair, of the clerk and customer actions.

Sometimes we will want to choose a rough merge algorithm of a particular kind, to favor one data stream over another quite consciously and explicitly. This will often be true when one of the merged streams is a TGM stream. In the Widget Warehouse system, we specified a function to produce a list of ALLOCATE and DELAY actions suffered by orders, a section of the list being output whenever a record appears in a TGM stream TL (Fig. 10.5). We might wish to ensure that the output will include all the records of OL that are available when the TL TGM is input. We can do this by the following rough merge of OL and TL:

```
RM itr
   RMGROUP sel (TL empty)
      RMNOTL sel (OL empty)
      RMNOTL alt (OL not empty)
         read OL;
         write OL to OL&TL;
      RMNOTL end
   RMGROUP alt (TL not empty)
      RMYESTL itr while (OL not empty)
         read OL;
         write OL to OL&TL;
      RMYESTL end
      write end-section to OL&TL;
      read TL;
   RMGROUP end
RM end
```

The effect of this rough merge is that when a TGM appears in TL, the OL input stream is read until it is empty before the *end-section* record is written to the merged stream. It is possible for a record of OL to be included in OL&TL before the *end-section* record even if it is written some time after the TGM in TL. The TGM behaves like a very polite person leaving a shop. On reaching the door, it looks to see whether there is another shopper wanting to use the same door, and, if so, holds the door open. While that shopper is going through the door, another shopper appears and goes through the door, and then another, and another. The unfortunate polite person gets no opportunity to stop holding the door until there is a gap in the traffic, perhaps long after he arrived at the door. The TGM record can get through only when there is a lull in the traffic on the OL stream.

10.7 TIMING AND GATHERED OUTPUTS

In an accounting system, we may wish to produce a daily list of balances at the close of business. One way of providing this function is shown in Fig. 10.6. When the TGM in TL indicates the close of business, the LISTER process writes a request record in RO to each ACCT process in turn; when the ACCT process reads the request, it writes a balance record in BAL, which the LISTER process waits for before writing the request record to the next ACCT process.

We may consider instead an alternative method (Fig. 10.7). TA is a TGM stream input to each ACCT process, signalling the end of the day's business. At first sight, it may appear that this is an adequate solution; but that is not so. There is no guarantee, even if the rough merges of A and TA in ACCT and of BAL and TL in LISTER are of the form discussed in the previous section, that all the balance records will arrive in time to

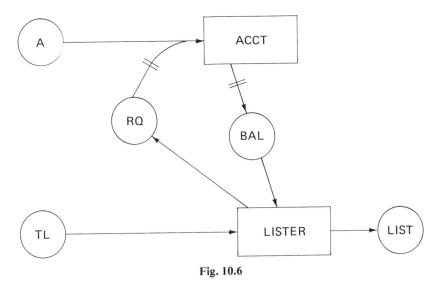

Fig. 10.6

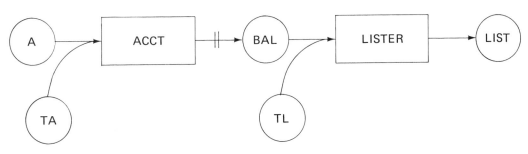

Fig. 10.7

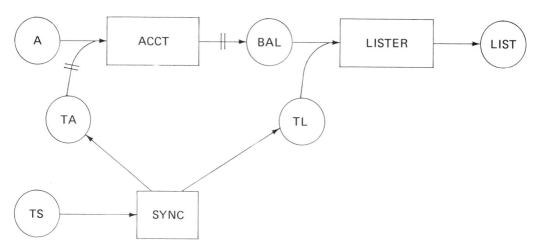

Fig. 10.8

be included in the daily LIST for the day in which they are written. Nor can we ensure their arrival by introducing a delay between the availability of TA and the availability of TL TGMs: we would still be relying on some assumptions about the relative speeds of the processes.

We need to specify some additional synchronization of the ACCT and LISTER processes, to ensure that all the balance records are written by ACCT processes before LISTER closes off the LIST for the day. We can provide this additional synchronization by introducing another process which writes the TA and TL streams, and has a special property. The SSD is shown in Fig. 10.8.

The process SYNC has the structure:

```
SYNC itr
   SYNCDAY seq
      read TS;
      write a TGM to each TA;
      wait for all TA TGMs to be read;
      write a TGM to TL;
      wait for the TL TGM to be read;
   SYNCDAY end
SYNC end
```

The operation *wait for a TGM to be read* is equivalent to *wait for the data stream to be empty*. Effectively, the SYNC process specifies that all ACCT processes must complete their business for the day before the LISTER process can complete its business.

This solution depends on:

—   the process SYNC as specified;

—   the rough merges in ACCT and LISTER being of the form shown in the preceding section;

— there being no buffering between a rough merge and the process which reads the merged stream it produces.

When we need to introduce a synchronization process like SYNC, we may mark it by a horizontal line in the SSD to indicate clearly that it has no purpose other than synchronization (Fig. 10.9).

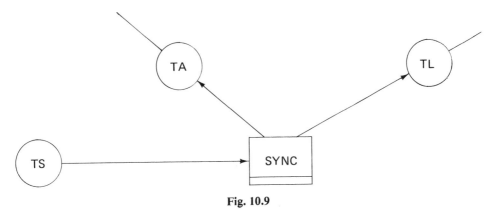

Fig. 10.9

11

The implementation step

11.1   THE IMPLEMENTATION TASK

The considerations that will be important in the implementation step vary greatly from one system to another. In one the developer is critically concerned to obtain fast enough response to some class of input records; in another he is most interested in the design of a database to hold many large state-vectors in a relatively small disk store; in another he needs to economize in main storage; in another he wants to make the best possible use of existing general-purpose software.

One consideration that will apply to almost all systems is the need to share processors among processes. JSD specifications typically involve many processes: one for each customer, one for each order, one for each *Daily Racket* reader, one for each elevator button. Almost always there are fewer processors available than there are processes in the specification. The question of how to share processors among processes then becomes an important implementation issue, and it brings others in its train. Rules must be established for the scheduling of the processes, so that each process gets processor time sufficiently often and in sufficient quantity; these rules must themselves be implemented in some way. When a large number of processes are sharing one processor, there is usually not enough main storage for the program text and state-vector of each process; so this storage too needs to be shared, and arrangements made for texts and state-vectors to be swapped between main and backing storage. It may be necessary to divide the program text of a process into pieces, each of which can be loaded into main storage when needed, and to do the same with state-vectors. The program texts need to be transformed, to allow for this sharing of processor time and space.

In this chapter we will be concerned chiefly with these problems of sharing processors among processes, and will pay little or no attention to other problems of implementation. This is not because we consider them unimportant, but because we are not offering any particular solutions. Other approaches to system development tend not to focus on the problems of process scheduling; either their specifications are written in terms of on-line transaction modules and batch programs, or they assume an implementation environment which can execute their systems directly. In the first case, they are forcing the specification into an implementation mold; in the second, they are limiting their applicability to systems which fit the implementation structure available. In JSD, we aim to write the specification in the form which fits the real world; subsequently, in the implementation step, we transform the specification to fit the machine.

The results of JSD implementation may be as conventional as the most conservative developer might wish. In a data processing system implementation, there may be a database of master records and batch and on-line programs to update them; in a control system implementation, there may be a cyclic executive invoking routines to test and update the values of a set of variables, or there may be a set of asynchronous processes running under the control of a special-purpose operating system. What is different in JSD implementation is the specification which provides its starting point, and the path by which the developer reaches the implementation goal. Different conventional implementations will be seen essentially as different schedulings of the processes of the SSD, with various accompanying transformations to make those schedulings practical and efficient.

Environments for which useful systems are developed usually provide some general-purpose software, such as an operating system, or a transaction-handler, or a teleprocessing monitor, or a batch program generator. Readers familiar with such environments may often find themselves, in this chapter, saying 'but now you are reinventing the operating system', or 'but this problem is already solved by CICS', or 'in our installation we generate programs of this kind automatically'. These objections are perfectly sound: there is no sense in wasting effort to recreate facilities which already exist, and if some part of the implementation task is already solved by existing software the developer should make it his business to know that, and to use the software properly. There are two reasons why we do not rely on such software in the implementations discussed in this chapter. The first reason is simply that it is not always available. The second is that such software can be approached much more intelligently and fruitfully by a developer who knows what he is trying to implement, and how, and hence what help he is seeking from the software. The parallel with programming languages is exact: the program designer must make the language his servant, not his master; the language must be used to express the design, not to preempt it; in the same way, general-purpose software must be the servant, not the master, of the implementation.

11.2   HI-RIDE ELEVATOR: IMPLEMENTATION—1

Before plunging into the problems of shared processors, we will first consider an implementation in which there is a dedicated processor available for each process of the specification.

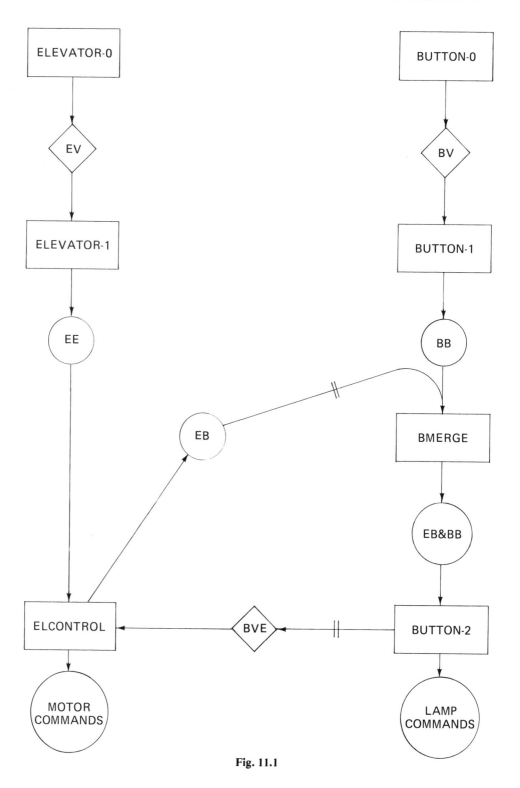

Fig. 11.1

Figure 11.1 shows the SSD for the simple version of the Hi-Ride Elevator system, with only one elevator. This is essentially the same as Fig. 9.27, except that we have shown the rough merge of the input streams to the BUTTON-2 processes as separate processes, BMERGE. There are 50 processes in the specification: a BUTTON-1, a BMERGE, and BUTTON-2 process for each of 16 buttons (5 up, 5 down, 6 in the elevator), and the 2 processes ELEVATOR-1 and ELCONTROL. Since microprocessors can be very small and cheap, we decide to implement this system on 50 processors.

Having freed ourselves from the need to share processors among processes, we need not consider questions of process scheduling: each process will schedule itself, by running as fast as it is able to on its dedicated processor. Nor need we consider the storage of state-vectors: the state-vector of each process is held as local variables within its processor. We are, however, concerned with these questions:

— How will we implement the inputs and outputs at the system boundary? That is, how will ELEVATOR-1 and BUTTON-1 processes obtain access to the EV and BV state-vectors of the real-world elevator and buttons respectively? Also, how will the MOTOR COMMANDS and LAMP COMMANDS be written by the ELCONTROL and BUTTON-2 processes?

— How will we implement the internal data stream and state-vector connections?

— If our implementation of the internal data streams does not provide the unlimited buffering that is assumed in a JSD specification, will the system be unable to run?

The first question is answered quite easily. The company's engineers agree that the floor sensors and button contacts can be brought out to data areas within the directly addressable storage of the ELEVATOR-1 and BUTTON-1 processors: ELEVATOR-1 has a 6-bit data area indicating the state of each floor sensor in one bit; BUTTON-1 has a 1-bit data area indicating whether the button is OPEN or CLOSED. They provide similar data areas for the COMMAND outputs. Two bits are needed for the MOTOR COMMANDS: one for UP/DOWN, and one for START/STOP. One bit is needed for each lamp, to represent LAMP ON and LAMP OFF. By setting these bits, the function processes ELCONTROL and BUTTON-2 issue their commands to the real world motor and the button lamps. Initially, the lamps are OFF and the motor is at STOP. From the point of view of the company's engineers, we have required them to treat the connections between the real motor and lamps and ELCONTROL and the BUTTON-2 processes as state-vector connections, instead of the implied data stream connections. If they prefer, we can easily implement the data stream connections directly, by writing pulses on output lines.

We will implement the internal connections of the system by data areas common to the connected processes. Thus there will be 16 BVE areas, each accessible to ELCONTROL and to the associated BUTTON-2 process, and so on. We will assume for the moment that the buffering of each internal data stream can be limited to one record, so that the common data areas are limited in size. We will return later to check this assumption.

When a data area is accessible to two processors, the hardware provides mutual exclusion; it is impossible for both processors to access the common area at the same time. This considerably simplifies the communication, but we must still take account of other requirements. Both the writing and the reading process will need to determine whether the single buffer is full (occupied by a record that has not yet been read) or empty. The writing process must wait when the buffer is full, and the reading process when it is empty. We must therefore provide a 1-bit flag associated with each record buffer, to indicate whether the buffer is full or empty, in addition to the bits which make up the record itself.

The EE data stream, between ELEVATOR-1 and ELCONTROL, can be implemented with a buffer of the flag only, since the records of EE have no data content. The *write* EE operation in ELEVATOR-1 is therefore:

```
WRITE-EE seq
    X := EE-flag;
    WRITE-EE-WAIT itr while (X = full)
        X := EE-flag;
    WRITE-EE-WAIT end
    EE-flag := full;
WRITE-EE end
```

and the *read* EE operation in ELCONTROL is:

```
READ-EE seq
    X := EE-flag;
    READ-EE-WAIT itr while (X = empty)
        X := EE-flag;
    READ-EE-WAIT end
    EE-flag := empty;
READ-EE end
```

The *write* EB operation in ELCONTROL and the *write* BB operation in BUTTON-1 are implemented similarly; in both cases, the records have no data content. The data stream EB&BB, however, is slightly more elaborate: each record has a 1-bit content, to indicate whether it is a VISIT or a REQUEST record. The *read* EB&BB operation in BUTTON-2 is therefore:

```
READ-EB&BB seq
    X := EB&BB-flag;
    READ-EB&BB-WAIT itr while (X = empty)
        X := EB&BB-flag;
    READ-EB&BB-WAIT end
    record := EB&BB-record;
    EB&BB-flag := empty;
READ-EB&BB end
```

The BMERGE process is very straightforward. The condition tests for EB empty and BB empty use the buffer flags; when a record is read, the appropriate 1-bit data record is written to the merged output stream EB&BB:

```
BMERGE itr
  BMERGE-BODY seq
    X := EB-flag;
    POSS-EBREC sel (X = full)
      EB-flag := empty;
      Y := EB&BB-flag;
      WRITE-EB&BB-WAIT itr while (Y = full)
        Y := EB&BB-flag;
      WRITE-EB&BB-WAIT end
      EB&BB-record := VISIT;
      EB&BB-flag := full;
    POSS-EBREC alt (X = empty)
    POSS-EBREC end
    X := BB-flag;
    POSS-BBREC sel (X = full)
      BB-flag := empty;
      Y := EB&BB-flag;
      WRITE-EB&BB-WAIT itr while (Y = full)
        Y := EB&BB-flag;
      WRITE-EB&BB-WAIT end
      EB&BB-record := REQUEST;
      EB&BB-flag := full;
    POSS-BBREC alt (X = empty)
    POSS-BBREC end
  BMERGE-BODY end
BMERGE end
```

Implementation of the state-vector connection BVE is even more simple. The operation *getsv* BVE(*button*) in ELCONTROL is implemented as:

$$sv := \text{BVE}(button);$$

while the operations in BUTTON-2 to set *outstanding* = *yes* and *outstanding* = *no* are implemented as:

$$\text{BVE} := yes; \quad \text{and} \quad \text{BVE} := no;$$

the hardware mutual exclusion being sufficient in this case to ensure that the obtained value of the state-vector is always a genuine value.

We have still to check our assumption that the limited buffering of the data streams will be sufficient to allow the system to operate satisfactorily. One potential danger is the danger of deadlock or circular waiting: process A is waiting for process B, and, simultaneously, process B is waiting for process A. We need to convince ourselves that our buffering limitation has not introduced deadlock into the system.

It is easy to see that there cannot be deadlock in a system consisting of just two processes connected by a single-buffer data stream, because they cannot both be waiting simultaneously; if the writer is waiting, it is because the buffer is full, and the reader cannot then be waiting; if the reader is waiting, the buffer is empty, and the writer cannot be waiting. This impossibility of deadlock extends to systems of many processes where there is no circular path. But the system we have built does have a circular path: from ELCONTROL to BMERGE, to BUTTON-2, and back to ELCONTROL. We need to be sure that this path cannot cause deadlock.

The path is, in effect, broken at two points. If the buffer EB is empty, BMERGE does not have to wait for it to become full, as can be seen from the text of BMERGE given above. So BMERGE cannot form an element in a circular waiting pattern. Also, the state-vector connection BVE cannot really cause waiting for any length of time: if one of the processes ELCONTROL and BUTTON-2 is waiting to access the common data area which implements their connection, this can only be because the other is executing an access operation to that area at the hardware level, and the mutual exclusion is in effect; the hardware access operation, once begun, will terminate soon, and the waiting will then end, irrespective of what is happening elsewhere in the system.

So we have not introduced deadlock. There is another potential danger: one of the processes might find itself indefinitely waiting for one of the buffers to become full or empty. Suppose, for example, that we had foolishly specified BMERGE so that it favored BB over EB to the extent that a record of EB was never read while there was a record of BB available. It would then be theoretically possible for a malevolent user to stand by a button pressing it with such speed and precision that there was always a BB record available to the BMERGE process for that button. This could be very serious: the resulting waiting by ELCONTROL could cause it to be indefinitely delayed. However, the difficulty is not a real difficulty, for several reasons:

— The rough merge in BMERGE is sufficiently fair: the EB record would be read by BMERGE after one BB record was read.
— The malevolent user would have to press his button several times per millisecond at least, and we may discount that possibility. (Perhaps we ought not to, remembering the activities of the phone phreaks of recent years!)
— The specification of ELCONTROL is such that the write EB operations occur only following a STOP and before the subsequent START; there would be no danger to life or limb even if ELCONTROL were indefinitely delayed at those points in its execution.

One final topic deserves some clarification. It might appear that we could implement the rough merge of EB and BB without the separate BMERGE processes by simply allowing the EB and BB stream for each BUTTON-2 process to use the same common area. The rough merge would be implemented by allowing ELCONTROL and BUTTON-1 both to write into the buffer for the merged stream EB&BB. This is not possible with the very rudimentary arrangements we are assuming for mutual exclusion at the hardware level, because the following sequence of events might then occur:

— ELCONTROL finds the buffer empty;
— BUTTON-1 finds the buffer empty;
— ELCONTROL places a VISIT record in the buffer and marks the buffer full;
— BUTTON-1 places a REQUEST record in the buffer and marks the buffer full.

The simplicity of the scheme we have used depends critically on the fact that only one process can write, and only one process can read, for each buffer. It also depends on the fact that there is only one record buffer for each data stream, so that reading and writing must alternate strictly. An implementation allowing more than one writing process, or multiple buffers, would require a much more powerful set of concepts. Readers who are interested in the subject may wish to consult chapter 3 of Brinch Hansen, *Operating System Principles*, Prentice-Hall.

11.3   HI-RIDE ELEVATOR: IMPLEMENTATION—2

Each microprocessor in the implementation of the preceding section is a bare machine. It has no operating system, no facilities for multi-tasking or multi-programming; it is capable of executing only one sequential process, and, by definition, there can be no concurrency within one sequential process; there is one program text, which is executed from beginning to end at whatever speed is possible for that process on that machine.

One way of reducing the number of processors needed is to simulate many processors on one processor; this can be done by multi-tasking, multi-programming, time-slicing, and various other techniques. As we will see later in this chapter, when we discuss some of these possibilities, we regard such methods as essentially equivalent to the provision of many processors. A virtual processor is as good as a real processor, and, if properly implemented, has the same characteristics.

Another way of reducing the number of processors needed is to transform the specification so that there are fewer sequential processes to be executed. This reduction in the number of processes is effective purely from the implementation point of view: there is no way we can reduce the number of processes specified without changing the model, the function, or both. However, we can make it appear to the machine that there is only one process to be executed, when in fact it is a composite of several specified processes.

As a gentle introduction to the necessary techniques of transformation, we will change our implementation of the Hi-Ride Elevator system to require 16 fewer processors. We will use only one processor for the BMERGE and BUTTON-2 processes for one button, thus reducing the number of processors per button from 3 to 2. The processes BMERGE and BUTTON-2 will be combined in such a way that they will appear to be one process, so that they can be executed on one processor.

The first step is to consider how the processes are to be scheduled; that is, how the time of one processor is to be shared between the two processes. Very roughly, a suitable scheduling is the following:

— give the processor to BMERGE until it has produced a record of EB&BB;
— then give the processor to BUTTON-2 until it has read that record of EB&BB, and is blocked waiting for another;
— then give the processor to BMERGE until it has produced another record of EB&BB, and so on.

This scheduling choice requires only a single record buffer for EB&BB, like the previous implementation on two processors. It has certain characteristics which we will explore further in a later section; for the moment we will simply accept it as a reasonable choice.

To implement this sharing of the processor, we need to make some changes to the texts of the processes BMERGE and BUTTON-2, to bring them under the control of the scheduler. The scheduler will be a new sequential process:

SCHEDULER **itr**
  SCHEDULE-CYCLE **seq**
    run BMERGE *until a record of* EB&BB *is written*;
    run BUTTON-2 *until the record has been read and*
                         another is needed;
  SCHEDULE-CYCLE **end**
SCHEDULER **end**

We will convert BMERGE and BUTTON-2 into subroutines which can be called by the scheduler using the operations:

CALL BMERGE-S (record);

and

CALL BUTTON-2-S (record);

The effect of calling BMERGE will be that the next record of EB&BB is placed by BMERGE in the record area which is the parameter of the call. The effect of calling BUTTON-2 will be that BUTTON-2 reads the record from the record area which is the parameter of the call, and returns when a further record is wanted.

We can show that BMERGE and BUTTON-2 are to share a processor (that is, 16 processors) by drawing a box around them in the SSD; and we can show the configuration of the scheduling in the shared processor by drawing a new kind of diagram: a SID, or System Implementation Diagram. Putting the SID and the relevant part of the SSD side by side, we have the arrangement shown in Fig. 11.2.

The vertical stripe on the box SCHEDULER in the SID indicates that it is a scheduling process, introduced at the implementation step (and so absent from the SSD). The double lines joining BUTTON-2 and BMERGE to SCHEDULER indicate that each of them is inverted with respect to one data stream and is a subroutine of SCHEDULER. It is not necessary to mark the double line with the name of the data stream: the identity of the data stream can be inferred from a comparison of the SSD and SID, by noting which SSD data stream (EB&BB) does not appear in the SID. The way in which the boxes BUTTON-2 and BMERGE are arranged below SCHEDULER does not imply any particular arrangement of the subroutine calls (such as 'BUTTON-2 is called before BMERGE'). The arrangement of the subroutine calls can be seen only from the text of the SCHEDULER process.

The conversion of BMERGE and BUTTON-2 into the required subroutines is carried out when they are coded into PL/I, COBOL, Pascal, or whatever is the implementation language. The conversion can be made by a precompiler or macro-processor,

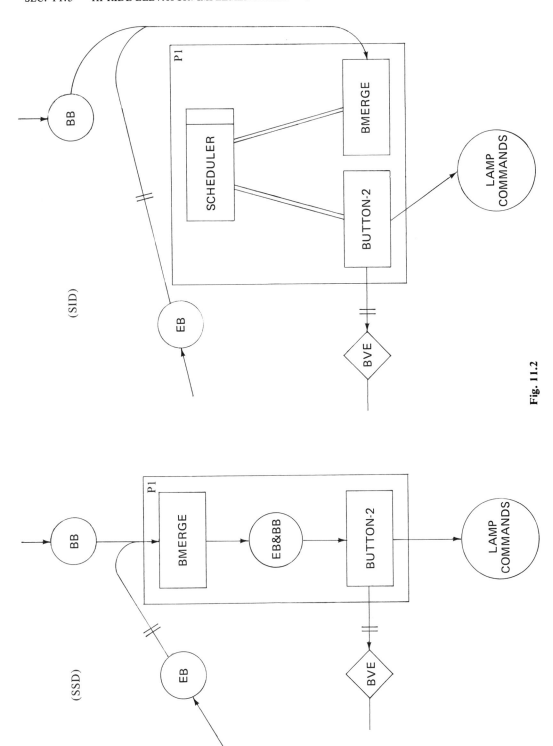

Fig. 11.2

or it can be made by hand: the best choice, if it is available, is to use a precompiler which can accept directives identifying the required transformations and can guarantee to perform the transformations correctly. In this chapter we will show the transformed processes in an adulterated version of structure text, purely to avoid any discussion of practical implementation languages. This adulterated version of structure text is never used in practice, and should be regarded merely as an unwelcome but expedient vehicle of explanation.

The text of BUTTON-2, in its original form, was given in Section 9.11, and the reader should compare it with the text below:

```
BUTTON-2-S subroutine (record)
   go to TP (text-pointer);
   TP(1):
   BUTTON-2 seq
      outstanding := no; OFF lamp;
      BUTTON-2-BODY itr
        REQUEST-GROUP seq
          EXTRA-VISIT-SET itr while (VISIT)
             text-pointer := 2; return; TP(2):
          EXTRA-VISIT-SET end
          REQUEST seq
             outstanding := yes; ON lamp;
             text-pointer := 3; return; TP(3):
          REQUEST end
          EXTRA-REQUEST-SET itr while (REQUEST)
             text-pointer := 4; return; TP(4):
          EXTRA-REQUEST-SET end
          VISIT seq
             outstanding := no; OFF lamp;
             text-pointer := 5; return; TP(5):
          VISIT end
        REQUEST-GROUP end
      BUTTON-2-BODY end
   BUTTON-2 end
BUTTON-2-S end
```

When BUTTON-2-S is first called by the scheduler, the first record of EB&BB is passed as the parameter (record). The value of text-pointer, by convention, is initially 1, so execution begins at TP(1), on taking the branch 'go to TP (text-pointer)'. The first 'read EB&BB' operation in the text of BUTTON-2, before BUTTON-2-BODY, has been removed, since the first record is already provided in the first call of the subroutine. Execution eventually reaches a point where the original text had a 'read EB&BB' operation; the transformed text has instead an operation to set a value in text-pointer, a return to the scheduler, and a label marking the text-pointer value. The next time the subroutine is called, execution will continue at the marked point, using the new record of EB&BB passed as the parameter. The effect of the code 'text-pointer := n; return TP(n):' is thus equivalent to the effect of 'read EB&BB'.

This transformation of BUTTON-2 is called 'inversion of BUTTON-2 with respect to EB&BB'. It transforms BUTTON-2 from a sequential process to a subroutine which handles one record of EB&BB on each call. Effectively, the subroutine mechanism is being used to suspend execution of the sequential process and to resume execution. Each 'return' statement in BUTTON-2-S is a suspension; each call of BUTTON-2-S by the scheduler is a resumption of its execution.

Here is the text of BMERGE similarly transformed:

```
BMERGE-S subroutine (record)
  go to TP (text-pointer);
  TP(1):
  BMERGE itr
    BMERGE-BODY seq
      X := EB-flag;
      POSS-EBREC sel (X = full)
        EB-flag := empty;
        record := VISIT;
        text-pointer := 2; return; TP(2):
      POSS-EBREC alt (X = empty)
      POSS-EBREC end
      X := BB-flag;
      POSS-BBREC sel (X = full)
        BB-flag := empty;
        record := REQUEST;
        text-pointer := 3; return; TP(3):
      POSS-BBREC alt (X = empty)
      POSS-BBREC end
    BMERGE-BODY end
  BMERGE end
BMERGE-S end
```

The text of the scheduler is:

```
SCHEDULER itr
  SCHEDULE-CYCLE seq
    CALL BMERGE-S (record);
    CALL BUTTON-2-S (record);
  SCHEDULE-CYCLE end
SCHEDULER end
```

The scheduler and the two subroutines together are now, from the machine's point of view, a single sequential process, and can therefore run on a single processor.

In implementing an inverted process, the developer must be careful to ensure that the state-vector of the process is preserved from the time that the process is suspended to the time that it continues execution. There are three particular points requiring attention:

— The local variables of the process, including the text-pointer, must be declared in such a way that they will not be discarded or lost when a *return* instruction is executed. They must be held in CONTROLLED or STATIC storage in PL/I, not in AUTOMATIC. In COBOL they may be held in WORKING-STORAGE, provided that the run-time environment preserves the WORKING-STORAGE of a sub-program from one CALL to another. Alternatively, they may be held in storage which is allocated at a sufficiently high level to guarantee preservation for the whole lifetime of the process, and passed as a parameter of the call statement. We will see in a later section that this last technique is sometimes needed for other reasons too.

— The 'return' instructions must not be written within text components which rely on hidden variables that cannot be preserved. Where a language specification manual states that it is forbidden to jump out of a text component and then jump back in again later, this is usually because there are such hidden variables: they may be program addresses or loop-control variables which are held in registers. This difficulty can always be overcome by writing the program text in a style which avoids the use of such components, implementing iterations and selections by labels and GO TO statements.

— The text-pointer value must be initialized to 1 before the process is first activated. There are various means of arranging for this; the choice will depend on how the local variables (including the text-pointer) are stored.

The inverted form of a process text must be thought of as 'object code', not as 'source code'. It is therefore entirely inappropriate to criticize an inverted text as 'unstructured': the GO TO statements are no more, and no less, unstructured than the branch instructions produced by a compiler; the initialization of the text-pointer is no more an offence against rules of elegance than the generation by a compiler of the relative initial address of a program.

The power of the inversion transformation is great. It puts a sequential process in a form which allows direct and explicit scheduling of its execution by a scheduler process which can be specified and written in almost any programming language. As we will see later, a sequential process can be inverted with respect to one data stream or to several, according to whether we want to suspend its execution only at the operation on one data stream or at the operations on several data streams.

11.4   SCHEDULING WITHOUT A SCHEDULER

Some readers will already have realized that we can dispense with the SCHEDULER process in our implementation of BMERGE and BUTTON-2 as a single process. One way is illustrated in Fig. 11.3. BUTTON-2 is inverted with respect to EB&BB, and is implemented exactly as before in the form of the subroutine BUTTON-2-S. BMERGE is not inverted, and acts effectively as the scheduling process for both. The '*write* EB&BB' operations in BMERGE are implemented as:

   CALL BUTTON-2-S (*record*);

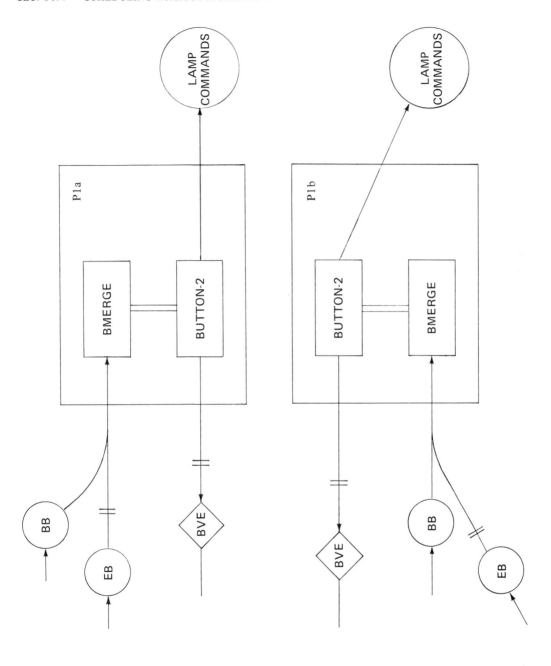

Fig. 11.3

Fig. 11.4

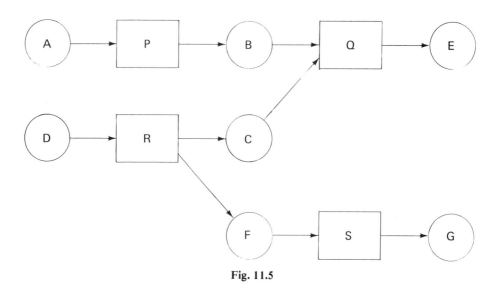

Fig. 11.5

The scheduling that is implemented is the following:

—   run BMERGE until it produces a record of EB&BB;
—   then run BUTTON-2 until it has read that record and is blocked waiting for another;
—   then run BMERGE again, until it produces another record of EB&BB, and so on.

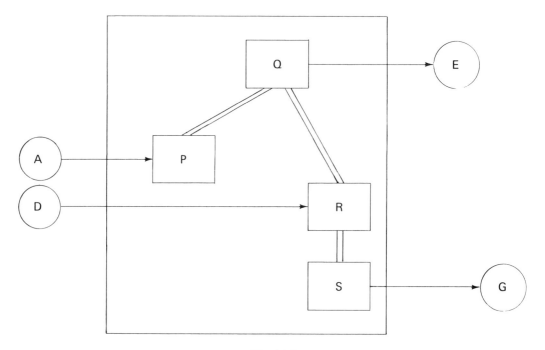

Fig. 11.6

Another way of dispensing with the scheduling process is shown in Fig. 11.4. Here it is BMERGE that is inverted with respect to EB&BB, and BUTTON-2 that acts as the scheduling process. The 'read EB&BB' operations in BUTTON-2 are implemented as:

CALL BMERGE-S (*record*);

The scheduling that is implemented is very slightly different from the scheduling of P1a; it is:

—   run BUTTON-2 until it is blocked waiting for a record of EB&BB;
—   then run BMERGE until it produces a record of EB&BB;
—   then run BUTTON-2 until it is again blocked waiting for a record of EB&BB, and so on.

We will return to this difference, and to some associated points, in the next section.

The technique of combining processes by inversion without adding a separate scheduling process can be applied to some quite large systems. Certainly, it can be applied to any system for which these conditions are true:

—   only data stream connection is used;
—   there is no rough merge in the system;
—   any two processes of the system are connected by only one path.

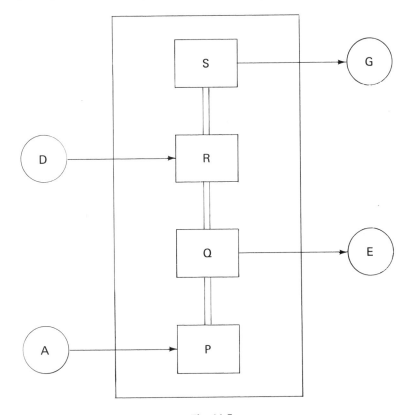

Fig. 11.7

Figure 11.5, for example, shows an imaginary system satisfying these conditions, and Fig. 11.6 shows an implementation.

Q is effectively the scheduling process for the system. P is inverted with respect to B, R is inverted with respect to C, and S is inverted with respect to F. The scheduling scheme implemented is:

— run Q until it is blocked waiting for a record of B or C;
— If Q is blocked waiting for a record of B, run P until P produces the record of B, then suspend P and continue to run Q;
— if Q is blocked waiting for a record of C, run R until it produces the record of C, then suspend R and continue to run Q;
— if R, while running, produces a record of F, suspend R and run S until it has read that record of F and is blocked waiting for another.

We can choose any process of the system as the effective scheduler. Figure 11.7 shows an implementation with S as the effective scheduler. R is inverted with respect to F; Q is inverted with respect to C; P is inverted with respect to B. The scheduling scheme implemented by this arrangement is, of course, different from that in which Q is the effective scheduling process.

11.5   SCHEDULING CHARACTERISTICS OF INVERSION

The purpose of inversion is to allow two or more sequential processes to be easily and conveniently scheduled on a single processor. Execution of the processes is interleaved, in a particular way, according to the structure of the scheduling process.

Suppose that we have two processes connected by a data stream,

and we choose to implement them on one processor by inversion with respect to A. Then the execution of each process can be shown as a line, with time running from left to right, divided into segments by the operations on that data stream: the line begins at the start of execution, and terminates at the end of execution.

P: s ──────→ wA ──────→ wA ──────────→ wA ──────→ wA ──────→ wA ───────

Q: s ──────→ rA──────→ rA ──────→ rA ──────────→ rA─────→ rA ───────

The markings wA and rA indicate the divisions between segments at write and read operations on A.

The interleaving of execution of P and Q, if P is inverted with respect to A and made a subroutine of Q, will be:

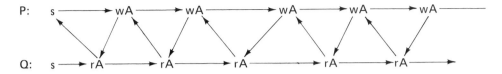

If we invert Q and make it a subroutine of P, we will need to discard the first *read* A operation in Q, and the interleaving will be:

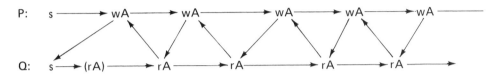

The difference between these two execution patterns is that in the first, where P is inverted, the initial segment of Q is executed immediately, and the initial segment of P is executed only when Q reaches a *read* A operation; in the second, it is P whose initial segment is executed immediately, while the initial segment of Q is executed only when P reaches a *write* A operation. This difference may, or may not, be immaterial. In the preceding section, we considered two implementations of part of the Hi-Ride Elevator system (Fig. 11.8).

The initial segment of BUTTON-2 contains the operations:

outstanding := *no*; OFF *lamp*;

If we choose the implementation P1a, these operations cannot be executed before BMERGE writes the first record of EB&BB; this in turn cannot occur before either BUTTON-1 writes a REQUEST record to BB or ELCONTROL writes a VISIT record to EB. The same is true of the implementation of P1 in Section 11.3, where the SCHEDULER process activates BMERGE before it activates BUTTON-2. The effect will be the following:

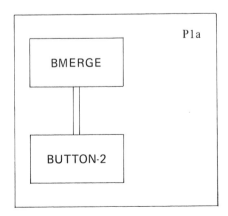
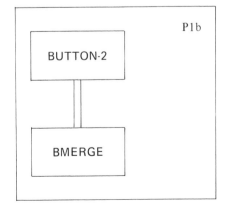

Fig. 11.8

— when the elevator system is installed, the initial value of *outstanding* is undefined, and so is the initial setting of the lamp;

— if the undefined value appears to ELCONTROL to be 'yes', the elevator will visit the floor immediately, even if no request has been made, and the lamp will then be turned off by BUTTON-2 even if it was already OFF;

— if the undefined value appears to be 'no', and the lamp is initially ON, an unfortunate early user of the elevator may believe that he need not press the button, and so may wait quite a long time for the elevator to arrive;

— if the first real request is made on the button before the elevator has visited the floor, and the lamp was initially ON, then when the request is made, the lamp will flicker off and come on again at once, as BUTTON-2 executes its initial segment followed by its REQUEST component.

These effects can be avoided by choosing the implementation P1b rather than P1a. The initial segment of BMERGE can be delayed without disadvantage until BUTTON-2 is blocked at a *read* EB&BB operation.

The different effects of the implementations P1a and P1b are, of course, both legitimate possible effects of the specification which is being implemented. We have not paid any explicit attention to the general question of how the system behaves during the initial period in which some processes have begun execution and some have not. We can avoid some, at least, of the difficulties by making these assumptions:

— Every process assigns defined values to every part of its state-vector at the beginning of its text, before executing any operation which communicates with any other process.

— The creation of a process is regarded as embodying execution of the process at least as far as the first communication with any other process.

— The state-vector of a process cannot be inspected until the process creation, as defined above, is complete.

— Execution of a system is preceded by creation of all those processes which are to be present initially and are not created by other processes.

If we choose an implementation which does not satisfy these assumptions, we must justify it explicitly.

11.6   IMPLEMENTING ROUGH MERGE WITH INVERSION

Suppose that we have the simple imaginary system shown in Fig. 11.9. This system does not satisfy the conditions given in Section 11.4 for combining all the processes by inversion without adding a separate scheduling process: the processes P and R are connected by two paths (P–B–R and P–C–Q–D–R). However, because R rough merges its input streams, we may still be able to schedule the system very simply.

Clearly, we can combine P and Q. Inverting Q, we obtain Fig. 11.10. The combined process consisting of P and Q will write the records of the data streams B and D in

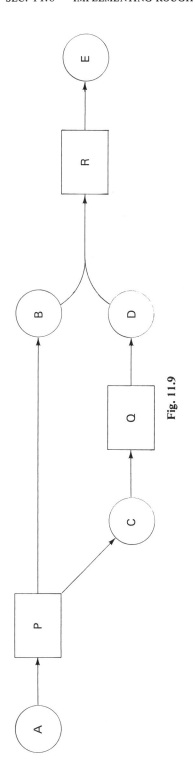

Fig. 11.9

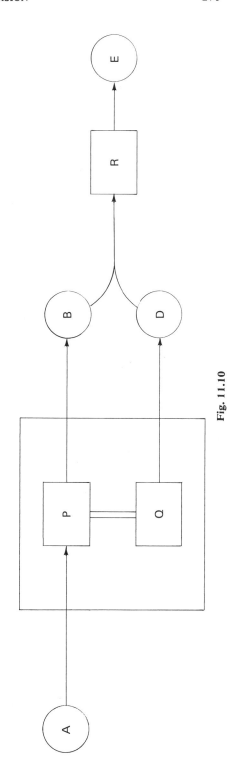

Fig. 11.10

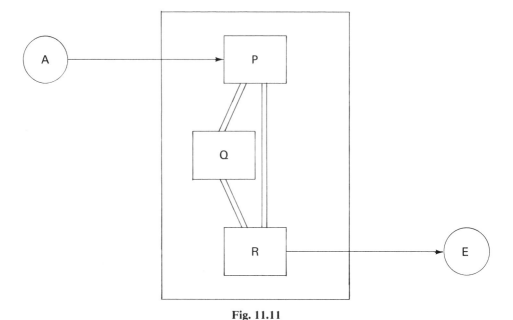

Fig. 11.11

some order. If this order is acceptable as the result of the rough merge in R, we can invert R with respect to the merged stream B&D, and make it a subroutine of the combined process—that is, of both P and Q (Fig. 11.11).

The essential additional condition is that accepting the records of B&D in the order they are written by P and Q scheduled as shown is a satisfactory implementation of the rough merge.

The notation for the connections to R is an obvious extension of the previously introduced notation for inversion.

11.7 CHANNELS

Suppose that we wish to use a separate scheduling process to implement the system:

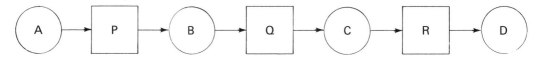

We can bring P under control of the scheduler by inverting it with respect to B; and we can bring R under control of the scheduler by inverting it with respect to C; but Q presents a difficulty.

We need to suspend execution of Q both at *read* B and at *write* C operations. This can easily be done by treating those operations as we have treated the *write* B and *read*

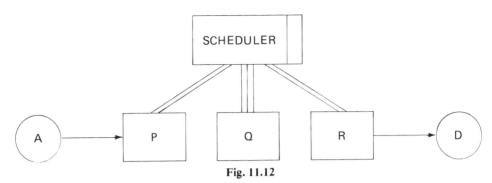

Fig. 11.12

C operations in P and R; but something more is needed. The scheduler must be able to determine whether Q is suspended at a *read* B or at a *write* C operation, so that it can call Q with appropriate parameters and can take the appropriate action when Q returns. This need does not arise when a process is inverted with respect to only one data stream: there can be only one reason for its suspension, and only one result when it returns after a call.

We will represent inversion with respect to two or more data streams by using a join with three or more lines. So the SID for the system is as shown in Fig. 11.12. We will call this kind of connection 'channel connection'. Q is connected by a channel to the SCHEDULER process; the treble line representing the connection indicates that Q is inverted with respect to two data streams.

For a process connected by a channel, the calling process can execute an operation:

 query Q;

which makes available the required information. The reason for suspension can then be evaluated in a condition in the calling process.

The SCHEDULER process might be:

```
SCHEDULER itr
  SCHEDULER-RECORD seq
    query Q;
    RECORD-TRANSFER sel (read B in Q)
      B-RECORD seq
        CALL P (B-record);
        CALL Q (B-record, C-record);
      B-RECORD end
    RECORD-TRANSFER alt (write C in Q)
      C-RECORD seq
        CALL Q (B-record, C-record);
        CALL R (C-record);
      C-RECORD end
    RECORD-TRANSFER end
  SCHEDULER-RECORD end
SCHEDULER end
```

The inversion necessary to give channel connection is a little more complex than inversion with respect to a single data stream (single inversion). Care must be taken with a number of points, including these:

— To provide the information required by query operations in the calling process, the inverted process must execute each segment in advance of the calling process executing its corresponding segment. For example, with the SCHEDULER shown above, Q must have executed its first segment and reached a *read* B or a *write* C operation before it is first called by SCHEDULER: only then can the first *query* C operation in SCHEDULER be effective.

— In Section 11.5, we discussed an implementation of single inversion in which the interleaving of the calling and called processes depends on whether the inversion is with respect to an input or to an output data stream. A conflict arises where a process is inverted with respect both to an input and to an output data stream, as in our present example. The conflict can be resolved by introducing an element of buffering, in the form of an additional record area for one of the data streams, and adjusting the interleaving as required.

— If a single record area is used for a data stream, and is passed as a parameter by the calling process, then the area must be kept intact for as long as needed by the called process. In our present example, if Q contains the sequence of operations:

read B(3); *write* C(6); *read* B(4); *read* B(5); . . .

then the call by SCHEDULER corresponding to the write C(6) operation must specify the same *B-record* parameter as the preceding call, and the value of *B-record* must not have been changed by SCHEDULER.

Sometimes we may combine two processes using one as the scheduler for the combination, and then invert the combination with respect to two or more data streams. For example, we might implement:

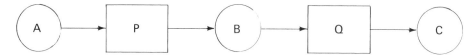

as shown in Fig. 11.13.

Q is then a subroutine of P, and the combined process P&Q is a subroutine of the SCHEDULER. *Read* B operations in Q return to P, while *write* C operations in Q return to the SCHEDULER. Some care is needed to implement these operations correctly, along with the *read* A and *write* B operations in P:

— There must be one text-pointer for the combined process; the values of this text-pointer are, essentially, the points in the text at which *read* A and *write* C operations appear. The entry-point coding for the combined process contains a GO TO statement which continues execution at the appropriate point when the combined process is called by the SCHEDULER.

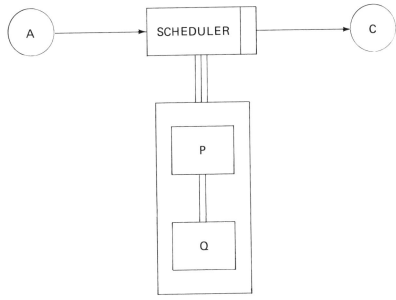

Fig. 11.13

— Separate text-pointers are used for P and Q to implement the *write* B and *read* B operations in P and Q respectively. It will not, usually, be possible to implement the *write* B operation as a CALL statement, since the return address for the CALL is likely to be lost if Q executes a *write* C operation.

The entry to the combined process is therefore:

P&Q **subroutine** (*A-record, B-record*)
   go to TP-PQ (*PQ-text-pointer*);
   TP-PQ(1):
   P **seq**

Read A operations in P and *write* C operations in Q are essentially of the form:

   PQ-text-pointer := *i; return*; TP-PQ(*i*);

PQ-text-pointer is the text-pointer for the combined process. Using separate text-pointers for P and Q to implement the operations on B, we implement the *write* B operations in P as:

   P-text-pointer := *j*;
   go to TP-Q(*Q-text-pointer*); TP-P(*j*):

In the text of *Q*, the entry-point is:

Q **seq**
  TP-Q(1):
  . . .

and the *read* B operations are implemented as:

Q-text-pointer := *k*;
go to TP-P(*P-text-pointer*); TP-Q(*k*):

Q-text-pointer must initially have the value 1; *P-text-pointer* does not require initialization.

Channel implementation may be greatly simplified in certain special cases. The most important of these cases arise where the pattern of operations on the data streams of the channel is fully predictable: there is then no need for query operations, since the information is already known.

11.8   SCHEDULING WITH BUFFERS

So far we have chosen implementations in which buffering of data streams is avoided. In the 50-processor implementation of the Hi-Ride Elevator system we had just one record area for each data stream; in the 34-processor implementation, we used inversion, with or without a separate scheduling process, to ensure that each record of EB&BB was passed to BUTTON-2 as soon as it was written by BMERGE, avoiding the need to buffer records which had been written but not yet read. In the imaginary system of the preceding section, we specified the SCHEDULER so that each record of B was written by P only when Q was ready to read it, and each record of C was read by R as soon as Q had written it.

It is not always possible to avoid buffering in the implementation. Consider the imaginary system shown in Fig. 11.14, which is slightly different from the system discussed in Section 11.6, where we implemented a rough merge by inversion. Here, R merges its inputs not by a rough merge, but by a data merge of some kind. The order in which the records of B and D are read by R is determined only by the structure of R, and cannot be assumed to be the order in which they are written by P and Q, whatever scheduling scheme is chosen.

To fix our idea of the system, we will suppose that:

— the input data stream A contains integer records in ascending order without duplicates;
— P writes alternate records of A to B and C, writing the first record to B;
— Q copies the records of C to D, adding 8 to each integer;
— R merges the records of B and D, eliminating duplicates, to give the output data stream E of records in ascending order.

An example of the contents of the data streams is:

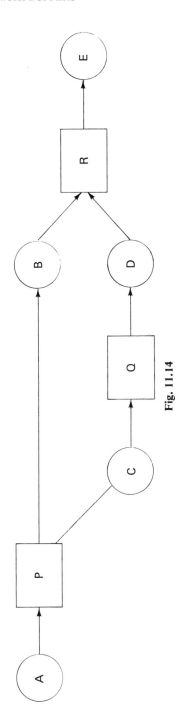

Fig. 11.14

A: 1, 5, 7, 10, 13, 17, 18, 25, 28, . . .
B: 1,   7,   13,   18,   28,   . . .
C: 5,   10,   17,   25,   . . .
D: 13, 18, 25, 33, . . .
E: 1, 7, 13, 18, 25, 28, . . .

The order of read operations executed in R, assuming that both B and D are read ahead, and that initially B is read first, is:

read B(1); *read* D(13); *read* B(7); *read* B(13); *read* B(18); . . .

Irrespective of the scheduling scheme we select, P cannot produce the B(18) record until it has produced the records C(5), C(10), and C(17). From these records, Q produces the records D(13), D(18), and D(25). At the point in the execution of the whole system at which R is about to read the record B(18), and has not yet read beyond the record D(13) in D, it is necessary that:

—   the records C(10) and C(17) are stored in a buffer; or
—   the records D(18) and D(25) are stored in a buffer; or
—   the records C(10) and D(25) are stored in a buffer.

Which of these occurs will depend on the scheduling of the process Q in relation to the process P; but some buffering is unavoidable.

The amount of buffering required in any system depends on the scheduling of the processes. We might have scheduled the Hi-Ride Elevator system so that buffering was needed for EB&BB, by running BMERGE in preference to BUTTON-2, so that BMERGE produced records of EB&BB while BUTTON-2 had still not read the earlier records; but, in that system, such a scheduling would have been perverse, and would have had some very undesirable consequences. In the present imaginary system, we might choose to run P and Q until they had produced 1000 records in each of the data streams B and D, before running R; we would then need buffering for 2000 records. But we can schedule

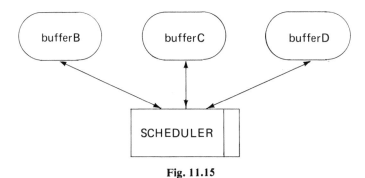

Fig. 11.15

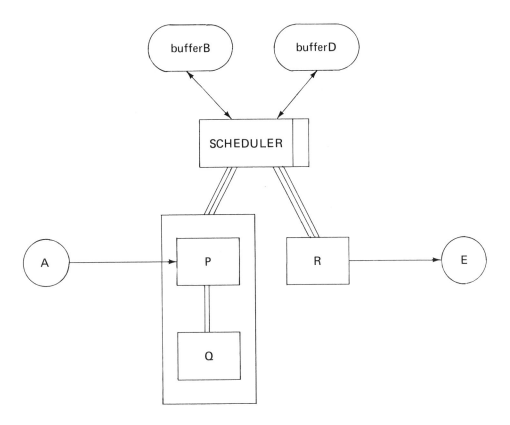

Fig. 11.16

the system so that much less buffering is needed: as soon as a record of B or D has been written, we can run R if it is blocked waiting for that record. A little calculation shows that the buffering needed will then be no more than 4 records in all.

We will place the buffers under control of the scheduling process. Assuming, for the moment, that we will need buffers for each of B, C, and D, we can show them by the notation in Fig. 11.15.

The buffers are accessible only to the scheduler. The scheduler writes to each buffer and reads from it; the read operations obtain the records in the order in which they were written. The scheduler can test whether a buffer is empty.

Figure 11.16 shows a SID showing a possible implementation for the system. Q is inverted with respect to C, and is a subroutine of P. The combined process consisting of P and Q is inverted with respect to both B and D. R is also inverted with respect to both B and D. No buffer is required for C, since records of C are passed directly from P to Q.

The SCHEDULER process might be:

```
SCHEDULER itr
  RECORD seq
    query R;
    R-READ sel (read B in R)
      R-READ-B sel (bufferB not empty)
        read bufferB (B-record);
        CALL R (B-record);
      R-READ-B alt (bufferB empty)
        query P&Q;
        B-FROM-PQ sel (write B in P&Q)
          CALL P&Q (B-record);
          CALL R (B-record);
        B-FROM-PQ alt (write D in P&Q)
          CALL P&Q (D-record);
          write D-record to bufferD;
        B-FROM-PQ end
      R-READ-B end
    R-READ alt (read D in R)
      R-READ-D sel (bufferD not empty)
        read bufferD (D-record);
        CALL R (D-record);
      R-READ-D alt (bufferD empty)
        query P&Q;
        D-FROM-PQ sel (write D in P&Q)
          CALL P&Q (D-record);
          CALL R (D-record);
        D-FROM-PQ alt (write B in P&Q)
          CALL P&Q (B-record);
          write B-record to bufferB;
        D-FROM-PQ end
      R-READ-D end
    R-READ end
  RECORD end
SCHEDULER end
```

The scheduler, in each instance of the component RECORD, provides the record needed by R if it can be provided from the buffer or from P&Q; if the required record cannot be provided, the next record produced by P&Q is placed in the buffer.

11.9   STATE-VECTOR SEPARATION

A very simple accounts system has the SSD:

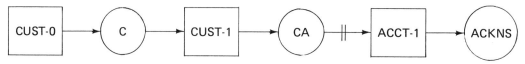

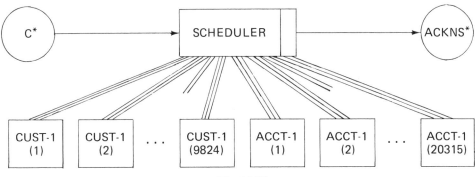

Fig. 11.17

There are many customers, CUST-O, modelled by processes CUST-1. Each customer has a number of accounts, modelled by processes ACCT-1. Transactions on an account are acknowledged by an embedded function which writes an output stream ACKNS. We would like to implement this system on a single processor, using a single input device for the input streams C, and a single output device for the output streams ACKNS. A possible SID is shown in Fig. 11.17.

The input and output streams C* and ACKNS* represent mergings of the individual streams C and ACKNS. The CUST-1 processes are inverted with respect to C and CA; the ACCT-1 processes are inverted with respect to CA and ACKNS. There is one CUST-1 process (and hence one CUST-1 subroutine implementing the inverted process) for each customer; and similarly there is an ACCT-1 subroutine for each account.

There is an obvious lack of economy here. We cannot avoid having many CUST-1 and ACCT-1 state-vectors, since no two customers and no two accounts need be in the same state at any time. But it is unnecessary to have many copies of the CUST-1 and ACCT-1 program texts: the executable text of every CUST-1 process is the same as the text of every other; the text of every ACCT-1 process is the same as the text of every other. We need only one copy of the CUST-1 and one copy of the ACCT-1 text. To achieve this economy, we must:

— separate the state-vectors from the program text;
— store the state-vectors somewhere accessible to the scheduler;
— bring together the required text and state-vector whenever a process is activated;
— replace the new value of the state-vector in the store when the process is suspended.

Choosing familiar symbols for the stored state-vectors, we can represent the required implementation as in Fig. 11.18. The CUST-1 SVFILE and ACCT-1 SVFILE are, of course, the 'customer master file' and 'account master file'; they may be implemented using database software or by any kind of file storage that can meet the accessing needs of the scheduling. When the SCHEDULER activates the CUST-1 process for customer 5173, it must execute the operations:

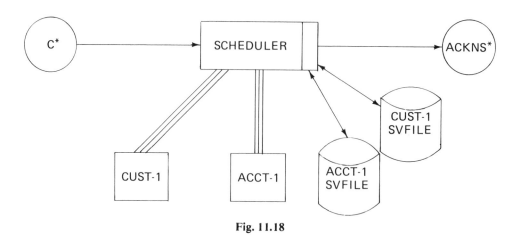

Fig. 11.18

loadsv CUST-1SV (5173) *into* CSV;
CALL CUST-1 (CSV, . . .);
storesv CSV *into* CUST-1SV (5173);

the *loadsv* operation retrieves the appropriate state-vector from CUST-1 SVFILE; the *storesv* operation replaces the new value after the activation and suspension of what is effectively CUST-1 (5173). The customer-id, 5173, is presumed to be a field in the input record of C*, indicating that it is a part of the input stream C for customer 5173.

When a process of the specification is used as a scheduling process, it may execute the necessary operations on the files of state-vectors. Another implementation of the system is shown in Fig. 11.19. ACCT-1 is inverted with respect to its input stream CA,

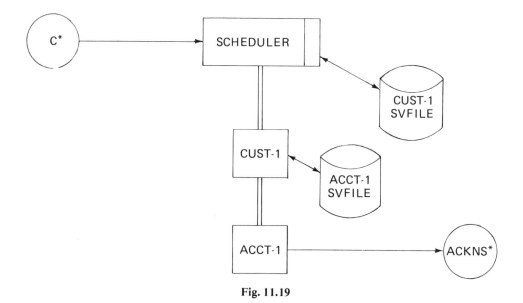

Fig. 11.19

and is a subroutine of CUST-1. The records of ACKNS* are written directly by
ACCT-1, it being assumed that some suitable implementation for this is provided. The
CUST-1 process is inverted with respect to its input stream C, and is a subroutine of the
SCHEDULER process. The operation *write* CA (*acct-id*) in CUST-1 is implemented by
the code:

> *loadsv* ACCT-1SV (*acct-id*) *into* ASV;
> CALL ACCT-1 (*ASV, CA-record*);
> *storesv* ASV *into* ACCT-1SV (*acct-id*);

An alternative way of handling separated state-vectors is for the *loadsv* and *storesv*
operations to be executed by the process which owns the state-vector. At the entry
point, before the GO TO statement which resumes execution, code is inserted to load the
state-vector whose identifier is in the input record:

> ACCT-1-S **subroutine** (*CA-record*)
>   *loadsv* ACCT-1SV (*CA-record-id*) *into local variables*
>   *and text-pointer*;
>
>   *go to* TP (*text-pointer*);
>   TP(1):
>   . . .

The return statements must then be preceded by the necessary *storesv* operation:

> . . .
> *text-pointer* := 3;
> *storesv local variables and text-pointer into*
>   ACCT-1SV (*CA-record-id*);
> *return*; TP(3):
> . . .

Clearly, this method is available only when the process is inverted with respect to input
streams rather than output streams, unless an additional parameter is passed giving the
identifier of the process instance which is being activated. Diagrammatically, we
represent the arrangement as:

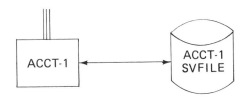

It is usual to choose this arrangement when a process is implemented as an 'on-line
transaction module'.

If two processes are in 1-1 correspondence, we may combine their state-vectors
into one. This will often be appropriate where we have specified a level-2 process
corresponding to a level-1 process. The system fragment:

may be implemented as shown in Fig. 11.20. The operation *write* CC in CUST-1 passes
as a parameter to CUST-2 the combined state-vector which it has itself received as a
parameter from the SCHEDULER process.

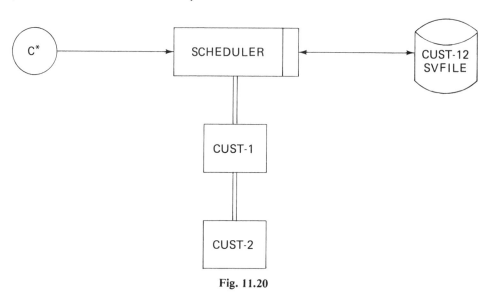

Fig. 11.20

11.10 WIDGET WAREHOUSE: IMPLEMENTATION—1

In Sections 9.18 and 9.19 we specified major functions for the Widget Warehouse
system. The resulting SSD, with some abbreviation of process names, and with the addition of an enquiry function ENQ which replies to enquiries about the orders, is shown in
Fig. 11.21. We will implement this system on a single processor, assuming the processor
to be dedicated, perfectly reliable, and perpetually running. We will remove some part of
this requirement in a later implementation.

One feature of this implementation task which we have not met before is the need
to provide a share of a processor to a process which loops inspecting a state-vector.
PROD-1, as specified in the initial model step in Section 8.11, loops inspecting the state-
vector of PROD-0. When it detects that an AVAIL action has occurred for PROD-0, it
writes a record to the data stream PP. Clearly, if we activate PROD-1, it will not
suspend itself before the next AVAIL action, and will thus monopolize the processor for
an unacceptably long time. The same problem is present, in an even more acute form, in
the BUTTON-1 process of the Hi-Ride Elevator system: BUTTON-1, once given the
processor, will not suspend itself until the button is pressed, and that may never happen.

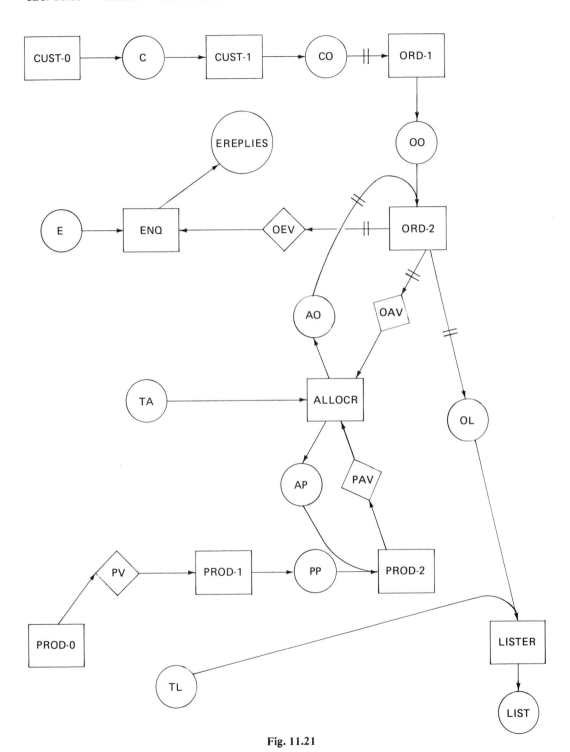

Fig. 11.21

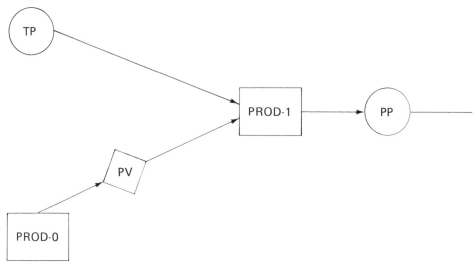

Fig. 11.22

We had no difficulty in implementing the Hi-Ride Elevator system, because we provided a processor for the sole use of each BUTTON-1 process; it was no disadvantage then that BUTTON-1 monopolized its processor while it waited for the button to be pressed, since no other process was waiting to use the same processor.

We need to change PROD-1 so that it will suspend itself sufficiently often. We can do this by providing it with another data stream, with respect to which it will be inverted. If we call this data stream TP, and choose to make it an input stream, the SSD is modified as in Fig. 11.22.

We must place *read* TP operations in the text of PROD-1; it will be suitable to cause PROD-1 to suspend itself on each *getsv* PV operation, so we place a *read* TP

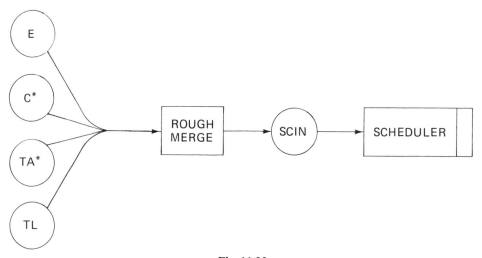

Fig. 11.23

operation following each of these. Now, when the inverted process PROD-1 is blocked at a *read* TP operation, the next call will cause it to execute a *getsv* PV operation, and possibly to write a record of PP, before returning to the calling process. We will arrange for the scheduler of the system to write the TP records to PROD-1 at a convenient frequency.

The data stream inputs to the system are C, E, TA, and TL. We will suppose that all of these inputs are merged into a single input stream to be read by the scheduler. Either, in an on-line system, the inputs from all the terminals are concentrated into one sequential message stream, or, in a more old-fashioned system, all the inputs go through one card reader. This supposition is really necessary if we are intending an implementation which is strictly on one processor, as opposed to an implementation on one hardware processor simulating many virtual processors. With only one processor, it is essential that all data stream input at the system boundary should be read by the scheduler, and not directly by processes of the SSD. If a process in the SSD reads input directly, then when that process is blocked waiting for that input stream to make a record available, the whole system is blocked. The problem is really the same problem as we saw with PROD-0, but in the case of data stream input it has an easier solution.

We can picture the system, therefore, as in Fig. 11.23. We will not consider the rough merge explicitly, but merely assume it to be fair enough.

A useful starting point in planning the scheduling of a system with significant data stream input is to diagram the structure of the input stream to the scheduler. The structure of SCIN may be as shown in Fig. 11.24. The meaning of this structure is that any of the record types can appear in the input at any time. This would be true if we provided a service round the clock, accepting input from any source at any time. We might instead place some restriction on the input. For example, we might allow enquiries and inputs from customers only during the hours of 9 a.m. to 5.30 p.m. each

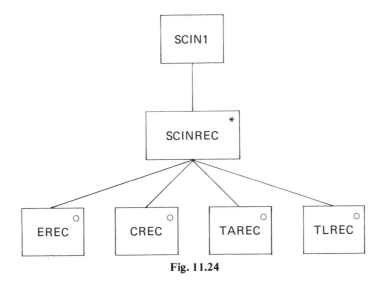

Fig. 11.24

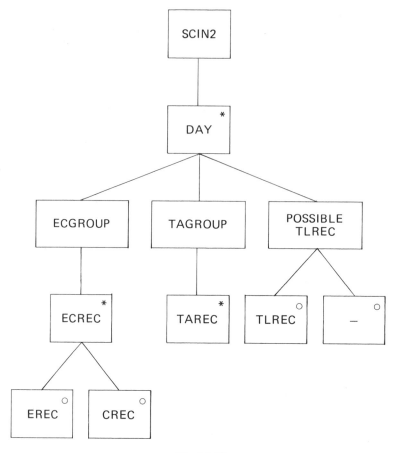

Fig. 11.25

day, and requests for allocation (TARECs) only between 6 p.m. and 9 p.m., and request for a LIST output only between 9.30 p.m. and 8.30 a.m. The structure of SCIN would then be as shown in Fig. 11.25.

We are not, of course, free to make arbitrary decisions here. Any restriction on the possibility of certain inputs at certain times is a part of the specification, and must be explicitly agreed with the user.

For our present implementation, we will assume the unrestricted structure of SCIN 1. We will also assume that the response requirements are these:

— ENQ replies should be produced as soon as possible, and should be based on an up-to-date state of the order model;

— allocation should be performed as soon as possible after the request (the TAREC) is entered;

— the LIST should be produced as soon as possible, consistent with the other requirements.

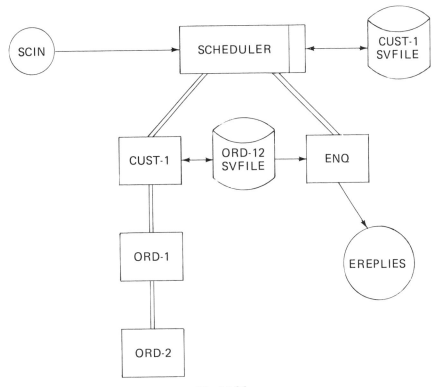

Fig. 11.26

We have intentionally stated rather vague requirements. We are left to make our own choices where there is conflict. This is a little unrealistic, but will allow us to explore various possibilities in discussing the implementation.

If the ENQ replies are to be produced 'as soon as possible', then the ENQ process must be activated as soon as an EREC is available in the SCIN stream. This implies that ENQ should be inverted and should be a subroutine of the scheduler. If the replies are to be based on 'an up-to-date state of the order model', then the CUST-1, ORD-1, and ORD-2 processes must similarly be scheduled as soon as input is available. The most direct way of achieving this is to make CUST-1, inverted with respect to C, a subroutine of the scheduler, and to allow CUST-1 to schedule ORD-1 and, indirectly, ORD-2, whenever it produces a CO record. ORD-2 is inverted with respect to its rough merged input stream OO&AO; its state-vector may be combined with that of ORD-1. The implementation so far is as shown in Fig. 11.26.

The output stream OL of ORD-2 does not appear in this partial implementation. That is because records of OL are ALLOC and DELAY, and cannot be written as a result of input records of OO, which contains only PLACE, AMEND, CANCEL, and DELIVER. (We must verify, in the specification of ORD-2, that nothing has been done to cause OL records to appear as a result of OO input: for example, by storing a DELAY record for output when a later AMEND or CANCEL is input.)

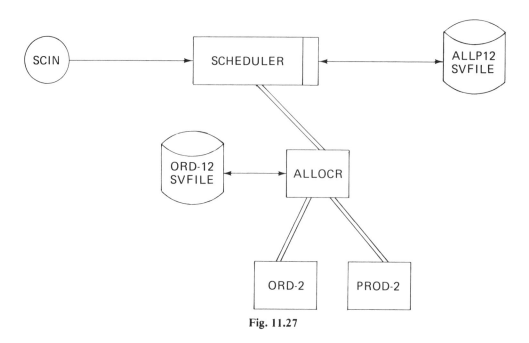

Fig. 11.27

The ALLOCR process is more complex. Its text is given in Section 9.18, omitting the *write* AP operation from the end of AGROUP-BODY which is discussed in Section 9.19. When the ALLOCR receives a TAREC, it executes the following sequence of operations:

— *getsv* PAV, determining the available stock for allocation;
— for those orders which are for the relevant product and are due for allocation:
    — *getsv* OAV to determine the quantity requested;
    — *write* DELAY or *write* ALLOCATE to AO, according to whether the allocation can be made;
— *write* an AP record, indicating the amount allocated in the AGROUP which has been executed.

The connections between ALLOCR and PROD-2 and between ALLOCR and ORD-2 both have the pattern which is often found in simple interacting functions: *getsv* followed by a *write* to the same process instance.

Since there is one ALLOCR for each instance of PROD-1 and PROD-2, we can conveniently combine their state-vectors, as we did for ORD-1 and ORD-2, giving a state-vector ALLP12. Inverting PROD-2 with respect to its rough merged input AP&PP, we can sketch the partial implementation as in Fig. 11.27.

PROD-1 is activated whenever a TP record is written. TP records are not a part of the input at the system boundary, but are to be written internally, according to the frequency of activation desired for PROD-1. It seems reasonable that PROD-1 should be

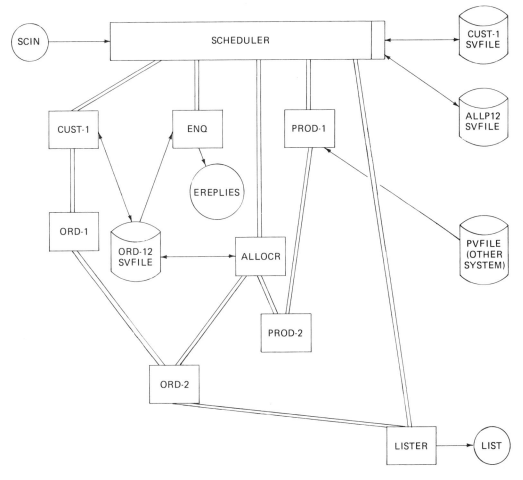

Fig. 11.28

activated whenever the associated ALLOCR is activated to execute an AGROUP. We may therefore write a TP record from the SCHEDULER whenever a TAREC is about to be written to an ALLOCR process. PROD-1 is inverted with respect to its TP input, and calls PROD-2 when it writes a PP output record. PROD-2 is thus a subroutine both of ALLOCR and of PROD-1.

It remains only to consider the LISTER. We may invert the LISTER process with respect to its rough merged input OL&TL, making it a subroutine both of the SCHEDULER and of ORD-2. The complete resulting implementation is shown in Fig. 11.28. It has been constructed rather hastily, and we will consider some of its defects in the next section.

11.11 WIDGET WAREHOUSE: IMPLEMENTATION—2

A major defect of the implementation developed in the preceding section is that response time to CREC and EREC inputs may be very bad, if they follow closely after a TAREC. When the scheduler reads the TAREC, it will activate the appropriate instance of the ALLOCR process, which will not suspend itself and return control to the scheduler until it has completed an AGROUP. This may require a large amount of elapsed time if there are many orders for the associated product due for allocation.

We can correct this defect by inverting ALLOCR with respect to both TA and AO data streams. It is then suspended at each *read* TA operation and also at each *write* AO operation, giving the scheduler an opportunity to activate some other process before the current AGROUP is complete. The relevant part of the implementation is now as shown in Fig. 11.29.

The ORD-2 processes are not now connected directly to the ALLOCR process; records of AO must pass through the scheduler, being written by ALLOCR and buffered by the scheduler before being read by ORD-2. Careful readers will notice that this implementation, unlike that of the previous section, allows the possibility that the ALLOCR process obtains an ORD-2 state-vector, and makes an allocation which then arrives at the ORD-2 process after an intervening CANCEL or AMEND record. We do not complain about this: the looseness of the scheduling was consciously permitted in the specification.

We can remove the looseness of scheduling by resolving that we will design the scheduler so that when ALLOCR writes a record of AO, the scheduler immediately activates the ORD-2 process to read that record. In this way, the scheduler can ensure that no CANCEL or AMEND record can intervene for the order between inspection of its state by ALLOCR and reading the resulting ALLOCATE or DELAY record.

An alternative implementation is also possible. We can introduce another input data stream, TOA, for ALLOCR, much as we introduced the stream TP for PROD-1. The process ALLOCR reads a record of TOA immediately before each *getsv* OAV operation. ALLOCR is inverted with respect to both TA and TOA, and thus is connected to the SCHEDULER by a channel. The records of TOA are written by the scheduler whenever it chooses to activate ALLOCR for one more order of the current AGROUP. The implementation of Fig. 11.28 is otherwise unchanged.

Whichever of these implementations we choose, the design of the SCHEDULER process becomes more complex than before. In the implementation of the previous section, the SCHEDULER needed to do nothing more elaborate than to activate ENQ for each EREC, ALLOCR for each TAREC, CUST-1 for each CREC, and LISTER for each TLREC. No records were buffered, and no process was suspended except when it was blocked waiting for an input record from SCIN. Now there are choices to be made, and in designing the SCHEDULER we must specify the algorithms for making them. If no input record is available in SCIN, the scheduler should activate an ALLOCR, if there is one, which is suspended in the middle of an AGROUP. If there is more than one ALLOCR so suspended, there must be some rule for deciding which is to be activated. A reasonable rule would be some kind of round robin: each suspended ALLOCR process is activated once in turn, so long as SCIN is empty. A list of suspended ALLOCR processes is maintained, addressed by a pointer which moves circularly around the list. In outline, the SCHEDULER might be:

```
SCHEDULER seq
    list := null; ptr := head of list;
    SCHEDULER-BODY itr
      SCHEDULER-PHASE sel (SCIN empty)
        POSSIBLE-ALLOCR sel (list is null)
        POSSIBLE-ALLOCR alt (list is not null)
          activate ALLOCR (ptr);
          query ALLOCR (ptr);
          POSSIBLE-ALLOCR-DELETE sel (read TA in ALLOCR (ptr))
            remove ALLOCR (ptr) from list;
          POSSIBLE-ALLOCR-DELETE alt (read TOA in ALLOCR (ptr))
          POSSIBLE-ALLOCR-DELETE end
          ptr := next in list;
        POSSIBLE-ALLOCR end
      SCHEDULER-PHASE alt (SCIN not empty)
        read SCIN;
        SCIN-RECORD sel (TAREC)
          query ALLOCR (TAREC-id);
          TARECORD sel (read TOA in ALLOCR (TAREC-id))
            {allocation already in progress: ignore TAREC}
          TARECORD alt (read TA in ALLOCR (TAREC-id))
            activate PROD-1 (TAREC-id);
            activate ALLOCR (TAREC-id);
            add ALLOCR (TAREC-id) to list;
          TARECORD end
        SCIN-RECORD alt (EREC)
          activate ENQ;
        SCIN-RECORD alt (CREC)
          activate CUST-1 (CREC-id);
        SCIN-RECORD alt (TLREC)
          activate LISTER;
        SCIN-RECORD end
      SCHEDULER-PHASE end
    SCHEDULER-BODY end
  SCHEDULER end
```

We have chosen, arbitrarily, to ignore a TAREC for a product whose allocation is already in progress. It would, perhaps, have been preferable to buffer the TAREC for future consumption when the current allocation for the product is complete.

The problem we have been considering in the case of the ALLOCR process exists also in the case of the LISTER process. If the LISTER contains an ordering clash, that is, if its rough merged OL input is not in the same sequence as the LIST output, then the LISTER process will run for a long time without suspension when it receives a TLREC.

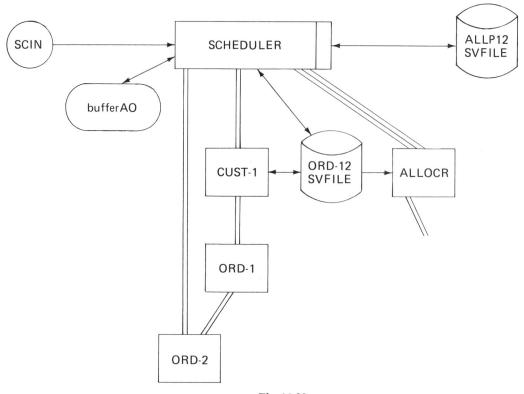

Fig. 11.29

The production of the output in LIST for one LIST GROUP, perhaps preceded by execution of a sort utility program, will monopolize the single processor to the exclusion of the other processes of the system.

We may be able to apply the same method to LISTER that we have applied to ALLOCR: we can introduce additional suspension points as operations on an additional data stream. But this method will not be successful if LISTER invokes a sort utility program: the sort utility may perhaps provide an opportunity to insert suspension points during its input and output phases, but not during execution of the central sorting phases. We are then compelled to adopt one of two schemes. Either we accept that input of a TLREC will make the system temporarily unavailable for processing of other input (perhaps restricting input of TLRECs to hours when little or no other input is provided), or we must use another processor in the implementation.

If we are implementing the system on a machine equipped with a multi-tasking supervisor, we will have no great difficulty in providing another processor. We simply run LISTER as a separate task from the SCHEDULER, passing the records of OL and TL to that separate task by whatever means the supervisor provides. We would specify a low priority for LISTER relative to the priority of SCHEDULER, to ensure that it does not reduce the performance of the rest of the system unacceptably.

11.12 PROCESS DISMEMBERING—1

In all the implementations considered so far, we have been able to keep the program text of each process intact. We have transformed it where necessary for inversion, and added some operations to handle state-vectors, but the text has always been kept in one piece. This is clearly very desirable, but it is not always possible.

In our implementation of the Widget Warehouse system, the ORD-2 process was transformed into a subroutine of ALLOCR and ORD-1, by inversion with respect to its rough merged input OO&AO. We assumed that there was no difficulty in implementing a common subroutine of this kind. Under different circumstances, however, it might be less simple:

— If we decide to run ALLOCR on a separate processor, we would make it a separate task, as we did with LISTER; there would be one task for each ALLOCR process. The supervisor might impose a rule that different tasks could not have common subroutines: ORD-2 could not be common to ALLOCR and ORD-1.

— If we create an implementation in which ALLOCR processes are run in a batch each evening, while CUST-1, ORD-1, ORD-2, and ENQ are run on-line during the day, we might similarly be precluded from using a common subroutine.

Provided that the state-vector of ORD-2 is separated from its program text, as it is, there is really no difficulty here. We merely create two copies of the program text of ORD-2, and use one as a subroutine of ALLOCR and the other as a subroutine of ORD-1. The two copies are identical, and share one state-vector which contains all the local variables of the process and its text-pointer. We must, of course, ensure that both copies are never simultaneously active: where ALLOCR runs on a separate processor, this would require us to use mechanisms for locking and unlocking the state-vector, regarded as a database record. However, this is not the problem we wish to discuss in this section.

The problem that concerns us in this section arises when we are prevented from keeping the whole of the text together. We may find, for example, that a 'transaction module' consisting of CUST-1, ORD-1, and ORD-2 is too large: a 'transaction monitor' may impose a size limit on the text of a transaction module. We would then need to find a way of reducing the size, and we will do so by cutting up, or dismembering, the text of ORD-2.

The structure of ORD-2 is essentially the structure shown in Appendix D. With the process inverted with respect to its rough merged input stream OO&AO, the text is, in outline:

```
ORD-2-S subroutine (OSV, O-record)
    go to TP (text-pointer);
    TP(1):
    ORD-2 seq
      PLACE seq
        text-pointer := 2; return; TP(2):
      PLACE end
```

```
        ORDER-BODY itr while (AMEND or DELAY)
          OBODY-ACTION sel (AMEND)
            AMEND seq
              text-pointer := 3; return; TP(3):
            AMEND end
          OBODY-ACTION alt (DELAY)
            DELAY seq
              write DELAY to OL;
              text-pointer := 4; return; TP(4):
            DELAY end
          OBODY-ACTION end
        ORDER-BODY end
        FINISH sel (CANCEL)
          . . .
        FINISH end
      ORD-2 end
    ORD-2-S end
```

For the copy of ORD-2 to be used in the transaction module with CUST-1 and ORD-1, the only input records that can appear are PLACE, AMEND, CANCEL, and DELIVER. The records DELAY and ALLOCATE cannot appear because they are written only by ALLOCR, which is not present in the transaction module. We can therefore safely remove from the text those parts which would be executed only when a DELAY or ALLOCATE record appears. The result is the reduced text:

```
ORD-2-S subroutine (OSV, O-record)
  go to TP (text-pointer);
  TP(1):
  ORD-2 seq
    PLACE seq
      text-pointer := 2; return; TP(2):
    PLACE end
    ORDER-BODY itr while (AMEND)
      ORDER-ACTION sel (AMEND)
        AMEND seq
          text-pointer := 3; return; TP(3):
        AMEND end
      OBODY-ACTION alt (else)
        TP(4):
      OBODY-ACTION end
    ORDER-BODY end
    FINISH sel (CANCEL)
      . . .
    FINISH end
  ORD-2 end
ORD-2-S end
```

The text-pointer label TP(4) must be retained, as must all the labels. Although DELAY and ALLOCATE records cannot be input to the copy of ORD-2 in the transaction module, the state of ORD-2 when the transaction module is activated may be the result of one of those records input to the other copy. The unnecessary condition on the selection OBODY-ACTION can be removed or replaced by the condition 'true' which can be evaluated at compile time rather than at run time.

Dismembering a process text in this way, like all JSD transformations, should be carried out on the text in the implementation language (PL/I, COBOL, etc.) or in object code; we show the transformation here in the structure text purely for purposes of explanation. Maintenance to the system must be performed on the original structure text, and the transformations repeated to obtain a changed object code version.

11.13 PROCESS DISMEMBERING—2

One of the defects of the Widget Warehouse system implementation discussed in Sections 11.10 and 11.11 was its dependence on a perfectly reliable, perpetually running, machine. In the next section we will consider an implementation which does not require the machine to run perpetually; it will, in fact, be a batch implementation. Before we begin to consider batch implementation, we must first explore another form of process dismembering.

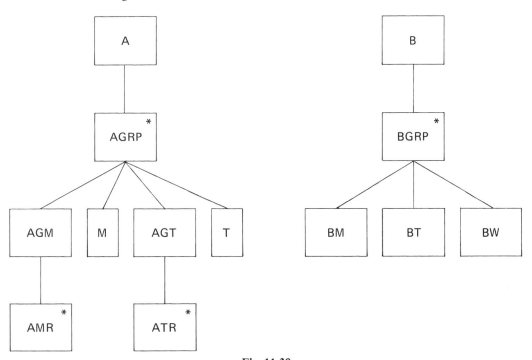

Fig. 11.30

Suppose that we have a very small system consisting of only one process:

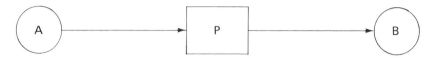

The structures of A and B are shown in Fig. 11.30.

The records AMR and ATR each contain an integer. The records M and T are effectively TGMs that have already been merged into the data stream A. For each AGRP in A there is a BGRP in B; BM is the total of the AMR records; BT is the total of the ATR records; BW is the total of both AMR and ATR records in the AGRP.

Using a little backtracking in the text of P, to simplify the explanations that will follow, we have:

```
P itr
  PGRP seq
    BW := 0;
    PGRPM seq
      BM := 0;
      PGM itr
        read A;
      PGM quit (M);
        BW := BW + AMR; BM := BM + AMR;
      PGM end
      PM seq
        {read A not needed}
        write BM;
      PM end
    PGRPM end
    PGRPT seq
      BT := 0;
      PGT itr
        read A;
      PGT quit (T);
        BW := BW + ATR; BT := BT + ATR;
      PGT end
      PT seq
        {read A not needed}
        write BT; write BW;
      PT end
    PGRPT end
  PGRP end
P end
```

The input records of A arrive steadily during the course of successive weeks. The M record arrives at 9 a.m. on Monday morning, and the T record at 9 a.m. on Thursday morning. We can, of course, choose to run the system on a dedicated, perpetually running, machine; but we decide that instead we would like to use the machine only once each week, on Thursday morning. Each Thursday morning we wish to execute one instance of PGRP, reading one instance of AGRP and writing one instance of BGRP.

We need to dismember the process P, and also the data streams A and B. Dismembering P, we have two parts of the process:

> P **itr**
>> *execute one PGRP*;
>
> P **end**

and

> PGRP **seq**
>> . . .
>
> PGRP **end**

The dismembering of A and B follows exactly the same pattern. We can implement the dismembered process P quite easily; the first part is implemented manually, following natural language instructions to the machine operator:

> Each Thursday morning, soon after 9 a.m., please run the program PGRP, using the latest generation of the input file AGRP.

The second part is the text of PGRP, implemented as a batch program. Dismembering of the input stream A consists of saving the input records until a T record appears, and presenting the saved records, with the T record, to the batch program in the form of a batch serial file. The T record can be supplied by the data preparation department at the appropriate time; in the batch serial file it is implemented as an end-of-file marker record. Dismembering the output stream B consists of no more than removing the paper from the printer when the batch program has produced the week's BGRP output.

This batch implementation is trivially easy, because of the relationship between the dismembering and the state-vector of P. The state-vector of P consists of:

— the text-pointer of P;
— the variables BM, BT, and BW.

The variables BM, BT, and BW are all local to PGRP. That is, their values are not carried over from one instance of PGRP to another. We do not need to remember values from one batch run to another. The text-pointer of P has only two values outside PGRP:

> TP(1):
> P **itr**
>> *execute one* PGRP;
>> TP(2):
>
> P **end**

These two values need not be distinguished in the implementation, because the meaning of the **itr** construct is that TP(2) is followed immediately by a branch to TP(1), with no intervening operation of any kind. Informally, the process is in the same state immediately after a PGRP as it was before the first PGRP. From the machine operator's point of view, this means that when he comes to carry out the next activity there is no scope for error: there is only ever one next activity that can be carried out.

It will be slightly more difficult to implement the system by two weekly batch programs, one to be run on Monday and one on Thursday. We dismember the process P into three parts this time:

```
P itr
  PGRP seq
    BW := 0;
    execute one PGRPM;
    execute one PGRPT;
  PGRP end
P end
```

and:

```
PGRPM seq
  . . .
PGRPM seq
```

and:

```
PGRPT seq
  . . .
PGRPT end
```

Dismembering the data streams is straightforward, as before, but we must take more care with the state-vector of P. First, the variable BW is global to PGRPM and PGRPT; the value of BW after running the batch program PGRPM must be preserved and made available to PGRPT. Second, the operator's instructions are a little more complex, and provide some scope for error:

> Each Monday morning, soon after 9 a.m., set the value of BW to 0, and then run the program PGRPM, using the latest generation of the input file AGRPM. Save the resulting value of BW. Then, on the following Thursday morning, run the program PGRPT, using the latest generation of the input file AGRPT and the saved value of BW.

We can simplify the operator's task in various ways. The operation BW := 0 can be moved into the beginning of the program PGRPM. The variable BW can be saved as a dataset in its own right and subjected to the same automatic control of dataset generations as the datasets AGRPM and AGRPT, if such control is provided in the machine's operating system. It may also be possible to ensure that the programs PRGPM and PRGPT can only be run alternately, starting with PRGPM, and that the dataset BW produced by PRGPM must be input to the following execution of PRGPT. All these mechanisms, provided by the operating system, are cumbersome and indirect ways of handling the state-vector of the process P after it has been dismembered: they allow the relationships which are explicitly shown in the text of P, and in the operations on its variables, to be implicitly maintained by constraining the execution of the dismembered parts. Systems for automatic generation of job control statements may provide a slightly more explicit way of achieving the same result.

We have presented this form of process dismembering as a means of obtaining a batch implementation, and we will often use it for that purpose. The essential precondition for its use is that the structure of the process to be dismembered corresponds to the required execution pattern. The process P which we have used as an example could not be dismembered into monthly batch programs, or batch programs to be run every two days: its structure contains no MONTH or TWO-DAY component. If we want to run P in monthly batches, we must build a separate scheduler for the system, and take care that the scheduler structure does have a MONTH component; P could then be inverted and made a subroutine of the scheduler, and the scheduler could be dismembered to give a monthly batch program. A standard application of this technique is in the implementation of on-line systems where service is provided for only a limited part of each day. The specification processes do not contain DAY components, but they can be scheduled by a scheduler which does, and which can be dismembered to give the required pattern of execution.

11.14 SID NOTATIONS FOR DISMEMBERING

If a process of the SSD, or a scheduler process, is dismembered, we will show its dismembered parts as separate boxes in the SID. The process name is suffixed by a small letter to distinguish the parts. If, for example, we dismember the ORD-2 process in the Widget Warehouse system implementation, we would show the parts of ORD-2 separately with suffixed names (Fig. 11.31).

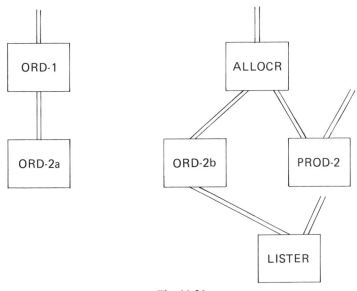

Fig. 11.31

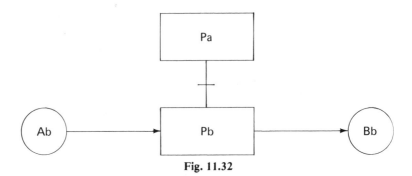

Fig. 11.32

When we use the second form of dismembering, discussed in the preceding section, we will need to show a new relationship between the dismembered parts. This relationship is called 'complete execution'; it is represented by a single line with a bar, as in Fig. 11.32.

Pa invokes or calls Pb, but not by the mechanism of process inversion; each call of Pb (the batch program PGRP) causes one complete execution of the text of Pb from beginning to end. The dismembered parts of the data streams are also shown with suffixed names. It is convenient sometimes to use special symbols to indicate serial and direct-access datasets. The version of this system in which P is dismembered into three parts is shown in Fig. 11.33.

Pc is the part:

P **itr**
  . . .
P **end**

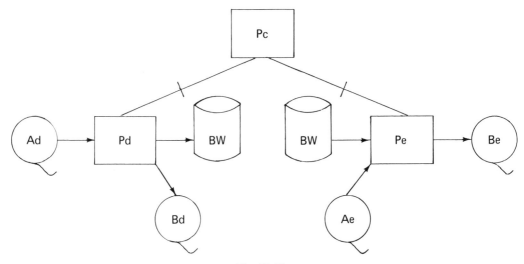

Fig. 11.33

Pd and Pe are respectively PGRPM and PGRPT. The control structure which determines the order of execution of Pd and Pe is not shown or implied in the diagram: it is shown explicitly in the text of Pc. The dataset BW is shown separately for Pd and Pe; a fully detailed version of the text of Pc would show the relationship between the instances, or generations, of BW produced by Pd and those input to Pe.

There is some scope for using more informative names in the boxes for parts of processes: in place of the bald 'Pe' we might write 'Pe(PGRPT)'.

11.15 WIDGET WAREHOUSE: IMPLEMENTATION—3

We are called into the office of the manager of the Widget Warehouse, where we learn that the implementations we discussed in the earlier sections of this chapter are unacceptable. The computer is very heavily loaded during the day with other systems: the purchasing and inventory system uses a lot of the available resources; more is consumed by the frequent printing of Snoopy calendars and the manager's own Predictive Roulette system, which he runs constantly in preparation for his regular visits to the local casino. Very little time is available for our own system during the day; it will be just possible to accept input for the C, E, TA, and TL streams, but the major processing must all be done in the evenings. Naturally, this will mean that the response time for enquiry processing by the ENQ process will be large, but the manager has decreed that this is inevitable, and must be accepted.

Returning to our earlier implementation, we see that quite a small change will solve the problem. We need to introduce another TGM input stream, TD, each record of which arrives when the day is finished and the computer is available for our major system to run. This is rough merged with the other input, and the structure of SCIN is now as shown in Fig. 11.34.

We must redesign the SCHEDULER so that the DAYBODY records are buffered during the day, and the system processes run only after the TD record has arrived. In outline, the new scheduler is:

```
NEWSCHED itr
  NSCHEDDAY seq
    DAYBODY itr
      read SCIN;
    DAYBODY quit (TD);
      write SCINREC to buffer;
    DAYBODY end
    TD seq
      {read SCIN not needed}
      write TD to buffer;
    TD end
    EVENING seq
      {run the system processes with all buffered input}
    EVENING end
  NSCHEDDAY end
NEWSCHED end
```

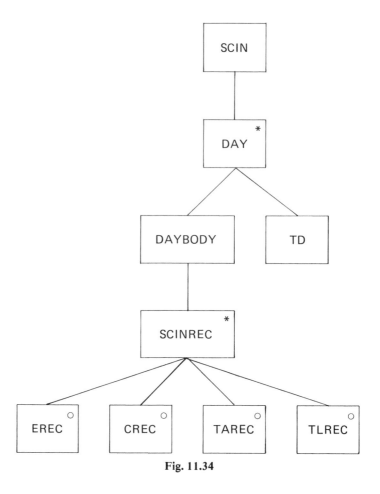

Fig. 11.34

We dismember this process into three parts, and arrive at the implementation shown in Fig. 11.35. NEWSCHEDb consists of the components DAYBODY and TD of NEWSCHED; NEWSCHEDc is the component EVENING; NEWSCHEDa is:

NEWSCHED **itr**
  NSCHEDDAY **seq**
    execute NEWSCHEDb;
    execute NEWSCHEDc;
  NSCHEDDAY **end**
NEWSCHED **end**

NEWSCHEDc may be almost the same as the simple SCHEDULER process of our first implementation. There is no benefit in the more complex scheduling of the second implementation, in which we took some trouble to suspend the ALLOCR and LISTER processes during AGROUPs and LIST GROUPs. The only change necessary is that BUFFERb, unlike SCIN, has an end-of-file marker, and this must be recognized by NEWSCHEDc. The structure of NEWSCHEDc is:

```
NEWSCHED-C seq
  read BUFFER-B;
  NEWSCHED-C-BODY itr while (not TD)
    NEWSCHED-C-REC sel (EREC)
      activate ENQ; read BUFFER-B;
    NEWSCHED-C-REC alt (CREC)
      activate CUST-1 (CREC-id); read BUFFER-B;
    NEWSCHED-C-REC alt (TAREC)
      activate PROD-1 (TAREC-id);
      activate ALLOCR (TAREC-id); read BUFFER-B;
    NEWSCHED-C-REC alt (TLREC)
      activate LISTER; read BUFFER-B;
    NEWSCHED-C-REC end
  NEWSCHED-C-BODY end
NEWSCHED-C end
```

In every important respect, this implementation is identical to our first simple implementation. We have merely arranged to delay running the system until each evening, saving the input records that arrive during the day. It is, as it were, a transaction-oriented system run in batch mode.

The state-vector of NEWSCHED consists of no more than the text-pointer value, indicating whether the next program to be run is NEWSCHEDb or NEWSCHEDc. The state-vectors of the system specification processes, of course, must be preserved from one instance of NSCHEDDAY to the next, as is usual with master files and databases. Some special care is needed with any process whose state-vector has not been separated. The only processes to consider are ENQ and LISTER. The ENQ process offers no difficulty: it is always suspended in the same state, being the state in which it is blocked waiting for an E record. We may therefore leave the ENQ process unchanged.

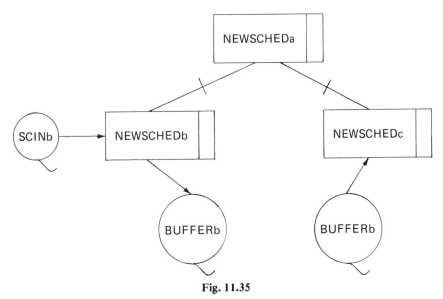

Fig. 11.35

The LISTER process, as specified in Section 9.18, can be similarly treated. If we had found a need to preserve state-vector values from one instance of NEWSCHEDc to another, we would merely have separated the state-vector from the text of the affected process, so that it could be held along with the other process state-vectors; we would also need to bring the state-vector together with the text when the process is activated, in the usual way.

11.16 WIDGET WAREHOUSE: IMPLEMENTATION—4

In an embarrassing interview, the manager tells us that even our new implementation is not good enough. After some unlucky evenings at the casino, he has disposed of the disk drives and replaced them by some used tape drives which he obtained at a low, low price. We must now design another implementation: NEWSCHEDa and NEWSCHEDb are still satisfactory, but we must redesign NEWSCHEDc.

Because we are limited to tape files, we must access process state-vectors serially, in the order they appear on tape. We can sort the files of state-vectors, and we can also sort the buffered data streams. Our purpose is to choose a scheduling of the system which correctly implements the specification and does not require an excessive amount of tape reading, writing, and sorting.

To keep the amount of tape activity reasonably small, we must schedule the system so that all processes of one type are activated in a single pass of the tape. For example, we might arrange to activate all the CUST-1 processes, then all the ORD-1 processes, and so on. This scheduling will, in general, conflict with the chronological ordering of the input records, and we must examine each conflict and its effects.

One general principle must be observed: the time ordering of data stream records must not be unnecessarily destroyed by sorting. Suppose, for example, that the input consists only of CRECs. We decide to sort the input into customer-id order, because that is the order of the CUST-1 state-vectors on tape. We must ensure that the chronological ordering is preserved within each customer-id. Similarly, if we take the CO output records from the CUST-1 processes, and sort them into order-id order, we must again preserve the chronological ordering within order-id. We will assume in everything that follows that every sort of a serial file preserves the input ordering within each instance of the sort key. If the available sort utility program does not allow this preservation as a default, we must append a sequence number to each input record and use that sequence number as the least significant field of the sorting key, thus forcing the sort to preserve chronological order.

Considering only the CREC and TAREC inputs, we can see at once a conflict of some severity. Suppose that a certain order is for widgets, and that the input stream to NEWSCHEDc contains these records for this order and product:

AMEND, TAREC, AMEND, . . .

We ought to activate the order process to read the first AMEND, then the ALLOCR process for widgets, then the order process to read the second AMEND. Unfortunately, activation of the order process for AMEND requires the ORD-2 state-vectors to be in order-id order, while activation of the ALLOCR process requires the ORD-2 state-vectors to be in product-id order. We could find ourselves passing the ORD-12SVFILE tape twice for every TAREC, with a sort after every pass. Clearly, this is not possible with the available resources. Nor is much gained by clever schemes in which the tape is kept in order-id order and each ALLOCR process scans the whole tape.

The only reasonable resolution of this problem is to defer activation of ALLOCR processes until all C inputs have been consumed by CUST-1 processes, and all resulting CO and OO records consumed by ORD-1 and ORD-2 processes. A TAREC input during the day is to be regarded as a request to perform the allocation in the evening, after other processing has been completed. The meaning of this decision in specification terms is that the rough merge of OO&AO input to ORD-2 is grossly favorable to OO input at the expense of AO input, and that the OAV connection between ALLOCR and ORD-2 gives ALLOCR a highly up to date—indeed, futuristic—view of the state of ORD-2.

The warehouse manager is in no position to object. He also agrees that we can treat ERECs similarly, issuing EREPLIES output on the basis of the state of ORD-2 after all other processing; and that the LISTER is to be run after all ALLOCR processes have run.

The input stream BUFFERb must therefore be separated out into its components C*b, Eb, TA*b, and TLb, and each component treated in a separate part of NEWSCHEDc. The outline structure of NEWSCHEDc is:

```
NEWSCHED-C seq
  NSC-C-A seq
    split BUFFERb into C*b, Eb, TA*b, TLb;
  NSC-C-A end
  sort C*b into customer-id order giving C*bSC;
  NSC-C-B seq
    activate CUST-1 processes;
  NSC-C-B end
  sort CO*b into order-id order giving CO*bSO;
  NSC-C-C seq
    activate ORD-1 and ORD-2 processes;
  NSC-C-C end
  sort TA*b into product-id order giving TA*bSP;
  sort ORD-12SVFILE into product-id/delay/quantity order
                                    giving ORD-12SVFILESPD;
  NSC-C-D seq
    activate PROD-1, PROD-2, ALLOCR, ORD-2 processes;
  NSC-C-D end
  sort Eb into order-id order giving EbSO;
  sort ORD-12SVFILE into order-id order giving ORD-12SVFILESO;
  NSC-C-E seq
    activate ENQ process;
  NSC-C-E end
  NSC-C-F seq
    activate LISTER process;
  NSC-C-F end
NEWSCHED-C end
```

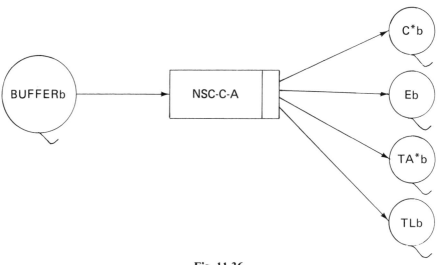

Fig. 11.36

NSC-C-A is a trivial program shown in Fig. 11.36. An end-of-file marker record is written to the end of each of the output files. It is possible for any output file to contain no records other than this marker.

NSC-C-B is a little more interesting (Fig. 11.37). CUST-1 is inverted with respect to its input stream C. The CUST-1 processes are activated in ascending order by customer-id, that being the order of the state-vectors on tape and the input records in the sorted file C*bSC. When activated, a CUST-1 process may write a record to CO*b.

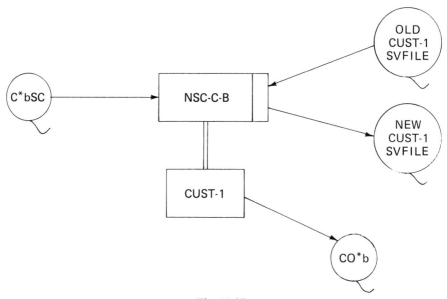

Fig. 11.37

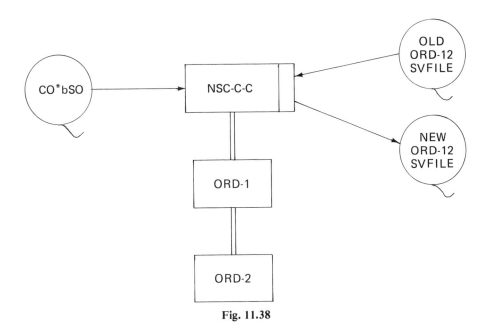

Fig. 11.38

NSC-C-B is the classical serial file update program. Each CUST-1 state-vector is read from tape; CUST-1 is activated as many times as there are CRECs for that customer in C*bSC (possibly zero times), and the new value of the state-vector written to the new state-vector file:

read C*bSC;
read OLD-CUST-1-SVFILE;
. . .
. . .
  NSC-C-B-CUST **seq**
    NSC-C-B-CUST-BODY **itr while** ($CREC\text{-}id = CSV\text{-}id$)
      CALL CUST-1 (CSV, CREC);
      read C*bSC;
    NSC-C-B-CUST-BODY **end**
    write CSV *to* NEW-CUST-1-SVFILE;
  NSC-C-B-CUST **end**
  read OLD-CUST-1-SVFILE;
. . .

NSC-C-C is similar to NSC-C-B (Fig. 11.38). ORD-1 is inverted with respect to its input stream CO; ORD-2 is inverted with respect to OO&AO. As we saw in a previous section, no OL output can be produced by ORD-2 as a result of OO input records. The ORD-1 and ORD-2 processes are activated in ascending order by order-id, that being the order of the state-vectors on tape and the records in the sorted file CO*bSO.

    NSC-C-D activates the PROD-1, PROD-2, ALLOCR, and ORD-2 processes (Fig. 11.39). The PVFILE from the other system is in product-id order, as is the sorted file of

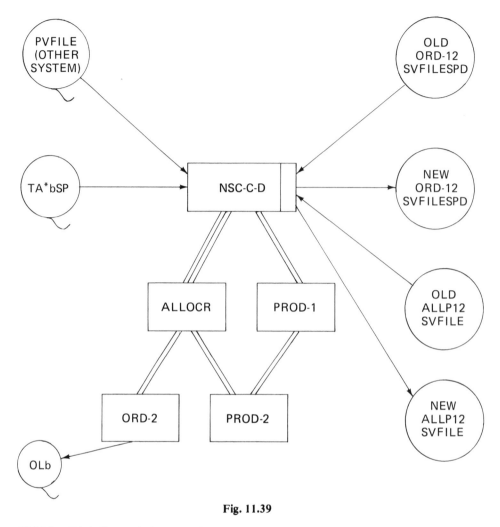

Fig. 11.39

TARECs, TA*bSP, and the sorted ORD-12SVFILE and the ALLP12SVFILE. Within product-id order, the ORD-12SVFILE is sorted so that the state-vectors are in reducing order of priority for allocation: delayed due orders, normal due orders, and orders not yet due for allocation. The ALLOCR process is inverted with respect to its TA input and also its OAV input regarded as a sequential data stream; each *getsv* OAV operation is regarded as a *read* operation on the data stream.

The structure of NSC-C-D is a straightforward JSP collating structure, matching inputs by product-id. Assuming, as we have done implicitly, that input errors have been eliminated by the input subsystem, we may concentrate our attention on the case of a product-id for which there is a TAREC, a PV state-vector, an ALLP12 state-vector, and zero or more ORD-12 state-vectors. The structure of the relevant component of NSC-C-D is:

```
RUN-ALLOCR seq
  {pid is product-id to allocate}
  CALL PROD-1 (ALLP12SV);
  CALL ALLOCR (ALLP12SV, dummy);
  RUN-ALLOCR-BODY itr while ((ORD-12SV-id = pid) and
                             (ORD-12SV due for allocation))
    CALL ALLOCR (ALLP12SV, ORD-12SV);
    write ORD-12SV to NEW ORD-12SVFILESPD;
    read OLD ORD-12SVFILESPD into ORD-12SV;
  RUN-ALLOCR-BODY end
  CALL ALLOCR (ALLP12SV, end-marker-for-OAV );
  {ALLOCR has completed an AGROUP}
  NOT-DUE-ORDER-SET itr while (ORD-12SV-id = pid)
    write ORD-12SV to NEW ORD-12SVFILESPD;
    read OLD ORD-12SVFILESPD into ORD-12SV;
  NOT-DUE-ORDER-SET end
  CONSUME-TA-SET itr while (TAREC-id = pid)
    read TA*bSP;
  CONSUME-TA-SET end
  write ALLP12SV to NEW ALLP12SVFILE;
  read OLD ALLP12SVFILE into ALLP12SV;
  read PVFILE;
RUN-ALLOCR end
```

The scheduler relies on knowledge of the structure of the ALLOCR process: it provides the equivalent of database access for the *getsv* OAV operations, including the end-marker to indicate the absence of further due orders for the product; it handles the ORD-12 state-vectors; it does not execute query ALLOCR operations, because ALLOCR is always blocked reading TA following the reading of the OAV end-marker, and at the beginning of each RUN-ALLOCR instance.

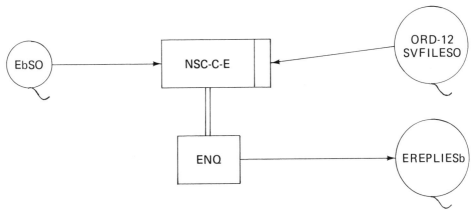

Fig. 11.40

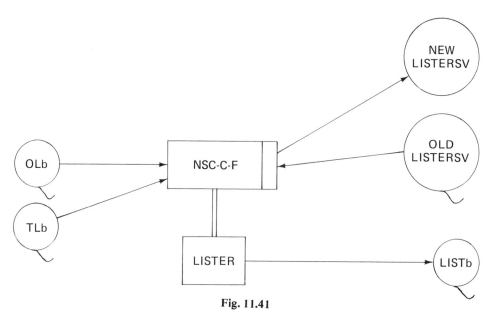

Fig. 11.41

NSC-C-E activates the ENQ process (Fig. 11.40). The ORD-12 state-vector file has been sorted back into order-id order: it will be the OLD ORD-12SVFILE in the next instance of NSC-C-C. The ENQ process is assumed to be unchanged in spite of the dismembering of the scheduling, and not to require separation of its state-vector.

NSC-C-F is shown in Fig. 11.41. The input file TLb may contain any number, including zero, of TLRECs. If it contains more than one, the surplus is ignored: the system has been scheduled in such a way that the rough merge of TLb and OLb must put any TLREC after all OLRECs; a second or further TLREC coming after all OLRECs would merely produce an empty LISTb. The state-vector of LISTER must be separated, since there may be zero TLRECs: LISTERSV would then contain, *inter alia*, all the OLRECs which will appear when a LIST GROUP is next produced.

NEWSCHED-C consists of 13 parts: there are 6 sort programs, 6 components NSC-C-A through NSC-C-F, and the sequence component NEWSCHED-C itself. We can reduce the amount of tape file passing if the sort utility is equipped with interfaces for input and output procedures. The effect of these interfaces is that the sort program can obtain its input file to be sorted by calling a subroutine to be supplied by the programmer, and can dispose of its output file similarly. We can use inversion to transform dismembered parts of the scheduler into such input and output subroutines. Looking at the early parts of the sequence NEWSCHED-C, we have the arrangement shown in Fig. 11.42.

If NSC-C-A is inverted with respect to its C*b output, it can be an input subroutine for the sort. Similarly, if NSC-C-B is inverted with respect to its C*bSC input, it can be an output subroutine for the sort (Fig. 11.43). The same kind of transformation can be made to the later parts of the dismembered scheduler. Each inversion of a part of the scheduler saves the writing, rewinding, and reading time for the tape file with respect to which the inversion is performed.

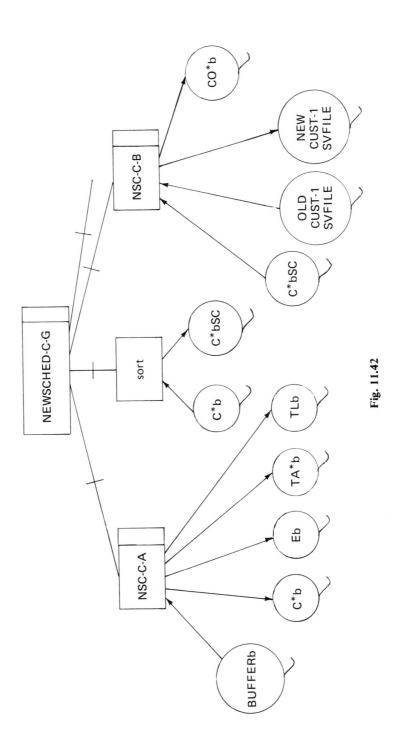

Fig. 11.42

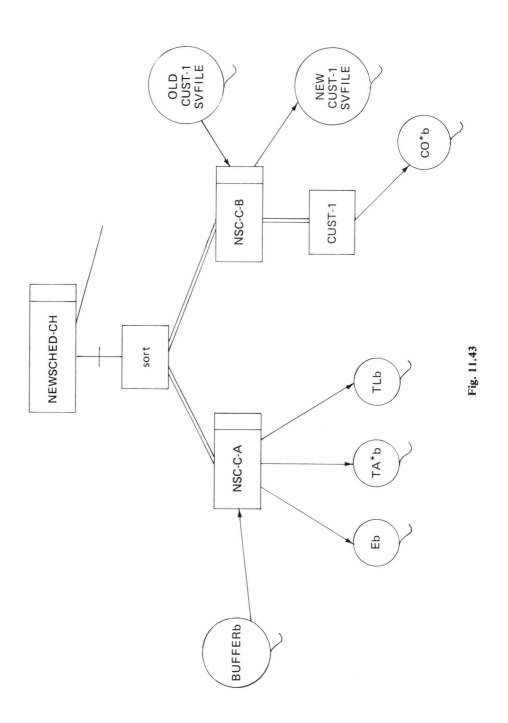

Fig. 11.43

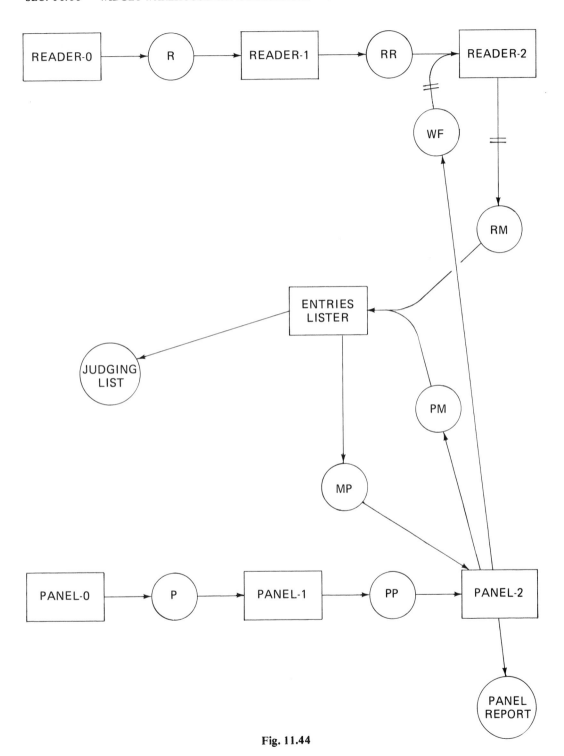

Fig. 11.44

11.17 *DAILY RACKET*: **IMPLEMENTATION**

We will implement the system specified in Sections 9.20 and 9.21. The SSD given in Section 9.20 is repeated in Fig. 11.44 for convenience. We will assume the second PANEL-2 structure given in Section 9.21, in which all the AWARD inputs are stored in a table before any of the SUBMIT records are read from the input stream MP.

We intend an implementation on a single processor, so we can usefully begin by considering the structure of the rough merged input stream to the scheduler (Fig. 11.45). No restriction has been placed here on the order of input, other than the restrictions already imposed by the specification of the behavior of the panel. Each RREC is a record of R*, and is either a SUBSCRIBE or an ENTER; the remaining records are records of P. We have not precluded the possibility that RRECs arrive between the time that the panel MEETs and the time that it DISPERSEs.

We decide on a scheduling in which the READER processes are as up to date as possible (there are some system functions which we have omitted for simplicity).

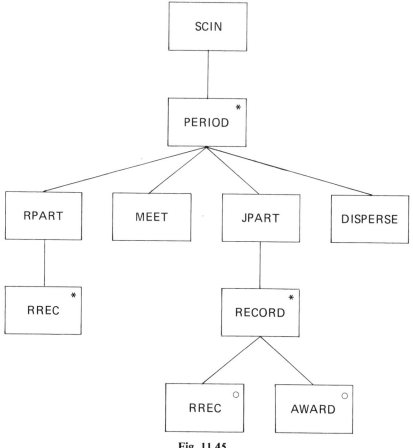

Fig. 11.45

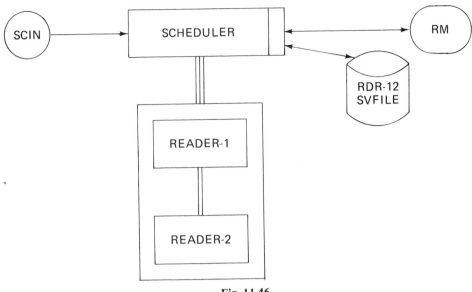

Fig. 11.46

Certainly, therefore, we will activate READER processes during RPART of SCIN. Inverting READER-1 with respect to R, and READER-2 with respect to RR&WF, we combine them into a single process which can be activated for each RREC of RPART. Since activation of READER-2 may cause an ENTER record to be produced in RM, the combined process will be connected to the scheduler by a channel (Fig. 11.46).

For the moment we will assume that the RM stream is buffered by the scheduler. We have combined the state-vectors of READER-1 and READER-2 in RDR-12SVFILE.

Looking at the process structures in the specification, we can see that the MEET record will indirectly cause PANEL-2 to write a record of PM to the ENTRIES LISTER process, which in turn will cause the completion of a SUBLIST of MP and the JUDGING LIST (MP is a copy of the JUDGING LIST). For a fair rough merge of the input to the ENTRIES LISTER, the PM record must arrive at that process after the buffered RM records. The question arises: ought we to buffer RM or not?

If we buffer RM, we can schedule the ENTRIES LISTER to produce a SUBLIST of the JUDGING LIST when the MEET record arrives in SCIN; when it does so, we will need to buffer MP, because the PANEL-2 process will not read MP until after the DISPERSE record arrives. If we do not buffer RM, but activate the ENTRIES LISTER on each RM record, we will need to buffer MP during the RPART of SCIN, and perhaps also the JUDGING LIST itself (unless we are happy for it to emerge gradually in the interval between successive judging sessions).

We decide that we will buffer RM. We will also combine PANEL-1 and PANEL-2, as we did READER-1 and READER-2, and invert the combined process with respect to the data streams P, MP, and PM. We are ignoring the PANEL REPORT and the output stream RM for now: neither can be written until the DISPERSE record appears. We have the arrangement shown in Fig. 11.47.

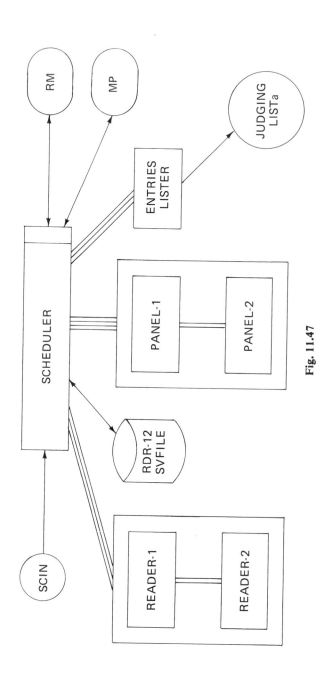

Fig. 11.47

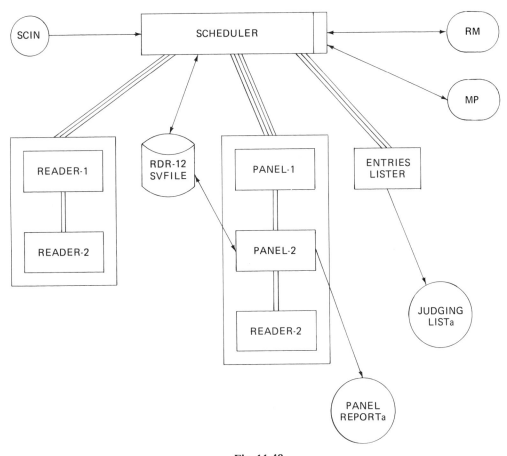

Fig. 11.48

ENTRIES LISTER is inverted with respect to RM&PM and MP; its output is shown as JUDGING LISTa, being a trivial dismembering of the list, consisting of a single SUBLIST. For a fair rough merge of RM&PM, the scheduler must empty the RM buffer, activating the ENTRIES LISTER, before passing the MEET record in PM to the ENTRIES LISTER. The JUDGING LISTa is produced while the ENTRIES LISTER is consuming the records of RM and PM. When the PM record has been consumed, the RM buffer is empty and the MP buffer is full.

During the JPART of SCIN, RRECs should be passed to the combined READER-1 and READER-2 process, and AWARDs to the PANEL-1 and PANEL-2 process. The PANEL-2 process is not yet blocked waiting to read MP, because the DISPERSE record has not yet appeared. When it does appear, and is passed to PANEL-1 and PANEL-2, the MP buffer will be emptied. PANEL-2 will produce records of WF and also the PANEL REPORT part for one session. Treating the PANEL REPORT as we did the JUDGING LIST, and using another copy of READER-2 as a subroutine of PANEL-2 (inverted with respect to its RR&WF input), we obtain the complete implementation

(Fig. 11.48). READER-2 cannot produce RM output as a result of WF input, so the inversion with respect only to RR&WF is adequate.

From this point, detailed specification of the scheduler and, perhaps, dismembering into a batch implementation, are straightforward; they are left as exercises for the energetic reader.

11.18 HI-RIDE ELEVATOR: IMPLEMENTATION—3

In Section 11.2 we developed an implementation for a simple version of the Hi-Ride Elevator system using 50 microprocessors. Then in the following section we reduced the number of processors required to 34, by combining the BUTTON-2 and BMERGE processes for each button. In this section we will consider implementation using only one hardware microprocessor for the whole system.

Let us suppose that the 50 microprocessor implementation is known to be satisfactory: it is correct, and the microprocessors are fast enough for the output commands to be issued quickly enough and the state changes of the buttons and sensors to be detected reliably. Then we can implement the system on a single hardware processor by a simple method of time-slicing. In JSD terms, this is still a 50-processor implementation: we are going to simulate 50 processors on one hardware processor.

The system must keep in the main storage of the processor:

— the 50 state-vectors, including common areas for communication between processes;
— the 5 different program texts (ELEVATOR-1, ELCONTROL, BUTTON-1, BUTTON-2, and BMERGE);
— a circular list of 50 entries, each entry containing a pointer to a state-vector and a pointer to a program text;
— a system initialization routine; and
— an interrupt-handling routine.

The time-slicing is implemented by a hardware clock which can be set to interrupt the processor and pass control to a specified location. The system initialization routine is:

> SYSINIT **seq**
>   *n := any of list*;
>   *set clock to interrupt every 60 microseconds, passing*
>   *control to* INTERRUPT; *wait for interrupt*;
> SYSINIT **end**

the interrupt-handling routine is:

> INTERRUPT **seq**
>   *n := next of list*;
>   *activate execution (state-vector (n), program text (n))*;
> INTERRUPT **end**

We have assumed that the processor is equipped with registers which allow the form of activation shown above; without such registers we will need some loading and storing of state-vectors.

The effect of such a scheme is to give each of 50 processes an equal share of the time of the single processor. If execution of the interrupt routine takes 5 microseconds, then each process will receive 55 microseconds of processor time every 3000 microseconds. If the speed of the single processor is P instructions per second, then each process is executing on a virtual processor whose average speed is $55P/3000$ instructions per second. However, this average is obtained at the cost of a zero speed for periods of 2945 microseconds at a time.

Clearly, we need to be satisfied that the system will operate satisfactorily under these conditions. If the period of zero speed is too long—perhaps because the worst case endangers the ability of ELCONTROL to respond fast enough to arrival of the elevator at a floor—we can reduce it by reducing the interrupt period. If we reduce the interrupt period from 60 to 30 microseconds, then the period of zero speed will be less than 1500 microseconds. This reduction is purchased at the cost of an increased proportion of the processor time being devoted to process switching in the interrupt routine: the average speed of the virtual processor now provided to each process is reduced to $25P/1500$ instructions per second, which is significantly less than $55P/3000$ instructions per second previously provided.

We are free to give different amounts of processor time to the different processes, if we wish. In each list entry we may hold a constant value $S(n)$, where S is the number of microseconds to be allocated to the process (n) when activated. The interrupt routine is now:

```
INTERRUPT seq
    n := next of list;
    set clock to interrupt after S(n) microseconds, passing
            control to INTERRUPT;
    activate execution (state-vector (n), program text (n));
INTERRUPT end
```

In the Hi-Ride Elevator system we would no doubt want to give a large number of microseconds to ELCONTROL on each activation, and much less time to each of the other processes.

11.19 HI-RIDE ELEVATOR: IMPLEMENTATION—4

The advantage of time-slicing is its extreme simplicity. The simulation of 50 processors is achieved by trivial devices of a general nature, which can be as easily applied to other systems. We demand no more from the interrupt mechanism than that it should interrupt execution only between successive machine instructions. Detailed examination of the system specification is not needed, except to assure ourselves that the supply of processor time to each process is sufficient for its requirements.

The disadvantage is that quite a lot of the processor time is likely to be wasted. If there is no outstanding request on any button when ELCONTROL is activated, and ELCONTROL is in course of executing WAIT-AT-GROUND, then the time devoted to ELCONTROL is devoted to a busy wait for events that cannot possibly occur: even if a button is pressed, the state of the associated button process will not change, since that process is not executing. We may therefore wish to consider a single-processor implementation more exactly tuned to the specified system. We will use the transformation

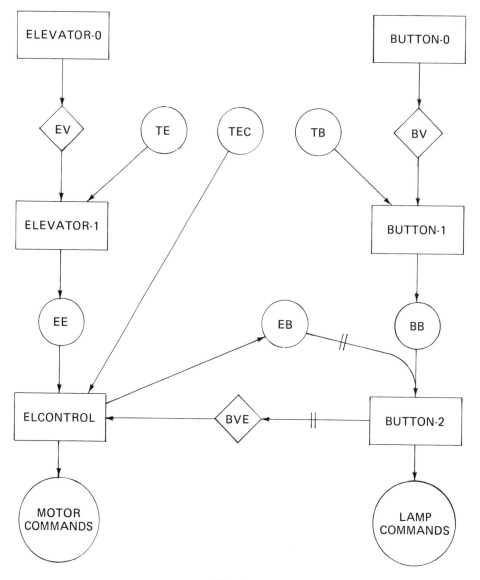

Fig. 11.49

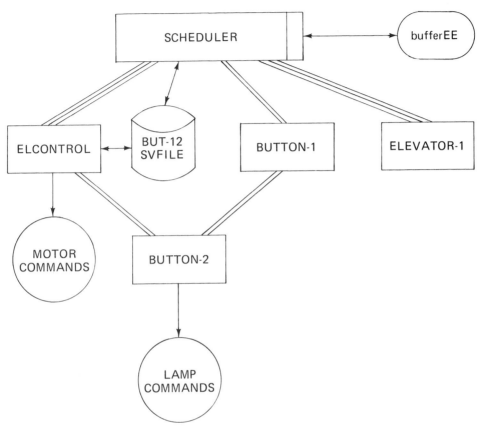

Fig. 11.50

techniques we have been discussing in earlier sections of this chapter to schedule the simple version of the Hi-Ride Elevator system on a single processor. We will implement the version with one elevator, specified in Section 9.13, in which the elevator waits at the ground floor when there are no outstanding requests, and reverses its direction of travel according to the currently outstanding requests.

The SSD is given in Fig. 9.27, but we must elaborate it a little. Data streams must be introduced for the processes ELEVATOR-1, BUTTON-1, and ELCONTROL, to cause suspension during busy wait loops. This is the technique we used in Section 11.10 for the process PROD-1 and in Section 11.11 for ALLOCR in the Widget Warehouse system. The resulting SSD is shown in Fig. 11.49. The data streams TE, TEC, and TB will be written by the scheduler. The read operations for these data streams are placed as follows:

— in ELEVATOR-1, whose text is shown in Section 8.8, we place an operation *read* TE before each *getsv* EV operation;

— in BUTTON-1, whose text is shown in Section 8.8, we place an operation *read* TB before each *getsv* BV operation;

— in ELCONTROL, whose text is shown in Section 9.13, we place an operation *read* TEC at the end of the iterated part of WAIT-AT-GROUND:

```
WAIT-AT-GROUND itr
    COMPLETE-SCAN seq
        . . .
    COMPLETE-SCAN end
    read TEC;
WAIT-AT-GROUND end
```

each instance of COMPLETE-SCAN, as its name implies, scans each button once.

BUTTON-2 may be inverted with respect to its rough merged input stream EB&BB, and made a subroutine of ELCONTROL and BUTTON-1. BUTTON-1 is inverted with respect to its TB input stream, and writes its output stream BB by calling BUTTON-2. ELEVATOR-1 is inverted with respect to its TE input and EE output streams. ELCONTROL is inverted with respect to its inputs EE and TEC: these are not rough merged by ELCONTROL, which therefore cannot be made a subroutine of ELEVATOR-1. The resulting SID is shown in Fig. 11.50.

The disk symbol for BUT-12SVFILE implies only direct access to the state-vectors; it does not imply the use of a disk device. Almost certainly, it will be necessary to hold the BUT-12SVFILE in main storage, where access will require microseconds rather than tens of milliseconds.

The SCHEDULER structure can be quite simple:

```
SCHEDULER itr
  SCHEDULER-PHASE seq
    BUTTON-SET seq
      b := 1;
      BUTTON-SET-BODY itr while (b ⩽ 16)
        RUN-BUTTON-1 seq
          loadsv BUT-12SV (b) into BSV;
          CALL BUTTON-1 (BSV, TBREC);
          storesv BSV into BUT-12SV (b);
        RUN-BUTTON-1 end
        b := b + 1;
      BUTTON-SET-BODY end
    BUTTON-SET end
    ELEVATOR-1 seq
      query ELEVATOR-1;
      ELEVATOR-1-BODY sel (read TE in ELEVATOR-1)
        CALL ELEVATOR-1 (TEREC, dummy);
      ELEVATOR-1-BODY alt (write EEREC in ELEVATOR-1)
        CALL ELEVATOR-1 (dummy, EEREC);
        write EEREC to bufferEE;
      ELEVATOR-1-BODY end
    ELEVATOR-1 end
```

```
         ELCONTROL seq
           query ELCONTROL;
           ELCONTROL-BODY sel (read TEC in ELCONTROL)
             CALL ELCONTROL (TECREC, dummy);
           ELCONTROL-BODY alt (read EE in ELCONTROL)
             ELCONTROL-EEREC sel (bufferEE empty)
             ELCONTROL-EEREC alt (bufferEE not empty)
               read bufferEE into EEREC;
               CALL ELCONTROL (dummy, EEREC);
             ELCONTROL-EEREC end
           ELCONTROL-BODY end
         ELCONTROL end
       SCHEDULER-PHASE end
     SCHEDULER end
```

Obviously, there is considerable scope for efficient representation in the handling of records by the SCHEDULER: none of the records referred to in the structure above contains any data. The BUTTON-1 processes are assumed to be numbered sequentially from 1 to 16, in addition to their existing identifiers as U1 to U5, D2 to D6, and E1 to E6.

The buffering of the EE records is not strictly necessary. An analysis of the specification shows that if everything in the mechanical system works correctly, then ELCONTROL must be blocked waiting to read EE at the time that ELEVATOR-1 writes an EEREC. It would therefore be possible to pass the record directly from ELEVATOR-1 to ELCONTROL without intermediate buffering. But it is probably preferable to use the very simple scheduling of the text given above, unless processor time is so precious that every nanosecond counts.

11.20 DATABASE DESIGN AND IMPLEMENTATION

We have paid remarkably little attention to database design and implementation. Partly, this is because we have been discussing problems in which the database is relatively simple; partly, because there is an extensive literature on the subject to which we have little to add (see, for example, C. J. Date, *An Introduction to Database Systems*, Addison-Wesley, or James Martin, *Computer Data-Base Organization*, Prentice-Hall); partly, because we believe that some of the concerns of database design are simplified by the JSD method and given a reduced, but more realistic, importance.

In JSD we regard a database as a collection of state-vectors of system processes: model processes, function processes, and, sometimes, scheduler processes. The content of each state-vector is determined by the needs of the process, and, where there is state-vector connection, by the information needs of other processes which inspect the state-vector. It is not much more sensible to set about designing a database before specifying the system processes than it would be to declare all the local variables of a program before specifying the executable text: the two are inextricably intertwined.

Just as we can dismember processes in JSD, so too we can dismember their state-vectors. We may decide that the state-vector of the ORDER process in the Widget Warehouse system is too large to be economically accessed on-line during the day, when customer inputs are accepted; so, just as we made two copies of the program text and eliminated from each those parts that could not be executed, so we may make two copies of the state-vector and eliminate from each those parts that cannot be referred to or updated.

Every process that shares a processor must have an explicit text-pointer in its state-vector. In JSD we have treated the text-pointer as an integer-valued variable, the values referring to numbered labels in the program text of the process. Yet in typical database designs, no such variable is to be found. This is because the role of text-pointer is usually assigned to a combination of other variables, which play that role in addition to their other roles. For example, in the READER-1 process of the *Daily Racket* system, the text-pointer will have values 1, 2, and 3, indicating that the reader has not yet SUBSCRIBEd, has SUBSCRIBEd but not yet ENTERed, and has ENTERed at least once. The correct value of the text-pointer can, perhaps, be deduced from such variables as name-and-address and most-recent-entry. If the former is blank, the text-pointer has the value 1; if the latter is null (say, $rank = 0$), and the former is not blank, the text-pointer has the value 2; otherwise the text-pointer has the value 3. This is clearly a very unsatisfactory substitute for the text-pointer: in more complex structures, such as the structure of the ORDER process shown in Appendix D, it leads to needless obscurity and error. It is often awkward to specify, and difficult to enforce, an appropriate null value for a substitute variable: the null value must be a value, but paradoxically an impermissible value, of the variable type. Worse, the number of combinations of values of the substitute variables is likely to be larger than the number of distinct values of the text-pointer. If there are 5 substitute variables, each regarded as having the value null or non-null for this purpose, there are 32 possible combinations. But these 32 combinations probably represent only 11 distinct values of the text-pointer. Immediately there is a self-inflicted problem: to determine which of the 32 combinations are valid (it is not valid to have a blank name-and-address but a non-null ranking in most-recent-entry), and which of the valid combinations are equivalent to one another. Developers who have not had difficulty with this problem are either using explicit text-pointers (or an equivalent representation), or else dealing with problems in which there is almost no dynamic content, so that the processes of the system are trivial and have only one or two distinct states.

For efficient implementation, it is necessary to provide access paths in the database. We have already seen, in the ALLOCR process of the Widget Warehouse system, how multiple state-vector connection leads to an explicit data structure indicating the required access path: the ALLOCR for a product must be able to obtain the ORDER state-vectors selectively (only orders for that product, and only orders due for allocation now) and in a certain sequence (delayed orders first, then normal orders, in descending sequence by quantity). Similar requirements arise from the scheduling of the system so that CO records are passed directly from the CUST-1 to the ORD-1 process; it would therefore be efficient to make a fast access path from any CUST-1 state-vector to the ORD-1 state-vectors for that customer.

SUMMARY OF CHAPTER 11

Different considerations are important in implementing different systems. Discussion here centers on process scheduling, on the sharing of processors among processes: this is the characteristic theme of JSD implementation. The results of JSD implementation are conventional and familiar, but they are reached by transforming the specification (11.1).

The Hi-Ride system can be implemented on 50 microprocessors, with state-vector and data stream connections implemented by shared data areas. Process scheduling is not a concern here, because each process has its own processor (11.2).

The number of processors can be reduced a little by sharing a processor between each pair of BMERGE and BUTTON-2 processes. The processes are inverted with respect to a connecting data stream, and become subroutines of a special-purpose scheduling process. Inversion is a transformation of the process text and can be readily mechanized. Sometimes, as here, it is possible to use one of the connected processes as the scheduler for the processor. For certain quite large systems this can be done, giving an implementation in the form of a hierarchy of subroutines (11.3, 11.4).

Inversion can be used to implement rough merging: the merging process becomes a subroutine of both (or all) processes which produce its merged input streams. Also, inversion with respect to more than one data stream is possible: this is called channel connection (11.5–7).

In some systems internal buffering of data streams is unavoidable. Buffers must then be provided in the implementation, and are placed under the control of the scheduler processes. The arrangement of buffering depends in part on the scheduling of the system processes (11.8).

Where there are many instances of a process, it is appropriate to separate the state-vectors from the process text: one copy of the state-vector is required for each process instance, but only one copy of the executable text is required for all of them. The state-vectors become 'master records', not necessarily one for one. Data stream operations for inverted processes can embody the operations to load and restore the state-vectors, giving the conventional pattern of retrieving, updating, and replacing a record (11.9).

Implementation of the Widget Warehouse system illustrates many of these techniques. Also, it illustrates the need to prevent a process which loops inspecting a state-vector from monopolizing the processor; this can be done by introducing an additional data stream to be written by the scheduler (11.10, 11.11).

JSD specification processes have long elapsed execution times, but practical machines can run only for a short time without break. For this and other reasons it is convenient to cut up, or dismember, processes into smaller pieces which can be loaded and executed conveniently. This dismembering, in various forms, is a standard JSD transformation. One very common case is the dismembering of a process into conventional batch programs that can be run periodically. Dismembering of a process is always accompanied by dismembering of its connected data streams. Dismembering is shown by appropriate notations in the System Implementation Diagram (SID) (11.12–14).

A further version of implementation of the Widget Warehouse system shows the use of dismembering to break continual execution into daily parts. This is effectively a batch arrangement of a transaction-orientated system (11.15).

More far-reaching changes are required if state-vectors are held in serial files. Process scheduling is then constrained by the need to activate processes in the order of the serial files, both state-vector files and files used to implement internal buffers of the system. Much sorting is required, but this is a matter of scheduling, not of specification (11.16).

An implementation of the *Daily Racket* system, partly batch and partly on-line, provides further illustration of process scheduling and transformation (11.17).

The Hi-Ride Elevator system can be implemented on one hardware processor time-sliced to simulate 50 processors. This is a relatively easy approach to implementation, but care must be taken to ensure that each process is running on a virtual processor of sufficient performance to give the necessary response times (11.18).

Alternatively, the same system can be implemented on one hardware processor by using the same transformation and scheduling techniques as we used for the other systems. Such an implementation can be viewed as the provision of a very special, highly tuned, operating system (11.19).

Database in JSD is primarily an implementation concern. The content of database records is determined by the local variables specified for model and function processes. The access paths are determined by the needs of function processes which use state-vector connection and the needs of process scheduling where separated state-vectors are involved (11.20).

PART III

VARIOUS TOPICS

This part of the book contains three short chapters. The first two contain brief discussions of the input subsystem and of system maintenance; the third is a largely retrospective chapter, looking at some aspects of JSD in the light of the material in the earlier parts.

Chapter 12 is about the input subsystem and errors. One important role of the input subsystem is to prevent invalid input from reaching the level-1 model processes. The input subsystem is a system in its own right, its inputs are all the sequences of messages that can possibly arrive from the real world, and its outputs are those that can be true according to the specified model of reality.

Chapter 13 is about system maintenance. One aspect of system maintenance is the development of new versions of parts of the system and the addition of new parts: the principles and methods of original development apply almost unchanged to this work. Another aspect is the substitution of new process texts for old while the processes are in course of execution. This aspect is clarified by the JSD insistence that system processes have long lifetimes; maintenance is eased by introducing processes whose lifetimes encompass both the old and the new versions.

Chapter 14 is a retrospective chapter. It contains observations on project management and documentation and on the role of data structures in JSD, together with some general comments on methodology.

12

The input subsystem and errors

12.1 ROLE OF THE INPUT SUBSYSTEM

As pictured in Fig. 12.1, the input subsystem is interposed between the real world entities and the processes which model them. In some systems, the input subsystem is null, or nearly so: the connections between the real world entities and the model are very direct, as in the Hi-Ride Elevator system, where the model processes directly inspect the physical states of the buttons and sensors. In other systems, the input subsystem may require a large development effort in its own right.

The role of the input subsystem can include:

— gathering and concentrating inputs from different sources to compose one or more input streams to the system proper;
— simplifying the human tasks to be performed in creating and submitting input to the system proper;
— detecting, and perhaps rectifying, errors in the input data to the system proper.

Strictly, we should have considered the input subsystem in the chapter about the initial model step. At least a preliminary specification of the input subsystem must be made in that step, since the input subsystem is the chief component in the connection between the real world and the model. We postponed consideration of it until now because we wanted to limit the complexity of the specifications discussed in subsequent chapters.

Some aspects and parts of the input subsystem may be independent of the system proper; conceptually, they are isolated from it, and can be specified and implemented almost without reference to it. For example, a teleprocessing network controller forms a part of the input subsystem for the application whose input is transmitted over the network; but the tasks of specifying and implementing the network may proceed with little or no interaction with the application development, beyond some highly abstract statements of traffic volumes and patterns. Other aspects and parts are tightly connected to the system proper. For example, interactive input with on-line error detection can be specified only in conjunction with the specification of the system model processes. We will be concerned in this chapter chiefly with the subject of errors; so we will be considering the input subsystem in close conjunction with the system proper.

334

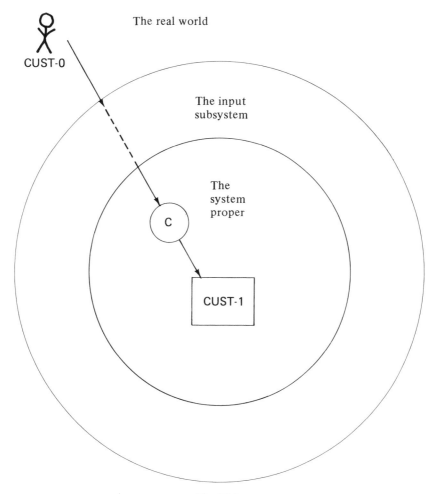

The real world

CUST-0

The input
subsystem

The
system
proper

C

CUST-1

Fig. 12.1

12.2   SOME DISTINCTIONS

A JSD model is a realization of an abstract description of the real world. The developer
must ensure, in the earliest steps of development, that this abstract description is true, in
the sense that real world happenings can be reasonably interpreted according to that
description. The inputs to the system bring news of events and actions in the real world,
and cause the processes of the model to simulate the behavior of the real world entities.
In specifying the model, we are specifying the ordered sets of events and actions which
are to be notified to the model and which it is to simulate.

The first distinction we make is between valid and invalid inputs, a distinction
familiar to practitioners of JSP program design. Input to a process is valid if it conforms
to the process specification, otherwise it is invalid. The specification of a reader in the

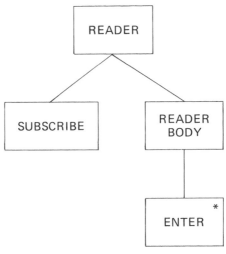

Fig. 12.2

Daily Racket system is as shown in Fig. 12.2. If input to this process consists of the messages:

    SUBSCRIBE, ENTER, ENTER, COMPLAIN, . . .

then it is invalid. The input:

    ENTER, ENTER, SUBSCRIBE, ENTER, . . .

is also invalid. Neither of these inputs conforms to the specification of the process. Notice that validity is a property of a set of messages, not only of a single message: the first of the inputs shown above is invalid because it contains the COMPLAIN message, which is not a part of the specified structure at all; the second consists of messages which are individually acceptable, but they are not in the specified ordering.

For a more complicated process, with more than one input stream, the validity of the input is a property of all the input streams taken together. For example, in the Widget Warehouse system, the structure of an order is based on a rough merge of the actions of the customer and the clerk. The input:

    ALLOCATE, PLACE, . . .

is not valid, although the ALLOCATE action may be a valid first action by the clerk, and PLACE is a valid first action by the customer.

Since validity is a property of input with respect to a specification, one degree of freedom available to the developer is to change the specification so that the definition of validity changes. He might, for example, change the specification of order to that shown in Fig. 12.3, in which case the input:

    ALLOCATE, PLACE, . . .

would become valid. In this chapter we will assume that no such changes are to be made to the specifications of the model processes, which we will regard as fixed. Given fixed

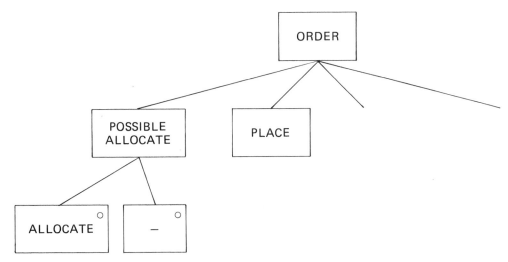

Fig. 12.3

specifications of the model, the developer has an absolute obligation to ensure that no invalid input can pass through the input subsystem to reach the system proper. This obligation is objective and technical: the specification defines without ambiguity what input is valid, and the input subsystem must detect and suppress all deviations from validity.

A second distinction is between true and false inputs. A true input is one which states that an action, or actions, have been performed when in fact they have been performed as stated. A false input is one which states that an action or actions have been performed when in fact they have not. For convenience, we will treat meaningless inputs as false: if an input message states that a customer of the Widget Warehouse has AMENDed the requested delivery date on an order to the 31 June, we will treat the message as false; if a message states that 'the mome raths outgrabe', and the real world for the system does not contain slithy toves or the Jabberwock as entities, we will treat the message as false. We would like to specify an input subsystem capable of detecting and rejecting all false inputs, but we cannot usually achieve this; some false inputs, in some systems, will be so plausible that they will pass any conceivable test of their truth or falsehood. Within the class of false inputs we may therefore make a subsidiary distinction between detected and undetected false inputs.

A third distinction is between desired and mistaken true inputs. A passenger in the Hi-Ride Elevator system presses the wrong button in the elevator: the input message is true, but the action was a mistake on the part of the passenger. A customer of the Widget Warehouse PLACEs an order for 50 gadgets because he thought he had a need for them; later he realizes that his need was actually for 50 tudgets. The input message was true: he really did order 50 gadgets, but it was a mistake. The distinction between mistaken and desired true inputs is in the mind of the person or organization in the real world that performs the action, not in any part of the system specification. The developer must take account of mistaken true inputs in the early steps of specification, by providing for corrective actions: that is one of the reasons for including AMEND and CANCEL as actions of the customer. But these corrective actions, and the mistakes they correct, are regarded in the specification as being just like other actions: there is nothing special about them. In particular, they do not require any special consideration in the input subsystem.

12.3   ELIMINATING INVALID INPUTS—1

We may view the connection between a real world entity and the process which models it as a chain of processes. At the real world end of the chain is some input device, which may be regarded as a process; at the model end of the chain is a JSD data stream or state-vector connection (Fig. 12.4).

Each process in the chain has an output stream in which it can produce error diagnostics. The input device is no exception: an on-line terminal equipped with a keyboard and a reader for plastic cards may display such messages as 'invalid card' or 'keyed number is not card number'; a punched card reader has lights to indicate conditions such as 'misfeed' or 'card jam'. The input device, P, and Q are processes of the input subsystem; E-0 is the real world entity; E-1 is the level-1 model process.

Each of the processes E-0, INPUT DEVICE, P, and Q must ensure that its output is valid input to the next process in the chain. Where E-0 is a human agent, or a highly unreliable physical object (such as the mechanical parts of a washing machine), we must specify and construct the input device so that the minimum constraint only need be satisfied by the output of E-0. For example, if E-0 is a person, and the input device is a keyboard, we usually require only that the person should be limited to striking any set of keys in any order with a force that is not enough to break the keyboard; if the input device is a punched card reader, we require only that decks of cards be placed in the input hopper, and that the operator should not pour cups of coffee into the machine. Later in the chain we may impose more stringent requirements: the stream B, for example, may be any sequence of characters from a specified character set, the requirement to emit only such a sequence being imposed on the input device; the process P may be required to emit only a sequence of messages, each of which is in a specified format; the process Q is required to emit only a sequence of messages which is valid input to the process E-1.

In a particularly simple case, the input device may be so robust, and the structure of E-1 so simple, that there is no need for any intermediate processes. For example, in the Hi-Ride Elevator system, we have:

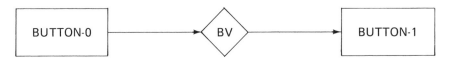

The physical button device has the states OPEN and CLOSED; the process BUTTON-1 is so specified that it can accept any sequence whatsoever of those states. There is no

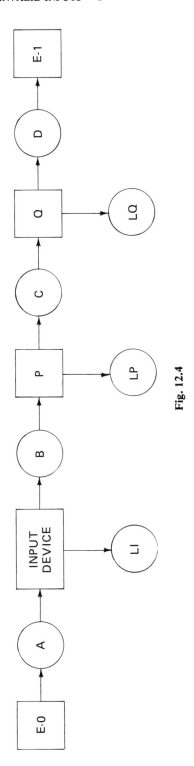

Fig. 12.4

significant possibility of invalid input to BUTTON-1. Notice that we are still relying on valid input to BUTTON-0 from the users of the elevator: we require that they limit themselves to pressing the button with reasonable force, and do not hit it with a sledgehammer or apply a high-voltage electric line to it.

12.4   ELIMINATING INVALID INPUTS—2

Where the model process has a non-trivial structure, valid input must satisfy constraints on the ordering of records as specified by the structure.

Suppose that P is a process of the input subsystem, writing a data stream RS which is input to the model process READER-1:

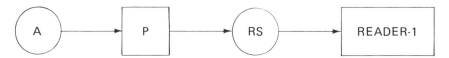

READER-1 has the structure of a *Daily Racket* reader, shown in Fig. 12.2 above. If the input stream A contains:

ENTER, SUBSCRIBE, ENTER, SUBSCRIBE, ENTER, ENTER;

then P must not merely copy A to RS, since RS would not then be valid input to READER-1. Instead P must make some change which will ensure that RS is valid for READER-1. There are many different changes and combinations of changes that could be made:

—   suppress the first three records;
—   suppress the first and fourth records;
—   swap the first and second records, and suppress the fourth record;
—   suppress the first and second records and swap the third and fourth records;

and many others. To specify the process P of the input subsystem is to specify the rules for choosing among these possible changes.

Theoretically, the choice is wide and there are several important factors:

—   Some errors are more likely results of the input procedures than others. It may be, for example, that records are very unlikely to be swapped in error, and that spurious records tend to come in groups. Suppressing the first three records would then be the change most likely to restore the input to what it should have been—that is, to the true statement of real world actions.
—   Some failures of the complete system may carry very high penalties. For example, it may be that to ignore an entry lays the *Daily Racket* open to punitive damages in the courts. It would then be wise to swap the first and second records and suppress the fourth, so avoiding suppressing any entry which may prove to have been real.

— If the model must be well up to date, it will be very unattractive to make any changes that rely on additional buffering of RS and hence additional delay in the scheduling of READER-1. Suppressing the first and fourth records does not require any buffering of RS: each record of A may be copied directly into RS if it can possibly be the next record in a valid RS; otherwise it is suppressed.

In practice, the last of these factors often dominates the specification of P. If the system is implemented as a batch system, with RS buffered for a week at a time, then P may apply changes within one week's records of RS; if the system is implemented as an on-line system, with on-line updating of the READER models, then the changes made by P will be limited to those that require no buffering.

12.5   ELIMINATING INVALID INPUTS—3

Suppose that we have a model process E-1, and a process P of the input subsystem; P writes a diagnostic output stream D:

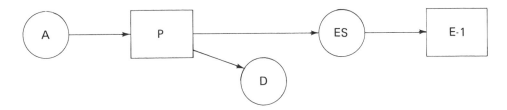

Records of incorrect format have been eliminated from A. The process P must be specified so that ES is valid input to E-1. It is also stipulated that P must accept or reject each record of A without waiting for the next record.

We begin by giving P the structure of ES, as if that were the structure of A. Then we place '*read* A' operations in the structure, using read ahead, and a '*write* ES' operation on each record component. At this point P is merely a process which copies its input to its output stream, assuming that its input has the structure of ES. We must now elaborate this structure so that valid input to P is A, ensuring that records of A which are not records of ES are not copied to the output. This elaboration may be tackled by two different approaches:

— by considering the possibility that each record of A might be wrong in various ways; it might be a spurious record wrongly inserted into A, it might be wrongly coded, or it might be itself a correct record whose presence indicates that the preceding record has been wrongly omitted;
— by assuming that the only possible kind of error is the insertion of spurious records into A.

The first approach is more general, because it allows for a wider variety of error diagnosis and repair; the second approach is less general, but can be systematized and even automated. We will illustrate the first approach in this section, and the second in the next.

Suppose that E-1 is the READER-1 process of the *Daily Racket* system. Then the structure of P, before elaboration, is:

```
P seq
  read A;
  SUBSCRIBE seq
    write AREC to ES; read A;
  SUBSCRIBE end
  READER-BODY itr
    ENTER seq
      write AREC to ES; read A;
    ENTER end
  READER-BODY end
P end
```

What if the first record is not a SUBSCRIBE message? Then it may be that one of the following errors (among other possibilities) has occurred:

(a)   The record has been wrongly encoded; it should be treated as if it were a SUBSCRIBE record.

(b)   The SUBSCRIBE record has been omitted in error; it should be supplied by P, using default values such as 'NO NAME' for the reader's name and address.

(c)   The record is a spurious insertion; it should be rejected.

There is no way of determining which error has in fact occurred, but the developer is free to choose which error is to be assumed. Depending on the choice made, the elaborated structure of P will be one of the following:

```
PA seq
  read A;
  SUBSCRIBE sel (SUBSCRIBE)
    write AREC to ES; read A;
  SUBSCRIBE alt (ENTER)
    write diagnostic 'record wrongly encoded ';
    write modified AREC to ES; read A;
  SUBSCRIBE end
  . . .
PA end
```

or:

```
    PB seq
      read A;
      SUBSCRIBE sel (SUBSCRIBE)
        write AREC to ES; read A;
      SUBSCRIBE alt (ENTER)
        write diagnostic 'SUBSCRIBE omitted';
        write default SUBSCRIBE record to ES;
      SUBSCRIBE end
      . . .
    PB end
```

or:

```
    PC seq
      read A;
      SUBSCRIBE sel (SUBSCRIBE)
        write AREC to ES; read A;
      SUBSCRIBE alt (ENTER)
        write diagnostic 'spurious record inserted';
        read A;
      SUBSCRIBE end
      . . .
    PC end
```

Similar choices can be made independently in different parts of a large structure. The specification of the process P can be viewed as a model of the behavior of an error-prone data input operator.

12.6   ELIMINATING INVALID INPUTS—4

If we are prepared to assume that the only possible kind of error is the insertion of spurious records into A, we can adopt a standard approach. With this approach, the elaboration consists of adding an iteration component following each '*read* A' operation in the unelaborated version of P. Each operation:

```
    read A;
```

becomes

```
    read A;
    INVAL-SET-N itr while (invalid for ES)
      write diagnostic; read A;
    INVAL-SET-N end
```

The problem now is to determine, for each of these iteration components, the explicit condition on the iteration. In a very simple case, the conditions will be obvious. For example, if E-1 is the READER-1 process of the *Daily Racket* system, then the elaborated structure of P is:

P **seq**
    read A;
    INVAL-SET-1 **itr while** (**not** SUBSCRIBE)
        write diagnostic; *read* A;
    INVAL-SET-1 **end**
    SUBSCRIBE **seq**
        write AREC *to* ES;
        read A;
        INVAL-SET-2 **itr while** (**not** ENTER)
            write diagnostic; *read* A;
        INVAL-SET-2 **end**
    SUBSCRIBE **end**
    READER-BODY **itr**
        ENTER **seq**
            write AREC *to* ES;
            read A;
            INVAL-SET-3 **itr while** (**not** ENTER)
                write diagnostic; *read* A;
            INVAL-SET-3 **end**
        ENTER **end**
    READER-BODY **end**
P **end**

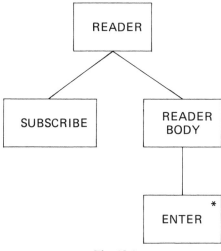

Fig. 12.5

The only record that can appear following the initial read operation, in a valid ES, is SUBSCRIBE; the only record that can appear following a SUBSCRIBE or an ENTER is ENTER. So the conditions on the three iteration components are (**not** SUBSCRIBE), (**not** ENTER), and (**not** ENTER).

For more complex structures, a systematic way of determining the conditions is needed. Barry Dwyer points out that a good way can be adapted from compiler theory (explained, for example, in Chapter 5 of A. V. Aho and J. D. Ullman, *Principles of Compiler Design*, Addison-Wesley). For each component X of the structure, we determine:

— FIRST(X), the set of records that can appear as the first record of X; and
— FOLLOW(X), the set of records that can appear following X.

For the structure shown in Fig. 12.5, we have:

FIRST(READER) = (SUBSCRIBE);
FOLLOW(SUBSCRIBE) = (ENTER);
FOLLOW(ENTER) = (ENTER).

The condition on the initial iteration component INVAL-SET-1, added following the *read ahead* operation, is:

while (not FIRST(READER))

The conditions on other iteration components, added following *read* operations which are placed at the end of AREC components, are:

while (not FOLLOW(AREC))

The FIRST and FOLLOW sets for a complex structure are determined by these rules (essentially as given by Dwyer):

(a)   If X is a record, then FIRST(X) = (X);
(b)   If X is a sequence component, with parts X1, X2, . . . , Xn, in that order, then:
    1.   FIRST(X) = FIRST(X1);
    2.   FOLLOW(X) = FOLLOW(Xn);
    3. $FOLLOW(Xj) = FIRST(X_{j+1})$ for $j = 1, 2, . . . , n-1$;
(c)   If X is a selection component, with parts X1, X2, . . . Xn, then:
    1.   FIRST(X) = (FIRST(X1) or FIRST(X2) or . . . FIRST(Xn));
    2.   FOLLOW(Xj) = FOLLOW(X)   for $j = 1, 2, . . . , n$;
(d)   If X is an iteration component whose iterated part is X1, then:
    1.   FIRST(X) = (FIRST(X1) or (FOLLOW(X));
    2.   FOLLOW(X1) = (FIRST(X1) or FOLLOW(X));
(e)   If X is the null component, then FIRST(X) = FOLLOW(X).

By repeatedly applying these rules, we can determine the FIRST set for the whole of a complex structure, and the FOLLOW sets for its elementary record components; these then give the necessary conditions. We will illustrate application of the rules to the imaginary structure shown in Fig. 12.6.

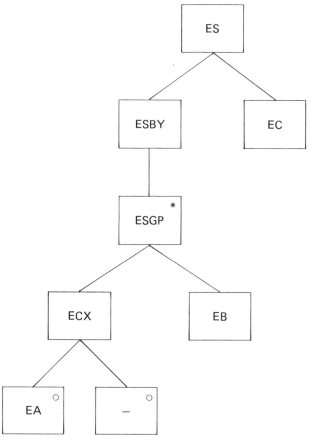

Fig. 12.6

We will assume that there is an end-of-file marker at the end of ES. So FOLLOW(EC) = (eof).

   (i)   FIRST(EA) = (EA); FIRST(EB) = (EB); FIRST(EC) = (EC); by rule (a).
  (ii)   FOLLOW(ESBY) = (EC); FOLLOW(ECX) = (EB); by (i) and rule (b3).
 (iii)   FOLLOW(EA) = (EB); FOLLOW(—) = (EB); by (ii) and rule (c2).
  (iv)   FIRST(—) = (EB); by (iii) and rule (e).
   (v)   FIRST(ECX) = (EA **or** EB); by (i), (iv), and rule (c1).
  (vi)   FIRST(ESGP) = (EA **or** EB); by (v) and rule (b1).
 (vii)   FOLLOW(ESGP) = (EA **or** EB **or** EC); by (ii), (vi), and rule (d2).
(viii)   FOLLOW(EB) = (EA **or** EB **or** EC); by (vii) and rule (b2).
  (ix)   FIRST(ESBY) = (EA **or** EB **or** EC); by (ii), (vi), and rule (d1).
   (x)   FIRST(ES) = (ES **or** EB **or** EC); by (ix) and rule (b1).

We have now determined FIRST(ES) and FOLLOW(EA), FOLLOW(EB), and FOLLOW(EC). The elaborated structure of P is therefore:

```
P seq
  read A;
  INVAL-SET-1 itr while (not (EA or EB or EC))
    write diagnostic; read A;
  INVAL-SET-1 end
  ESBY itr while (EA or EB)
    ESGP seq
      ECX sel (EA)
        EA seq
          write EA to ES;
          read A;
          INVAL-SET-2 itr while (not EB)
            write diagnostic; read A;
          INVAL-SET-2 end
        EA end
      ECX alt (not EA)
      ECX end
      EB seq
        write EB to ES;
        read A;
        INVAL-SET-3 itr while (not (EA or EB or EC))
          write diagnostic; read A;
        INVAL-SET-3 end
      EB end
    ESGP end
  ESBY end
  EC seq
    write EC to ES;
    read A;
    INVAL-SET-4 itr while (not eof)
      write diagnostic; read A;
    INVAL-SET-4 end
  EC end
P end
```

The benefit of a systematic approach of this kind is obvious. The disadvantage is that it presupposes a very limited class of error, the introduction of spurious records into an otherwise correct data stream. This presupposition may not be harmful if the input subsystem is on-line: indeed, it may be positively beneficial. The on-line operator has the opportunity to amend and resubmit a rejected record, to insert the previously omitted preceding record, or to be grateful that a truly spurious insertion has been rejected. But if the input subsystem is not on-line, and an error other than a spurious insertion occurs, the behavior of P as specified above may be rather undesirable. It will, certainly, not pass invalid input to E-1; but it may reject records that ought, in some sense, to have been accepted. For example, suppose that the data stream A contains the records:

EA, EA, EA, EB, EB, EA, EC, eof;

The second and third records will be suppressed in INVAL-SET-2, since EA can be followed only by EB. If, in fact, the second record was mis-keyed, and should have been EB, we may feel a little disgruntled. The treatment of the EC record is worse. The EC record will also be suppressed in INVAL-SET-2, along with the end-of-file marker. P will then be blocked waiting for another record of A, which will never come; E-1 will be similarly blocked, waiting for a record of ES.

    The lesson, well known to JSP practitioners, is that detection of input errors must always favor one class of error over others. There must always be an error type which is the preferred diagnosis: input streams containing only this type of error will be repaired with an apparently magical insight; but when other types occur, the diagnosis and repair will seem to be insanely perverse.

12.7 ERROR DETECTION AND SCHEDULING

The technique discussed in the preceding sections could be applied in a different way. We could connect the process P of the input subsystem to the model process E-1 as if P were an interacting function (Fig. 12.7).

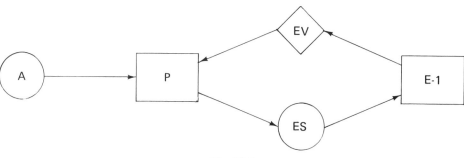

Fig. 12.7

    To determine whether a record of A should be suppressed or copied to ES, P inspects the state-vector of E-1. The values of the text-pointer of E-1, we will assume, are the points at which it has *read* ES operations. The structure of P can then be simplified:

```
P itr
  AREC seq
    read A;
    getsv EV;
    AREC-BODY sel (AREC is in set of acceptable records
                           for current value of E-1 text-pointer)
      write AREC to ES;
    AREC-BODY alt (else)
    AREC-BODY end
  AREC end
P end
```

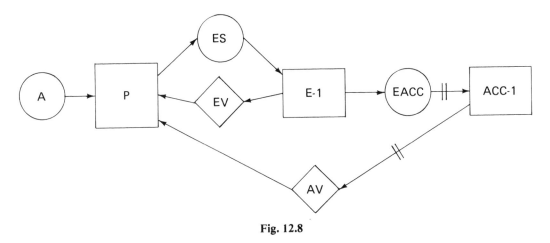

Fig. 12.8

The set of acceptable records for each value of E-1's text-pointer is made exactly as before; P contains a table in which these sets are listed.

Correct operation of P now requires that E-1 should be fully up to date when P obtains its state-vector. If we accept this obligation, we can solve a wider class of problems than before. Suppose that E-1 models a customer, and that a customer has many accounts, the accounts being marsupial entities of customer. The initial model SSD is then:

The validity of the input stream ES now depends not only on the state of E-1, but, in some cases, also on the state of ACC-1. Using the technique as applied in the preceding

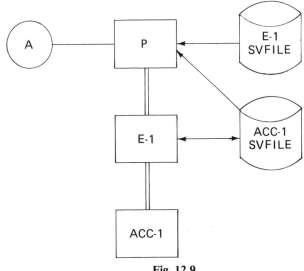

Fig. 12.9

sections, we would be compelled to replicate this model, both of E-1 and of ACC-1, in the input subsystem. Instead, we may use the interacting function connection (Fig. 12.8).

P now relies on both E-1 and ACC-1 being fully up to date. An implementation of the connections could be as shown in Fig. 12.9. Part of the input subsystem has thus been integrated with part of the system proper. If P is scheduled to execute on-line, we have on-line data input and validation.

12.8   FALSE INPUTS

Some false inputs will be invalid, and suppressed for that reason. Some others can be detected by redundancy checks. For example, check digits may be appended to input fields to reduce the chance that a mis-keyed input record will be accepted; an input for actions such as AMEND in the Widget Warehouse system may be required to carry the old as well as the amended value of the affected variable; inputs may be time-stamped to increase the chance of detecting misordering. And there are other techniques, such as on-line interactive data input, or machine-readable turn-around documents.

But however hard we try to detect false inputs, they will sometimes get through the net. When a false input is eventually detected, perhaps a long time afterwards, there must be some means of mitigating the damage that has been done.

It is not, in general, possible to repair the damage completely: that would require that every part of the system directly or indirectly affected by the false input be restored to its previous state and executed again with corrected input. Both inside the system and in the real world to which it is connected it would be necessary to undo everything that had been done as a result of the error. Suppose, for example, that a customer of the Widget Warehouse is a victim of a false input: the quantity of his order for gadgets is wrongly AMENDed from 500 to 50. As a result, gadgets will have been allocated to some other customers who, presumably, must be asked to return them. Some of those wrongly allocated gadgets will have been consumed, or passed on to other organizations. Complete restoration of the state of the system and of the real world is manifestly impossible.

In some cases, false inputs can be treated much like mistaken true inputs; the falsely reported action is regarded as if it had really occurred, and some correcting action is performed to bring the state of the model closer to the state of the real world. A correcting action is not special, and has no special technical privileges. It is not permissible, for example, to provide a 'facility' for arbitrarily changing the values of local variables in process state-vectors; it becomes no more permissible when use of the 'facility' is restricted to the president of the company, or the systems programming group, or the database administrator. A correcting action is a real world action, like any other; like any other, it must be an action of some entity modelled in the system, and must be properly specified within the structure of that entity's model process. If it is intended to affect other entities, it must do so through the normal mechanisms of the specification, by writing records to data streams which they read.

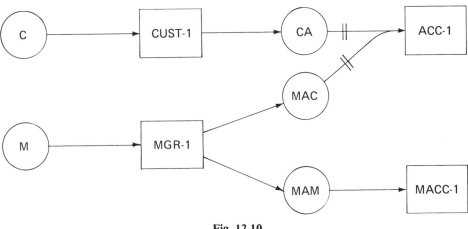

Fig. 12.10

A simple example of a correcting action is provided by the treatment of false inputs in a bank system. Inevitably, some errors will occur in handling debits and credits to customers' accounts. A sum of money may be debited to one customer's account that should have been debited to another's. The bank manager must be able to transfer money between customers' accounts to correct this kind of error. An SSD for the system is shown in Fig. 12.10.

The manager is modelled by the process MGR-1. Actions of the manager include transferring money between his own account, modelled by MACC-1, and any customer's account. The manager now has the ability to correct errors arising from false input by performing his own specified actions.

Specification of correcting actions of this kind is a task in the earliest development steps, not the latest. When the developer recognizes, in the initial model step, that some correcting actions must be provided for some class of false inputs, he must return to the entity action and entity structure steps to specify them.

The result of a correcting action is usually imperfect, in the sense that the damage is not fully repaired. For example, in the bank system, it might be that interest is charged on overdrawn accounts. If a false input causes a customer's account to appear overdrawn, and interest is charged, it is necessary for the manager to refund the interest as well as the sum originally wrongly debited. But the interest has already been credited to some other account. The manager and the developer may well decide that it is not worth while to correct this error also. The result of the correction will then be that the customer's account balance has been corrected, but not the interest account. From the customer's point of view, a more important defect in the correction may be that his name now appears on a historic list of overdrawn accounts; in some systems, the consequences might be serious.

13

System maintenance

13.1 THE MAINTENANCE PROBLEM

During the useful lifetime of a system, its specification will certainly change. There will be new functional requirements, and old functional requirements will be modified or replaced; there will also be changes to the real world which require corresponding changes to the model embodied in the system. We are using the word maintenance here to denote the activity of changing the system to meet these changes in specification.

System maintenance demands change both to the specification and to the implementation. Just as in program maintenance, we must be willing to go back to the earliest affected development stage and follow the necessary change through from there. If the Widget Warehouse manager decides that customers must confirm their orders after placing them, then presumably CONFIRM will be an action of customer, and the change must be followed through from the very first development step, the entity action step. If there is to be a new rule for controlling the Hi-Ride Elevators, then the change must start at the function step, and be carried through to the implementation.

Sometimes, a maintenance task may be very easy. The commonest case is the addition of a function process to the system, connected to the model only by state-vector inspection. If the necessary local variables are already present in the model process' state-vectors, the addition can be made without any disturbance to the existing system specification; the implementation, too, is likely to be largely undisturbed.

More often, it will be necessary to change an existing function process, or even to change the model. Such changes are inevitably difficult. Changing a process during its lifetime is like changing a program during its execution. It makes very little difference that the process is suspended, its state-vector safely stored in a disk file, and the machine switched off: as we have seen throughout earlier chapters, we must still think of it as being a program in course of execution, just as if it were engaged in executing an input procedure to get the next record from a keyboard, disk, tape, or card reader. When the manager of the Widget Warehouse decides to change the rules for order processing, the developer is confronted with the task of changing the text of all the order processes: but there are ten, or a hundred, or a thousand order processes in course of execution. As some reach the end of their text, and complete execution, others begin;

there is no point in time at which the ORD-12SVFILE will be empty, at which there will be no order process executing its text.

This difficulty is not created by JSD; it will not disappear if the developer chooses another method. JSD merely reveals it in a clear form, and makes it more explicit and so easier to tackle correctly. JSD helps in another way too. Much system maintenance may be expected to affect only the system functions, leaving the model unchanged. Because the model and function aspects of the specification are well separated, change is likely to be more localized.

13.2   ONE PROCESS INSTANCE

In Section 9.5 we specified a weekly report on the entries sent in by *Daily Racket* readers:

WEEK *nnn* ENTRIES REPORT

ENTRIES THIS WEEK—*eeeee*
TOTAL ENTRIES SO FAR—*ffffff*

The report is produced by a function process WKENTRPT (Fig. 13.1).

The structure of the rough merged input RE&TW is shown in Fig. 13.2, and this is also the structure of WKENTRPT, with some components added for the computation and printing of the output.

Suppose that we are required to change the report so that a new line is printed each week:

BEST WEEK SO FAR—*mmm*—*ggggg* ENTRIES

The line shows the largest number of entries that has occurred in any one week, and the week number of that occurrence. It is relatively trivial to specify the required new version of the process WKENTRPT: new local variables are needed for the largest number that has occurred so far, and for the associated week number, and operations to assign new values to them when appropriate.

The new function process—let us call it WKENTRPTN—has a different text from the old, and a different set of local variables in its state-vector. To make the change, we must find a way of replacing the text and state-vector of WKENTRPT by the text and state-vector of WKENTRPTN, and of initializing the values of WKENTRPTN's state-vector to take account of the current values accumulated by WKENTRPT; and we must do this without disrupting the system.

The change will be easy if we can find a moment in the system execution at which:

—   WKENTRPT is suspended; and
—   the state-vector of WKENTRPT contains only a small amount of information, all of which is compatible with WKENTRPTN; and
—   these conditions will persist for long enough for the change to be made.

Clearly, a suitable moment would be one at which WKENTRPT has produced all of its

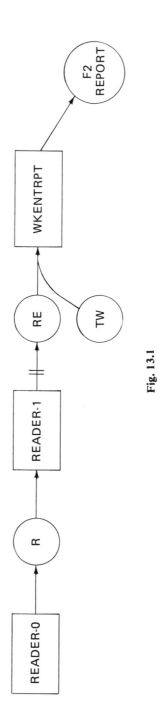

Fig. 13.1

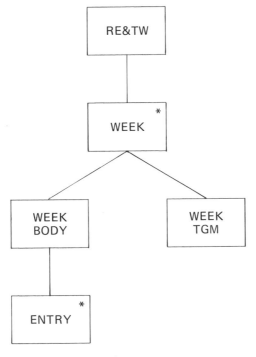

Fig. 13.2

output for one WEEK, and has not yet read the first ENTRY record for the next week. The values of the week number and the total of entries so far are present in the state-vector of WKENTRPT; since no ENTRY record has yet been read for the next week, the other variables, including the text-pointer, may be ignored.

In the likely batch implementation, WKENTRPT will have been dismembered. There will be a batch program, corresponding to one instance of WEEK in WKENTRPT, which is scheduled to be run when the WEEK TGM appears; the scheduler will have buffered the RE input on disk or tape; the state-vector of WKENTRPT will have been dismembered, and the part which is not local to one instance of WEEK will be held as a disk record. With this implementation, the (dismembered) text and state-vector of WKENTRPTN can be substituted for those of WKENTRPT at any time between one batch run and the next.

In a different implementation, WKENTRPT might be more severely dismembered. There might be a part for ENTRY, and another for WEEK TGM. That is, the counts of entries are updated as each ENTRY occurs in READER-1, and the week's report is printed when the WEEK TGM appears. By good fortune, we find that we need to replace only the second of these dismembered parts of WKENTRPT, and the problem is much the same as before.

The maintenance task is simple. There is only one instance of the WKENTRPT process. Its structure provides an obvious place (the end of a WEEK) to change over from the old to the new. The scheduling of the process makes it easy to identify the moment at which that place in the structure is reached, and gives plenty of time to make the substitution.

13.3   MULTIPLE PROCESS INSTANCES

There are two aspects to a maintenance change. The new process specification must be developed, and the old must be replaced by the new. The two aspects are intimately related, because we must find a point in the process structure at which the old and the new are compatible, and we must make the change at that point.

Sometimes the only way to make the change is to specify a combined structure, combining the old and the new process specifications, and containing the necessary structural mechanism for changing from old to new. Suppose, for example, that we wish to change the F1 function specified in Section 9.6 for Widget Warehouse orders. The structure of the function process is shown in Fig. 13.3.

There is one instance of this process for each ORDER. It produces an exception report when the order is amended more than once without an intervening delay. We wish to change the specification: the report should be produced when the order is delayed more than once without an intervening amendment.

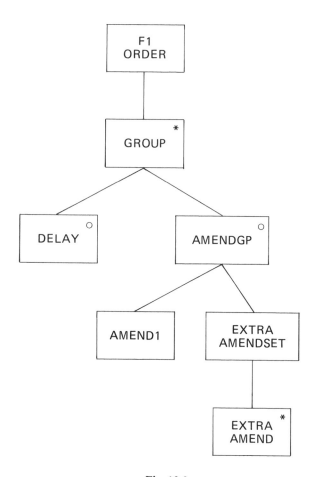

Fig. 13.3

Following the approach of the preceding section, we look for a suitable point in the structure at which the change can be made. Obviously, it is at the end of a GROUP. But there are many F1-ORDER processes, all at different points in their execution. It would be impossible to find a moment when all F1-ORDER processes are simultaneously at the end of a GROUP. So we must specify a combined structure. The necessary structure is shown in Fig. 13.4.

Instead of replacing the old process by a completely new process, we will replace it by the combined process. The text of COMF1-ORDER begins:

COMF1-ORDER **seq**
 OLD-PART **itr while** (*false*)
  ...

The condition (*false*) is, by definition, never satisfied. As soon as any instance of the process reaches the node at the beginning of OLD-PART, it will terminate its OLD-PART and begin its NEW-PART component. Each F1-ORDER process will therefore change over to the new specification as soon as it can.

For this change to work properly, we must be sure that the combined process is entirely compatible with the old. The old state-vectors must be extended, reformatted, or translated into the new, and this must be done either automatically at the appropriate point in COMF1-ORDER or by explicit manipulation of the state-vectors when the old text is replaced by the combined text. Treatment of state-vectors is easiest when the combined version is identical to the old, or is an extension of it that can be accommodated within the existing variable-length format.

The text of COMF1-ORDER must be implemented in the same way as F1-ORDER was implemented, and can then replace it at any time when it is not being executed for any process instance.

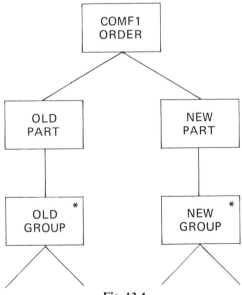

Fig. 13.4

Eventually, none of the process instances will be executing OLD-PART. It will then be possible to make a further change, in which the combined process is replaced by the new process: the OLD-PART component is dropped, and only the NEW-PART remains. The same considerations apply to this second change as to the first: the process texts and state-vectors must be compatible.

In some cases, the combined process will be more complex than a simple sequence of the old followed by the new; this greater complexity is a reflection of a real world difficulty in accomplishing an orderly change from the old to the new. In a system for life assurance, the rules governing life policies may be changed in some substantial respect: the structure of the policy entity is changed as a result. It is not possible to regard the composite structure as a sequence of the old followed by the new; nor is it possible to avoid the problem by leaving existing policies unchanged and using the new rules for all new policies: the lifetime of a policy is too long for that. One possible approach to a solution is to regard the combined process as a selection (Fig. 13.5).

The selection condition will require backtracking. The first jump out of OLD POLICY is at the very beginning:

POLICY **posit** (*old policy*)
  OLD-POLICY **seq**
POLICY **quit**;
   . . .

Thus, any policy which begins its lifetime after the combined process is substituted for the old process will execute NEW POLICY, not OLD POLICY. Because the jump is at the beginning of OLD POLICY, there are no side-effects to consider. The heart of the specification question, however, is this: where else can there be jumps out of OLD POLICY into NEW POLICY, and what side-effects have to be dealt with for each jump, and how? In application language: at what points in an old policy can it be converted into a new policy? what must happen to the previously accumulated rights and obligations of the old policy when it is converted? at what points in the new policy may a converted old policy start its new life?

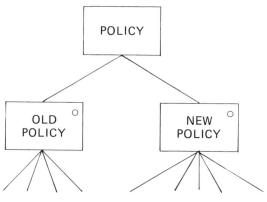

Fig. 13.5

The answers to these questions are to be sought in the real world of the system, not in technical considerations. But the formulation of the problem in terms of jumps from one structure into another, and the associated side-effects, will probably help greatly to clarify the issues.

13.4 EXTENDING EXISTING SYSTEMS

When an existing system must be extended, by enlarging its model of reality, by adding more functions, or both, the developer is faced with a fundamental choice: whether to make the extension in JSD terms or to adopt the methods of the original system development. The choice will depend chiefly on the scale of the extension that is planned. If it is small, it will probably be sensible to adopt the original methods: the cost of doing otherwise would be greater than any possible benefits. If it is large, it will be right to invest in the partial respecification needed for the extension.

The main work of respecification is concerned with making explicit the model of the real world on which the existing system is based. The entities and their actions must be identified, and entity structures specified. Sometimes, this can be done directly from the original functional specification, especially where the writer of the specification has included material which he, perhaps, regarded as useful background explanation, and the JSD developer would regard as an informal statement of the real world description. Sometimes, the task will be more difficult. The specification may be purely functional, leaving the model of reality to be inferred from the statement of the functions. Or, less helpfully, the specification may be cast in terms of the implementation, describing the on-line transaction modules and the batch programs of the system. It will then be necessary to piece together the actions of each entity from the separate fragments describing how the master record for that entity is updated; the entity structure must be derived from an examination of the system scheduling, which shows the ordering of the various updates to the master record.

An important tool in understanding existing systems is a clear grasp of the various transformations used in the JSD implementation step. We have discussed these transformations at length in an earlier chapter, from the point of view of the developer who uses them. But they can also be regarded as explanations of how an existing implementation is related to its explicit or implicit specification. Where the same field in a database record is updated by operations in different programs or modules, there must have been dismembering of the process whose state-vector contains that field. Where the current values of various fields in a record are tested before one is updated, those values are effectively indicating the current value of the process text-pointer. Where a database record exists in one instance only, it is either part of the state-vector of an entity of which there is only one instance, or else it is part of the state-vector of a dismembered function process. The developer will need to apply this kind of analysis either to follow an existing specification through to its implementation or, in some cases, to infer the specification from its implementation.

When respecification is very hard, a compromise may be possible. The existing system can itself be regarded as a real world; its master records are themselves regarded as the entities. An abstract description of this real world can be made, ignoring some of the actions of those entities, if the connections between the existing system and the extension can be restricted to certain points in time. We saw an example of this approach in the Widget Warehouse system, where the connection between the purchasing system and the order allocation system was restricted to the point at which the main batch updating program of the purchasing system had just been run. It was then possible to specify the product stock entity in a highly abstract way, ignoring all the actions, such as stock issues, receipts, and wastage, which take place between the completion of one instance of the batch updating program and the next. The connection between the two systems was a state-vector connection: regarding the product stock record as a real world entity, the model process, PRODUCT-1, inspected its state-vector directly. We might instead have made a data stream connection, embedding some suitable write operation in the PRODUCT-0 entity itself—that is, in the appropriate part of the batch updating program.

14

Retrospect

14.1 MANAGING A JSD PROJECT

From a management point of view, a JSD project has three main phases. In the first phase, consisting of the entity action and entity structure steps, an abstract description of the real world is made. In the second phase, consisting of the initial model, function, and system timing steps, the abstract description is realized as a process model, and the currently known functions are specified on the basis of this model. The third phase consists of the implementation step, and converts the specification into a practical set of executable programs matched both to the response requirements of the specification and to the number and power of the available processors. A major checkpoint should occur at the end of each phase. At the end of the first and second phases, the check is concerned to establish the fit between the specification and the user's needs; at the end of the third phase, the check is primarily technical, addressing questions of convenience and efficiency of system execution, and the correctness of the implementation with respect to the specification.

One of the benefits of JSD is that it demands a clearer separation of skills on the part of the development team. The first two phases are focused on the user, on his world, on his view of his world, and on what help he wants from the system. The developer in these phases needs some formal skills; he must be able to express process structures correctly, and he must understand the forms of process communication and be able to specify them correctly. These skills are not difficult to acquire. What is more significant in the first two phases is that the developer must be able to communicate well with the user, and to reach very quickly an understanding of the user's world and his needs. Above all, he must be really interested in these things. Many people who have worked as systems analysts have lacked this interest; they have become analysts only because that seems to be the road to promotion and success, and would, in their hearts, have preferred to remain programmers. These people are easily identified. They prefer to have their desk in the computer center, not in the user's offices. They fill their bookshelves with manuals on software subjects: database systems, programming languages, even operating systems. They rush through the tedious business of finding out what the user wants as quickly as possible, often far too quickly, so that they can progress to the really interesting work of database definition. They write program specifications which are actually programs, expressed in an informal programming language such as English.

These people are in the wrong job. The primary division in system development work is between the work which is focused on the user and the work which is focused on the computer. In JSD, this is the division between the first two phases and the third phase. The third phase is technical, and concerned with the computer. It is only a very slight exaggeration to say that the third phase has nothing at all to do with the user of the system. The third phase in JSD provides a demanding technical task that must be carried out by people whose interests lie in that area. Essentially, these are the people who want to be programmers, and the people who enjoy the technical aspects of system design.

Within each phase, it is usually possible to partition the work to be done into a number of individual tasks. A JSD model often consists of largely disconnected entity types; the specification of each type may be treated as a separate task, although there must obviously be a further activity in which the model is considered as a whole. Functions are more easily separated. It is often possible to consider a function, together with those parts of the model to which it is connected, in almost complete isolation from the rest of the system. In the third phase, individual tasks can be separated after the scheduling of the system has been determined in general. In particular, processes running on separate processors, whether real or simulated, can be separately implemented; and dismembered parts of one process can also be separately implemented. In this sense, JSD implementation gives rise to a number of distinct programming tasks in the traditional way; but the tasks themselves are different from the traditional tasks because they manipulate existing processes rather than creating new ones, at least so far as the processes of the specification are concerned; the implementation of scheduling processes is very much a traditional program design and implementation task, in which inverted specification processes play the part of previously programmed subroutines.

Estimating project cost and duration is always difficult. There is some reason to hope that it may be a little easier with JSD, because the JSD form of specification provides some measure of problem size. The estimates may take into account:

— the number of entity types in the model;
— the number of actions in each entity structure;
— the number of nodes in each entity structure;
— the number of simple embedded functions;
— the number of simple imposed functions;
— the number of interacting functions;
— the number of process types in the SSD;
— the number of processors, real or simulated, to be used, and hence the number and complexity of the scheduling processes to be implemented;
— the complexity of the necessary transformations, measured by the number of data streams in each inversion;

and other factors too. At the outset of a project, only a very rough estimate can be made of any of these factors. Confidence in the estimates can be improved either by comparing the system to be developed with other, already known, systems, or by carrying out a preliminary development project in which each step is taken far enough to allow a reasonable assessment of the associated quantities.

In some projects it is very desirable to start by constructing a prototype of the system to be developed. A prototype can be constructed for a particular critical part of the system, or for the system as a whole. For example, in some systems the human engineering of the input subsystem is critical; the success of the system depends largely on the comfort and efficiency of interactive procedures. It may then be worth while to build a prototype of that part of the system, to experiment with screen formats, editing functions, and menus; only a very limited simulation of the system proper is needed to drive such a prototype. In some systems, it may be desirable to build a prototype of the complete system. JSD offers two obvious approaches to prototyping the whole system:

— complete the system specification, but implement it in the quickest and cheapest way irrespective of running cost;
— complete the model specification, but experiment with the functions to be added to the model.

Before deciding to build any prototype system, it is necessary to formulate the questions which use of the prototype is intended to answer. A prototype intended for experimentation with system functions would be very different from one intended for experimentation with system performance.

Sometimes it will be very attractive to deliver the system incrementally, starting with a limited specification and building up to the full specification over the course of several increments. The natural way to do this in JSD is to specify the whole of the model initially; then, in successive increments, to specify additional functions and to implement enough of the model to support the functions provided. When the model itself consists of a number of disconnected parts, as it often will, it may be right to begin by specifying only some of the real world entities; functions based on that partial model can then be specified before the model is completed.

14.2   DOCUMENTATION

We have described the various development documents of a JSD project in earlier chapters. Each development step produces documentation as a by-product; the documentation is the tangible output of the step, and embodies and records the decisions that were made there. In addition, there may be a need for user manuals, and for introductory and overview documents of various kinds. In this book, we have considered only the technical documentation that emerges directly from the development procedure.

Technical documentation serves a number of different purposes. One purpose is to provide quick and accurate answers to specific questions about the system. Some of these answers can be found in the basic technical documentation. If we wish to know whether a customer of the Widget Warehouse can CANCEL an order after it has been

ALLOCATEd, we need only to look at the entity structure for an order; if we wish to know the rules for controlling an elevator in the Hi-Ride Elevator system, we look at the ELCONTROL process structure. Sometimes, the questions will be harder to answer. If we wish to know all the places in the implemented Widget Warehouse system where the ORD-12 state-vector is accessed, we must look first at the SSD, then at the implementation diagram, then, perhaps, at the executable program texts. There is some scope here for what we might call automated secondary documentation, such as cross-reference lists, in which such information is automatically extracted from the documentation produced by the developer.

Another important purpose of documentation is to record the reasons for development decisions. This is particularly valuable when changes are made to the system. Few experiences in development are more disquieting than to recollect that some proposed change has previously been rejected, for a reason that is now forgotten. Peter Naur, in *Concise Survey of Computer Methods*, published by Studentlitteratur, recommends in the context of program development:

> Write down all arguments entering into the program development process, including possibilities that were rejected, immediately while the development is going on. As far as possible, include the reasoning behind the design choices made.
>
>   If at all possible, use a typewriter when writing down the design considerations. It is not necessary that the resulting script is neat and perfect, as long as the corrections are clear.

Naur has conducted an experiment in program development in which the developers were required to do all their thinking seated at a typewriter; the result is that every piece of formal documentation is, as it were, only the last paragraph in the description of the thinking which created it.

This approach seems highly desirable in system development generally. The central principles are that the documentation should contain a history of the development, not merely its product; and that neatness and precision of format are not of overriding importance. Obviously, documentation that is unreadable is of no value whatsoever; but it is a cardinal mistake to demand such perfection of format that the developer is encouraged to minimize the documentation in order to minimize the weight of that burden.

Where possible, documentation that must be maintained, such as structure specifications, should be capable of manipulation and reproduction by machine. Structure diagrams contain no information that is not contained in the associated structure text. It is therefore very useful to be able to store structure specifications in text form, and print or display them in diagrammatic form. Changes to the structure can then be made to the text form, and the changed diagram produced mechanically. A similar technique would be useful for system specification and implementation diagrams, but we have offered no textual form of these.

When diagrams must be maintained manually, the most useful tools are scissors and paste, and a photocopying machine.

Elaborate interactive systems for creating and manipulating diagrams have some advantages, but they have dangers too. For many people, playing with an interactive computer system is a delicious entertainment: even a text editor is as much fun as Space Invaders; certainly, it is easier fun than thinking. The computer is a help in interactive development, but it is also an irrelevant distraction. If you find that sitting down at a computer terminal is a more attractive prospect than sitting down with a pencil and paper, you should be suspicious of your reasons. The computer is also dangerous here because every input, however ill-considered, is awarded the accolade of a uniformly perfect format; there is no equivalent in the display produced by the computer of the hasty scribble, or the untidy pencilled diagram marred by multiple and almost illegible corrections. We are therefore strongly tempted to consider each task complete when the very first draft has been stored in the machine; we resist the temptation only when the defects of the content are ugly enough and obvious enough to mar the computer-produced beauty of the form.

14.3   DATA STRUCTURES IN JSD

It is possible, and not entirely unreasonable, to regard a system as no more than a large program. One might then hope to apply the same design and development method to programs and systems alike; if a program can be designed by specifying input and output data structures and combining them to form a program structure, surely the same technique could be applied to a system? Could we not say that a database, which is the internal data of a system, has the purpose of mediating between input and output data structures when these are in conflict? It would follow then that the system developer should be centrally concerned with the data structures of input, output, and the database.

It may, or may not, be possible to build such an approach to system development, but it would certainly not be JSD. Data structures do not play a central role in JSD; rather, they play different supporting roles in different steps of the JSD procedure.

In the initial model step, the simplest and most convenient arrangement, which we adopt whenever possible, is to connect a real world entity to its level-1 process by data stream connection. The entity structure is then reflected in the data structure of the stream and also in the structure of the level-1 process. In a sense, the stream data structure is important here; but we need not consider it separately from the entity structure, which has already been specified. Where we are forced to use state-vector connection between a real world entity and its level-1 process, as in the Hi-Ride Elevator system, we have slightly more use for a data structure showing the succession of values of the state-vector which are obtained by the *getsv* operations in the level-1 process; but here again the data structure is so closely related to the already specified entity structure that the gain from considering it separately is small. Similar arguments hold for data stream connections within the initial model: the data stream connecting an entity such as the bank customer with a marsupial such as the customer's account has a structure already specified in the previous step.

Structures of data streams are more significant, and more useful to the developer, where a process has more than one input data stream, whether rough merged or not. In

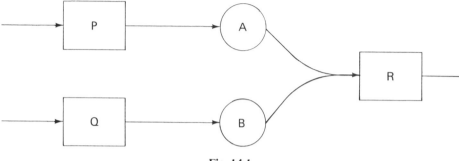

Fig. 14.1

the SSD fragment in Fig. 14.1 the streams A and B carry the abstractions of the processes P and Q respectively which must be merged in the structure of the process R. It is useful, both in constructing and in checking the specification of R, to view the structure of R as a composition of the structures of A and B. This is especially true when A and B have non-trivial structures and R rough merges them; we need then to check that the structure of R accommodates all the possible interleavings of A and B that can arise from the rough merge. In the initial model step the structures of A and B will be structures of previously specified entities: we saw an example in Section 7.14, where A and B were CUS-ORDER and CLK-ORDER, and their composition R was the ORDER process. In the function step the structures of A and B are likely to be new abstractions of the processes P and Q rather than restatements of existing specifications.

In the function step generally, data structures may play a role very like their role in program design. The output of a function process which produces a periodic report is a

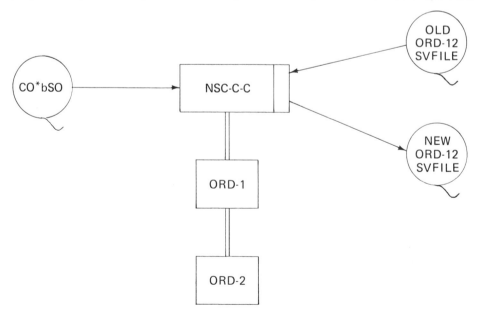

Fig. 14.2

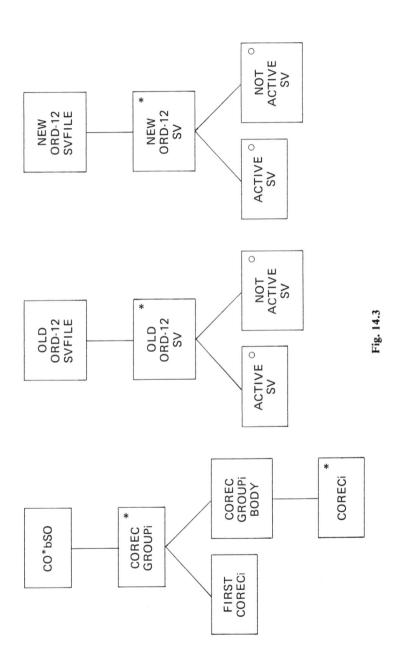

Fig. 14.3

data stream whose structure must be explicitly specified; the function process structure must compose this output with the inputs to the function. Inputs to a function which are obtained by state-vector connection often require explicit structuring of a non-trivial nature, as we saw in Section 9.9; the resulting structures constitute 'views' of the database which must be provided, directly or indirectly, in the implementation.

In speaking of a database we do not necessarily mean the kind that is found in data processing systems, implemented on disk drives or other backing storage devices. We mean quite generally the stored state-vectors of the system processes. The ELCONTROL processes in the Hi-Ride Elevator system are function processes which inspect the BUTTON-2 and BUTTON-SERVICE state-vectors in different sequences and combinations at different points in their execution. In a single-processor implementation it may be desirable to pay as much attention to the access paths to these state-vectors as is usually paid to access paths in a disk-stored database. For example, the state-vectors may be directly accessible by identifier (because ELCONTROL must examine the states of the buttons associated with the floor at which the elevator has just arrived), and also linked into an 'outstanding list' and a 'not outstanding list' (because ELCONTROL must scan for outstanding requests while the elevator is waiting). The analogy with techniques of storing disk records, directly accessible by identifier and linked into sequentially retrievable sets, is obvious.

The patterns of process activation established in the implementation step give rise directly to data structures to be imposed on the database and also to data structures to be imposed on the system's internal buffers. For example, the scheduler dismembered part, NSC-C-C, discussed in Section 11.6, has the SID shown in Fig. 14.2.

The ORD-1 and ORD-2 processes are activated in ascending sequence by order-id, which is the sequence into which the buffer part CO*bSO has been sorted. Simplified a little, the structures to be imposed are as shown in Fig. 14.3.

An active ORD-12 SV is one for which there is a COREC GROUP in CO*bSO: that is, one for which there is at least one COREC. More elaborate scheduling schemes will give rise to more elaborate data structures for both buffers and state-vectors. Specification of these data structures is a part of the task of developing the scheduler, which is itself essentially a task of program design entirely within the implementation step. The structures form no part of the system specification: they describe a reality which is purely technical.

14.4   SOME METHODOLOGY

The subject of computer system development is excessively disadvantaged by infatuation with destructively polysyllabic terminology. One of the most notable examples is the almost universal substitution of the word 'methodology' for the word 'method'. A method is a way of doing something; methodology is, or should be, the study and science of method. The penalty paid for the substitution is, arguably, that we discuss methodology less than we should because its name has been stolen.

One way to characterize a method is by the structure it imposes on development decisions. Here we mean 'decisions' in a very wide sense: the developer makes a decision when he records, and resolves to use, some fact about the subject matter of the system or about the system itself, or when he makes a choice among alternative possibilities. So it is a decision that the *Daily Racket* panel meets before it judges each group of entries; it is a decision that the Hi-Ride elevator is to wait at the ground floor when there are no outstanding requests; it is a decision that the file of ORD-12 state-vectors is to be sorted into ascending sequence by order-id; it is a decision that the instruction '$b := b + 1$' is to be executed at a particular point in the structure of the Hi-Ride Elevator system scheduler.

Different decisions have different properties, depending on their intrinsic nature and their place in the method's decision structure. Some questions we may ask about a decision are:

— How liable is it to error? Is there a high likelihood that it will be made wrongly?
— What is its subject matter? Is it about the real world, or about the system being developed? Is it about the specification or about the implementation?
— How easily can it be made? Does someone already know the right choice?
— How soon will we find out if the decision is made wrongly?
— How much later development depends on this decision? How much work will be wasted if this decision is made wrongly?
— Does a choice here imply some other choice elsewhere? Is another decision implicit in this one?
— Is this an independent decision, or must it be made in conjunction with others?

Merely to ask these questions is to suggest some principles of methodology, and some criteria for evaluating alternative methods. We claim that JSD is a sound development method, and that its underlying ideas can be justified by appeal to such methodological principles:

— Easier decisions should be made before difficult decisions. In JSD, the first decisions are about the real world that provides the subject matter of the system. The system's prospective users already have a model of that real world in mind, and can give authoritative guidance to the developer in formulating the abstract description in the first two development steps.
— The most error-prone decisions should be deferred as long as possible. Decisions about the system to be built are always error-prone, because by definition they are decisions about something that does not yet exist. JSD defers these decisions: specification decisions about the system are deferred to the function step; implementation decisions to the end of development.
— Implicit decisions should be avoided; it should always be clear to the developer what is being decided at each step, and there should be no hidden commitments incurred which may later prove difficult or even impossible to discharge. The classic traditional hidden commitments are a commitment to a model of reality implicit in a functional specification, and a commitment to constraints on the functional specification implicit in a configuration of on-line transaction modules and batch updating of sequential files. JSD avoids these implicit commitments by

  making the model of reality explicit before the functions are specified, and by
  making the functional specification explicit before designing the implementation.

— If a decision is error-prone, it should be subjected to the earliest possible confirmation or refutation. In JSD, the entity and action lists are immediately tested in the
   entity structure step, and the result is tested again in the function step. The decision that a function process can be connected in a certain way into the SSD is
   immediately tested by the specification of its structure.

— Whenever possible, decisions should be independent of one another: they should
   be orthogonal. A JSD description of reality in terms of entities and their behavior
   is very loosely connected; it is usually quite easy to change one part of the description without affecting other parts. The functions are connected only to the model
   in most cases, not to each other, so they can be specified independently.

Neither the principles nor their application can be absolute. In any development, there
are always difficult decisions, and scope for mistakes; decisions are never completely
orthogonal; there is always some possibility that an early wrong decision will remain
undetected for too long. But a good method should structure the decisions so that the
expected cost of mistakes is as low as possible.

14.5   NOT TOP-DOWN

JSD is not top-down. This is a proud claim, not an embarrassed confession. For many
people, 'top-down' is a synonym of 'good': a development method, if it is to claim
serious consideration, must be able to claim that it is 'top-down' and, preferably,
'structured' too. The esteem in which top-down methods are held is greatly strengthened
by the good repute of their more academically flavored cousin, stepwise refinement.

  The fundamental idea of top-down development is that the object to be developed,
whether it is a small program or a large system, can best be regarded as a hierarchy.
The top-down developer begins by stating the highest level of the hierarchy, the
decomposition into a small number of large objects; then, each of these is further
decomposed into a small number of smaller objects, and so on, until the lowest level is
reached. The name 'top-down' is appropriate because development begins at the top of
the hierarchy and works down, level by level, until the bottom is reached. The hierarchy
may be a hierarchy of subroutines, or it may be a hierarchy of data-flow diagrams; in
either case there is a level-by-level decomposition from the top level downwards.

  Top-down is a reasonable way of describing things which are already fully
understood. It is usually possible to impose a hierarchical structure for the purposes of
description, and it seems reasonable to start a description with the larger, and work
towards the smaller aspects of what is to be described. But top-down is not a reasonable
way of developing, designing, or discovering anything. There is a close parallel with
mathematics. A mathematical textbook describes a branch of mathematics in a logical
order: each theorem stated and proved is used in the proofs of subsequent theorems. But
the theorems were not developed or discovered in this way, or in this order; the order of
description is not the order of development.

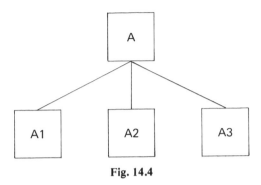

Fig. 14.4

When the developer of a system, or of a program, already has a clear idea of the completed result in his mind, he can use top-down to describe on paper what is in his head. This is why people can believe that they are performing top-down design or development, and doing so successfully: they confuse the method of description with the method of development. The development has been performed in some hidden way, perhaps by contemplation of the problem, perhaps by speculating on possible solutions and their implications; when the top-down phase begins, the problem is already solved, and only details remain to be decided.

A development method must allow the developer to solve problems to which he does not already know the solution, to develop systems which he cannot yet see in his mind's eye. Top-down is the worst possible method from this point of view, because it compels the developer to make the largest and most far-reaching decisions at the beginning, when, one must assume, he knows least about the problem. Each step in a top-down development is taken in the context determined by the previous higher-level steps; if the first step in decomposing A results in three smaller objects (Fig. 14.4), then the context of the following steps is fixed to that extent: they are directed to the decomposition of A1, A2, and A3. If the first step was ill-chosen, nothing can be done at any later step to retrieve the error; the developer must press on with a design he now knows to be bad, or he must return to the very first step and begin the development again. The work done at later steps is likely to be useless if the top-level decomposition is changed; something will have been gained in understanding of the problem, and something of the lower levels may survive by sheer good fortune. But nothing more.

This jaundiced view of top-down decomposition is corroborated by the often made suggestion that a substantial software development project should be tackled twice: once to do it, and once to do it properly. The earliest stages of top-down development deal, by definition, in unknowns: the decision to decompose A into A1, A2, and A3 is inevitably imprecise and vague, because those parts will not become precise until the development is completed. The brilliant top-down developer is one who completes the development in his mind's eye before committing himself to writing down even the top level of decomposition. Where developers are merely skilled and competent, rather than brilliant, the consequences of their early decisions emerge only at the end of the project: hence the appealing suggestion that it could all be done properly the second time around.

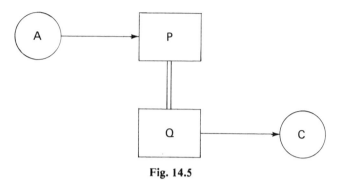

Fig. 14.5

We may also question the applicability of hierarchical structure as such. Certainly a JSD entity structure is hierarchical (a tree is a special case of a hierarchy without common sub-components): but it is notable that we specify an entity structure only when its lowest-level components, the actions, are already defined and known; and the same is true of function process structures. Elsewhere in JSD, hierarchical structures of subroutines appear only in the implementation step. If we specify:

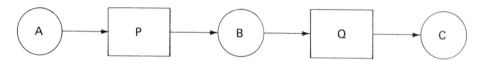

we may implement it as in Fig. 14.5.

The specification was a network, albeit a trivial network, and the implementation is a hierarchy. It would be quite wrong to consider this hierarchical structure at the outset of the development, treating P as the top and Q as the lower level. We might as easily have chosen to implement as in Fig. 14.6. Which is now the top, and which the bottom? Careful study of top-down specifications and designs often—perhaps always—reveals that implementation has played a determining role from the outset of development; what purports to be a pure specification, free from considerations of how the system will be implemented, is in fact largely a statement of an intended implementation of the final

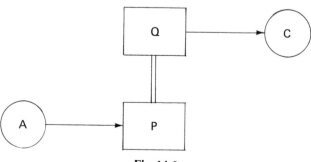

Fig. 14.6

system. In some approaches it is positively expected that the implementation steps are merely the final steps in the top-down or stepwise development. It follows that the very first, top-level, step in the development is the first, top-level, step in the implementation. It hardly seems sensible to expect the developer of a system to make the largest implementation decision at the very beginning of development, when it is not yet known what is to be implemented.

Appendix A

JSD glossary

Abstraction: description of a reality, purposefully omitting certain aspects.

Action: an event in which one or more entities participate by performing or suffering the action.

Backtracking: a technique for handling lack of information for a run-time decision, by making an assumption and subsequently, if it proves wrong, abandoning it.

Blocked: waiting for an input record, and so unable to proceed until it becomes available.

Boundary (Model): a conceptual boundary dividing those aspects of reality which are modelled from those which are ignored.

Boundary (System): a boundary, crossed by data stream and state-vector connections, dividing the system from the reality in which it is embedded.

Channel: an implementation device by which a process is inverted with respect to two or more data streams simultaneously.

Collate: to merge two or more data streams by comparing key values in their records.

Conversational constraint: a particular interleaving of data stream operations in two processes, having the pattern of a conversation in which one process writes a question and the other writes a reply, alternately.

Data merge: a merge of two or more data streams based on the data values in their records.

Data stream: an ordered set of records or messages by which two processes communicate, the records being read by one process in the order in which they were written by the other.

Data structure diagram: a structure diagram representing the ordering of records in a data stream or of successive state-vectors.

Dismembering: a transformation in which the text or state-vector of a process, or a data stream, is broken into a number of parts for convenience and efficiency in execution.

Dynamic model: a model embodying a specification of the actions of entities and the time ordering of those actions.

Elementary: a type of data or process component which is not further decomposed and appears as a leaf of a structure diagram.

Embedded function: a function which is provided by embedding the required output operations directly into the structure of a model process.

Entity: an object in the real world which participates in a time-ordered set of actions.

Entity action step: the first step in JSD development procedure, in which the entities and the actions in which they participate are listed.

Entity structure step: the second step in JSD development procedure, in which structure diagrams are drawn for the entities, showing the time-orderings of the actions in which they participate.

Fixed merge: a merge of two or more data streams according to fixed rules and not depending on the values in their records.

Function: an action or set of actions performed by the system and resulting in the production of output.

Function process: a process which is added to the system for the purpose of producing output, as opposed to a model process.

Function step: the fourth step in JSD development procedure, in which functions are added to the specification.

Getsv: an operation executed by one process which obtains the current value of the state-vector of another process.

Implementation step: the sixth step in JSD development procedure, in which the specification is transformed so that it can be conveniently and efficiently executed.

Imposed function: a function which is provided by a function process obtaining data from the model by directly inspecting the state-vectors of model processes.

Initial model step: the third step in JSD development procedure, in which model processes are specified for the entities of the real world, and connections are specified between these processes and the entities they model.

Interacting function: a function which interacts with the model processes by writing data stream records which they read and so affecting their states.

Inversion: a transformation in which a sequential process is converted into a procedure, invoked once for each record of each data stream with respect to which the process is inverted.

Iteration: a type of data or process component consisting of one part occurring zero or more times for each occurrence of the iteration.

Level-0: the real world with which the system is concerned.

Level-1: the direct model of the real world.

Level-2: a further modelling of the level-1 model, for purposes of specifying particular functions.

Loadsv: an operation executed by a scheduler process which loads into main storage the state-vector of a process to be activated.

Marsupial entity: an entity which emerges from the structure of another entity, especially when several interleaved instances exist of the marsupial entity within one instance of the other.

Minimal structure: a structure which describes exactly the time-ordering constraints on the actions of an entity, but imposes no further structure beyond those constraints.

Model: an abstraction which has been realized, especially by a set of sequential processes.

Model process: a sequential process forming a part of the model, as opposed to a function process.

Process: execution of a program text from beginning to end, or a particular instance of such execution.

Processor: a device used in implementation, capable of realizing a single process execution.

Program structure diagram: a structure diagram representing the ordering of the parts of a program.

Query: an operation which interrogates a suspended process and determines the reason for its suspension.

Read: an operation which waits for, and accepts, the next record of an input data stream.

Real world: the context in which the subject matter of the system exists.

Rough merge: a merge of two or more data streams according to the order in which the records become available for reading.

Scheduling: an interleaving of two or more process executions so that they may be treated as a single process execution and realized on a single processor.

Selection: a type of data or process component consisting of two or more parts of which one occurs once for each occurrence of the selection.

Separation of state-vectors: a transformation in which the local variables of a process, including the text-pointer, are separated from the executable part of the text and stored and retrieved explicitly as a data object.

Sequence: a type of data or process component consisting of one or more parts each of which occurs once for each occurrence of the sequence.

Sequential data stream: *see* data stream.

Sequential process: *see* process.

State-vector: the local variables of a process, including the process text-pointer.

Static model: a model which does not show time-ordering.

Storesv: an operation executed by a scheduler process which stores the updated state-vector of an activated process.

Structure diagram: a diagram representing the tree structure of a data stream or program text.

Structure text: a textual representation of the tree structure of a data stream or program text, showing conditions on the iteration and selection components.

Synchronization process: a process introduced in the system timing step which synchronizes processes by writing two or more time grain marker streams.

System implementation diagram: a diagram showing how a system is implemented.

System specification diagram: a diagram showing the processes of the system, and the connections among them.

System timing step: the fifth step in JSD development procedure, in which additional synchronization necessary for correct system output is specified.

Text-pointer: a variable whose value indicates the point in its text reached by a process.

Time grain marker: a record indicating the arrival of a point in real world time.

Transformation: systematic conversion of a part of a system into a form better suited to convenient and efficient execution on available hardware and software.

Tree: a type of structure used extensively in JSD for data and programs.

Write: an operation which places the next record into an output data stream.

Appendix B

JSD notations

1 **STRUCTURE DIAGRAMS**

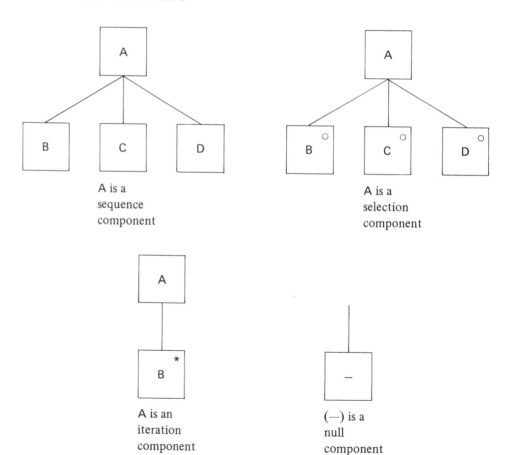

A is a
sequence
component

A is a
selection
component

A is an
iteration
component

(—) is a
null
component

2 STRUCTURE TEXT

A seq
  B;
  C;
  D;
A end

A is a
sequence
component

A sel *(cond-B)*
  B;
A alt *(cond-C)*
  C;
A alt *(cond-D)*
  D;
A end

A is a
selection
component

A itr while *(cond-B)*
  B;
A end

A is an
iteration
component

A posit
  x;
A quit *(cond-1)*;
  y;
A quit *(cond-2)*
  z;
A admit
  w;
A end

A is a selection
component with
backtracking

A itr
  x;
A quit *(cond-1)*;
  y;
A quit *(cond-2)*;
  z;
A end

A is an iteration
component with
backtracking

3 SYSTEM SPECIFICATION DIAGRAM

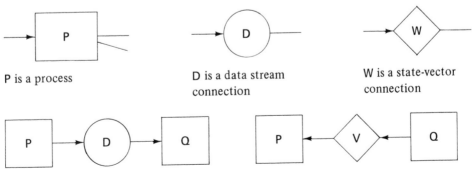

P is a process

D is a data stream
connection

W is a state-vector
connection

One P connected to one Q by a data
stream D written by P and read by Q

One P connected to one Q by P directly
inspecting the state-vector of Q

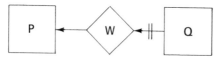

One P connected to many Q by P directly
inspecting the state-vectors of the Qs

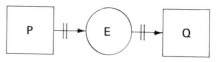

Many P connected to many Q by data
streams E written by the Ps and read by
the Qs

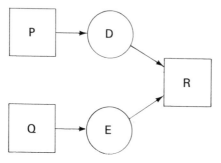

R merges its input data streams D and
E by fixed or data merge

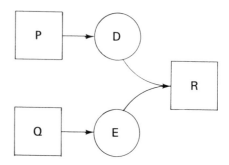

R merges its input data streams D and E
by rough merge

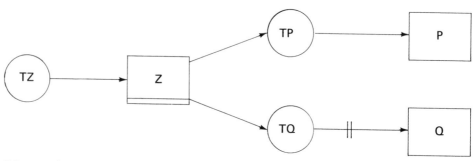

Z is a synchronization process which writes Time Grain Marker streams TP and TQ to the
processes P and Q to synchronize their execution

4   SYSTEM IMPLEMENTATION DIAGRAM

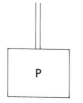

P is a process inverted with respect to one
of its data streams

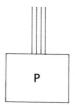

P is a process inverted with respect to
three of its data streams

S is a special-purpose scheduling process
not present in the system specification,
introduced in the implementation step

B is a circular buffer

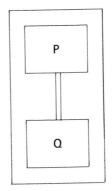

ABC-SVFILE is a direct-access file of
state-vectors of process ABC, which
have been separated from the program
text of ABC

P and Q inverted are treated as a single
sequential process for purposes of
implementation. Q inverted is a
subroutine of P

Q is inverted with respect to two data
streams and its state-vector has been
separated. The scheduling process S
retrieves and stores the state-vectors
of Q

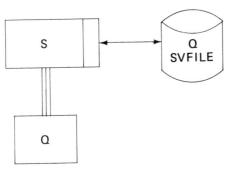

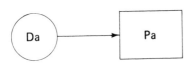

Pa is a dismembered part of a process P;
it reads Da, a dismembered part of a data
stream D read by P

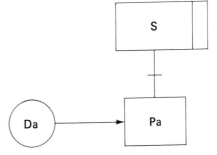

The dismembered part Pa of process P is
executed some number of times by the
scheduling process S

Appendix C

The *Daily Racket* competition

1   ENTITY AND ACTION LISTS (6.4, 6.9)

READER: SUBSCRIBE, ENTER
PANEL: AWARD, MEET

2   ACTION DESCRIPTIONS (6.10)

SUBSCRIBE: become a regular customer by paying for a year's copies of the paper; action of READER. Attributes: date, name, address, . . .

ENTER: make an entry in the competition and send it to the *Daily Racket*; action of READER. Attributes: ranking, fee, verse, . . .

AWARD: award a prize to an entry; action of PANEL. Attributes: ranking, verse, prize-type, . . .

MEET: come together, usually about once a week, to receive and judge entries; action of PANEL. Attributes: date, . . .

3   ENTITY STRUCTURES (7.8)

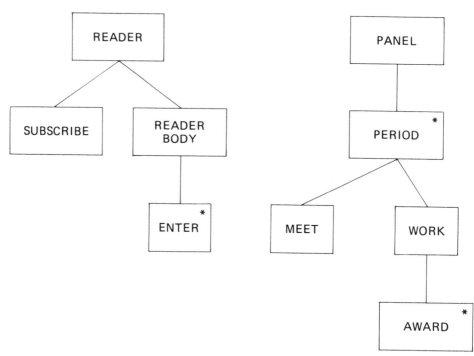

4 INITIAL MODEL (8.5, 8.10)

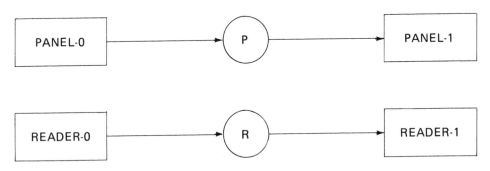

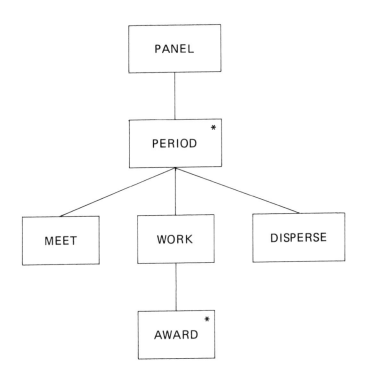

5   MAJOR FUNCTIONS (9.20, 9.21)

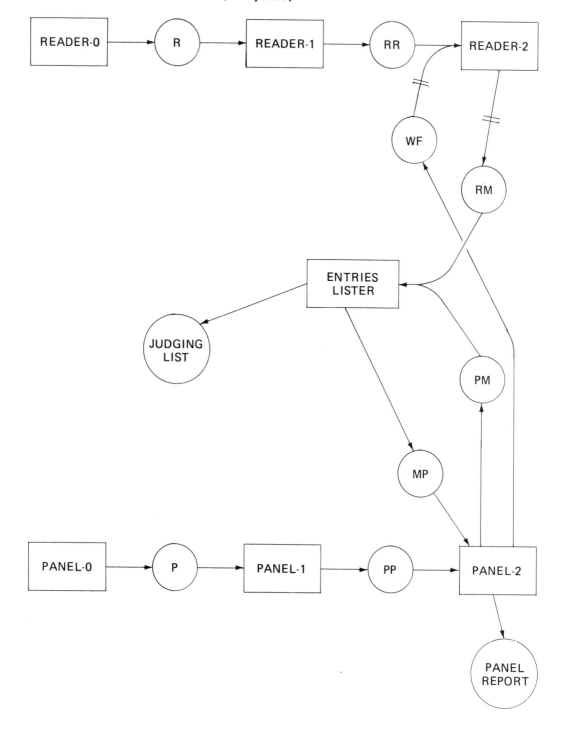

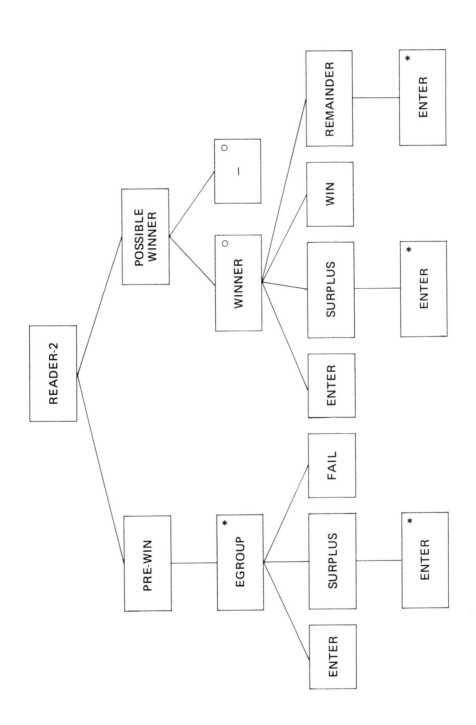

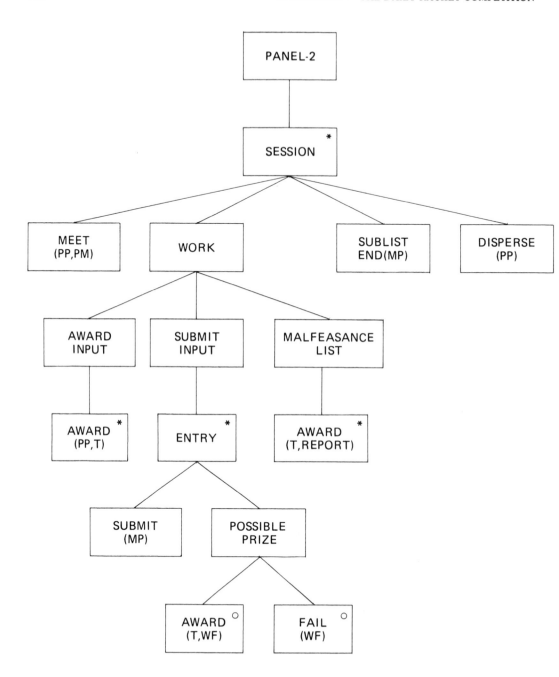

6   IMPLEMENTATION (11.17)

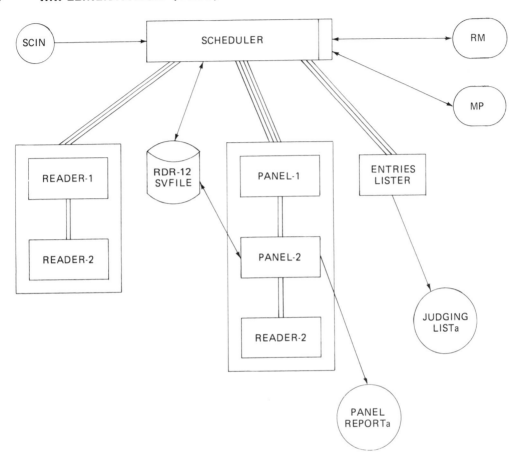

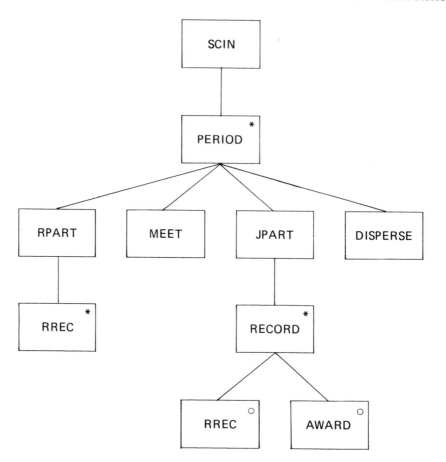

Appendix D

The Widget Warehouse Company

1   ENTITY AND ACTION LISTS (6.11)

        CUSTOMER: PLACE, AMEND, CANCEL, DELIVER
          CLERK: DELAY, ALLOCATE
          ORDER: PLACE, AMEND, CANCEL, DELIVER, DELAY, ALLOCATE
        PRODUCT: ALLOCATE, DELIVER

2   ACTION DESCRIPTIONS

        PLACE: convey an order to the company for allocation and delivery. Action
                of CUSTOMER and ORDER.
                Attributes: product-id, quantity, requested date, . . .
       AMEND: change the quantity or requested date of an order; product-id
                cannot be changed. Action of CUSTOMER and ORDER.
                Attributes: code (new quantity or new requested date), quantity or
                date, . . .
      CANCEL: cancel an order. Action of CUSTOMER and ORDER.
                Attributes: . . .
       DELAY: delay an order because stock is not available for it to be allocated.
                Action of CLERK and ORDER.
                Attributes: . . .
    ALLOCATE: allocate product stock to an order. Action of CLERK, ORDER, and
                PRODUCT.
                Attributes: quantity, . . .
     DELIVER: deliver ordered product to a customer. Action of CUSTOMER,
                ORDER, and PRODUCT.
                Attributes: date, quantity, . . .

3   ENTITY STRUCTURES

Non-automated System (7.13)

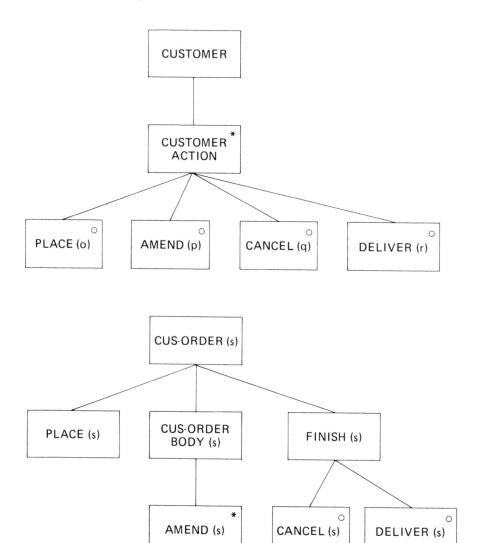

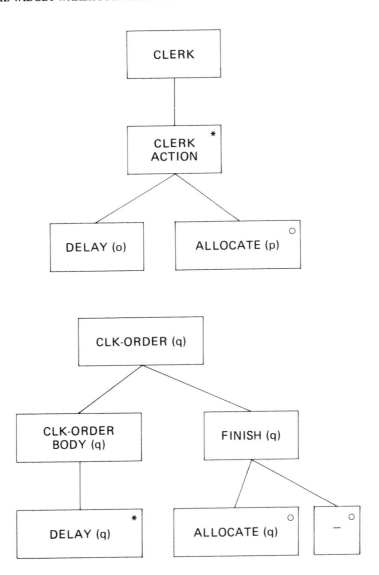

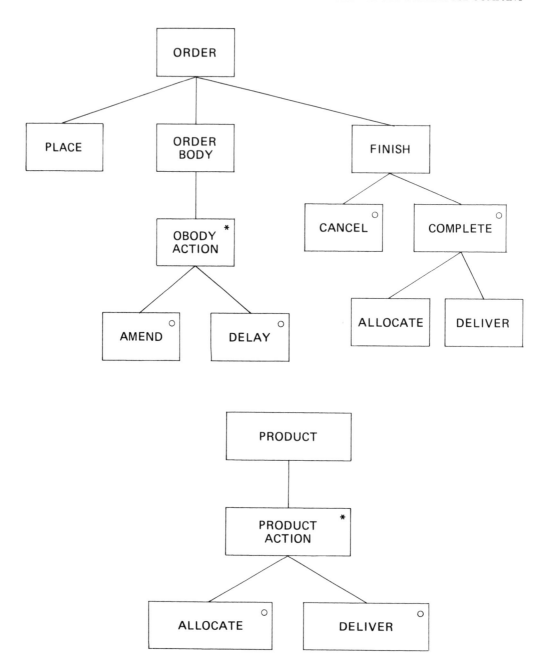

Automated System (7.15)

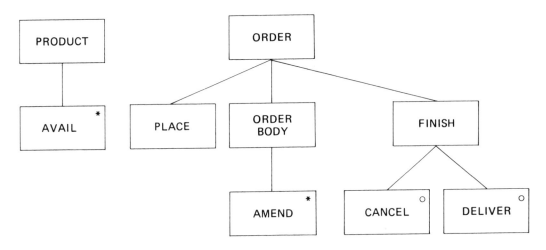

4   **INITIAL MODEL**

Automated System (8.11)

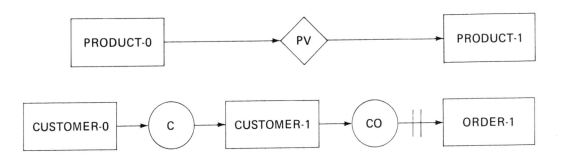

```
PRODUCT-1 seq
  getsv PV;
  PRODUCT-1-BODY itr
    AVAILABILITY-AT-DATE-I seq
      AVAIL; i := j (where PV = DATEj);
      getsvPV;
      AVDATE-BODY itr while (DATEi)
        getsv PV;
      AVDATE-BODY end
      AVAILABILITY-AT-DATE-I end
    PRODUCT-1-BODY end
  PRODUCT-1 end


CUSTOMER-1 seq
  read C;
  CUSTOMER-1-BODY itr
    CUSTOMER-ACTION sel (PLACE(i))
      PLACE; write PLACE to CO(i); read C;
    CUSTOMER-ACTION alt (AMEND(j))
      AMEND; write AMEND to CO(j)); read C;
    CUSTOMER-ACTION alt (CANCEL(k))
      CANCEL; write CANCEL to CO(k); read C;
    CUSTOMER-ACTION alt (DELIVER(1))
      DELIVER; write DELIVER to CO(1); read C;
    CUSTOMER-ACTION end
  CUSTOMER-1-BODY end
CUSTOMER-1 end


ORDER-1 seq
  read CO;
  PLACE; read CO;
  ORDER-1-BODY itr while (AMEND)
    AMEND; read CO;
  ORDER-1-BODY end
  FINISH sel (CANCEL)
    CANCEL; read CO;
  FINISH alt (DELIVER)
    DELIVER; read CO;
  FINISH end
ORDER-1 end
```

Non-automated System (8.15)

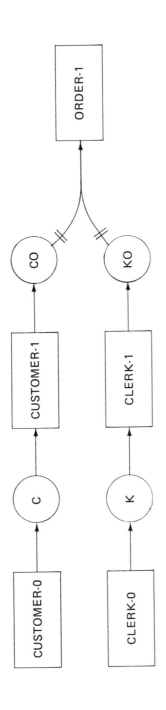

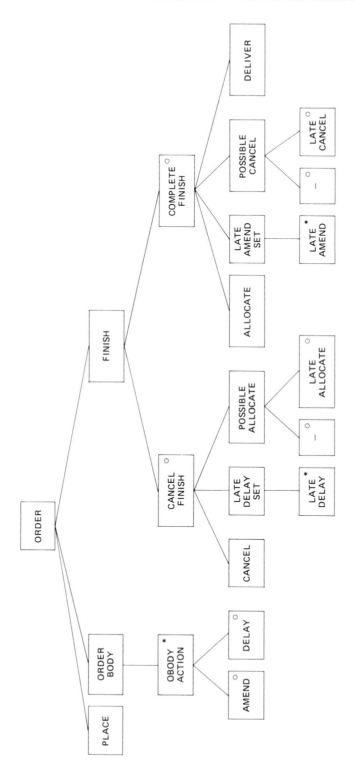

5   MAJOR FUNCTIONS (9.18, 9.19)

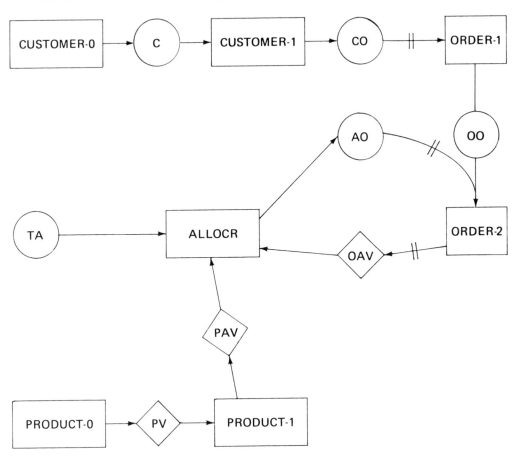

ALLOCR **itr**
  AGROUP **seq**
    read TA;
    getsv PAV; *available* := *quantity in* PAV;
    AGROUP-BODY **seq**
      getsv OAV;
      DELAY-GROUP **itr while** (DELAYED)
        DELAY-ORDER **sel** (*requested* ⩽ *available*)
          available := *available* − *requested*;
          write ALLOCATE *to* AO (OAV);
        DELAY-ORDER **alt (else)**
          write DELAY *to* AO (OAV);
        DELAY-ORDER **end**
        getsv OAV;
      DELAY-GROUP **end**

```
NORMAL-GROUP itr while (not end-of-OAVs)
    NORMAL-ORDER sel (requested ⩽ available)
        available := available – requested;
        write ALLOCATE to AO (OAV);
    NORMAL-ORDER alt (else)
        write DELAY to AO (OAV);
    NORMAL-ORDER end
    getsv OAV;
  NORMAL-GROUP end
 AGROUP-BODY end
 AGROUP end
ALLOCR end
```

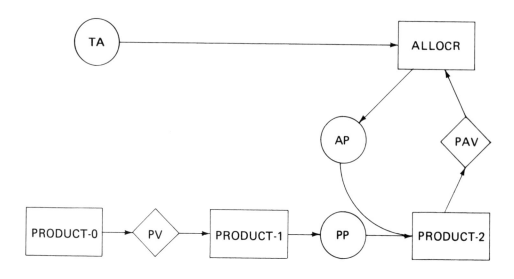

```
PRODUCT-2 seq
    quantity := 0;
    read PP & AP;
    PRODUCT-2-BODY itr
      PRODUCT-2-RECORD sel (PP record)
          quantity := quantity in PP record;
      PRODUCT-2-RECORD alt (AP record)
          quantity := quantity – allocated;
      PRODUCT-2-RECORD end
      read PP & AP;
    PRODUCT-2-BODY end
PRODUCT-2 end
```

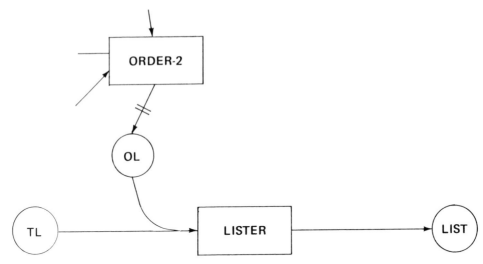

6   IMPLEMENTATION (11.10, 11.11, 11.15, 11.16)

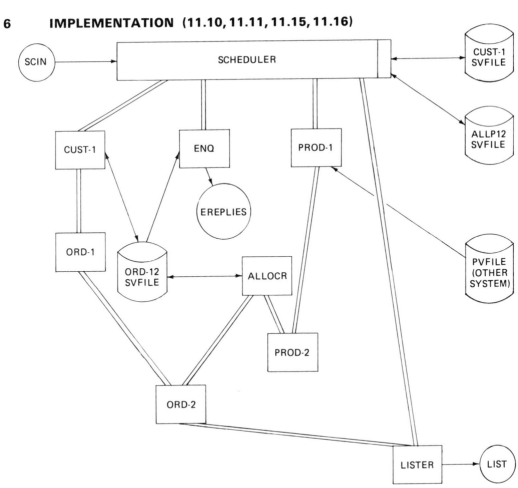

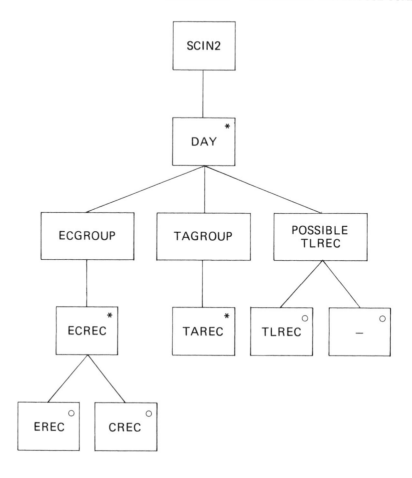

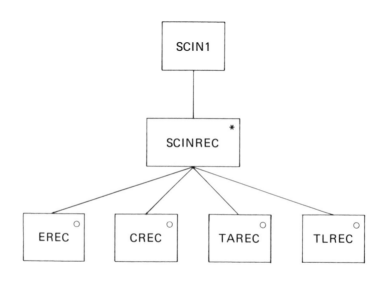

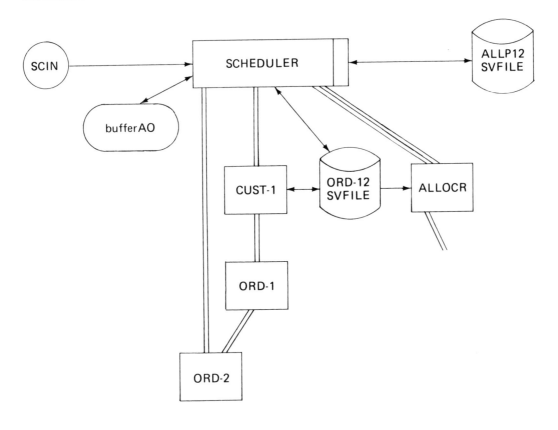

```
SCHEDULER seq
   list := null; ptr := head of list;
   SCHEDULER-BODY itr
      SCHEDULER-PHASE sel (SCIN empty)
         POSSIBLE-ALLOCR sel (list is null)
         POSSIBLE-ALLOCR alt (list is not null)
            activate ALLOCR (ptr);
            query ALLOCR (ptr);
            POSSIBLE-ALLOCR-DELETE sel (read TA in ALLOCR (ptr))
               remove ALLOCR (ptr) from list;
            POSSIBLE-ALLOCR-DELETE alt (read TOA in ALLOCR (ptr))
            POSSIBLE-ALLOCR-DELETE end
            ptr := next in list;
         POSSIBLE-ALLOCR end
      SCHEDULER-PHASE alt (SCIN not empty)
         read SCIN;
         SCIN-RECORD sel (TAREC)
            query ALLOCR (TAREC-id);
            TARECORD sel (read TOA in ALLOCR (TAREC-id))
               {allocation already in progress: ignore TAREC}
```

```
        TARECORD alt (read TA in ALLOCR (TAREC-id))
            activate PROD-1 (TAREC-id);
            activate ALLOCR (TAREC-id);
            add ALLOCR (TAREC-id) to list;
        TARECORD end
      SCIN-RECORD alt (EREC)
        activate ENQ;
      SCIN-RECORD alt (CREC)
        activate CUST-1 (CREC-id);
      SCIN-RECORD alt (TLREC)
        activate LISTER;
      SCIN-RECORD end
    SCHEDULER-PHASE end
  SCHEDULER-BODY end
SCHEDULER end
```

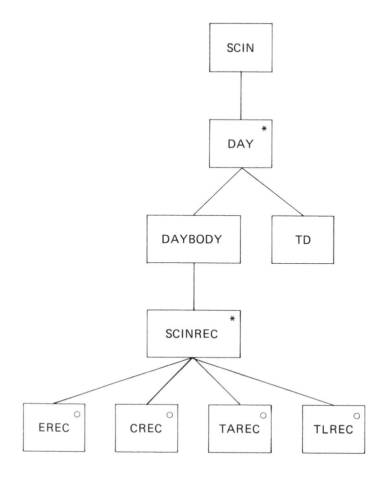

```
NEWSCHED itr
  NSCHEDDAY seq
    DAYBODY itr
      read SCIN;
    DAYBODY quit (TD);
      write SCINREC to buffer;
    DAYBODY end
    TD seq
      {read SCIN not needed}
      write TD to buffer;
    TD end
    EVENING seq
      {run the system processes with all buffered input}
    EVENING end
  NSCHEDDAY end
NEWSCHED end
```

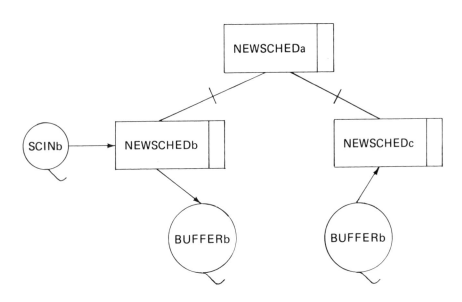

```
NEWSCHED itr
  NSCHEDDAY seq
    execute NEWSCHEDb;
    execute NEWSCHEDc;
  NSCHEDDAY end
NEWSCHED end
```

NEWSCHED-C **seq**
  NSC-C-A **seq**
    split BUFFERb *into* C*b, Eb, TA*b, TLb;
  NSC-C-A **end**
  sort C*b *into customer-id order giving* C*bSC;
  NSC-C-B **seq**
    activate CUST-1 *processes*;
  NSC-C-B **end**
  sort CO*b *into order-id order giving* CO*bSO;
  NSC-C-C **seq**
    activate ORD-1 *and* ORD-2 *processes*;
  NSC-C-C **end**
  sort TA*b *into product-id order giving* TA*bSP;
  sort ORD-12SVFILE *into product-id/delay/quantity order*
                                   giving ORD-12SVFILESPD;
  NSC-C-D **seq**
    activate PROD-1, PROD-2, ALLOCR, ORD-2 *processes*;
  NSC-C-D **end**
  sort Eb *into order-id order giving* EbSO;
  sort ORD-12SVFILE *into order-id order giving* ORD-12SVFILESO;
  NSC-C-E **seq**
    activate ENQ *process*;
  NSC-C-E **end**
  NSC-C-F **seq**
    activate LISTER *process*;
  NSC-C-F **end**
NEWSCHED-C **end**

Appendix E

The Hi-Ride Elevator Company

1   ENTITY AND ACTION LISTS (6.13, 6.15)

    BUTTON: PRESS
ELEVATOR: ARRIVE(m), LEAVE(n).

2   ACTION DESCRIPTIONS

      PRESS: be depressed and released once; action of BUTTON.
           Attributes: ...
ARRIVE(m): arrive at FLOOR(m), either from above or from below; action of
           ELEVATOR.
           Attributes: floor-number, ...
  LEAVE(n): leave FLOOR(n), either upwards or downwards;
           action of ELEVATOR.
           Attributes: floor-number, ...

3   ENTITY STRUCTURES (7.6)

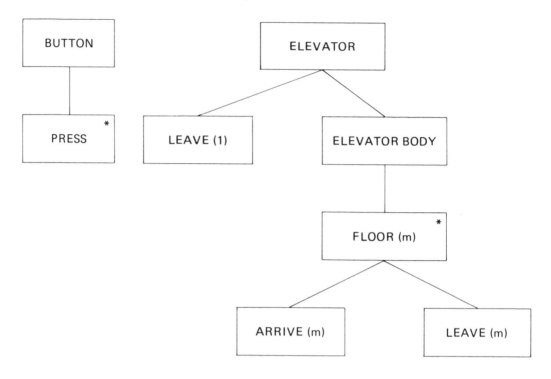

—　the value of (m) must always be in the range 1 to 6 inclusive;
—　for the first instance of FLOOR(m), the value of (m) must be 1 or 2;
—　in any two successive instances of FLOOR(m), the values of (m) must be identical, or must differ by 1.

4   INITIAL MODEL (8.8)

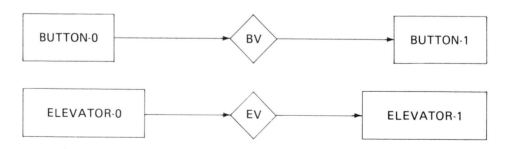

BUTTON-1 **seq**
  getsv BV;
  OPENSET1 **itr while** (OPEN)
    getsv BV;
  OPENSET1 **end**
  BUTTON-BODY **itr**
    PAIR **seq**
      DEPRESS;
      CLOSEDSET **itr while** (CLOSED)
        getsv BV;
      CLOSEDSET **end**
      RELEASE;
      OPENSET **itr while** (OPEN)
        getsv BV;
      OPENSET **end**
    PAIR **end**
  BUTTON-BODY **end**
BUTTON-1 **end**

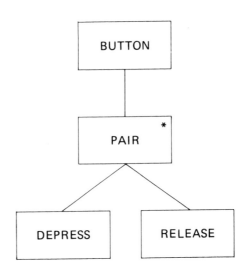

ELEVATOR-1 **seq**
  $m := 1$; *getsv* EV;
  AT1SET **itr while** (AT1)
    getsv EV;
  AT1SET **end**
  LEAVE(1);
  NATSET1 **itr while** (NAT)
    getsv EV;
  NATSET1 **end**
  ELEVATOR-BODY **itr**
    FLOOR-M **seq**
      $m := j$ *where* $EV = ATj$;
      ARRIVE(m);
      ATMSET **itr while** (ATm)
        getsv EV;
      ATMSET **end**
      LEAVE(m);
      NATSET **itr while** (NAT)
        getsv EV;
      NATSET **end**
    FLOOR-M **end**
  ELEVATOR-BODY **end**
ELEVATOR-1 **end**

5   MAJOR FUNCTIONS (9.11, 9.13, 9.14)

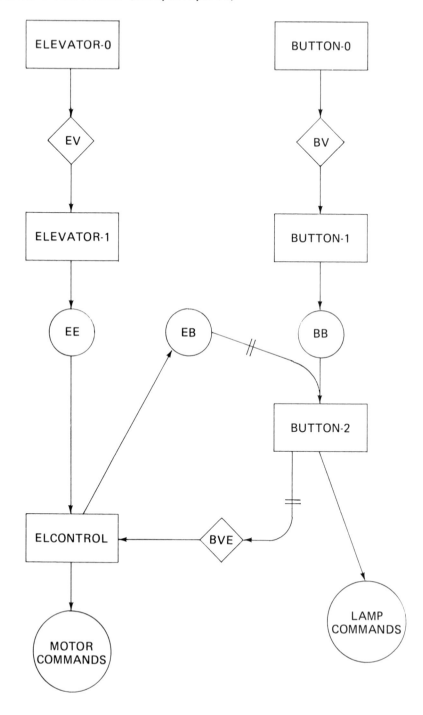

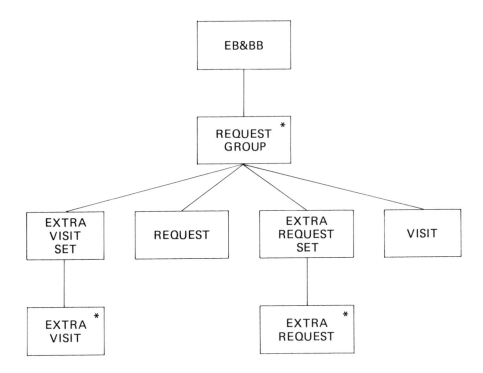

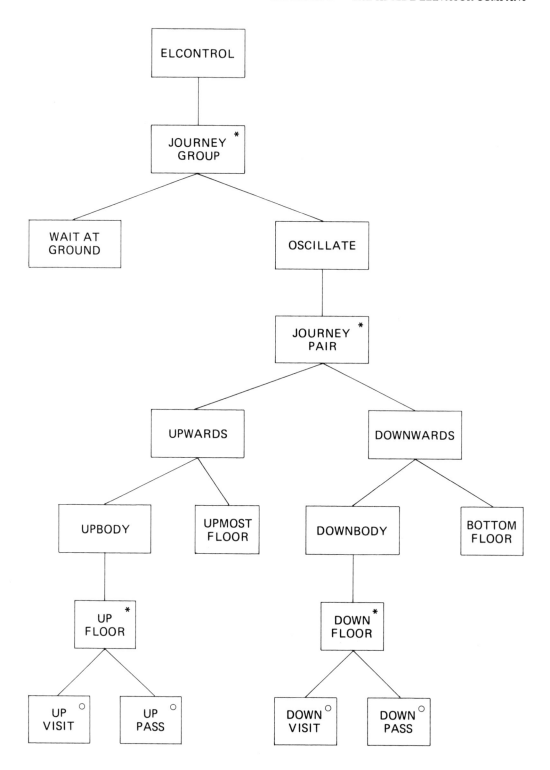

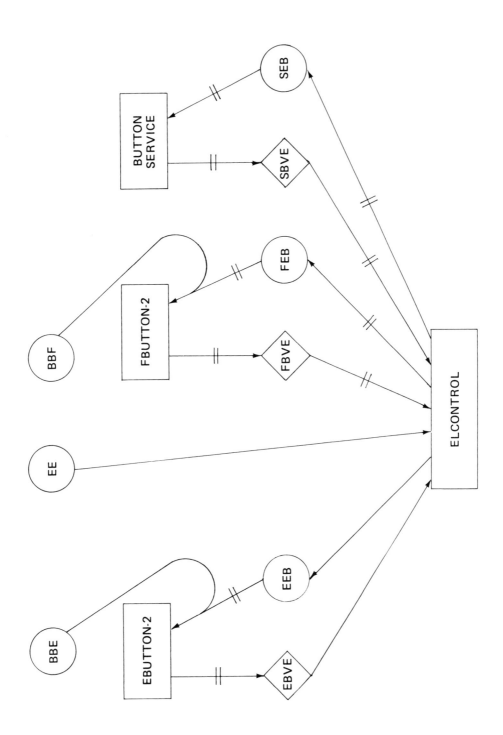

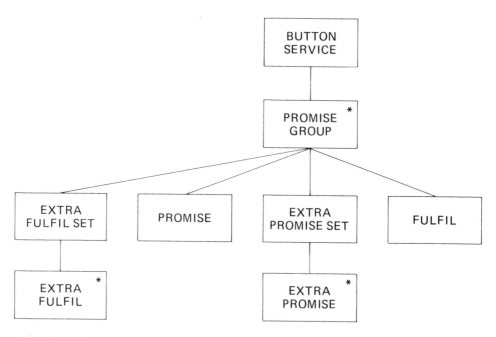

6   IMPLEMENTATION (11.19)

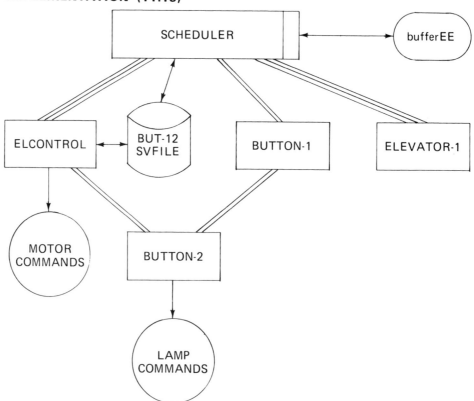

```
SCHEDULER itr
  SCHEDULER-PHASE seq
    BUTTON-SET seq
      b := 1;
      BUTTON-SET-BODY itr while (b ≤ 16)
        RUN-BUTTON-1 seq
          loadsv BUT-12SV (b) into BSV;
          CALL BUTTON-1 (BSV, TBREC);
          storesv BSV into BUT-12SV (b);
        RUN-BUTTON-1 end
        b := b + 1;
      BUTTON-SET-BODY end
    BUTTON-SET end
    ELEVATOR-1 seq
      query ELEVATOR-1;
      ELEVATOR-1-BODY sel (read TE in ELEVATOR-1)
        CALL ELEVATOR-1 (TEREC, dummy);
      ELEVATOR-1-BODY alt (write EEREC in ELEVATOR-1)
        CALL ELEVATOR-1 (dummy, EEREC);
        write EEREC to bufferEE;
      ELEVATOR-1-BODY end
    ELEVATOR-1 end
    ELCONTROL seq
      query ELCONTROL;
      ELCONTROL-BODY sel (read TEC in ELCONTROL)
        CALL ELCONTROL (TECREC, dummy);
      ELCONTROL-BODY alt (read EE in ELCONTROL)
        ELCONTROL-EEREC sel (bufferEE empty)
        ELCONTROL-EEREC alt (bufferEE not empty)
          read bufferEE into EEREC;
          CALL ELCONTROL (dummy, EEREC);
        ELCONTROL-EEREC end
      ELCONTROL-BODY end
    ELCONTROL end
  SCHEDULER-PHASE end
SCHEDULER end
```

Index